Teen Talkback with Interactive Booktalks!

Teen Talkback with Interactive Booktalks!

ॐॐ

Lucy Schall

LIBRARIES UNLIMITED

AN IMPRINT OF ABC-CLIO, LLC
Santa Barbara, California • Denver, Colorado • Oxford, England

Library of Congress Cataloging-in-Publication Data

Schall, Lucy.
  Teen talkback with interactive booktalks! / Lucy Schall.
    pages cm
  Includes bibliographical references and index.
    ISBN 978-1-61069-289-2 (hardcopy) — ISBN 978-1-61069-290-8 (ebook)   1. Book talks—United States.   2. Teenagers—Books and reading—United States.   3. Young adult literature—Bibliography.   4. Fiction genres—Bibliography.   5. Young adults' libraries—Activity programs.   6. Reading promotion—United States.   I. Title.
    Z1003.15.S327   2013
    021.7—dc23   2013000241

ISBN: 978-1-61069-289-2
EISBN: 978-1-61069-290-8

17   16   15   14   13   1   2   3   4   5

This book is also available on the World Wide Web as an eBook.
Visit www.abc-clio.com for details.

Libraries Unlimited
An Imprint of ABC-CLIO, LLC

ABC-CLIO, LLC
130 Cremona Drive, P.O. Box 1911
Santa Barbara, California 93116-1911

This book is printed on acid-free paper ∞

Manufactured in the United States of America

*To Bob Schall,
whose ability to think outside the box
of traditional education continues to inspire
kids, teachers, and me.*

Contents

Acknowledgments

I thank Barbara Ittner, my editor, for her insight, encouragement, and patience; Lisa Kurdyla of VOYA for her encouragement and support; and Joice Imel of the Meadville Public Library for her suggestions about teen reading and book selection.

The staffs of the following libraries and media centers have provided me with resources and support: St. Petersburg Public Libraries in St. Petersburg, Florida; the growing teen section in the Meadville Public Library; and the Meadville Middle School and High School Media Center in Meadville, Pennsylvania.

Teaching Books.net has generously provided me with much information as well as suggestions for additional sources.

Introduction

B ooktalks, and book trailers, and book guides. OH MY!
Young Adult book promotion and support are reaching new levels of quantity and quality online. Each librarian and media specialist has many choices to involve teens, but do they have time to gather and consider them? *Teen Talkback with Interactive Booktalks!* offers easy access to many of those online tools, as well as interactive booktalks and read alouds. It is organized by genre categories suggested by Diana Tixier Herald in *Teen Genreflecting 3: A Guide to Reading Interests*: Issues; Contemporary; Action/Adventure/Survival; Mystery/Suspense; Fantasy; Heritage; and Multiple Cultures. Of course, books classified in one genre often fit in another also. That point came home to me very quickly when I was presenting a title as a journey book, and a young man immediately said, "Every book is a journey book."

The bibliography information for featured books, published primarily between 2008 and 2012, and "Related Works" includes the author name, book title, publisher and date of publication, number of pages, price and ISBN, a bracketed fiction, nonfiction, graphic novel or reference designation, and a reading level suggestion.

C	=	children
M	=	middle school
J	=	junior high
S	=	senior high
A	=	adult
G	=	girls
B	=	boys
CG	=	cross-gender

Cross-gender designations indicate titles that appeal to both boys and girls, and may also include the phrases "with high interest for boys" or "with high interest for girls." The abbreviation "pa." indicates paperback.

Remember! Since teen readers, like adults, have a broad range of purpose and preference in their reading, these reading level designations are only *suggestions*. The **Theme/Topic** listing and the **Summary** give the book's basic content and ideas. Following the summary is a brief **Values Statement** that explains what values or ideals the work's content and themes address.

Next is the **Interactive Booktalk**. Booktalks highlight good books teens might overlook in a well-developed library collection. They advertise both the book and the library. Teachers supplementing textbook information will find that booktalking makes that supplemental reading list a personalized reference document, as students note their preferences during the presentation. Booktalks in this volume can be considered "ready-mades" or springboards for writing another booktalk according to personal style or purpose. Presenter directions are in italics. Short enough to hold a teen audience's attention, several booktalks from different genres can be included in one 45-minute program. Individual booktalks might introduce or conclude a class period or library program. If the group to whom you are speaking does not react well to interaction, these talks can easily be adapted to "just listening." Passing the books around before or after the presentation may provide an interactive experience strong enough to "sell" the book. If an alternative booktalk or book trailer is available online, the Web address(es) will follow the booktalk. And, always check *Book Trailers for All* (http://booktrailersforall .com). Teresa Schauer describes her journey to founding this Web site in "Book Trailers for All," an article that appeared in the February, 2012, issue of *VOYA*.

The **Read Aloud/Talkback** section following the booktalk lists at least five specific passages for sharing aloud, reflecting for discussion or writing, or presenting dramatic readings or performances. The Read Aloud/Talkback entries, according to the book's plan, include a chapter, section, division or page designation, a beginning and ending phrase for locating the passage, and a brief comment on the content and a discussion question or activity suggestion for teen involvement or reaction. Some passages also include attention-getting statements for classroom or book display posters. Other passages can act as booktalks. If available, Web addresses for discussion guides and author interviews are listed. These are valuable sources for those interested in pursuing additional discussion material or "from the horse's mouth" information or advice for writing groups.

Booktalking Tips

Every booktalker has a distinct style and favorite methods. The following are some suggestions I can pass on from my own experience.

Read every book you booktalk.

Booktalk only the books you respect and with which you feel comfortable.

Include books from several genres. Tell your audience how a book from one genre relates to a book in another.

If you are planning a full program of booktalks, invite your audience to select the books they want to hear about from the books that you bring.

Display the books so that the covers hold the audience's attention.

Hand out an annotated list at the beginning of the program for the audience to refer to, mark, and visit later.

Keep the booktalk short.

Hold the book while you speak.

Have extra copies so that (if you are lucky) you have a replacement for the one snatched by an eager reader, especially if you circulate the books.

Keep in mind that in this age of testing and assemblies, 45-minute presentations may not be possible. Adapt as needed.

Use technology and the teen customers who know it so well to extend your booktalks. You might want to train some of those teens to be booktalkers.

For excellent step-by-step advice, consult another Libraries Unlimited publication: *The Booktalker's Bible: How to Talk about the Books You Love to Any Audience* (2003) by Chapple Langemack.

Related Works include sources for expanded learning or further reading. The listings include books as well as short stories, plays, poems, articles, and Web sites. These sections will help build book programs, units of study, and inter-genre relationships. They also will guide instructors, librarians, and parents to additional reading or information sources. If a booktalk for one of the books in Related Works appears in this book, the chapter name and page numbers are provided; if it appears in one of my previous booktalk books, the book title will be included in the reference with the appropriate page numbers: *Booktalks Plus* (2001), *Booktalks and More* (2003), *Teen Genre Connections* (2005), *Booktalks and Beyond* (2007), *Genre Talks for Teens* (2009), or *Value-Packed Booktalks* (2011). Be sure to check on more related titles at **Your Next Read** (http://www.yournextread.com/us/). Additional free resource suggestions are available in Elizabeth Duffy's "Free Stuff for Your Library," an article that appears in the June 2012 issue of *VOYA*. The index of *Teen Talkback with Interactive Booktalks!* includes authors, titles, and topics for a quick overview of a work's relationships to others mentioned in this volume.

The professional recommendations from *VOYA, Booklist, School Library Journal*, the *ALAN Review*, as well as award lists and YALSA'a "best" booklists are still most valuable to me. Recommendations and suggestions from my reading family, friends, audiences, and librarians keep growing. Getting involved in and excited about teen books, they are even more aware that teen publication is a distinct publication division, rather than an add-on to the children's section or an adapted adult publication. But as my one of my friends observed, "You know those teen books aren't just for teens. They're just really good books." Hopefully, this volume gives you useful tools for motivating more readers, as you continue to explore recent texts and encourage "customers" to share their opinions and excitement.

Issues

Issues books confront topics, such as identity, abuse, dependency, dysfunctional families, and disease. Often, they are the most controversial. The situations they present, however, are common news stories. Issues books allow us to go beyond the horror and contemplate the courage and faith required to work through brutality, confusion, and sorrow. Seeing characters face devastating events often help some teens cope in their own lives and make other teens realize how fortunate they are.

Courage

Brown, Jennifer. Hate List.

New York: Little, Brown and Co., 2009. 408p. $16.99.
ISBN 978 0 316 04144 7. [fiction] JS, CG with high interest for girls

Themes/Topics: School shootings, high school, emotional problems, family crisis, forgiveness

Summary/Description

Sixteen-year-old Valerie returns to high school for her senior year after her boyfriend maims or kills several classmates and a teacher in a school attack at the end of their junior year. His targets are on a Hate List he compiled with Valerie. Valerie is shot in the leg as she defends a classmate and tries to stop the shooting. Suspected of instigating the event, she is assigned to Dr. Hieler for outpatient sessions. Val confesses feelings of guilt, anger, and grief as she faces a suspicious and angry student body, the girl she saved but hated, and her parents' failing marriage. Admitting her responsibility, she can move on with her life.

Values: Valerie learns the importance of remembrance, apology, and forgiveness.

Booktalk

Valerie Leftman is starting her senior year. What can she expect? (*Wait for answers.*) At the end of her junior year, a bully harassed her and broke her MP3 player. Valerie told her boyfriend Nick. He shot the bully. Then he opened fire on the entire cafeteria. He chose some victims, but others were just at the wrong place at the wrong time. And, before he killed himself, he shot Valerie. Was shooting Valerie an accident? A failed double suicide? An act of revenge because Valerie shielded one of his targets? No one is sure, even Valerie. Is Valerie going to get lots of sympathy? (*Wait for a response.*) No. Valerie has to face the survivors who know that Valerie started Nick's *Hate List*.

Book trailer available @ http://www.youtube.com/
watch?v=KWNGIRTU2u4

Read Aloud/Talkback

1. Chapter 9, pages 166 to 169, beginning "She stood at the end . . ." and ending the chapter. Val realizes that she is losing Stacy's friendship. *Talkback*: Have both girls changed?
2. Chapter 17, page 224, beginning "I had changed . . ." to end of chapter. Val realizes that her mother sees her as a danger to others. *Talkback*: How do you react to "unfair"?
3. Chapter 28, pages 293 to 295, beginning "He pulled his eyes . . ." and ending with the chapter. Valerie confronts her father over his affair with his secretary and her part in the shooting. *Talkback*: How does this passage speak to responsibility?
4. Chapter 39, pages 363 to 372, beginning with the chapter and ending ". . . drifting off to sleep." Valerie visits Ginny Baker in the hospital. *Talkback*: Describe Ginny's character.
5. Part 4, page 398, beginning "I saw . . ." and ending ". . . without the other." Valerie realizes the balance between winning and losing. *Talkback*: Do you agree with Valerie's conclusion about winners and losers?

Educator Guide available @ http://www.hachettebookgroup
.com/_assets/guides/EG_9780316041447.pdf

Author interviews available @

http://www.hachettebookgroup.com/EEC12C6B14EB4EA080
A2CCD17100F373.aspx

http://authorsunleashed.blogspot.com/2010/02/interview-with-
jennifer-brown.html

http://oldpeoplewritingforteens.wordpress.com/2009/12/10/
interview-with-hate-list-author-jennifer-brown-and-book-
giveaway/

http://teens.dbrl.org/2012/02/22/exclusive-interview-with-author-
jennifer-brown/

http://www.jenniferbrownya.com/faq.htm

Related Works

1. **Koja, Kathe. *Buddha Boy*.** New York: Farrar, Straus and Giroux/
Frances Foster Books, 2003. 117p. $16.00. ISBN 0 374 30998
1. [fiction] MJS, CG with high interest for boys (*Booktalks and
Beyond*, 2007, pages 40 to 43.) When bullies harass a new student
and obvious misfit, his friend defends him and realizes that he can
make a difference.

2. **Mikaelsen, Ben. *Touching Spirit Bear*.** New York: HarperCollins
Publishers, 2001. 241p. $15.95. ISBN 0 380 97744 3. [fiction] MJS,
CG with high interest for boys (*Booktalks and More*, 2003, pages
80 to 82.) Fifteen-year-old Cole Mathews accepts a Circle of Justice
alternative which includes reconciliation with his victim.

3. **Myers, Dean. *Shooter*.** New York: HarperTempest, 2004. 223p.
$16.99. ISBN 0 06 029520 1. [fiction] JS, CG with high interest for
boys. A friendship among three outcasts and unchecked bullying
lead to a fatal school shooting.

4. **Pixley, Marcella. *Freak*.** New York: Farrar Straus and Giroux/
Melanie Kroupa Books, 2007. 131p. $16.00. ISBN-13: 978 0 374
32453 7. [fiction] MJS, G (*Genre Talks for Teens*, 2009, pages 37 to
39.) Twelve-year-old Miriam fights her worst enemy, discovers that
they share problems, and prevents her from being raped. The girl
apologizes.

5. **Strasser, Todd. *Give a Boy a Gun*.** New York: Simon & Shuster,
2000. 146p. $16.00. ISBN 0 689 81112 8. [fiction] MJS, CG with
high interest for boys (*Booktalks and More*, 2003, pages 116 to 118.)
Bullied and teased by the school jocks, two boys execute a terrorist
act in their school.

ℭℨℨ

de la Peña, Matt. I Will Save You.

New York: Ember/Random House Children's Books, 2010. 310p. $8.99pa.
ISBN 978 0 383 73828 6. [fiction] CG with high interest for boys

Theme/Topics: Mental illness, schizophrenia, dysfunctional families, friendship, California.

Summary/Description

Kidd Ellison, whose alcoholic mother killed his abusive father and then herself, runs away from a juvenile mental institution, lives on the beach, and does maintenance work with Red who sees him as a son. Kidd falls in love with Olivia, an upper-class girl, who is vacationing on the beach. Devon, Kidd's other personality, threatens to destroy both relationships. He steals, tells Kidd that Olivia will abandon him, and threatens to hurt her. To protect her, Kidd throws Devon (himself) over a cliff on the beach. Throughout the story, Kidd thinks that he is in solitary confinement for killing Devon. He is in a hospital bed. Red, Olivia, and his counselor are by his side.

Values: Kidd's work ethic and sensitivity lead to strong friendship and love, but his recurring mental illness teaches him that he must commit to full treatment.

Booktalk

Ask how many people in the group go away for the summer and make new friends.

Discuss how many of those friendships are successful or lasting.

Kidd Ellison needs some friends. His mother killed his father and then herself. He lives in a mental hospital. But he is tired of waiting for someone to help him. One summer, he runs away and finds friends. His boss Red treats him like a son and gives him all kinds of advice. The beautiful Olivia seems to really like him. (*Does he have a chance for success?*) Kidd thinks so, but a friend from the mental hospital finds him. Devon. Devon is way more streetwise than Kidd. He tells Kidd how things really are. Devon knows that when Olivia finds out who Kidd really is she will dump him. When Red finds out some of the things Kidd has done, Red will fire him. Devon wants Kidd to himself, even if it means killing Olivia. Kidd knows about evil. It killed his parents, but he promises Olivia "I Will Save You."

Book trailer available @ http://www.youtube.com/
watch?v=yAddza4Xwl4

Read Aloud/Talkback

1. "What I Remember about My Mom," pages 26 to 28. Kidd lists random memories. *Talkback*: What is your reaction to Kidd's mother and their relationship?
2. "Philosophy 3: About How a Bad Thing Can Turn Good," pages 88 to 90. Kidd reflects on his mother's beating. *Talkback*: Did something good come from something bad?
3. "There were riptide warning . . ." pages 155 to 160. Devon tries to drown Kidd. *Talkback*: What does Devon reveal about himself and Kidd?
4. "Dreams from Solitary Confinement," pages 204 to 211. Kidd hears Red and Olivia talking. *Talkback*: Is this a dream?
5. "On the Morning of the Grunion," pages 280 to 282, beginning with "On the morning . . ." and ending ". . . campsite exit." Red decides to reconnect with Maria. *Talkback*: How are Kidd and Red alike? Different?

Discussion guide available @ http://www.randomhouse.com/
catalog/teachers_guides/9780385738279.pdf

Related Works

1. **Bray, Libba. *Going Bovine*.** New York: Delacorte Press, 2009. 479p. $17.99. ISBN 978 0 385 73397 7. [fiction] S, CG with high interest for boys (*Value-Packed Booktalks*, 2011, pages 4 to 5.) In a coma, 16-year-old Cameron learns how much his family loves him.
2. **Hartnett, Sonya. *What the Birds See*.** Cambridge, MA: Candlewick Press, 2002. 196p. $15.99. ISBN 0 7636 2092 0. [fiction] JS, G. Surrounded by irresponsible adults, nine-year-old Adrian is drawn into a neighbor girl's tragic fantasy.
3. **Hautman, Pete. *Invisible*.** New York: Simon & Shuster Books for Young Readers, 2005. 149p. $15.95. ISBN 0 689 86800 6. [fiction] JS, CG (*Genre Talks for Teens*, 2009, pages 29 to 32.) A brilliant loner spies on beautiful girls, talks to his deceased friend, and burns himself.
4. **Leavitt, Martine. *Heck Superhero*.** Asheville, NC: Front Street, 2004. 144p. $16.95. ISBN 1 886910 94 4. [fiction] MJ, CG with high interest for boys (*Booktalks and Beyond*, pages 28 to 30.) Thirteen-year-old Heck, abandoned by his depression-prone mother, moves back and forth between real and superhero worlds.

5. **Rapp, Adam.** *Under the Wolf, Under the Dog*. Cambridge, MA: Candlewick Press, 2004. 310p. $16.99. ISBN 0 7636 1818 7. [fiction] S/A, CG. Seventeen-year-old Steve Nugent, writing a journal in a facility for drug users and possible suicides, recalls his own personal physical and emotional deterioration in reaction to those events.

Cʒʡ

Frost, Helen. **Hidden.**

New York: Farrar, Straus and Giroux/Frances Foster Books, 2011. 147p. $16.99.
ISBN 978 0 374 38221 6. [novel in verse] JS, G

Themes/Topics: Kidnapping, interpersonal relationships, camps, memory, blame, Michigan

Summary/Description

Eight-year-old Wren Abbott is accidentally kidnapped during a robbery. She hides in the robber's garage where Darra, the robber's daughter, leaves food and water. Wren escapes through the cat door. The father is arrested, and the mother divorces him. At 14, both girls meet at Camp Oakwood, recognize each other, and work through their mutual hostility.

Values: Both girls realize that they can take responsibility for only their own behavior as they confront their anger and begin to develop a friendship.

Booktalk

Fourteen-year-old Wren and Darra meet at camp. They remember each other, but they have never seen each other. How is that possible? Six years before, Darra's father stole a car and accidentally kidnapped Wren who was (*Point to the cover of the book and draw out the response "Hidden."*) in the back. Darra knew Wren was there. She left food and water. Then, Wren escaped, and Darra's dad went to prison. Wren blames Darra. Darra blames Wren. Neither one wants to talk to or even see each other. But the question is how long can that explosive blame and anger stay (*Point to the cover and wait for the response, again.*) hidden?

Alternative booktalk available @ http://www.mackinbooktalk.com/viewBook.aspx?bookId=1910

Book trailer available @ http://animoto.com/play/ QsA0g8FFn2q1CZqYjGueJg

Read Aloud/Talkback

1. "Block and Parry," pages 78 to 79. Wren describes lifesaving class. *Talkback*: How does lifesaving class have a double meaning?
2. "In the Sun," pages 101 to 102. Wren and Darra begin their friendship. *Talkback*: Why are the questions and answers with double meanings important?
3. "Old Shipwrecks," pages 105 to 107. Darra describes a Camp Oakwood tradition. *Talkback*: What is your view of this tradition?
4. "I Hold the Letter," page 114. Darra reads the father's letter telling her that he will be released from prison. *Talkback*: How does the reality of the father's release differ from Darra's fantasy about it?
5. In the last words of the long lines of Darra's poems, Parts Two and Three. Frost gives Darra an additional voice through these end words. "Diving Deeper: Notes on Form" explains her method and purpose. *Talkback*: What does this form add to the novel? Try to use the same form to describe a scene or recall an event in your own life.

Author interviews available @ http://www.helenfrost.net/ section.php?section=links

Related Works

1. **Christopher, Lucy. *Stolen*.** New York: Scholastic Inc./Chicken House, 2010. 304p. $17.99. ISBN 978 0 545 17093 2. [fiction] JS, CG with high interest for girls (Adventure/Survival, pages 102 to 104.) Sixteen-year-old Gemma is kidnapped by a man who has stalked her since she was 10.
2. **Frost, Helen. *The Braid*.** New York: Farrar, Straus and Giroux/ Frances Foster Books, 2006. 95p. $16.00. ISBN 0 374 30962 0. [novel in verse] JS, G (*Genre Talks for Teens*, 2006, pages 100 to 103.) Two teenage sisters, caught up in the Highland Clearances of the 1850s are separated and tell their stories and struggles in alternating narrative poems.
3. **Frost, Helen. *Keesha's House*.** New York: Farrar, Straus and Giroux/Frances Foster Books, 2003. 116p. $16.00. ISBN 0 374 34064 1. [novel in verse] JS, CG (*Booktalks and Beyond*, 2007, pages 21 to 24.) Seven teenagers share their troubles, in a house extended to homeless kids.

4. **Henry, April. *Girl, Stolen*.** New York: Henry Holt and Co., 2010. 213p. $16.99. ISBN 978 0 8050 9005 5. [fiction] JS, CG with high interest for girls (Action, Adventure, Survival/Trust, pages 102 to 104.) A teenage girl is accidentally kidnapped, held for ransom, and saved by her captor's son.

5. **Simmons, Michael. *Pool Boy*.** Brookfield, CT: Roaring Brook Press/A Neal Porter Book, 2003. 164p. $23.90. ISBN 0 7613 2924 2. [fiction] JS, CG with high interest for boys (*Booktalks and Beyond*, 2007, pages 54 to 56.) Fifteen-year-old Brett becomes a pool boy after his father goes to jail for insider trading.

ॐ ॐ

Handler, Daniel (text). Maira Kalman (art).
Why We Broke Up.

New York: Little, Brown and Company, 2011. 355p. $19.99.
ISBN 978 0 316 12725 7. [fiction] S, G

Themes/Topics: Dating, souvenirs, love, letters, virginity, seduction, trust, movies

Summary/Description

Min Green writes a letter to her ex-boyfriend, Ed Slaterton, in which she describes how each item in the box she is leaving on his doorstep impacted their breakup. She belongs to an artsy high school clique. Ed is cocaptain of the high school basketball team. He becomes her trophy date. Min thinks that she is drawing him into her quirky movie and cooking interests, but he is slowly seducing her as he cheats on her with another girl. She breaks up with him when she learns about "the other girl" and discovers that Al, the boy she considered her very good friend, is actually in love with her

> **Value:** Min is slowly distinguishing among friendship, infatuation, and love, as she learns to appreciate her own beauty and strengths.

Booktalk

Ask how many people know someone who has broken up with a girlfriend or boyfriend. Wait for responses. Ask how the person reacted.

Min's break up with her trophy date Ed becomes an event. (*Open to the pictures as you talk.*) She puts every item that reminds her of their relationship—theater ticket, sugar, earrings, notes, and bottle caps—in a box and drops it on Ed's doorstep. And, of course, there is a letter. It explains to this high school hero, the cocaptain of the high school basketball team, her story, his story, and the end of their story. Min is thorough, step by step, page by page, and her letter becomes a book to tell *poor* unsuspecting Ed *Why We Broke Up*.

Book trailer available @ http://www.youtube.com/watch?v=dC34V0akNec&feature=related

Read Aloud/Talkback

1. Pages 18 to 20, beginning "I had a feeling . . ." and ending ". . . sweet late night." Min meets Ed for the first time, and he asks her out. *Talkback*: What does this memory reveal about Min? After reading the entire book, do you react differently?
2. Pages 58 to 59, beginning "'Out!'" and ending with the chapter. Ed charms the clerk and buys the camera. *Talkback*: After reading this passage, how would you distinguish between charming and unreliable?
3. Page 175, the entire paragraph. Min asks Ed for her lost umbrella. *Talkback*: Is Min talking about an umbrella? Does she actually have any hope of getting the umbrella back?
4. Pages 248 to 263. Min recalls Halloween Saturday. *Talkback*: Why is Halloween Saturday an important setting for this section?
5. Pages 315 to 320. Al confesses his jealousy and love. *Talkback*: After reading his chapter, how would you describe the difference between Al and Ed?

Author interviews @

http://www.mediabistro.com/galleycat/daniel-handler-maira-kalman-on-why-we-broke-up_b47009
http://www.youtube.com/watch?v=Ff_wxHeyRI8&feature=related

Why We Broke Up project available @ http://www.youtube.com/watch?v=AMl_Pr51Xgk

Related Works

1. **Booth, Coe. *Kendra*.** New York: Scholastic, 2008. 292p. $16.99. ISBN-13: 978 0 439 92536 5. [fiction] JS, G (*Value-Packed Booktalks*, 2011, pages 24 to 26.) When her mother rejects her for a more exciting professional life, Kendra becomes sexually active with a manipulative and unfaithful boyfriend.

2. **Flake, Sharon G. *Who Am I without Him? Short Stories about Girls and the Boys in Their Lives***. New York: Hyperion Books for Children/Jump at the Sun, 2004. 168p. $15.99. ISBN 078680693 1. [fiction, short stories] JS, G (*Booktalks and Beyond*, 2007, pages 19 to 21.) Ten short stories explore the male/female relationship.

3. **Murdock, Catherine Gilbert. *Dairy Queen Trilogy***. Boston, MA: Houghton Mifflin Co. [fiction] JS, CG with high interest for girls (*Value-Packed Booktalks*, 2011, pages 63 to 68.)

Dairy Queen. 2006. 275p. $16.00. ISBN-13: 978 0 618 68307 9. To pass English, star athlete D. J. writes an explanation of her summer which involves her family dynamics and her love life.

The Off Season. 2007. 277p. $16.00. ISBN-13: 978 0 618 93493 5. In her junior year, D. J. deals with her continuing romance, her friend's sexual orientation, her family's many problems, and her growing athletic success.

Front and Center. 2009. 254p. $16.00. ISBN-13: 978 0 618 95982 8. In this last novel, D. J. learns to accept people as they are, as she acknowledges her own strength and leadership role.

☙❧

Harmon, Michael. Brutal.

New York: Alfred A. Knopf, 2009. 227p. $16.99.
ISBN-13: 978 0 375 84099 9. [fiction] JS, CG

Themes/Topics: High schools, social isolation, bullies, fathers and daughters, mothers and daughters, singers, moving households, California

Summary/Description

When her mother takes her medical talents to a South American jungle, Poe Holly, a punker who sang in a Los Angeles band, moves in with the perfectionist father she has not seen for 16 years. He lives in Benders Hollow, the perfect small town, and is the counselor at Benders High, where the in-crowd sets the rules and bullies newcomers. Poe's socially inept neighbor is a target. School politics prevent Poe, the school's best singer, from being the choir's head soloist. When Poe's neighbor suffers a brutal beating triggered by Poe's choir conflicts, she uses her obnoxious personality and some detective work to find justice. She also works through her personal conflicts with her parents and her own bullying behavior.

Values: Instead of criticizing others, Poe takes responsibility for her attitudes and actions.

Booktalk

Poe Holly is a punker. She used to sing with an LA band. Now, she is taking her attitude and her black fingernails to Benders Hollow, California. Her do-good doctor mom gets a call from a South American jungle to save the world. Poe has to live with her perfectionist father whom she hasn't seen—even a picture—in 16 years. How do you think that will work out? (*Wait for answers.*) The entire town looks like Dad's house and car—perfect! If a person can't keep up that appearance, there's trouble. What do you think the high school is like? (*Wait for answers.*) A select few run Benders High. Their parents run the town. But trouble is Poe's middle name. And if anyone—her mom, dad, or townies—gives her or her outsider friends a hard time, she gives back with more. Words, pranks, fists are all part of the bully game. Everyone, even Poe, is willing to go *Brutal*.

Audio booktalk available @ http://www.hclib.org/teens/booklistaction.cfm?list_num=1067

Book trailer available @ http://www.youtube.com/watch?v=RUja3yz9Oj8

Read Aloud/Talkback

1. Chapter 1, pages 1 to 3, beginning with the chapter and ending with ". . . pissed off." Poe talks about her mother. *Talkback*: What do you learn about Poe and her mother from this passage?
2. Chapter 4, pages 24 to 25, beginning with "We didn't talk . . ." and ending with ". . . making it different." Poe reacts to her father with her mother's advice. *Talkback*: Do you agree with Poe?
3. Chapter 7, pages 59 to 63, beginning with "Teachers are supposed . . ." and ending with the chapter. Poe discusses a teacher's role with her father. *Talkback*: Do you agree with Poe, her father, or neither one?
4. Chapter 16, pages 134 to 136, beginning with the chapter and ending with ". . . then walked inside." Velveeta confronts Poe about her attitude. *Talkback*: How did you react to Velveeta's conversation with Poe?
5. Chapter 24, pages 193 to 195. Poe's father reacts to Poe's behavior in the counseling meeting. *Talkback*: Why is this conversation a turning point in the story?

Read aloud available @ http://www.youtube.com/
watch?v=_aEg9R0M97U

Related Works

1. **Bruchac, Joseph.** *The Way*. Plain City, OH: Darby Creek Publishing, 2007. 164p. $16.95. ISBN-13: 978 1 58196 062 4. [fiction] MJS, CG with high interest for boys (*Value-Packed Booktalks*, 2011, pages 213 to 215.) Cody LeBeau, an Abenaki Indian, deals effectively with bullying when his uncle teaches him martial arts and self-respect.

2. **Coy, John.** *Box Out*. New York: Scholastic Press, 2008. 289p. $16.99. ISBN 13: 978 0 439 87032 0. [fiction] JS, CG with high interest for boys (*Value-Packed Booktalks*, 2011, pages 58 to 60.) Sophomore Liam Bergstrom is called up to the varsity, but is shunned when he refuses to participate in the Christian athletic program.

3. **Pixley, Marcella.** *Freak*. New York: Farrar, Straus and Giroux/Melanie Kroupa Books, 2007. 131p. $16.00. ISBN-13: 978 0 374 32453 7. [fiction] MJS, G (*Genre Talks for Teens*, 2009, pages 37 to 39.) When 12-year-old Miriam faces the girl who bullies her, she discovers that neither of them has a supportive adult for help.

4. **Prose, Francine.** *Bullyville*. New York: HarperTeen, 2007. 260p. $16.99. ISBN-13: 975 0 06 057497 0. [fiction] MJ, CG with high interest for boys (*Genre Talks for Teens*, 2009, pages 16 to 19.) After his father dies in the Twin Towers terrorist attack, 13-year-old Bart Rangely attends an exclusive boys' school and confronts a bullying campaign.

5. **Schwartz, John.** *Short: Walking Tall When You're Not Tall at All*. New York: Roaring Brook Press/Flash Point, 2010. 132p. $16.99. ISBN 978 1 59643 323 6. [nonfiction] JS, CG. Schwartz, a short person, warns us "abnormal people that difference is good, and negative labels are often commercial hype." Pages 59 to 72 present criteria for examining the bias of scientific studies, and "The Beginning," his concluding chapter on pages 111 to 114, emphasizes that "It's always *our* decision who we are."

ॐ

Keller, Julia. Back Home.
New York: Egmont, 2009. 194p. $15.99.
ISBN 978 1 60684 005 4. [fiction] JS, CG

Themes/Topics: Brain damage, family problems, soldiers, veterans, Iraq War

Summary/Description

Thirteen-year-old Rachel Browning's father is injured in Iraq. He loses a leg and an arm. Brain trauma takes away his drive for recovery. As the family lives with this helpless, difficult, and sometimes angry stranger, Rachel becomes stronger. She adapts to a string of home health care professionals and therapists, helps her mother who is trying to earn a living for the family, learns what makes real friends, and realizes that even though her family loves her father, everyone benefits when professionals care for him away from home.

Value: Rachel learns about coping, true friends, and family unity.

Booktalk

Ask for a volunteer to read Chapter 1, pages 1 and 2, beginning with the chapter and ending ". . . came back home." Thirteen-year-old Rachel doesn't have the world at her fingertips anymore. Neither that fort, nor anything else, is safe enough. Her father went to Iraq. An enemy attack took his leg and arm and, worse, a part of his brain, the part that tells his body to fight back and keep going. How might that affect a family? (*Wait for responses.*) Officials tell Rachel's family that her father survived. The man who comes back though doesn't look, smell, or sound like that father. He is silent, stubborn, scary, and dirty. This man can tear the family apart, because this man brings the war *Back Home*.

Read Aloud/Talkback

The entire story is suitable for read aloud. The five specific suggestions are as follows:

1. Chapter 2, pages 23 to 24, beginning with "I didn't blame . . ." and ending with ". . . plenty for now." Rachel reflects on adulthood. *Talkback*: Do you agree with Rachel?
2. Chapter 5, pages 83 to 86, beginning with "When Dad was . . ." and ending with the chapter. Rachel reflects on her father's pictures from Iraq. The ideas introduced here conclude the narrative, pages 193 to 194, beginning with "These days . . ." and ending with the chapter. *Talkback*: What do you feel the sky symbolizes?
3. Chapter 7, pages 133 to 135, beginning with "Just what *is* a body . . ." and ending with ". . . to have things." Rachel contemplates the qualities that make an individual. *Talkback*: What elements do you think define each person?

4. Chapter 9, pages 178 to 180, beginning with "Life is about . . ." and ending with ". . . could escape." Rachel explains the choices her father's injury brings. *Talkback*: How do you react to Rachel's attitude about choices?

5. Chapter 9, pages 185 to 186, beginning with "And so Dad . . ." and ending with ". . . hear him, either." Rachel explains her feelings about her father going to a facility. *Talkback*: What does Rachel communicate about her father and the family?

Author interviews available @

http://www.zulkey.com/2009/11/how_did_you_decide_to_2.php
http://llnw.wbez.org/archives/audio/848/2009/09/848_20090917c.mp3

Related Works

1. **Aronson, Marc and Patty Campbell (eds.).** *War Is: Soldiers, Survivors, and Storytellers Talk about War*. Cambridge, MA: Candlewick Press, 2008. 200p. $17.99. ISBN 978 0 7636 3625 8. [anthology: nonfiction and fiction] S, CG (*Value-Packed Booktalks*, 2011, pages 27 to 29.) Twenty selections explore war from the points of view of protestors, correspondents, soldiers, and military family members.

2. **Beah, Ishmael.** *A Long Way Gone: Memoirs of a Boy Soldier*. New York: Farrar, Straus and Giroux/Sarah Crichton Books, 2007. 229p. $22.00. ISBN-13: 978 374 10523 5. [nonfiction] JS/A, CG with high interest for boys (*Genre Talks for Teens*, 2009, pages 98 to 100.) Orphaned Ishmael describes his journey from refugee, to boy soldier, and finally to a representative for peace in a UN rehabilitation camp.

3. **Hobbs, Valerie.** *Sonny's War*. New York: Farrar, Straus and Giroux/Frances Foster Books, 2002. 215p. $16.00. ISBN 0 374 37136 9. [fiction] JS, CG (*Teen Genre Connections*, 2005, pages 230 to 233.) Fourteen-year-old Cory sees her life changing in the midst of the Vietnam War. Her brother Sonny, a bitter Vietnam veteran, returns home with a leg wound and a drug habit.

4. **McCormick, Patricia.** *Purple Heart*. New York: Harper Collins Publishers/Balzar & Bray, 2009. 199p. $1699. ISBN 978 0 06 1730900. [fiction] JS, CG with high interest for boys (Action/Adventure/Survival, pages 89 to 91.) Eighteen-year-old Matt Duffy, awarded a Purple Heart, struggles through a brain trauma to remember what happened.

5. **Myers, Walter Dean.** *Sunrise over Fallujah*. New York: Scholastic Press, 2008. 304p. $17.99. ISBN 13: 978 0 439 91624 0. [fiction] JS, CG with high interest for boys (*Genre Talks for Teens*, 2010, pages 98 to 100.) Private Robin Perry (aka Birdy) relates his experiences as a member of a Civil Affairs Unit in the Iraq invasion.

King, A. S. **Please Ignore Vera Dietz.**
New York: Alfred A. Knopf, 2010. 323p. $16.99.
ISBN 978 0 375 86586 2. [fiction] S, CG with high interest for girls

Themes/Topics: Friendship, secrets, death,
father/daughter relationships

Summary/Description

Told in the voices of 18-year-old Vera, Vera's father, and Vera's neighbor and best friend, Charlie Kahn, the story centers on Vera's coming of age after Charlie's death. Vera secretly loves Charlie who comes from an abusive home. She works through grief and the resentment she holds for his choosing a vicious, detention-riddled crowd of friends who bully her. She deals with her mother divorcing her father and essentially abandoning her, and she manages her heavy academic schedule and a 40-hour-per-week pizza job. Vera comes from an alcoholic family and drinks to cope. Her father discovers that she is drinking and dating an older man. He joins her in therapy, and they learn to communicate their feelings and fears. To move on, the father disposes off all the mother's belongings. Vera reconciles her feelings for Charlie.

Values: Vera learns the importance of self-respect in
love for friends and family.

Booktalk

Ask how many people in the group know someone who goes to school but doesn't socialize. Ask them to explain why the person doesn't get involved in activities. Eighteen-year-old Vera Dietz doesn't get involved in school either. She works a 40-hour week—no time for high school drama. She has enough drama in her life. When she was 12, her mother left for good. Last August, her best friend Charlie died—mysteriously. That was way worse than Mom leaving. Vera talked to Charlie more than she did Mom or Dad. But Charlie had started hanging with another crowd, a crowd that pounded Vera into the ground. What would be your reaction to a friend like that? (*Wait for responses.*) Vera felt the same. Now, dead lots-of-nerve-Charlie is telling Vera to clear his name. Invisible Vera becomes drunk Vera. Her Dad starts talking to her. At work, a college dropout is interested in her, too. But Vera wants to say "Please Ignore Vera Dietz."

Book trailer available @ http://www.randomhouse.com/
book/196759/please-ignore-vera-dietz-by-as-king

Shelf talk available @ http://www.as-king.com/Please%20
Ignore%20Vera%20Dietz%20Shelftalker.pdf

Read Aloud/Talkback

1. "The Funeral," page 5, beginning with the chapter and ending with ". . . for being dead?" Vera reacts to Charlie's eulogy. *Talkback*: What is your impression of Charlie?
2. "A Brief Word from Ken Dietz (Vera's Dad)" and "Ken Dietz's Avoiding Your Destiny Flow Chart," pages 23 to 27. Vera's father explains his background and offers a life flowchart to Vera. *Talkback*: Do you agree with Ken Dietz's perception of a successful life?
3. "A Brief Word from the Dead Kid," pages 49 to 50. Charlie explains how he accepted his destiny. *Talkback*: What do Charlie and Ken Dietz have in common?
4. "Ken Dietz's Flow Chart of Destructive Behavior," page 128. The chart shows the path of alcoholism and the alternatives. *Talkback*: Do you agree with Ken Dietz's chart?
5. "Drive Car, Deliver Pizza—Tuesday—Four to Eight" and "A Brief Word from the Pagoda," pages 297 to 299, beginning with "My delivery . . ." and ending with the end of the Pagoda statement. Vera ponders the appropriate signs for people. *Talkback*: Why does the Pagoda disagree with Vera? What is your reaction?

Discussion guide available @ http://www.as-king.com/
Please%20Ignore%20Vera%20Dietz%20
Discussion%20Guide.pdf

Related Works

1. **Alexie, Sherman, and Ellen Forney (illus.). *The Absolutely True Diary of a Part-Time Indian*.** New York: Little, Brown & Company, 2007. 228p. $16.99. ISBN-13: 978 0 316 01368 0. [fiction] JS, CG with high interest for boys (*Genre Talks for Teens*, 2009, pages 269 to 272.) Arnold Spirit (a.k.a. Junior) leaves the

reservation school and enrolls in a more prosperous white school that can help him break the family cycle of alcoholism.

2. **Davis, Deborah.** *Not Like You*. New York: Clarion Books, 2007. 268p. $16.00. ISBN-13: 978 0 618 72093 4. [fiction] JS, G (*Genre Talks for Teens*, 2009, pages 9 to 11.) Fifteen-year-old Kayla denies that she will ever be like her alcoholic and irresponsible mother, but finds herself following a destructive path.

3. **Rottman, S. L.** *Stetson*. New York: Viking, 2002. 192p. $16.99. ISBN 0 670 03542 4. [fiction] JS, CG with high interest for boys (*Teen Genre Connections*, 2005, pages 23 to 25.) Seventeen-year-old Stetson separates himself and his sister from his alcoholic father.

4. **Soto, Gary.** *The Afterlife*. New York: Harcourt Brace and Company, 2003. 161p. $16.00. ISBN 0 15 204774 3. [fiction] JS, CG with high interest for boys (*Teen Genre Connections*, 2005, pages 294 to 296.) Stabbed in a restroom, 18-year-old Jesús moves from life to the afterlife and briefly touches those left behind.

5. **Tharp, Tim.** *The Spectacular Now*. New York: Alfred A. Knopf, 2008. 294p. $16.99. ISBN 978 0 375 85179 7. [fiction] S, CG with high interest for boys (*Value-Packed Booktalks*, 2011, pages 11 to 13). Sutter Keely, a life-of-the-party senior, denies his destructive behavior and alcoholism.

ᘓᘔ

Silvey, Craig. Jasper Jones.
New York: Alfred a Knopf, 2009. 312p. $16.99.
ISBN: 978 0 375 86666 1. [fiction] S, CG

Theme/Topics: Abuse, suicide, prejudice, rebellion, incest, recluses, small town, dysfunctional families, secrets, interpersonal relations, Vietnam War

Summary/Description

Jasper Jones, the town outcast, knocks on the 13-year-old Charlie Bucktin's window in the middle of the night and leads him to a beaten and hanged girl. The girl, Laura Wishart, is Jasper's girlfriend and the daughter of the shire president. Charlie has a crush on her sister, Eliza. Jasper knows that he will be accused of the murder and persuades Charlie to help him bury Laura in a deep pond. Laura's parents find her missing. A fruitless search ensues. Jasper and Charlie search for the murderer and discover their own shocking family secrets. Eliza tells Charlie about their father's sexual abuse and the incestuous pregnancy that lead to her sister's suicide. Charlie tells Eliza about the burial. Jasper leaves town. The town assumes that the rebellious Laura ran away. Eliza burns down her family's house in revenge against her parents, but the town blames Jasper, even though he is gone.

Values: Jasper Jones forces Charlie to choose trust and loyalty over obedience to questionable authority.

Booktalk

Ask what people expect when someone knocks on the door. Ask what they would expect if someone knocked on their bedroom window in the middle of the night.

Thirteen-year-old Charlie hears that knock on the window in the middle of the night. It is Jasper Jones, the town outcast. He needs help. Charlie, the bookworm, the kid the bullies love to pick on, goes with him. Jasper leads him to his secret glade. There, Charlie sees Laura Wishart, the shire president's daughter hanged and dead with Jasper's rope. Why would Jasper bring Charlie here? (*Wait for responses.*) Charlie becomes part of the crime, a witness to forbidden love, and an unwilling keeper of horrible secrets. Who or what can help him? The town authorities? The wisdom of his books? His protective parents? Or *Jasper Jones*?

Book trailers available @ http://www.craigsilveyauthor.com/
index.php?option=com_content&view=article&id=60&Ite
mid=55

Read Aloud/Talkback

1. Chapter 1, pages 5 to 6, beginning with "Jasper Jones . . ." and ending with ". . . far better world for it." Charlie relates Jasper's reputation and his father's reaction. *Talkback*: Why are Jasper's reputation and the works of Mark Twain so closely related?

2. Chapter 2, pages 62 to 63, beginning with "See, I always thought . . ." and ending with ". . . this season." Charlie notes how Jasper and Charlie are seen in sports. *Talkback*: How would you account for how differently the town reacts to Jasper on and off the field?

3. Chapter 3, pages 83 to 85, beginning with "And then they . . ." and ending with ". . . to hurt somebody." Charlie tries to understand a murderer by reading about past cases. The passage ties to the passage in Chapter 9, pages 308 to 309, beginning with "I wipe my eyes . . ." and ending with ". . . still inside." *Talkback*: What do you conclude about violent acts from these passages? Do you agree with Charlie's conclusions?

4. Chapter 5, page 151, beginning with "I bin made to feel . . ." and ending with ". . . are you?" Jasper explains his view of life. *Talkback*: Do you agree with Jasper?

5. Chapter 6, pages 206 to 207, beginning with "*Sorry* means you feel the . . ." and ending with ". . . locked away." Charlie ponders the meaning of sorry. *Talkback*: How would you explain the meaning of sorry?

Reading Group guide available @
http://www.allenandunwin.com/_uploads/BookPdf/
ReadingGroupGuide/9781741757743.pdf

Author interviews available @
http://www.youtube.com/watch?v=P72HGCm—mY&feature=related
http://www.youtube.com/watch?v=Cv8u5IBlt04&feature=related
http://www.youtube.com/watch?v=2XuV6dY-n8U&feature=related

Author read aloud available @ http://www.youtube.com/
watch?v=nK2MDx6lPa8&feature=related

Related Works

1. **Blackman, Malorie. *Naughts & Crosses*.** New York: Simon & Schuster Books for Young Readers, 2005. 387p. $15.95. ISBN 1 4169 0016 0. [fiction] JS, CG (*Booktalks and Beyond*, 2007, pages 16 to 19.) Sephy Hadley, a dark-skinned cross, and Callum McGregor, a light-skinned naught, become romantically involved in a prejudiced society.

2. **Brooks, Kevin. *Lucas: A Story of Love and Hate*.** New York: Chicken House, 2002. 432p. $16.95. ISBN 0 439 45698 3. [fiction] JS, CG with high interest for boys (*Booktalks and Beyond*, 2007, pages 4 to 6.) Sixteen-year-old Caitlin McCann decides to help Lucas, a stranger with no friends, family, or last name.

3. **Schmidt, Gary D. *Lizzie Bright and the Buckminster Boy*.** New York: Clarion Books, 2004. 219p. $15.00. ISBN 0 618 43929 3. [fiction] MJS, CG (*Booktalks and Beyond*, 2007, pages 251 to 254.) A young minister's son challenges the prejudices and greed of a small New England town by befriending the smart and rebellious Lizzie Bright, part of a poor community founded by former slaves.

4. **Schmidt, Gary D. *Trouble*.** New York: Clarion Books, 2008. 297p. $16.00. ISBN-13: 978 0 618 92776 1. [fiction] MJS, CG (*Genre Talks for Teens*, 2009, pages 292 to 295.) A family blames a Cambodian refugee for their son's death, but then discovers that their daughter was responsible.

5. **Zusak, Markus.** *The Book Thief.* New York: Alfred A. Knopf, 2006. 552p. $21.90. ISBN 0 375 93100 7. [fiction] JS, CG with high interest for girls (*Genre Talks for Teens*, 2009, pages 241 to 243.) Death tells the story of Liesel Meminger, the daughter of a communist in Hitler's Germany, and the foster couple who quietly defy the government.

Faith

෫ඁ

Avasthi, Swati. Split.

New York: Alfred A. Knopf, 2010. 280p. $16.99.
ISBN: 978 0 375 86340 0. [fiction] JS, CG with high interest for boys

Themes/Topics: Abuse, dysfunctional family, brothers

Summary/Description

Sixteen-year-old Jace fights with his father for attacking his mother. His father beats him up and throws him out of the house. He leaves Chicago and flees to Albuquerque to live with his brother Christian, who left home five years ago. With the help of Miriam, Christian's girlfriend, the brothers open up to each other. After a last attempt to help their mother escape fails, the truth about Jace abusing his girlfriend and stealing comes out. At first, Christian throws him out. Miriam invites him to stay with her. They share their suffering, anger, and fear, and take responsibility for their actions. Jace reveals his past to a new girl he wishes to date. Christian moves to a larger apartment to accommodate Jace, and the three are learning to be a family.

Values: Sixteen-year-old Jace and his brother learn the importance of openness, trust, and honesty, as they deal with their history of family violence.

Booktalk

Ask how many in the group think that violence runs in families?

Sixteen-year-old Jace hits his father. Why? Because he knows that his father hit his mother. Who do you think wins? (*Wait for answers.*) So, Jace is out of the house. He is bloody and beaten. He has a camera, a car, $3.84 in his pocket, his brother's address, and no plan—just one hope.

He is going to drive to Albuquerque and find Christian, the brother who left five years ago. Will Christian let Jace in? Will he even know him? And, when Christian finds out about Jace's not so squeaky clean past, will he let him stay? After all, Jace was Dad's favorite. Maybe, violence is genetic. Can Jace find a home or, once again, have to fight and *Split*?

Book trailer available @ http://www.randomhouse.com/
book/6457/split-by-swati-avasthi#blurb_tabs

Read Aloud/Talkback

1. Chapter 3, pages 16 to 17, beginning with the chapter and ending with ". . . looks like today." Jace recalls father's sportsmanship lesson. *Talkback*: How does the father's advice to Jace apply to the father also?
2. Chapter 6, pages 52 to 58. In this chapter, Christian and Jace discuss the rules for staying. *Talkback*: What makes this talk between the brothers so difficult?
3. Chapter 12, pages 106 to 109, beginning with "I'm back in the . . ." and ending with ". . . tick by us." Jace recalls beating Lauren. *Talkback*: In this scene, is either Lauren or Jace taking responsibility?
4. Chapter 19, pages 165 to 166, beginning with "You're an interesting . . ." and ending with "Jace, sir." Dakota comments on Jace's "charm." *Talkback*: Assess Jace's charm.
5. Chapter 31, pages 263 to 264, beginning with "I always thought . . ." and ending with the chapter. Jace and Miriam talk about the mother's abuse. *Talkback*: How does this passage address responsibility?

Readers Guide available @ http://www.randomhouse.com/
catalog/teachers_guides/9780375863400.pdf

Author interviews available @

http://www.swatiavasthi.com/
http://www.bookbundlz.com/BBArticle.aspx?articleId=43
http://marjoleinbookblog.blogspot.com/2010/07/author-inter
viewsswati-avasthi.html
http://agoodaddiction.blogspot.com/2010/03/author-interview-
swati-avasthi.html
http://trythisbookonforsize.blogspot.com/2012/06/interview-with-
author-swati-avasthi.html
http://www.bookreporter.com/authors/swati-avasthi/news/inter
view-030910
http://whatsonthebookshelf-jen.blogspot.com/2011/12/hug-author-
author-interview-swati.html

http://www.whorublog.com/?p=832

http://dreamingdreamsnomortaleverdared.blogspot.com/2012/01/
swati-avasthi-takeover-giveaway.html

http://www.childrensliteraturenetwork.org/blog/interviews/tag/
swati-avasthi/

Related Works

1. **Dessen, Sarah. *Dreamland***. New York: Viking, 2000. 250p. $15.99. ISBN 0 670 89122 3. [fiction] JS, G (*Booktalks and More*, 2003, pages 73 to 75.) Caitlin O'Koren allows her abusive boyfriend to control her life.

2. **Flake, Sharon G. *Who Am I without Him?: Short Stories about Girls and the Boys in Their Lives***. New York: Hyperion Books for Children/Jump at the Sun, 2004. 168p. $15.99. ISBN 078680693 1 [fiction, short stories] JS, G (*Booktalks and Beyond*, 2007, pages 19 to 21.) Ten short stories emphasize that a girl must find strength in herself before she finds it in a boyfriend.

3. **Flinn, Alex. *Breathing Underwater***. New York: HarperCollins Publishers, 2001. 263p. $15.95. ISBN 0 06 029198 2. [fiction] JS, CG (*Teen Genre Connections*, 2005, pages 19 to 21.) Sixteen-year-old Nick Andreas is sentenced to six months of family violence and anger management classes after he beats his girlfriend.

4. **Grace, Amanda. *But I Love Him***. Woodbury, MN: Flux/Llewellyn, 2011. 264p. $9.95pa. ISBN 978 0 7387 2594 9. [fiction] S, CG with high interest for girls. A young girl becomes trapped in an abusive and dangerous relationship.

5. **Klass, David. *You Don't Know Me***. New York: Farrar, Straus and Giroux/Frances Foster Books, 2001. 262p. $17.00. ISBN 0 374 38706 0. [fiction] JS, CG (*Booktalks and More*, 2003, pages 31 to 33.) A young man, abused by his mother's live-in boyfriend, mistrusts everyone around him, but learns that he does not know his mother.

❧❧

Christopher, Lucy. Flyaway.

New York: Scholastic Inc./Chicken House, 2011. 336p. $16.99.
ISBN: 978 0 545 31771 9. [fiction] MJ, CG

Themes/Topics: Swans, illness, death, family relationships, interpersonal relationships

Summary/Description

Isla and her father welcome the wintering swans at the lake every year. In one outing, the father falls ill and is taken to the hospital. He needs a heart valve replaced. Struggling with her grief and fear, Isla meets Harry, a cancer ward patient preparing for a bone marrow transplant. She looks out the hospital window and spots a lone whooper struggling to fly. Isla creates a flying machine for her art class, and enables the swan to fly and reunite with the flock. Her success inspires Harry to live, encourages the father to recover, and strengthens Isla's relationships with her grandfather and brother.

Value: The story confirms the importance of nature, family, and friendship.

Booktalk

Ask what the group associates with the phrase "flying away"? Isla and her father welcome the swans to their winter home every year. This year, her father runs toward the swans. He falls. Father and daughter are in the back of an ambulance, then in the hospital where her grandmother died six years ago. The doctors say that the father needs a heart operation. Will her father, like her grandmother, *Flyaway*? (*Wait for responses.*) As she waits and worries in that place filled with tubes and machines, she makes friends with Harry. Harry isn't like her other friends. He is as fascinated by the birds as she is. Like her father, he needs a risky procedure. Is he about to *Flyaway*? From the hospital window, she and Harry see a swan struggling to fly. If the swan flies away, it will join the flock and live. (*Ask how the meaning of flyaway is changing and wait for a response.*) Life and death are blending, and Isla may be the one to *Flyaway*.

Author booktalk available @ http://www.youtube.com/watch?v=p84vzm6f0lY

Read Aloud/Talkback

1. "The Beginning," pages 1 and 2. Isla describes how the arrival of the swans bonds the family. *Talkback*: How does this introduction establish a mystical quality?
2. Chapter 13, page 68. Isla dreams about the dying swans. *Talkback*: What is your reaction to Isla's dream?
3. Chapter 29, pages 141 to 142, beginning with "Swans *are* amazing . . ." and ending with the chapter. Isla's father explains the "swan song." *Talkback*: How do Isla and her father view the swan song? How do you view it?

4. Chapter 61, pages 278 to 281, beginning with "Like last time . . ." and ending with ". . . I can help her." Isla panics when she sees her father and directs her efforts to the swans. *Talkback*: Isla runs from her father's room to help the swans. Do you agree with her reaction?

5. Chapter 69, pages 307 to 310. Isla presents her flying machine to the class. *Talkback*: What does Isla learn from her presentation? What do you learn?

Author interview available @ http://www.lucychristopher.com/ questions

Related Works

1. **Frost, Helen. *Diamond Willow*.** New York: Farrar, Straus and Giroux/Frances Foster Books, 2008. 109p. $16.00. ISBN-13: 978 0 374 31776 8. [novel in verse] M, G (*Value-Packed Booktalks*, 2011, pages 239 to 241.) In a series of diamond-shaped verses with small bolded messages within them, 12-year-old Willow tells about her coming of age tied to her birth and her lead dog.

2. **Hiaasen, Carl. *Hoot*.** New York: Alfred A. Knopf, 2002. 292p. $15.95. ISBN 0 375 82181 3. [fiction] MJ, CG with high interest for boys (*Teen Genre Connections*, 2005, pages 37 to 39.) Roy Eberhardt's curiosity draws him into a fight to save burrowing owls and a friendship with abused children.

3. **Sonnenblick, Jordan. *After Ever After*.** New York: Scholastic Press, 2010. 272p. $16.99. ISBN 978 0 439 83706 4. [fiction] MJS, CG (*Value-Packed Booktalks*, 2011, pages 8 to 10.) Jeffrey Alper, from *Drums, Girls and Dangerous Pie*, may not pass eighth grade. The challenge forces him to work through his feelings about family, cancer, and friendships. He concludes that every life is important.

4. **Sonnenblick, Jordan. *Drums, Girls and Dangerous Pie*.** New York: Scholastic Press, 2005. 288p. $16.99. ISBN 0 439 75519 0. [fiction] MJS, CG. Thirteen-year-old Steven, a talented drummer, learns to handle his conflicts and emotions, as he helps his family cope with his four-year-old brother's battle with leukemia.

5. **Tan, Shaun. *Lost and Found*.** New York: Scholastic Inc./Arthur A. Levine Books, 2011. 128p. $21.99. ISBN 978 0 545 22924 1. [illustrated fiction] MJS, CG (Fantasy/New Powers, pages 193 to 195.) "The Red Tree," the first short story, illustrates how a girl finds one sprout of hope in an overwhelming world.

༕༡

Connelly, Neil. The Miracle Stealer.

New York: Scholastic, Inc./Arthur A. Levine Books, 2010. 240p. $17.99.
ISBN 978 0 545 13195 7. [fiction] JS, CG with high interest for girls

Themes/Topics: Illness, families in crisis, grief,
miracles, faith, hope

Summary/Description

Nineteen-year-old Andi Grant's six-year-old brother Daniel is
deemed a miracle worker because as a three-year-old he survived
entrapment in a collapsed well. The community and media pressure
split their family. The father leaves. Andi conflicts with her mother who
believes Daniel is blessed. Andi constructs a "fraud" miracle to destroy
Daniel's credibility and force people to leave him alone. Her plan goes
wrong. Daniel saves her life, and she begins a healing journey with her
family, boyfriend, and community.

Values: Andi opens herself to love and hope while distinguishing
spiritual belief from superstition.

Booktalk

*Ask how many people in the group believe in miracles and compare their
responses.* Nineteen-year-old Andi lives in Paradise, Pennsylvania, with
a miracle worker, her six-year-old brother Daniel. People say that he
walks on water, brings dead babies to life, and cures alcoholism. Andi
worries that his adoring followers will either kill him or drive him crazy.
They have been whipped up by a profit-crazy press, driven away her
father, and built a wall between Andi's believing mother and Andi. What
would you do? (*Wait for responses.*) Andi won't leave Daniel. She decides to take control. Her plan will expose her brother as a fraud and the
adoring crowds will disappear. But the forces that Andi doesn't believe
in might not look too kindly on *The Miracle Stealer*.

Read Aloud/Talkback

1. Chapter 1, page 2, beginning with "In the hospital . . ." and ending
    with ". . . back from the dead." Andi distinguishes between an
    observer and a witness. *Talkback*: How would you distinguish
    between an observer and a witness?

2. Chapter 3, pages 33 to 40. In this chapter, Andi witnesses Daniel's entrapment and rescue. *Talkback*: What is your reaction to the events that Andi describes and to Andi?

3. Chapter 4, pages 41 to 42, beginning with "The Scarecrow's talk . . ." and ending with ". . . superstitious crap." Andi writes an article to debunk the miracle workers. *Talkback*: On page 46, beginning with "You're trying . . ." and ending with ". . . their mind." Gayle reacts to Andi's article. How did you react?

4. Chapter 5, page 79, beginning with "He froze . . ." and ending with ". . . making sense." Andi's father leaves. *Talkback*: In the context of faith and belief, how is the departure of Andi's father ironic?

5. Chapter 16, page 230, beginning with "It took me a good . . ." and ending with the novel. Andi explains where she stands on faith. *Talkback*: How did you react to Andi's "maybe"?

Author interview available @ http://chavelaque.blogspot .com/2010/10/q-neil-connelly-author-of-miracle.html

Related Works

1. **Connelly, Neil. *St. Michael's Scales*.** New York: Arthur A. Levine Books, 2002. 32p. $16.95. ISBN 0 439 19445 8. [fiction] MJS, CG (*Teen Genre Connections*, 2005, pages 59 to 61.) Fifteen-year-old Keegan Flannery decides to atone for his twin brother's death and his mother's subsequent mental illness by killing himself.

2. **Hautman, Pete. *Godless*.** New York: Simon & Shuster Books for Young Readers, 2004. 198p. $15.95. ISBN 0 689 86278 4. [fiction] JS, CG (*Genre Talks for Teens*, 2009, pages 27 to 29.) Jason Bock, disillusioned by his parents' religion, begins one centered on the town water tower and finds new insights about belief, faith, and religion.

3. **Rylant, Cynthia. *God Went to Beauty School*.** New York: Harper-Tempest, 2003. 56p. $15.89. ISBN 0 06 009434 6. [poetry] JS, CG (*Teen Genre Connections*, 2005, pages 84 to 85.) In 23 poems, Rylant characterizes God as an almighty being who puts the world in motion and discovers the pain and beauty in His creation.

4. **Spires, Elizabeth. *I Heard God Talking to Me: William Edmondson and His Stone Carvings*.** New York: Farrar, Straus and Giroux, 2009. 56p. $17.95. ISBN-13: 978 0 374 33528 1. [biography in verse] JS/A, CG (*Value-Packed Booktalks*, 2011, pages 241 to 243.) In 23 poems, Elizabeth Spires personifies the creations and expresses the vision of William Edmondson, who began carving in the 1930s after God spoke to him.

5. **Zevin, Gabrielle. *Elsewhere*.** New York: Farrar, Straus and Giroux, 2005. 277p. $19.95. ISBN 0 374 32091 8. [fiction] MJS, G (*Booktalks and Beyond*, 2007, pages 188 to 190.) Death allows 16-year-old Liz to experience and enjoy many lives instead of just one.

ℭℰ

Freitas, Donna. **The Survival Kit.**
New York: Frances Foster Books, 2011. 353p. $16.99.
ISBN 978 0 374 39917 7. [fiction] JS, G

Themes/Topics: Grief, death, identity, coming of age, interpersonal relationships

Summary/Description

Sixteen-year-old Rose Madison is a beautiful, popular cheerleader who dates the captain of the football team. Her grief over her mother's death and her father's subsequent drinking makes her withdraw from her "perfect" high school life and focus on "Rose's Survival Kit," her mother's last gift to her. As she works through its contents—an iPod play list, a picture of peonies, a crystal heart, a paper star, a box of crayons, and a tiny handmade kite—she rediscovers her friends, finds romance with the family landscaper who also lost his father to cancer, discovers her strengths, understands and helps others through their personal crises, and comes to terms with her mother's death.

Values: In her grief, Rose discovers the joy and responsibility of love.

Booktalks

Sixteen-year-old Rose Madison is beautiful and popular. She is the cheerleader who dates the captain of the football team. But the attention hasn't made her a snob. She has no enemies, and her best friend is not even part of the in-group. She has it all together, until her mother dies of cancer. Her brother goes away to college and her dad starts drinking. Rose is used to success, happiness, and family support. It's all gone. What now? (*Wait for answers.*) Those things are all possible, but Rose is blinded by her grief. She can't see any answers to "What now?," but there are some. And she begins to find them in her mother's last gifts to her, a beautiful sparkling gown and a package labeled "Rose's Survival Kit."

Read Aloud/Talkback

1. Chapter 5, pages 33 to 37. Rose finds the survival kit and explains it in relation to her mother and family. *Talkback*: What is your reaction to this chapter?

2. Chapter 9, page 61, beginning with the chapter and ending with ". . . find out either." Rose reflects on her breakup with Chris Williams. *Talkback*: What does this paragraph tell you about Rose's relationship with Chris?

3. Chapter 12, pages 87 to 88, beginning with "During one of our . . ." and ending with ". . . continued on his way." Will and Rose discuss the garden. *Talkback*: What does this conversation reveal about Will and Rose?

4. Chapter 25, pages 204 to 205, beginning with "I know . . ." and ending with ". . . with him, too?" Rose wonders about her feelings for Will. *Talkback*: Why is Rose's question so important?

5. Chapter 35, pages 316 to 318, beginning with "When I got home . . ." and ending with the chapter. *Talkback*: Why is the jacket decision a turning point for Rose?

Related Works

1. **Averett, Edward. *The Rhyming Season*.** New York: Clarion Books, 2005. 214p. $16.00. ISBN 0 618 46948 6. [fiction] JS, G (*Booktalks and Beyond*, 2007, pages 65 to 68.) After her basketball-star brother dies, Brenda Jacobsen discovers her own strength by leading the girls' basketball team to a championship.

2. **Flake, Sharon G. *Who Am I without Him? Short Stories about Girls and the Boys in Their Lives*.** New York: Hyperion Books for Children/Jump at the Sun, 2004. 168p. $15.99. ISBN 078680693 1. [fiction, short stories] JS, G (*Booktalks and Beyond*, 2007, pages 19 to 21.) Ten short stories explore the female/male relationship.

3. **Koertge, Ron. *Shakespeare Bats Cleanup*.** Cambridge, MA: Candlewick Press, 2003. 116p. $15.99. ISBN 0 7636 2116 1. [fiction, poems] MJS, CG (*Booktalks and Beyond*, 2007, pages 73 to 74.) Fourteen-year-old Kevin Boland is diagnosed with mono, stops playing baseball, and starts writing poems which reflect on his mother's death, his father's writing career, his initiation into dating, and the parallels between baseball and poetry.

4. **Sandell, Lisa Ann. *A Map of the Known World*.** New York: Scholastic Press, 2009. 304p. $16.99. ISBN-13: 978 0 545 06970 0. [fiction] JS, G (*Value-Packed Booktalks*, 2011, pages 20 to 22.) Cora, a talented cartographer, enters her freshman year following the car

crash death of her rebellious brother. The boy whom her parents blame for his death helps her and her family heal.

5. **Swanson, Julie A.** *Going for the Record*. Grand Rapids, MI: Eerdmans Books for Young Readers, 2004. 217p. $8.00. ISBN 0 8028 5273 4. [fiction] JS, G (*Teen Genre Connections*, 2005, pages 68 to 70.) Seventeen-year-old Leah qualifies for the Olympic soccer team at the same time that she finds out that her father has cancer, and decides to balance her life away from competitive sports.

ᘓᘔ

Schmidt, Gary D. Okay for Now.

New York: Houghton Mifflin Harcourt/Clarion Books, 2011. 360p. $16.99.
ISBN: 978 0 547 15260 8. [fiction] MJS, CG

Themes/Topics: Small town life, dysfunctional families, creativity, loss, survival, John James Audubon, Vietnam War, Apollo space missions, Joe Pepitone of the New York Yankees

Summary/Description

Doug Swieteck, from *The Wednesday Wars*, moves to a small town in upstate New York before his eighth grade year because his abusive father is fired. Doug becomes fascinated with the plates of John James Audubon's Birds of America on display in the town library. They lead him to friendships with Mr. Powell, a librarian who teaches him how to draw, Lil Spicer, who gets him a delivery job in her father's delicatessen, and the customers on his delivery route, including the eccentric writer, Mrs. Windermere. These people, his teachers, his father's boss, and Doug's hero, Joe Pepitone, help him find his personal strengths and deal with his father's treachery, his brothers' attitudes, his oldest brother's return from Vietnam, and finally Lil Spicer's cancer diagnosis.

Values: Art and community help Doug face personal challenges.

Booktalk

Ask how many in the group have heard about John James Audubon. Show some of Audubon's work. Ask them how they might react to some of the illustrations.

Twelve-year-old Doug Swieteck is moving to stupid Marysville, New York, because his father decked his boss. Doug doesn't draw and he can't read, but some smart aleck girl kind of dares him to go into the local library, and as Doug says, "What would you do?" That's where he sees the picture of *The Arctic Tern*. (*Show the picture.*) It kind of takes his breath away. (*Ask for a volunteer to read Read Aloud/Talkback 1.*) So, Doug goes back to the library to get another look. Doug would ask . . . (*Try to get them to finish the sentence with "What would you do?"*) He discovers that there are lots more smart alecks in that stupid town, and lots more Audubon pictures where they shouldn't be, and some almost nice people who might help him get them back, and maybe he is wrong about everything. He decides to take things day by day. After all . . . (*Try to get them to finish the sentence with "What would you do?"*) And, maybe, things will be just *Okay for Now*.

Booktalk available @ http://www.youtube.com/watch?v=QeLgtt81XGU

Author interview available @ http://www.youtube.com/watch?v=mtv3UOi9HNg

Read Aloud/Talkback

The entire book is suitable for read alouds.

1. Chapter 1, pages 19 to 20, beginning with "I went over . . ." and ending with ". . . my back pocket." Doug sees Audubon's *Arctic Tern*. *Talkback*: What does his reaction reveal about him?

2. Chapter 3, pages 80 to 83, beginning with "We waited . . ." and ending with ". . . will you build?" Principal Peattie and Mr. Ferris give their orientation speeches. *Talkback*: Which speech appeals to you? Why?

3. Chapter 3, pages 96 to 102, beginning with "The police came back. . ." and ending with ". . . horizon settle." Doug describes people's reactions to his brother being suspected of robbery. *Talkback*: What does the description say about Doug?

4. Chapter 4, pages 130 to 134, beginning with "On Saturday mornings . . ." and ending with ". . . get back to her." Doug's customers react to his carrying *Jane Eyre*. *Talkback*: Do the reactions surprise you?

5. Chapter 6, pages 200 to 202, beginning with "The So-Called Gym Teacher eyed me . . ." and ending with "He's okay for now." Doug and his wrestling partner defy the gym teacher. *Talkback*: How does the incident affect each person?

Educator guide and webcasts available @ http://www.hmh
books.com/schmidt/resources.html

Related Works

1. **Bauer, Joan.** *Close to Famous*. New York: Penguin/Viking, 2011.
   250p. $16.99. ISBN 978 0 670 01282 4. M, G (Contemporary/
   Friendship, pages 54 to 56.) Twelve-year-old Foster's cooking skills
   help her adjust to her new small town.
2. **Bronte, Charlotte.** *Jane Eyre*. New York: Penguin Putnam, Inc./
   Signet Classic, 1997. 461p. $4.95pa. ISBN 0 451 52655 4. S/A, G.
   This 19th-century novel follows Jane Eyre through her challenging
   childhood and young adulthood.
3. **Manfredi, Angi.** "A Lot of Things Goin On," *VOYA*. (October,
   2012): 314 to 316. Gary Schmidt explains his writing career and the
   views that influence his writing.
4. **Schmidt, Gary D.** *The Wednesday Wars*. New York: Clarion
   Books, 2007. 264p. $16.00. ISBN-13: 978 0 618 72483 3. [fiction]
   MJS, CG (*Genre Talks for Teens*, 2009, pages 56 to 59.) Holling
   Hoodhood learns that his English teacher is a human being and that
   he can apply Shakespeare's themes to his personal life.
5. **Sonnenblick, Jordan.** *Zen and the Art of Faking It*. New York:
   Scholastic Press, 2007. 272p. $16.99. ISBN-13: 978 0 439 83707 1.
   [fiction] MJ, CG (*Value-Packed Booktalks*, 2011, pages 42 to 44.)
   Fourteen-year-old San Lee, a new eighth-grade student, poses as a
   Zen Buddhist to fit into his new school, impress a girl in his social
   studies class, and hide his father's criminal past.

CJ꙳꙰

Shulman, Mark. Scrawl.

New York: Roaring Brook Press/A Neal Porter Book, 2010. 234p. $16.99.
ISBN 978 1 59643 417 2. [fiction] JS, CG with high interest for boys

Themes/Topics: Self-perception, poverty, bullies, high schools,
diaries, anger

Summary

After vandalizing the school with his friends, Tod is assigned a daily
detention in a hot, empty room with Mrs. Woodrow, a guidance
counselor. He must write his story in a notebook. His entries reveal his
friendships, bullying, criminal acts, as well as his anger, compassion,

intelligence, and creativity. This daily diary and Mrs. Woodrow's reaction to it helps him unravel his situation within the school where an in-group that includes teachers persecutes him; his own friends, jealous of any success or other friends, betray him; and his grief over his father estranges him from his mother and stepfather. By the end of the story, Tod proves his worth to himself, his school community, and his family through his writing and his costume design for a student written/ produced play which his former friends try to destroy.

Values: Tod learns to value his own talents and the talents of others.

Booktalk

Ask a member of the group to read aloud Tuesday, October 19, entry from the beginning to ". . . as the rest of us." (Pages 3 to 4.) Then ask, "What do you think of Tod?" Wait for responses. Maybe, Tod Munn should be in the criminal system. He likes to steal, vandalize buildings, and beat people up. Nice guy. Then, he meets Mrs. Woodrow who wants to read what he has to say. Most people stay away from him. There is another new woman in his life, Luz Montoya, a "spooky goth girl." Do these ladies offer Tod compassion and understanding? (*Wait for an answer.*) No. Just work. And suddenly, the life that Tod, future kingpin criminal—He will tell you about it right here (*Point to the book*)—had so figured out becomes one big *Scrawl*.

Book trailer available @ http://us.macmillan.com/scrawl/ markshulman

Read Aloud/Talkback

1.   Friday, October 22, pages 11 to 16. In this entry, Tod complains about the school, describes his friends, and states his view of life. *Talkback*: What details in this passage reveal Todd's hunger, fear, and sensitivity?

2.   Friday, October 29, pages 33 to 38. Tod encounters Luz Montoya and the cafeteria lady. *Talkback*: How does Tod see himself in relation to others in the school?

3.   Monday, November 1, pages 38 to 41. Tod explains why art class is a waste of time. *Talkback*: After reading the passage, what is your reaction to Tod and to art class?

4.   Friday, November 5, pages 57 to 58. Tod questions the assignment and labels himself a loser. *Talkback*: Why do you think that Tod is angry with Ms. Woodrow?

5. Wednesday, December 8, pages 228 to 230. Tod confronts Mrs. Woodrow about her interest in him. *Talkback*: What does this last section tell about Mrs. Woodrow and Tod?

Author interviews available @

http://yaauthorscafe.blogspot.com/2010/12/scrawl-by-mark-shulman.html

http://eluper.livejournal.com/143004.html

http://janasbooklist.blogspot.com/2010/11/interview-with-scrawl-author-mark.html

http://cynthialeitichsmith.blogspot.com/2011/02/new-voice-mark-shulman-on-scrawl.html

http://middlegradeninja.blogspot.com/2010/11/7-questions-for-mark-shulman.html

Author blog available for Scrawl @ http://mackids.squarespace.com/mackidssquarespacecom/2010/9/13/where-the-trouble-began-scrawl.html

Related Works

1. **Anderson, Laurie Halse.** *Twisted*. New York: Viking Press, 2007. 250p. $16.99. ISBN-13: 978 0 670 06101 3. [fiction] JS, CG (*Genre Talks for Teens*, 2009, pages 1 to 4.) Senior Tyler Miller builds muscles and a bad boy reputation after he is arrested for graffiti, required to work outdoors to pay for the damages, and attracts the attention of the sister of the boy who bullies him.
2. **Brooks, Kevin.** *Black Rabbit Summer*. New York: Scholastic/Chicken House, 2008. 496p. $17.99. ISBN-13: 978 545 05752 3. [fiction] JS, CG with high interest for boys (*Value-Packed Booktalks*, 2011, pages 112 to 113.) After an alcohol- and drug-filled reunion with childhood friends, 16-year-old Pete Boland unravels the resulting mystery of two missing persons.
3. **Bruchac, Joseph.** *The Way*. Plain City, OH: Darby Creek Publishing, 2007. 164p. $16.95. ISBN-13: 978 1 58196 062 4. [fiction] MJS, CG with high interest for boys (*Value-Packed Booktalks*, 2011, pages 213 to 215.) Cody LeBeau, an Abenaki Indian, deals with bullying in his high school, but believes he is a loser until his uncle, an accomplished martial arts fighter, helps him develop self-confidence and strength.
4. **Northrup, Michael.** *Gentlemen*. New York: Scholastic Press, 2009. 234p. $16.99. ISBN-13: 978 0 545 09749 9. [fiction] JS, CG with high interest for boys (*Value-Packed Booktalks*, 2011, pages

116 to 118.) Three friends suspect that their English teacher killed their fourth most troublesome group member.

5. **Pixley, Marcella.** *Freak*. New York: Farrar, Straus and Giroux/ Melanie Kroupa Books, 2007. 13: 978 0 374 32453 7. [fiction] MJS, G (*Genre Talks for Teens*, 2009, pages 37 to 39.) Twelve-year-old academically precocious Miriam, harassed by the popular crowd, eventually confronts and then defends her worst enemy.

✿✿

Stork, Francisco X. The Last Summer of the Death Warriors.

New York: Scholastic Inc./Arthur A. Levine Books, 2010. 352p. $17.99.
ISBN-13: 978 0 545 15133–7. [fiction] JS, CG with high interest for boys

Themes/Topics: Revenge, cancer, death, family relationships, interpersonal relationships

Summary/Description

Pancho and D.Q. meet at St. Anthony's Orphanage. Pancho wants to find and kill the man responsible for his mentally retarded sister's death. D.Q. is dying from brain cancer. The priest hires Pancho as D.Q.'s aid. He prepares the room where D.Q. wishes to die and stays with him through the treatments arranged by D.Q.'s controlling mother. The job enables Pancho to leave the orphanage and find his sister's killer. In a series of experiences, he learns to appreciate honesty, life, and love. He finds the man responsible for his sister's death, but understands that killing him will end his own life and violate the feelings that his sister had for the only man who showed her affection. Pancho returns to D.Q., supports his decision to return to St. Anthony's against the mother's wishes, and begins to plan his own future.

Values: Honesty and personal responsibility teach Pancho and D.Q. about love and give their lives meaning.

Read Aloud/Talkback

What do you think of when you hear *Death Warrior*? (*Wait for responses.*) This story is about two boys: a poor Latino boy with death on his mind and a rich Anglo boy with a desire to live. Pancho, the Latino, is determined to murder the man he believes killed his sister. D.Q., the Anglo, has brain cancer and wants Pancho to be his aide during the chemo, the throwing up, and the deterioration. Pancho can handle that. The problem is that D. Q. never shuts up. Why do you think that Pancho would take that job? (*Wait for responses.*) His motivation is different. It will place Pancho closer to the person he wants to kill. D. Q.'s fight to live as well as he can as long as he can complicates Pancho's plan to kill as quickly as he can. Life is not easy for either *Death Warrior*, and they don't make it easy for each other. Their battles may mean *The Last Summer of the Death Warriors*.

Alternative booktalk available @ http://www.scholastic.com/teachers/article/last-summer-death-warriors-booktalk

Book trailers available @

http://www.youtube.com/watch?v=kH2ZVcsww_0
http://www.youtube.com/watch?v=WKwog3fPBuE

Read Aloud/Talkback

1. Chapter 4, pages 24 to 27, beginning with "Pancho slipped . . ." and ending with the chapter. D. Q. explains his plan to die. *Talkback*: How does this conversation affect you?
2. Chapter 6, pages 37 to 38, beginning with "Do you want . . ." and ending with ". . . and circumstances." D. Q. explains the "no whining" rule. *Talkback*: Do you agree with the "no whining" rule?
3. Chapter 11, pages 79 to 81, beginning with "Pancho closed his eyes." and ending with the chapter. D. Q., Father Concha, and Pancho explore the duty to live. *Talkback*: How is the duty to live related to the quality of life?
4. Chapter 24, pages 195 to 196, beginning with "1. Who is . . ." and ending with ". . . time given to you." D. Q. reads the "Death Warrior Manifesto." *Talkback*: What is your reaction to the manifesto?
5. Chapter 30, page 290, beginning with "While Juan kept . . ." and ending with ". . . she didn't." Pancho sees Helen's portrait of D. Q. *Talkback*: Why is the portrait significant to both boys?

Discussion guide available @ http://www.franciscostork.com/death_warriors_questions.php

Author read aloud available @ http://www.youtube.com/watch?v=ACsb2p7SHf0

Author interviews available @

http://bwibooks.com/articles/francisco-stork.php
http://www.bookreporter.com/authors/francisco-x-stork/news/interview-030110

Author journal available @ http://www.franciscostork.com/
journal/

Related Works

1. **Bray, Libba.** *Going Bovine*. New York: Delacorte Press, 2009. 479p. $17.99. ISBN 978 0 385 73397 7. [fiction] S, CG with high interest for boys (*Value-Packed Booktalks*, 2011, pages 4 to 5.) A dying, cynical teenager discovers that love is most important.

2. **Halpin, Brendan.** *Forever Changes*. New York: Farrar Straus and Giroux, 2008. 181p. $16.95. ISBN 13: 978 0 374 32436 0. [fiction] JS, G. Eighteen-year-old cystic fibrosis patient Brianna Pelletier makes peace with death and decides to live a normal life.

3. **Sedgwick, Marcus.** *Revolver*. New York: Roaring Brook Press, 2010. 204p. $16.99. ISBN: 978 1 59643 592 6. [fiction] JS, CG with high interest for boys (*Value-Packed Booktalks*, 2011, pages 97 to 101.) Fourteen-year-old Sig chooses between the Bible and the gun when threatened by his dead father's enemy from the Alaskan gold rush.

4. **Sonnenblick, Jordan.** *After Ever After*. New York: Scholastic Press, 2010. 271p. $16.99. ISBN: 978 0 439 83706 4. [fiction] MJS, CG (*Value-Packed Booktalks*, 2011, pages 8 to 10.) Cancer survivor Jeffrey Alper loses his friend to leukemia and concludes that no life is pointless.

5. **Soto, Gary.** *The Afterlife*. New York: Harcourt, Inc., 2003. 161p. $16.00. ISBN 0 15 204774 3. [fiction] JS, CG with high interest for boys (*Teen Genre Connections*, 2005, pages 294 to 296.) Stabbed in a restroom, 18-year-old Jesús learns how much his family loves him and celebrates his cousin's decision not to avenge his death. The novel is a sequel to the 1997 publication *Buried Onions*.

Contemporary

As teens face everyday life with school activities, jobs, and sometimes family problems, they can make regrettable decisions and begin to wonder who they are. In their journeys, socializing, and working, they clarify their identities and find whom they can trust. As they become more confident, they even might find someone to love.

Identity

❦❧

Dessen, Sarah. **What Happened to Goodbye.**
New York: Penguin Group Inc./Viking, 2011. 402p.
ISBN: 978 0 670 01294 7. [fiction] JS, G

Themes/Topics: Divorce, identity, high school, friendship

Summary/Description

After her parents' divorce, 17-year-old McClean moves from town to town with her father, who "fixes" restaurants. She assumes a new identity with each move and grows more isolated from her mother whom she blames for the divorce. In Lakeview, because of Dave, a brilliant and genuine neighbor with whom she begins to fall in love, McClean establishes true friendships. Her father announces another move, and her mother demands that McClean spend more time with her. McClean's turbulent reaction forces the parents to see how their decisions have ruptured McClean's life. They allow her to stay in Lakeview with her friends before she moves on to college.

Values: McClean learns the importance of personal identity and the power of personal actions.

Booktalk

Why do we have the words hello and goodbye in our language? (*Wait for answers.*) Is letting people know that you are arriving or leaving that important? (*Wait for answers.*) Since her parents' divorce, McClean Sweet's whole life is about packing her bag and moving on. Her father moves from town to town and rehabilitates failing restaurants. She is great at hello. Each time she moves, she says hello as a new person. Eliza Sweet becomes Lizbet or Beth and fits right in. But since her family broke apart, Ms. Sweet doesn't say goodbye. She just leaves. In Lakeview, she becomes McClean again. Why? What do you think that means? (*Wait for answers.*) These Lakeview people seem to worry about what they do, but not what other people think about it. Her brilliant neighbor Dave is one of those people. Life looks good here, maybe with Dave. Or will he, like the boyfriends of those other Sweet girls, someday be wondering *What Happened to Goodbye*?

Book trailer available @ http://www.youtube.com/watch?v=TZ qM26CAAaU&feature=related

Read Aloud/Talkback

1. Chapter 2, pages 18 to 19, beginning with "Our relationship . . ." and ending with ". . . from nothing." McClean talks about her relationship with her mother. *Talkback*: What is your reaction to McClean's reflections about her mother? Consider the last sentence in the passage.
2. Chapter 2, pages 28 to 29, beginning with "My home page . . ." and ending with ". . . no surprise." McClean describes how the divorce affected her relationships. The book title occurs in the passage. *Talkback*: In this passage, McClean says that she had gotten ". . . smart about dealing with people." Do you agree?
3. Chapter 2, pages 46 to 47, beginning with "I smiled . . ." and ending with the chapter. McClean tells Dave that her name is McClean. *Talkback*: What is the significance of McClean's decision?
4. Chapter 5, page 132, beginning with "Everyone is something." and ending with ". . . between them." McClean reflects on Riley's response about Dave. *Talkback*: Why is the statement "Everyone is something" so important to McClean?
5. Chapter 16, pages 366 to 69, beginning with "I'd brought it to my . . ." and ending with ". . . the world around us." McClean uses the quilt from her mother and the town model to distinguish her past and present. *Talkback*: What do the quilt and the model clarify for McClean?

Reading group guide available @ http://www.teachervision
.fen.com/tv/printables/penguin/tl-guide-sarah-dessen.pdf

Author interview available @ http://sarahdessen.com/book/
what-happened-to-goodbye/

Related Works

1. **Anderson, Laurie Halse.** *Prom*. New York: Viking Press, 2005. 215p. $16.99. ISBN 0 670 05974 9. [fiction] JS, G (*Booktalks and Beyond*, 2007, pages 56 to 58.) 18-year-old Ashley discovers her leadership and planning abilities while working on the prom.
2. **Brooks, Martha.** *Mistik Lake*. New York: Farrar, Straus and Giroux/ Melanie Kroupa Books, 2007. 207p. $16.00. ISBN-13: 978 0 374 34985 1. [fiction] S, G (*Genre Talks for Teens*, 2009, pages 4 to 6.) In Mistik Lake, the family's summer retreat, 17-year-old Odella unravels her fractured family's secrets and discovers love.
3. **Cabot, Meg.** *Teen Idol*. New York: HarperCollins Publishers, 2004. 293p. $16.89. ISBN 0 06 009617 9. [fiction] MJS, G (*Booktalks and Beyond*, 2007, pages 61 to 63.) The author of a teen advice column learns her true friends and her people skills when she guides a movie star around her high school.
4. **Dessen, Sarah.** *Lock and Key*. New York: Viking, 2008. 422p. $18.99. ISBN-13: 978 0 01088 2. [fiction] JS, G (*Value-Packed Booktalks*, 2011, pages 13 to 15.) As Ruby lives with her high-achieving sister and gets to know her coping-with-life-problems neighbor, she learns to respect herself and take responsibility for her happiness.
5. **Vivian, Siobhan.** *Same Difference*. New York: Scholastic/Push, 2009. 287p. $18.99. ISBN-13: 978 0 545 00407 7. [fiction] JS, G (*Value-Packed Booktalks*, 2011, pages 53 to 56.) During a college summer art institute, 16-year-old Emily learns to respect her own talent and the feelings of friends and family even if they hide behind carefully developed personas.

СЯ⬝Ꮯ

Hautman, Pete. **How to Steal a Car.**
New York: Scholastic Press, 2009. 176p. $16.99.
ISBN-13: 978 0 545 11318 2. [fiction] JS, CG with high
interest for girls

Themes/Topics: Family dysfunction, stealing cars,
conduct of life

Summary/Description

Fifteen-year-old Kelleigh Monahan picks up a set of dropped car keys and begins her addiction to stealing cars. As the thefts escalate, she reveals a life in an affluent but emotionally bankrupt family and social network. At first, she rationalizes her actions as joy riding or helping friends. Then, she works on commission with a car thief. Stealing cars is the only thing that makes her think she is going somewhere.

Values: Kelleigh sees the adults in her life as cold and dishonest. She has little or no self-respect or life direction.

Booktalk

Ask the group how they picture a car thief. Fifteen-year-old Kelleigh isn't old enough to drive a car. Her high-profile lawyer father can buy her any car she wants. Her perfect mother drives Kelleigh anywhere she wants to go. Kelleigh's really good friends make sure that she always has company. She has $20,000.00 of her own saved for college, but Dad is going to pay the bill anyway. She gets $100.00 a month to spend on anything she wants. Is that a good life? (*Wait for a reaction.*) But Kelleigh wants more. She wants to stand out, and Kelleigh goes after what she wants. When she has a book review due, she picks the biggest book. (*Hold up a copy of* Moby Dick.) When she has an opportunity to get extra credit (even though she doesn't need it) by writing a how-to essay, she takes it. She decides to write an essay with a real-life reward and even do hands-on research. But this stand-out project can lead to way more than high grades, Daddy's money, or popularity. This project may lead her to a jail cell. Golden Kelleigh can't get caught, or can she? Is she smarter and faster than anyone when she decides to complete her independent study on *How to Steal a Car*?

Alternative booktalk available @ http://www.scholastic.com/teachers/article/how-steal-car-booktalk

Book trailer available @ http://www.youtube.com/watch?v=3Je mimtxh9A&context=C44f66b3ADvjVQa1PpcFPEwPklA3yOGSt pLb_RFrVT_DxU-3c61XI=

Read Aloud/Talkback

This book has no chapter numbers. The passages are designated by page numbers.

1. Pages 11 to 12, beginning with "How I usually . . ." and ending with ". . . my mom." Kelleigh describes the way she dresses. *Talkback*: What do Kelleigh's dressing choices say about her? Be specific.
2. Pages 13 to 14, beginning with "I did not . . ." and ending with ". . . again." Kelleigh explains her perfect mother. *Talkback*: Is this passage important? Use specifics to support your statement.
3. Pages 23 to 25, beginning with "When I was nine years old . . ." and ending with "Even your closest friends." Kelleigh describes her dolphin meltdown at 13. *Talkback*: What does Kelleigh reveal about herself in the dolphin meltdown?
4. Page 166, beginning with "I think . . ." and ending with ". . . disappointment." Kelleigh explains her attraction to a professional car thief. *Talkback*: What does this brief passage reveal about Kelleigh? Relate it to details in the rest of the story.
5. Pages 169 to 170, beginning with "I got in the car . . ." and ending with the novel. Kelleigh expresses why stealing cars attracts her. *Talkback*: What is your reaction to the story's conclusion?

Discussion guide available @ http://www.petehautman.com/
how-to-steal-a-car.html

Author interviews and read aloud available @
http://minnesota.publicradio.org/display/web/2009/09/15/
hautman/

Related Works

1. **Anderson, Laurie Halse. *Twisted*.** New York: Viking Press, 2007. 250p. $16.99. ISBN-13: 978 0 670 06101 3. [fiction] JS, CG (*Genre Talks for Teens*, 2009, pages 1 to 4.) Senior Tyler Miller builds muscles and catches the attention of the most popular girl in school after he is arrested for graffiti and sentenced to work outdoors. The subsequent events challenge his family's upwardly mobile lifestyle.
2. **Dessen, Sarah. *Just Listen*.** New York: Penguin Group/Speak, 2006. 371p. $8.99pa. ISBN-13: 978 0 14 241097 4. [fiction] JS, G (*Genre Talks for Teens*, 2009, pages 24 to 27.) In this "girl who has everything story," high school model learns to express her feelings and trust her choices when she is befriended by Owen Armstrong, the "Angriest Boy in School."
3. **Hautman, Pete. *Godless*.** New York: Simon & Schuster Books for Young Readers, 2004. 198p. $15.95. ISBN 0 689 86278 4. [fiction] JS, CG (*Genre Talks for Teens*, 2009, pages 27 to 29.) Disillusioned by his parents' church, Jason Brock starts his own religion centered

on the town water tower and discovers the dark side of himself and his fellow worshipers.

4. **Hautman, Pete. *Invisible*.** New York: Simon & Schuster Books for Young Readers, 2005. 149p. $15.95. ISBN 0 689 86800 6. [fiction] JS, CG (*Genre Talks for Teens*, 2009, pages 29 to 32.) Loner 17-year-old Doug Hanson acts out his unhappiness with stalking, fire, and threats.

5. **Tharp, Tim. *The Spectacular Now*.** New York: Alfred A. Knopf, 2008. 294p. $16.99. ISBN 978 0 375 85179 7. [fiction] S, CG with high interest for boys (*Value-Packed Booktalks*, 2011, pages 11 to 13.) Sutter Keely, a life-of-the-party senior, denies his destructive behavior and hides his father's desertion of the family.

ᘓᘔ

Kelly, Tara. Amplified.

New York: Henry Holt and Co., 2011. 293p. $16.99.
ISBN 978 0 8050 9296 7. [fiction] JS, G

Themes/Topics: Rock music, rock groups, interpersonal relations, mental health, independence, Santa Cruz (California)

Summary/Description

Seventeen-year-old Jasmine Kiss defies her dominant father and pursues her dream of becoming a rock musician rather than going immediately to college. Her father refuses her any financial support. She joins a band and moves into a home with three male rock musicians. She also gets a job in a psychic reading establishment run by the mother of the band's singer and the bassist who is getting over a romance and friendship gone bad. Jasmine becomes close friends with the singer and almost becomes the bassist's girlfriend; but she realizes that first she must overcome her stage fright, become a polished performer, and find out who she is.

Values: Jasmine learns the value of true friendship, integrity, personal identity, and openness.

Booktalk

Seventeen-year-old California girl, Jasmine Kiss just graduated from high school and is accepted at Stanford. But Stanford is her dad's plan, not hers. Jasmine wants to join a rock band. Going to Stanford is the safe path, the one her cardiologist Dad will finance. Joining the rock band, if she can find one to take her, means paying her own bills. Dad will throw her out. What should she do? (*Wait for answers.*) Jasmine leaves home. When she gets as far as Santa Cruz, her car breaks down. The mechanic is an obnoxious jerk, but guess what? (*See if anyone can guess that he is part of a rock band.*) If she can make his band, she also can get a good rent rate in the "band" house. Three guys who live there are the rest of the band. The really big catch is something that Jasmine lies about. Her audiences have been either her lifelong friend or her stuffed animals. But what do you think she tells the boys in the band? (*Wait for answers.*) So the comfortable, protected, leader-of-the-pack-rich-girl becomes homeless, laughed at, and broke, and nobody feels sorry. Suddenly, life is *Amplified*.

Read Aloud/Talkback

1. Chapter 7, pages 78 to 79, beginning with "A string of thoughts . . ." and ending with ". . . starved to death." Jasmine recalls her father's advice about succeeding. *Talkback*: Do you agree with Jasmine's father? What does her thought reveal about their relationship?

2. Chapter 8, pages 98 to 100, beginning with "I took a few minutes . . ." and ending with ". . . too good to be true." Tina gives Jasmine a reading. *Talkback*: How do you react to Tina's reading? Did it require supernatural powers?

3. Chapter 17, pages 254 to 256, beginning with "Nile grinned at me . . ." and ending with the chapter. Jasmine and Sean fight over Jasmine's working with Nile. *Talkback*: Who is right?

4. Chapter 18, pages 270 to 272, beginning with "I just wanted . . ." and ending with ". . . I fit." Jasmine reflects on her life after her disastrous meeting with Nile. *Talkback*: Why do you think that the experience with Nile is so upsetting?

5. Chapter 19, page 292, beginning with "I'm tired of . . ." and ending with ". . . know that." Sean and Jasmine talk about their relationship. *Talkback*: Do all the comments of Sean and Jasmine apply to both or just one of the speakers?

Discussion starter quiz available @ http://www.goodreads
.com/quizzes/12326-amplified-by-tara-kelly

Author reactions available @ http://thetaratracks.com/blog/

Author interview available @ http://www.thereadiacs.com/
interview-with-tara-kelly

Related Works

1. **Dessen, Sarah. *Lock and Key*.** New York: Viking, 2008. 422p. $18.99. ISBN-13: 978 0 670 01088 2. [fiction] JS, G (*Value-Packed Booktalks*, 2011, pages 13 to 15.) Seventeen-year-old Ruby tries to run away from the affluent life her long-lost sister offers her, but is persuaded to stay by her new down-to-earth-coping-with-life boyfriend.
2. **Earls, Nick. *48 Shades of Brown*.** New York: Houghton Mifflin, 2004. 288p. $6.99pa. ISBN 0 618 45295 8. [fiction] S, CG (*Teen Genre Connections*, 2005, pages 75 to 77.) Sixteen-year-old Dan, sheltered and intellectual, stays with his 20-something Aunt Jacq in Australia, and confronts responsibility and his own sexual awakening.
3. **Lloyd, Saci. *The Carbon Diaries, 2015*.** New York: Holiday House, 2008. 330p. $17.95. ISBN-13: 978 0 8234 2190 9 [fiction] JS, CG with high interest for girls (*Value-Packed Booktalks*, 2011, pages 166 to 168.) In the midst of an environmental meltdown, Laura realizes her ability to help others, her love for a bandmate, and a stronger relationship with her family.
4. **Nolan, Han. *Born Blue*.** New York: Harcourt, 2001. 177p. $17.00. ISBN 0 15 201916 2. [fiction] JS, CG (*Teen Genre Connections*, 2005, pages 13 to 15.) Placed in an abusive foster home, Janie bonds with seven-year-old Harmon, who introduces her to the music of lady blues singers around whom she focuses her life.
5. **Stork, Francisco X. *Marcelo in the Real World*.** New York: Scholastic/Arthur A. Levine Books, 2009. 320p. $17.99. ISBN-13: 978 0 545 05474 4. [fiction] S, CG (*Value-Packed Booktalks*, 2011, pages 243 to 246.) Eighteen-year-old autistic-like Marcello learns to value the truth, even though it might hurt or offend his father.

৩৯

Sachar, Louis. The Cardturner: A Novel about a King, a Queen, and a Joker.

New York: Delacorte Press, 2010. 336p. $17.99.
ISBN 978 0 385 73662 6. [fiction] JS, CG with high interest for boys

Themes/Topics: Duplicate bridge, interpersonal relationships, intergenerational relationships, coming of age

Summary/Description

Between his junior and senior high school years, Alton Richards works as his blind, rich, and sick great uncle's cardturner in duplicate bridge. He becomes close to the uncle, fascinated by the game, and drawn to Toni Castaneda, the granddaughter of the uncle's favorite bridge partner. When the uncle dies, Alton and Toni are haunted by his uncle and her grandmother. With the voices they hear, they carry out the couple's dream of winning a national championship and discover their own feelings for each other. Sachar, an avid bridge player, explains the bridge terms in sections that he signals with a whale graphic. The symbol recalls his own impatience with Herman Melville's extensive nature explanations in Moby Dick. For the non-bridge player, he provides quick explanations in boxed text. An appendix expands on the story's bridge decisions and situations.

Values: Alton learns the importance of sincerity, integrity, and independence.

Booktalk

Ask how many in the group play card games. Ask how many know anything about playing bridge. Alton Richards knows nothing about cards, but he is holding a losing hand. He is between his junior and senior years. His best friend stole Alton's girlfriend. Alton has no job, and Dad loses his. Without money, Alton can't fill out college applications. His parents volunteer him to drive his old, sick, blind, and rich uncle to bridge club four days a week. This is the "favorite" uncle whom Alton barely knows. And what is the parents' motivation? (*Wait for the "He may leave them money" answer.*). Alton will be his uncle's cardturner. A what? Alton has no clue about what he is supposed to do. His uncle has no patience. For minimum wage, Alton enters a crazy world, which includes a beautiful girl who hears voices, and a murky family past that stretches to a U.S. president. Who knew that turning cards would bring this much angst and so little payoff? So Alton has to make another move. If he is going to be a winner, he has to be a player, not just *The Cardturner*.

Book trailers available @

http://www.youtube.com/watch?v=tb5UkQdbsFI
http://www.youtube.com/watch?v=MimxuKjL0ZY

Read Aloud/Talkback

1. Chapter 10, page 35, beginning with the chapter and ending with ". . . suits for you." Uncle Lester illustrates the importance of context in memory. *Talkback*: Can you compose an example parallel to Uncle Lester's that applies to your own life?

2.   Chapter 13, pages 46 to 47. Alton's mother tells him about the Castaneda family. *Talkback*: How does Alton's mother define "nuts"? Do you agree?
3.   Chapter 31, pages 120 to 124, beginning with "Based on all the . . ." and ending with the chapter. Trapp and Alton discuss perception and reality. *Talkback*: Do you agree with Trapp? Why or why not?
4.   Chapter 36, pages 144 to 147. Trapp explains the synchronicity concept. *Talkback*: Have you ever had an experience with synchronicity?
5.   Chapter 76, pages 314 to 315, beginning with "My dad . . ." and ending with the chapter. Alton decides to be his own man. *Talkback*: Do you believe in the new Alton?

Discussion guide available @ http://www.provolibrary .com/images/stories/books-reading/book-club/PDF_Guides/ Cardturner.pdf

Author interview available @ http://www.youtube.com/ watch?v=7vUpO5cgZ1w

Related Works

1.   **Levin, Betty. *The Unmaking of Duncan Veerick*.** Asheville, NC: Front Street, 2007. 212p. $16.95. ISBN-13: 978 1 932425 96 3. [fiction] MJ, CG with high interest for boys (*Genre Talks for Teens*, 2009, pages 135 to 138.) Thirteen-year-old Duncan helps an elderly woman and becomes involved in protecting her possessions from her nephew.
2.   **Lubar, David. *Dunk*.** New York: Clarion, 2002. 249p. $15.00. ISBN 0 618 19455 X. [fiction] JS, CG with high interest for boys (*Teen Genre Connections*, 2005, pages 79 to 81.) Fifteen-year-old Chad Turner learns about love and life when he experiences the complicated world of Bozo with a mentor who has lost his family and career.
3.   **Luper, Eric. *Big Slick*.** New York: Farrar, Straus and Giroux, 2007. 234p. $16.00. ISBN-13: 978 0 374 30799 8. [fiction] JS, CG with high interest for boys (*Genre Talks for Teens*, 2009, pages 77 to 79.) Sixteen-year-old Andrew Lang shifts his poker habit from a negative to a positive after his father confronts him about stealing.
4.   **Peet, Mal. *Keeper*.** Cambridge, MA: Candlewick Press, 2003. 225p. $15.99. ISBN 0 7636 2749 6. [fiction] JS, CG with high interest for boys (*Booktalks and Beyond*, 2007, pages 75 to 77.) A famous goalkeeper learns his skills from a ghostly mentor.

5. **Sonnenblick, Jordan.** *Notes from the Midnight Driver*. New York: Scholastic Press, 2006. 272p. $16.99. ISBN 0 439 75779 7. [fiction] JS, CG with high interest for boys (*Genre Talks for Teens*, 2009, pages 82 to 84.) After driving drunk over a neighbor's lawn gnome, 16-year-old Alexander Gregory is sentenced to community service, where he learns about life from a rest home resident who plays "gotcha."

Standiford, Natalie. Confessions of the Sullivan Sisters.

New York: Scholastic Press, 2010. 320p. $17.99.
ISBN 978 0 545 10710 5. [fiction] JS, G

Themes/Topics: Family relationships, grandmothers, sisters, coming of age, social status

Summary/Description

On Christmas, the Sullivan children's tyrannical grandmother announces that someone in the family has offended her, and unless the person confesses by New Years Day, she will cut the family out of the will. The family assumes that the three sisters of the six children are guilty. Norrie (17) confesses that she loves a graduate student. She ran away from the Debutant Cotillion to be with him for three days in New York. Jane (16) confesses to exposing the family secrets on myevilfamily. com. Sassy (15) confesses to killing her grandmother's fifth husband. Each confession explains how these acts relate to the grandmother's behavior. On New Year's Day, the grandmother reveals that the girls' youngest brother is the offender and then confesses her own faults and offenses.

Values: The story illustrates the importance of family ties, heritage, and honesty.

Booktalk

Norrie, Jane, and Sassy are three of the wealthy Sullivans. Their rich grandmother is one of the most powerful women in the city. She is known as Almighty. On Christmas, the Sullivans learn that one of them has offended Almighty. Grandma will cut the entire family out of her will if the guilty party doesn't come forward and confess to Almighty's lawyer by New Years Day. There is plenty of guilt to go around: a forbidden romance, a tell-all blog, and a sudden death. Ginger and Daddy-o, the Sullivan parents, tell Norrie, Jane, and Sassy to confess and repent. But their offenses have a "why." A big part of the "why" is Grandma. The girls have to decide. (*Wait for a response after each of the following questions.*) Should they cave to save the family fortune? Should they claim their independence and tell Grandma to back off? Is it possible to do both? The answer is in the *Confessions of the Sullivan Sisters*.

Book trailer available @ http://www.youtube.com/watch?v=j_m_8y_eNj8&feature=youtube_gdata

Read Aloud/Talkback

1. Chapter 2, pages 14 to 15, beginning with "Brooks and his friend . . ." and ending with ". . . want that?" Norrie describes the appealing Brooks. *Talkback*: After reading the passage, what do you think makes a person attractive?
2. Chapter 8, pages 58 to 61, beginning with "Now on to . . ." and ending with ". . . fell asleep." Norris reacts to the Almighty ordering her to invite Brooks to the Debutante Ball. *Talkback*: What is your reaction to Almighty's argument?
3. Chapter 8, pages 206 to 207, beginning with "Sister Mary Joseph . . ." and ending with the chapter. Jane goes to the principal's office. *Talkback*: Is the suspension fair?
4. Chapter 12, pages 232 to 236. Jane admits to her own evil. *Talkback*: Is Jane evil?
5. Chapter 13, pages 311 to 313. Almighty writes her own confession to the girls. *Talkback*: Will things change after the grandmother's confession?

Jane's evil blog available @ http://www.myevilfamily.com/

Author interviews available @

http://dailyfig.figment.com/2010/10/21/interview-with-natalie-standiford/

http://foreveryoungadult.com/2010/08/30/between-two-lockers-with-natalie-standiford/

http://thebookscout.blogspot.com/2010/09/blog-tour-natalie-standiford-interview.html

http://www.youtube.com/watch?v=Jy8uT8IbVZ4

http://www.readingangel.com/2010/09/interview-and-giveaway-natalie.html

Related Works

1. **Clarke, Judith. *One Whole and Perfect Day*.** Honesdale, PA: Front Street, 2006. 250p. $16.95. ISBN-13: 978 1 932425 95 6. [fiction] JS, CG with high interest for girls (*Genre Talks for Teens*, 2009, pages 41 to 44.) Lily, labeled the sensible one in her eccentric family, hopes for one day of togetherness, but finds that freedom and coincidence may be more productive than plans and rules.

2. **Cushman, Karen. *The Loud Silence of Francine Green*.** New York: Clarion Books, 2006. 225p. $16.00. ISBN-13: 978 0 618 50455 8. [fiction] MJ, G (*Genre Talks for Teens*, 2009, pages 21 to 24.) Thirteen-year-old Francine Green, a conformist from a conformist family, attends a Catholic school in California and finds herself questioning rigid rules and prejudices during the early 1950s.

3. **Koja, Kathe. *Headlong*.** New York: Farrar, Straus and Giroux/ Frances Foster Books, 2008. 195p. $16.95. ISBN-13: 978 0 374 32912 9. [fiction] JS, G (*Value-Packed Booktalks*, 2011, pages 15 to 17.) Two girls from very different backgrounds form a close friendship, in spite of the pressures from family and school.

4. **Schmidt, Gary D. *Trouble*.** New York: Clarion Books, 2008. 297p. $16.00. ISBN-13: 978 0 618 92766 1. [fiction] MJS, CG (*Genre Talks for Teens*, 2009, pages 292 to 295.) Fourteen-year-old Henry Smith learns the sins of his prominent well-established family after his brother is killed in a car accident.

5. **Simmons, Michael. *Pool Boy*.** Brookfield, CT: Roaring Brook Press/A Neal Porter Book, 2003. 164p. $23.90. ISBN 0 7613 2924 2. [fiction] JS, CG with high interest for boys (*Booktalks and Beyond*, 2007, pages 54 to 56.) After his father is convicted of insider trading, 15-year-old Brett becomes a pool boy and learns the satisfaction of work and self-reliance.

Vivian, Siobhan. Not That Kind of Girl.

New York: Scholastic Press, 2010. 336p. $16.99.
ISBN 978 0 545 16915 8. [fiction] S, G

Themes/Topics: Interpersonal relations, coming of age, character, decision making, peer pressure

Summary/Description

Senior Natalie Sterling is the high-achieving student council president, whose best friend was humiliated by a football player in their freshman year. Natalie defends her friend, closes herself off from high school social life, and expects her friend to do the same. Freshman Spencer, who claims the right to display her sexuality, forces Natalie to question her life and goals. At the same time, Natalie begins to secretly meet a football star with very different life goals, and her best friend rebels against Natalie's expectations. Spencer becomes involved in a sexting scandal, and Natalie's love life becomes gossip fodder. Natalie, with Spencer's help, regains control of her life when she realizes that each person is responsible for and grows from their judgments, actions, and consequences. Some content may be controversial.

Value: Natalie learns to rely on her own judgment rather than the judgment of others.

Booktalk

Senior Natalie Sterling is at the top of her class and running for student council president. Her chances of winning are good, but the dumb jock running against her decides that elections are basically about sex. What should she do about her opponent? (*Wait for responses.*) Natalie is going to be her sensible, strong, and achieving self. She learned about taking the high road from her best friend who almost ruined her life via a star football player. Natalie saved her because she knew her friend was *Not That Kind of Girl.* (*Point to the cover as you are speaking.*) Now, Natalie is saving someone else she believes is (*Point to the cover and wait for the response.*) *Not That Kind of Girl.* This rescue is a freshman without a clue about what she is doing to her reputation. But the "victim" seems to want trouble, not help. She can't understand why Natalie doesn't want trouble too, especially when it's all muscle and drop-dead gorgeous. And, maybe, Natalie is not that sure that she, herself, is *Not That Kind of Girl.*

Author reading/booktalk available @ http://www.youtube.com/watch?v=HEdltRAVLXA

Author interviews available @

http://us.reachout.com/blog/interview-siobhan-vivian-author-of-not-that-kind-of-girl

http://holes-in-my-brain.blogspot.com/2011/02/author-interview-siobhan-vivian.html

Read Aloud/Talkback

1. Chapter 3, pages 29 to 31, beginning with the chapter and ending with ". . . that day." Autumn and Natalie meet and become friends. *Talkback*: What is the basis of the friendship?
2. Chapter 12, pages 112 to 113, beginning with "My little thing?" and ending with the chapter. Natalie puts Connor down after he helps her. *Talkback*: Is Natalie fair to Connor?
3. Chapter 26, pages 216 to 221. Autumn and Natalie confront each other about their friendship. *Talkback*: What do you find out about both girls?
4. Chapter 40, page 312, beginning with "Autumn took my . . ." and ending with the chapter. Autumn gives Natalie advice about bad decisions. *Talkback*: Do you agree with Autumn?
5. Chapter 41, page 317, beginning with "It didn't matter . . ." and ending with the chapter. Natalie concludes that her own opinion of herself is the most important. *Talkback*: Do you agree with Natalie?

Related Works

1. **Anderson, Laurie Halse. *Prom*.** New York: Viking Press, 2005. 215p. $16.99. ISBN 0 670 05974 9. [fiction] JS, G (*Booktalks and Beyond*, 2007, pages 56 to 58.) Eighteen-year-old Ashley Hannigan runs the prom and discovers that she may be college material.
2. **Dessen, Sarah. *Just Listen*.** New York: Penguin Group/Speak, 2006. 371p. $8.99.pa. ISBN-13: 978 0 14 241097 4. [fiction] JS, G (*Genre Talks for Teens*, 2009, pages 24 to 27.) Shunned by her peer group and struggling with family problems, Annabel Green meets an outcast who teaches her to express her opinions and trust her choices.
3. **Lockhart, E. *The Disreputable History of Frankie Landau-Banks*.** New York: Hyperion, 2008. 342p. $16.99. ISBN-13: 978 078683818 9. [fiction] JS, CG with high interest for girls (*Value-Packed Booktalks*, 2011, pages 51 to 53.) Frankie Landau-Banks, a student in a highly competitive boarding school, refuses to be marginalized by the popular and privileged senior boys in a secret society.
4. **Vivian, Siobhan. *A Little Friendly Advice*.** New York: Scholastic/Push, 2008. 248p. $16.99. ISBN-13: 978 0 545 00404 6. [fiction] JS, G (*Value-Packed Booktalks*, 2011, pages 22 to 24.) The main character becomes a responsible person independent of her parents' personal decisions, and realizes that friendship is not ownership.

5. **Vivian, Siobhan.** *Same Difference*. New York: Scholastic/Push, 2009. 287p. $18.99. ISBN-13: 978 0 545 00407 7. [fiction] JS, G (*Value-Packed Booktalks*, 2011, pages 53 to 56.) Emily learns to respect her own talents and the feelings of friends and family, as she evaluates life's rewards and failures.

Friendship

෯ඐ

Acampora, Paul. **Rachel Spinelli Punched Me in the Face.**

New York: Roaring Brook Press, 2011. 168p. $15.99.
ISBN 978 1 59643 548 3. [fiction] MJ, CG with high interest for boys

Themes/Topics: Friendship, moving, single-parent families, small town life, trumpet, volunteering, forgiveness, Connecticut

Summary/Description

When his mother deserts the family, 14-year-old Zachary and his policeman father, both trumpet players, move to Connecticut where they find a town similar to an extended family. Their neighbors are Teddy Spinelli, a prodigy trumpet player, and his 14-year-old younger sister Rachel. She attacks anyone who picks on or calls Teddy retarded. Teddy bonds with Zachery and pushes him to practice the trumpet and volunteer to restore the local park. Rachel becomes jealous of Zachary's time with Teddy and resents that her deceased mother's final concern was that their father would take care of Teddy. She reaches out to Zachary for help with her anger and frustration. When Zachary's mother shows up for a visit, Zachary rejects her, but Rachel and Teddy persuade him to give his feelings time.

Values: Zachary learns the value of friendship, dedication, and decisiveness.

Booktalk

Who in this room has a superpower? (*Wait for an answer.*) The Spinelli family has two people with superpowers. Teddy, the 17-year-old that the bullies call a retard, is an outstanding trumpet player. Rachel, his

14-year-old sister, has rage, and she'll use it on anyone who picks on her brother. For her, detention is an extracurricular activity. Superpowers aren't always positive. Fourteen-year-old Zachary is the new kid in town, their neighbor. He thinks that he is powerless, maybe even wishy-washy. His mother dumped him and his father without a word. So they moved to Falls, Connecticut, and are starting over. His father is the town policeman. In Falls, everybody seems to magically know everyone else's business. So the entire town has . . . (*Wait for the response of superpowers.*) And Zachary discovers one or two of his own when *Rachel Spinelli Punch(es Him) in the Face*.

Read Aloud/Talkback

1. Chapter 5, page 33, beginning with "As Rachel walked away . . ." and ending with ". . . ferocious girl?" Zachary is attracted to Rachel. *Talkback*: Is Zachary or his father right about Rachel?
2. Chapter 6, pages 39 to 40, beginning with "Things are going . . ." and ending with the chapter. Zachary participates in a discussion about how life works. *Talkback*: Mrs. Yee gives her view of life. Do you agree? How does her advice apply to Zachary?
3. Chapter 7, page 53, beginning with "Rachel knelt down . . ." and ending with ". . . she told him." Rachel makes friends with Skipper. *Talkback*: What does the encounter with Skipper reveal about Rachel?
4. Chapter 9, pages 70 to 71, beginning with "What was your . . ." and ending with ". . . around here." Rachel tells Zachary about her mother. *Talkback*: What does Rachel reveal about her family situation?
5. Chapter 18, page 157, beginning with "We loved . . ." and ending with ". . . off the ride." Zachary's father confronts Zachary's mother. *Talkback*: How do you feel about what Zachary's father says?

Related songs available @ http://paulacampora.com/punch2.html

Author interviews available @

http://mackids.squarespace.com/mackidssquarespacecom/2011/9/19/an-interview-with-nancy-mercado-and-paul-acampora.html

http://thiskidreviewsbooks.com/tag/paul-acampora/

Related Works

1. **Bauer, Joan. *Hope Was Here*.** New York: G. P. Putnam's Sons, 2000. 186p. $16.99. ISBN 0 399 23142 0. [fiction] MJS, G (*Booktalks and More*, 2003, pages 258 to 260.) A 16-year-old waitress, whose

mother deserted her, arrives in a new town with her aunt and takes on the challenge of the diner life.

2. **Blacker, Terence.** *Boy2Girl*. New York: Farrar, Straus and Giroux, 2004. 295p. $16.00. ISBN 0 374 30926 4. [fiction] MJ, CG with high interest for boys (*Booktalks and Beyond*, 2007, pages 58 to 61.) Sam Lopez moves to London to live with his cousin's family and undergoes an initiation that involves his posing as a girl.

3. **Naylor, Phyllis Reynolds.** *Cricket Man*. New York: Atheneum Books for Young Readers/Ginee Seo Books, 2008. 196p. $16.99. ISBN 978 1 4169 4981 7. [fiction] JS, CG (*Value-Packed Booktalks*, pages 18 to 20.) Kenny Sykes moves into a new neighborhood, saves crickets from dying in the family pool, reinvents himself as a superhero called Cricket Man, and discovers his power to help others.

4. **Sonnenblick, Jordan.** *Zen and the Art of Faking It*. New York: Scholastic Press, 2007. 272p. $16.99. ISBN-13: 978 0 439 83707 1. [fiction] MJ, CG (*Value-Packed Booktalks*, 2011, pages 42 to 44.) Fourteen-year-old Sam Lee poses as a Zen Buddhist to fit into his new school and impress a girl in his social studies class.

5. **Spinelli, Jerry.** *Stargirl*. New York: Alfred A. Knopf, 2000. 186p. $15.95. ISBN 0 679 88637 0. MJS, CG with high interest for girls (*Booktalks and More*, 2003, pages 8 to 10.) Leo Borlock recalls the new 10th grader named Stargirl who captivated and alienated the student body.

ʚ̃ɞ̃

Bauer, Joan. **Close to Famous.**

New York: Penguin Group/Viking, 2011. 250p. $16.99.
ISBN 978 0 670 01282 4. [fiction] M, G

Themes/Topics: Cooking, acting, rebirth, conduct of life, learning disabilities

Summary/Description

Twelve-year-old Foster and her mother flee the mother's abusive boss, an Elvis impersonator for whom she sings backup. They settle in Culpepper where a couple offers them a small trailer while they rebuild their lives. Foster can't read but hones her cooking skills via the cooking channel, and dreams of having her own cooking show. Her mother hopes to become a headliner. Foster meets Macon who aspires to produce documentaries. Macon works for Miss Charleena, an aging actress who hopes to return to Hollywood. As Foster bakes her way to fame and a part time job, she and her mother receive the support that allows Foster to learn to read and her mother to confront her abuser.

Values: Foster learns the importance of courage, persistence, quality, and generosity.

Booktalk

Ask how many people in the group like to cook and why. Cooking brings people together. Cooking could be a path to popularity, but 12-year-old Foster wants fame. Foster dreams about having her own cooking show, and she is that gifted. When Foster and her mother run out of Memphis with an abusive Elvis impersonator in pursuit, Foster's dream turns into a nightmare. Until they almost fall off a cliff and land in the little town of Culpepper. Then, with Foster's help, things start to turn around. How is that possible? (*Wait for the answers.*) Her cupcakes and muffins connect her to a famous actress, a wanna-be documentary producer, and a determined do-gooder. They all have their dreams, challenges, and can-do attitudes. Together, they stir up some hopes, joys, and fears that take them *Close to Famous*.

Alternative booktalk, author interview, and cupcake recipes available @ http://www.joanbauer.com/close_to_famous.html

Booktalk available @ http://www.youtube.com/watch?v=vx44yntO-WQ

Booktrailer available @ http://www.youtube.com/watch?v=vx44yntO-WQ

Read Aloud/Talkback

1. Chapter 4, pages 24 to 25, beginning with "Mama put on . . ." and ending with ". . . I'm a loser." Foster illustrates Huck's abuse. *Talkback*: Why is Huck dangerous? Be specific.
2. Chapter 20, pages 142 to 143, beginning with "What book do . . ." and ending with ". . . just said to me." Miss Charleena and Foster talk about her reading. *Talkback*: What do Foster and Miss Charleena teach each other?
3. Chapter 21, pages 146 to 147, beginning with "I went into the . . ." and ending with "I stood too." Miss Charleena and Foster view Charleena's big scene about inner strength. *Talkback*: How does this scene apply to Foster?

4. Chapter 25, pages 178 to 181, beginning with "We walked . . ." and ending with ". . . to tell me that." Lester takes Foster fishing. *Talkback*: What does fishing teach Foster about patience, persistence, and positive thinking?

5. Chapter 35, page 250, beginning with "I'll tell you . . ." and ending with the novel. Foster reflects on tough things. *Talkback*: What is Foster's attitude toward ". . . tough things"? Do you agree?

Author information available @ http://www.joanbauer.com/report.html

Discussion guide and book club start-up suggestions @ http://www.teachervision.fen.com/tv/printables/penguin/tl-guide-close-to-famous.pdf

Related Works

1. **Bauer, Joan. *Hope Was Here***. New York: G. P. Putnam's Sons, 2000. 186p. $16.99. ISBN 0 399 23142 0. [fiction] MJS, G (*Booktalks and More*, 2003, pages 258 to 260.) A 16-year-old waitress, raised by her aunt because her mother deserted her, uses her work to define her life.

2. **Bauer, Joan. *Peeled***. New York: G. P. Putnam's Sons, 2008. 248p. $16.99. ISBN-13: 978 0 399 23475 0. [fiction] MJS, CG with high interest for girls (*Value-Packed Booktalks*, 2011, pages 121 to 123.) Hildy Biddle, high school reporter, uses her father's advice and the cooperation of her family and town to foil a dishonest land developer.

3. **Bauer, Joan. *Rules of the Road***. New York: G. P. Putnam's Sons, 1998. 201p. $15.99. ISBN 0 399 23140 4. [fiction] MJS, CG with high interest for girls (*Booktalks Plus*, 2001, pages 114 to 116.) Sixteen-year-old Jenna Boller acquires poise and an eye for quality when she drives for the owner of Gladstone Shoes.

4. **Schwartz, John. *Short: Walking Tall When You're Not Tall at All***. New York: Roaring Brook Press/Flash Point, 2010. 132p. $16.99. ISBN 978 1 59643 323 6. [nonfiction] JS, CG. Schwartz uses his experiences as a short person to warn us that difference is good, and negative labels are often a product of commercial hype.

5. **Sonnenblick, Jordan. *After Ever After***. New York: Scholastic Press, 2010. 272p. $16.99. ISBN 978 0 439 83706 4. [fiction] MJS, CG (*Value-Packed Booktalks*, 2011, pages 8 to 10.) Eighth grade cancer survivor, Jeffrey Alper, meets new challenges when a standardized test threatens to keep him from graduating.

ℭℨ℩

Ehrenhaft, Daniel. **Friend Is Not a Verb.**

New York: Harper Collins Publishers/Harper Teen, 2010. 241p. $15.99.
ISBN 978 0 06 113106 6. [fiction] JS, CG with high interest for boys

Themes/Topics: Interpersonal relations, bands, brothers and sisters, fugitives from justice, family life, New York City

Summary/Description

Sixteen-year-old Henry (Hen) Birnbaum strives for fame in a band and a chance with the glamorous band leader Petra, who dumps him as a base player and boyfriend. Complicating his quest are the new feelings he has for his next door neighbor/best friend, Emma, and his curiosity about his sister's yearlong disappearance. Tutored in both base and life by Gabriel, his sister's friend and fellow fugitive, he is reinstated in the band, and discovers that Petra dumped him because she sees that Hen and Emma really love each other. He also learns that his parents knew where his sister was hiding for a year. When his sister disappears again, she contacts Hen but not her parents and makes restitution for their crime which was stealing money from Gabriel's father. Hen learns all actions have consequences. Content and situations may be considered controversial.

Values: Hen and Emma value friendship, sincerity, quality, honesty, and family.

Booktalk

Ask for a volunteer to read pages ix to xii. How do you see the speaker? (*Wait for some responses*.) Behind that symbolic port-o-john door, Hen finds a lot of you-know-what to sort out in his and his family's life. But he also finds some good people in there too, and every one of them, including Hen, discovers that the important thing in life is knowing that *Friend Is Not a Verb*.

Read Aloud/Talkback

1. Part I, Chapter 1, pages 13 to 14, beginning with "Whenever I suffer . . ." and ending with ". . . wasn't Emma's fault." Hen describes Emma. *Talkback*: Is Emma girlfriend material?

2. Part I, Chapter 3, page 40, beginning with "I glared at . . ." and ending with ". . . stretched awkwardly." Gabriel explains the shift in the meaning of friend paralleling today's complicated life. Title is included. *Talkback*: Do you agree with Gabriel's view of the word friend?

3. Part II, Chapter 14, pages 176 to 179, beginning with "I stopped listening . . ." and ending with ". . . would be paradise." Hen starts to appreciate Emma. *Talkback*: Should Hen admire Emma for the letter?

4. Part III, Chapter 18, page 226, beginning with "It's not a neat . . ." and ending with the chapter. Hen and Gabriel discuss the ending. *Talkback*: What does this passage say about journey?

5. "Epilogue," pages 227 to 229. Hen reflects on the importance of honesty. *Talkback*: Using a scale of 1 to 5, with 1 meaning highly disagree and 5 highly agree, rate this statement: "There's probably no connection at all between Journey and a valuable life lesson." Compare your ratings with the ratings of others. Explain your choice.

Related Works

1. **Castellucci, Cecil.** *Beige*. Cambridge, MA: Candlewick Press, 2007. 307p. $16.99. ISBN 978 0 7636 3066 9. [fiction] S, G. Fifteen-year-old Katy, a reserved French Canadian, stays with her aging punk star father in Los Angeles and finds friendship and the excitement of a band.

2. **Earls, Nick.** *48 Shades of Brown*. New York: Houghton Mifflin, 1999, 2004. 288p. $6.99pa. ISBN 0 618 45295 8. [fiction] S, CG (*Teen Genre Connections*, 2005, pages 75 to 77.) A shy 16-year-old spends a year with his eccentric aunt and falls in love.

3. **Green, John.** *An Abundance of Katherines*. New York: Dutton Books, 2006. 215p. $16.99. ISBN 0 525 47688 1. [fiction] JS, G (*Genre Talks for Teens*, 2009, pages 44 to 46.) A self-absorbed child prodigy embarks on a journey to find a true-love formula, and discovers that friendship, honesty, and integrity beat fame and popularity.

4. **Nye, Naomi Shihab.** *Going Going*. New York: Harper Collins/ Greenwillow Books, 2005. 232p. $16.89. ISBN 0 06 029366 7. [fiction] JS, CG with high interest for girls (*Genre Talks for Teens*, 2009, pages 59 to 61.) Sixteen-year-old Florrie crusades to save small businesses and old buildings, but discovers that people can be ignored and destroyed as easily as real estate.

5. **Zevin, Gabrielle.** *Memoirs of a Teenage Amnesiac*. New York: Farrar, Straus and Giroux, 2007. 271p. $17.00. ISBN-13: 978 0 374 34946 2. [fiction] JS, G. High school junior, Naomi Paige Porter, hits her head in a fall and forgets her life from puberty on. She

reevaluates her feelings about her popular boyfriend, divorced parents, new stepparents, old friends, academic achievement, and her extracurricular activities, and realizes that her true love is her lifelong friend and co-yearbook editor.

Halpin, Brendan. Shutout.

New York: Farrar, Straus and Giroux, 2010. 181p. $16.99.
ISBN 978 0 374 36899 9. [fiction] MJ, G

Themes/Topics: Soccer, friendship, interpersonal relations, family life, high schools

Summary/Description

Fourteen-year-old Amanda Conant and her longtime friend Lena try out for the varsity soccer team. Very tall Amanda does not make varsity. Very short Lena does. The selection sweeps Lena into the popular crowd. Amanda, feeling jealous, bitter, and isolated, grudgingly accepts her junior varsity status. As she works with the team, she finds new friends, a perceptive and supportive coach, and new self-confidence about her height through yoga. Lena is pressured into bad choices that culminate in an all night drinking party and an entire varsity team suspension before the championship game. The junior varsity plays instead. Although they lose, Amanda stars in their surprisingly close challenge. Her cheering section includes her blended family, Lena, and a possible new boyfriend.

Values: Amanda acquires self-confidence as she learns about true friendship and the importance of family.

Booktalk

Fourteen-year-old Amanda and her best friend Lena rule the soccer field. They are trying out for varsity soccer this year. They are sure they are going to make it. They are half right. Short, pretty Lena makes varsity. Five-foot, 10-inch, size-11 shoe, Amanda is . . . (*Point to the title and say "Shutout."*) She makes junior varsity. That hurts. OK. They won't be at practice together. They will share classes. Wrong. Amanda gets assigned to bonehead math. Their schedules are completely different. So Amanda is . . . (*Wait for the response as you point to the title.*) *Shutout*. There is always lunch, but varsity soccer puts Lena in a new social league, the upper-class in-group. That means Amanda is . . . (*Wait *for the response of Shutout.*) That table doesn't have seats for losers like Amanda. Lena's friends tie up Lena's phone. Amanda is . . . (*Wait for the response of Shutout.*) Amanda is in a new game with a new field and new rules and she is *Shutout*.

Read Aloud/Talkback

1. "Warm-up," pages 3 to 5. Amanda introduces herself. *Talkback*: What is your impression of Amanda?

2. "Preseason," Chapter 3, pages 22 to 24. Lena is cut out from the varsity soccer. *Talkback*: At this point, what effect are adults having on Amanda? Is she ungrateful?

3. "Preseason," Chapter 8, pages 59 to 63, beginning with "Then Beasley . . ." and ending with the chapter. The coach's speech and approach surprises Amanda. *Talkback*: After reading about this coaching session, how would you describe Beasley?

4. "Soccer Season," Chapter 4, pages 100 to 102, beginning with "As much as . . ." and ending with the chapter. Amanda confesses going to the party. *Talkback*: Did Amanda do the right thing? Is her parents' reaction appropriate?

5. "Postseason," Chapter 7, page 183, beginning with "You really can . . ." and ending with the book. Amanda reflects on the "what if game." *Talkback*: Do you agree with Amanda's reaction to "what if"?

Related Works

1. **Coy, John. *Box Out*.** New York: Scholastic Press, 2008. 289p. $16.99. ISBN-13: 978 0 439 87032 0. [fiction] JS, CG with high interest for boys (*Value-Packed Booktalks*, 2011, pages 58 to 60.) When sophomore Liam Bergstrom is called up to varsity, he questions coaching techniques and playing time tied to religious beliefs.

2. **Hamm, Mia, and Aaron Heifetz. *Go for the Goal: A Champion's Guide to Winning in Soccer and Life*.** New York: HarperCollins Publishers, 1999. 222p. $21.00. ISBN 0 06 019342 5. [nonfiction] MJS, CG with high interest for girls (*Booktalks and More*, 2003, pages 132 to 134.) Mia Hamm speaks primarily to girls interested in soccer, but Part I focuses on working hard, sacrificing for success, following a passion, concentrating, and maintaining physical fitness.

3. **Peet, Mal. *Keeper*.** Cambridge, MA: Candlewick Press, 2003. 225p. $15.99. ISBN 0 7636 2749 6. [fiction] JS, CG with high interest for boys (*Booktalks and Beyond*, 2007, pages 75 to 77.) El Gato,

the world's best goalkeeper, relates his ghostly path to soccer fame that also led him to his balance in life.

4. **Schwartz, John.** *Short: Walking Tall When You're Not Tall at All*. New York: Roaring Brook Press/Flash Point, 2010. 132p. $16.99. ISBN 978 1 59643 323 6. [nonfiction] JS, CG. Schwartz uses his experiences as a short person to warn all of us that we are "abnormal," "below-average" people, difference is good, and that negative labels are often a product of commercial hype. "The Beginning," his concluding chapter on pages 111 to 114, emphasizes that "It's always *our* decision who we are."

5. **Swanson, Julie A.** *Going for the Record*. Grand Rapids, MI: Eerdmans Books for Young Readers, 2004. 217p. $8.00pa. ISBN 0 8028 5273 4. [fiction] JS, G (*Teen Genre Connections*, 2005, pages 68 to 70.) A 17-year-old soccer star, qualifying for the World Cup and Olympic teams, rethinks her focus when her dad develops cancer.

ᘓᘔ

Vernick, Audrey. Water Balloon.

New York: Clarion Books/Houghton Mifflin Harcourt, 2011. 310p. $16.99.
ISBN 978 0 547 59554 2. [fiction] MJ, G

Themes/Topics: Divorce, interpersonal relationships, families, father/daughter, change

Summary/Description

Thirteen-year-old Marley stays with her compulsive father for the summer when her mother decides to travel. Because the newly divorced parents support two households, the father arranges a babysitting job for Marley with twins, does not replace his broken computer, and cancels his internet connection. Marley's two best friends are involved in a theater camp where they are making friends with older teens. Because Marley clings to their childhood rituals, they consider her an embarrassment. Jack, the boy next door, offers her friendship, understanding, and a romantic interest. With some humor and introspection, Marley manages the twins, accepts that her father dates the twins' mother, separates herself from exploitive friends, and bonds with Jack.

Values: Self-reliance and empathy help Marley to change, mature, and move on.

Booktalk

Thirteen-year-old Marley Baird faces a losing summer. Mom and Dad have just completed their "friendly divorce." No one asks how friendly Marley feels. Marley's two best friends are sharing experiences in a theater camp without Marley. Mom decides that Marley will spend the summer with her compulsive, dandelion-digging dad while Mom takes a trip to reconnect with friends. What would your reaction be? (*Wait for responses.*) Dad can't afford a computer and won't buy a cell phone. But the topper is Marley's new job. She has to earn her own money by babysitting twins. Dad arranged a job without asking her. What would your reaction be? (*Wait for responses.*) Since no one is talking to Marley about major decisions, Marley isn't talking much either. Then, she discovers Jack, her father's neighbor. He is cute, kind, and blue-eyed, and he likes to talk to Marley. End of story? No, beginning of story, one that kind of stops and starts with a crazy *Water Balloon*.

Book trailers available @

http://www.youtube.com/watch?v=mteZvgNNnGc
https://sites.google.com/a/harwood.org/2012–2013-dcf/home/
    vernick-audrey-water-balloon

Read Aloud/Talkback

1. "I'm in Danger, People," pages 16 to 17, beginning with "I'm such a mess . . ." and ending with ". . . angry silence." Marley describes the gradual change that brought her parents' divorce. *Talkback*: Should Marley have noticed the changes?
2. "I'm in Danger, People," pages 23 to 24, beginning with "Much to my . . ." and ending with the chapter. Marley reflects on being solitary. *Talkback*: Are school activities overrated?
3. "My Normal Abnormal Way," page 166, beginning with "God, Marley . . ." and ending with ". . . true that hurts." Leah confronts Marley about her attitude. *Talkback*: How would you react to Leah's assessment?
4. "This Limbo," pages 176 to 177, beginning with "The sun's rays . . ." and ending with the chapter. Marley reflects on change and uncertainty. *Talkback*: How would you interpret "play the game" in each of the situations that Marley describes?
5. "Brave as I'll Ever Be," pages 300 to 301, beginning with "Wisdom's a no show." and ending with ". . . light blue eyes." Marley recalls her mother's life lessons. *Talkback*: Is Marley right about her mother's nursery school wisdom?

Discussion questions and activities available @
https://sites.google.com/a/harwood.org/2012–2013-dcf/home/
vernick-audrey-water-balloon

Author interviews available @

http://cynthialeitichsmith.blogspot.com/2011/09/new-voice-audrey-
vernick-on-water.html

http://lyndamullalyhunt.blogspot.com/2011/09/interview-with-
water-balloon-author.html

http://bibliolinks.wordpress.com/2012/06/25/marvelous-middle-
grade-monday-water-balloon-by-audrey-vernick/

http://patzietlowmiller.com/2011/11/05/an-author-you-should-
know-audrey-vernick/

Related Works

1. **Castellucci, Cecil. *Beige*.** Cambridge, MA: Candlewick Press, 2007. 307p. $16.99. ISBN 978 0 7636 3066 9. [fiction] S, G. A reserved French Canadian teen stays with her aging punk star father in Los Angeles, gains an unlikely friend, and a new relationship with her parents. Subject matter requires a mature audience.

2. **Dessen, Sarah. *Keeping the Moon*.** New York: Viking, 1999. 228p. $15.99. ISBN 0 670 88549 5. [fiction] JS, G (*Booktalks and More*, 2003, pages 82 to 84.) Fifteen-year-old Nicole Sparks (Colie) discovers a different life and her potential in a summer with her single, overweight, eccentric Aunt Mira instead of her goal-driven celebrity mother.

3. **Garfinkle, D. L. *Storky: How I Lost My Nickname and Won the Girl*.** New York: G. P. Putnam's Sons, 2005. 184p. $16.99. ISBN 0 399 24284 8. [fiction] MJ, CG with high interest for boys (*Booktalks and Beyond*, 2007, pages 63 to 65.) High school freshman "Storky" Pomerantz seeks popularity with his peers and acceptance from his father, but finds one good friend as well as attention and respect from his stepfather.

4. **Hobbs, Valerie. *Tender*.** New York: Farrar, Straus and Giroux/ Francis Foster Books, 2001. 256p. $18.00. ISBN 0 374 37397 3. [fiction] MJS, G (*Teen Genre Connections*, 2005, pages 48 to 49.) When her grandmother dies, 15-year-old Live Trager lives with her father and learns to pay her own way.

5. **Siobhan, Vivian. *A Little Friendly Advice*.** New York: Scholastic/ Push, 2008. 248p. $16.99. ISBN-13: 978 0 545 00404 6. [fiction] JS, G (*Value-Packed Booktalks*, 2011, pages 22 to 24.) Sixteen-year-old Ruby clarifies her relationships with the friends who dominate her, the father who deserted her, and her new, good listener boyfriend.

Love

ᘓᘔ

Brody, Jessica. The Karma Club.

New York: Farrar, Straus and Giroux, 2010. 258p. $16.99.
ISBN 978 0 274 33979 1. [fiction] JS, G

Themes/Topics: Friendship, revenge, conduct of life

Summary/Description

Senior Madison Kasparkova is dumped by her boyfriend for a social standout. Madison attends a retreat at the Napa Valley Spiritual Center for Inner Growth, distorts the director's message, and organizes her friends into *The Karma Club*, a revenge squad, to restore balance to their lives. Their plans not only hurt their enemies, but also produced personal disasters for the girls. Madison revisits the Napa Valley Center, and the director tells her that each person controls his or her own life, not the life of others. With additional advice from her father, she begins living positively and confesses her escapades to her new boyfriend whom she misjudged as a snob. He helps Madison and her friends avoid an attempted blackmail, and the group redirects their energies with positive results.

Values: Madison and her friends learn the importance
of integrity and independence.

Booktalk

Ask how many in the group have heard of Karma. Explain if no one can.

Madison, a senior, is just discovering Karma. Madison works hard for popularity. She even gets her boyfriend's picture in a national magazine. The couple achieves star quality. That should be a good thing. What should happen? What do you think does happen? (*Wait for answers to both questions.*) The article makes Madison's boyfriend a target for the most beautiful girl in school. The high school goddess wins him, and Madison is out for revenge. Her friends have been done wrong, too. They decide to help Madison set the universe in balance just like Karma says. What should happen? (*Wait for answers.*) What goes around comes around, and what comes around may be just a little more than they can handle in *The Karma Club*.

Book trailer, book launch video, and karma activities available @ http://www.jessicabrody.com/books/teen-fiction/the-karma-club/about-the-book/

Read Alouds/Talkbacks

1. "Prologue," pages 3 to 4. Madison explains Karma. The prologue is also appropriate for a *booktalk*. *Talkback*: Does Madison's explanation of Karma agree with the opening line? Be sure to cite specifics from the passage in your explanation.

2. "The Heather Campbell of Colonial High," page 21, beginning with "I'm not surprised . . ." and ending with ". . . Ryan Feldman." Madison explains Angie's aversion to popularity. *Talkback*: Do you agree with Madison? Be specific.

3. "Napa Valley Spiritual Center for Inner Growth," pages 57 to 61, beginning with "The next morning . . ." and ending with ". . . source of purest joy." Madison gives her initial impressions of Karma. *Talkback*: What do you learn about Karma? What do you learn about Madison? Be specific.

4. "Returning to Ground Zero," page 224, beginning with "If we don't give . . ." and ending with "It's not." Madison realizes she is just like the people she attacks. *Talkback*: What is Madison's realization and why is it important?

5. "The New Godfather," pages 238 to 239, beginning with "For a brief moment . . ." and ending with ". . . bring you success." Madison accepts her father's advice to do the opposite. *Talkback*: How can you apply the advice of Madison's father to your own life?

Jessica Brody's advice for writers @ http://www.jessicabrody .com/for-writers/advice/

Related Works

1. **Cabot, Meg. *Teen Idol*.** New York: HarperCollins Publishers, 2004. 293p. $16.89. ISBN 0 06 0096179. [fiction] MJS, G (*Booktalks and Beyond*, 2007, pages 61 to 63.) When Junior Jenny Greenley guides movie star Luke Striker around her high school, she sees her world with new eyes and finds her true friends and people skills.

2. **Dessen, Sarah. *Just Listen*.** New York: Penguin Group/Speak, 2006. 371p. $8.99pa. ISBN 978 0 14 241097 4. [fiction] JS, G (*Genre Talks for Teens*, 2009, pages 24 to 27.) When high school model, Annabel Greene, keeps silent about an attempted rape by her best friend's boyfriend, is isolated by her social group, and

befriended by the "Angriest Boy in School," she learns how to confront issues in her life.

3. **Dessen, Sarah. *Lock and Key***. New York: Viking, 2008. 422p. $18.99. ISBN-13: 978 0 670 01088 2. [fiction] JS, G (*Value-Packed Booktalks*, 2011, pages 13 to 15.) When Ruby moves in with the sister she has not heard from in 10 years, she learns that she must take responsibility for her own happiness by embracing love, openness, and giving.

4. **Lockhart, E. *The Disreputable History of Frankie Landau-Banks***. New York: Hyperion, 2008. 342p. $16.99. ISBN-13: 978 078683818 9. [fiction] JS, CG with high interest for girls (*Value-Packed Booktalks*, 2011, pages 51 to 53.) Marginalized by an elite, male, secret society, Frankie Landau-Banks launches pranks that almost get her expelled, but do not change her attitude toward power.

5. **Zevin, Gabrielle. *Memoirs of a Teenage Amnesiac***. New York: Farrar, Straus and Giroux, 2007. 271p. $17.00. ISBN-13: 978 0 374 34946 2. [fiction] JS, G (*Genre Talks for Teens*, 2009, pages 61 to 64.) High school junior Naomi Paige reevaluates her life and her popular boyfriend after a hit on the head wipes away her memory from puberty on.

ᘉ ᘉ

Day, Susie. My Invisible Boyfriend.

New York: Scholastic Press, 2010. 288p. $16.99.
ISBN-13: 978 0 545 07354 7. [fiction] JS, G

Themes/Topics: Interpersonal relationships, fantasy boyfriends, England, private schools

Summary/Description

Fifteen-year-old Heidi Ryder is the only one in her social group without a boyfriend. Used to fantasizing over a fictional ace detective whose series was canceled, she creates gingerbread Ed, a fictional boyfriend, inspired by a cookie given to her by her boss. Her friends communicate with him via Internet and draw Heidi into their own feelings and romances. The complications lead to Heidi discovering a real boyfriend, her boss's son, and the group reaffirming their strong friendship.

Values: Heidi and her friends learn the importance of belonging in genuine friendship.

Booktalk

Read aloud pages 2 to 3, beginning with "You know your life . . ." and ending with ". . . belong." That is 15-year-old Heidi Ryder talking. New school. Great friends. Life is good, until the party. Everyone has a boyfriend, everyone except you know who. (*What should she do?*) Heidi cooks up one. She has the perfect recipe. (*Read "Recipe for an Imaginary Boyfriend" on page 23.*) (*Do you agree with the recipe?*) Unfortunately, computers make her creation a little more real and her life little more complicated. Her friends find him on the Web. They talk to him, want to meet him, maybe even want to date him. Has she cooked up Mr. Fabulous or Mr. Frankenstein? Is he her dreamboat or nightmare? Let Heidi tell you. Her life becomes a saga/mystery/comedy: *My Invisible Boyfriend.*

Alternative booktalk available @ http://www.scholastic.com/teachers/article/my-invisible-boyfriend-booktalk

Book trailer available @ http://www.youtube.com/watch?v=Ai_gRSiuiL4

Read Aloud/Talkback

1. Pages 69 to 72, beginning with "I'm kind of desperate . . ." and ending with ". . . girly thoughts." Heidi unveils gingerbread Ed to Betsy and Teddy. *Talkback*: Do you agree with Betsy?
2. Pages 83 to 84, beginning with "After dinner . . ." and ending with ". . . care of herself." Heidi reflects on Gingerbread Ed and belonging. *Talkback*: Can you fix Heidi's dilemma?
3. Pages 119 to 120, beginning with "OK, so it's sort . . ." and ending with ". . . it doesn't sting." Heidi realizes why she wants everyone to like Ed. *Talkback*: How does Heidi's realization affect the novel?
4. Pages 138 to 139, beginning with "My hands are . . ." and ending with ". . . like that before." Heidi sees Teddy's costume drawings. *Talkback*: Is Heidi right to be proud?
5. Page 257, beginning with "That's what I . . ." and ending with ". . . me at all." Heidi thinks about what she needs in a boyfriend. *Talkback*: How would you describe the difference between what Heidi has and what she needs in a boyfriend? Rewrite her boyfriend recipe.

Author read aloud available @ http://www.youtube.com/watch?v=nh32Wi6dp2I&feature=related

Author interviews available @ http://www.susieday.com/interviews/

Related Works

1. **Blacker, Terence.** *Boy2Girl*. New York: Farrar, Straus and Giroux, 2004. 295p. $16.00. ISBN 0 374 30926 4. [fiction] MJ, CG (*Booktalks and Beyond*, 2007, pages 58 to 61.) Sam agrees to pose as a girl for a peer initiation, gains friends, and teaches his peers about relating to girls.

2. **Freitas, Donna.** *The Possibilities of Sainthood*. New York: Farrar, Straus and Giroux/Frances Foster Books, 2008. 272p. $16.95. ISBN-13: 978 0 374 36087 0. [fiction] JS, G (*Value-Packed Booktalks*, 2011, pages 37 to 40.) Fifteen-year-old Antonia Lucia Labella strives to be the Patron Saint of Kissing, but does not need the persona to find a boyfriend.

3. **Juby, Susan.** *Alice I Think*. New York: Harper Tempest, 2003. 290p. $16.89. ISBN 0 06 051544 9. [fiction] JS, G. Alice, home-schooled by her eccentric parents, enters high school to please her therapist and becomes a misfit and a target.

4. **Korman, Gordon.** *Jake, Reinvented*. New York: Hyperion, 2003. 213p. $15.99. ISBN 078681957-X. [fiction] JS, CG. Thinking his happiness lies with a girl from the in-crowd, an academic nerd becomes a party animal with disastrous results.

5. **Sonnenblick, Jordan.** *Zen and the Art of Faking It*. New York: Scholastic Press, 2007. 272p. $16.99. ISBN-13: 978 0 439 83707 1. [fiction] MJ, CG (*Value-Packed Booktalks*, 2011, pages 42 to 44.) Fourteen-year-old San Lee creates a "Buddha Boy" identity to fit into his new school.

ध्रुव

Eulberg, Elizabeth. The Lonely Hearts Club.

New York: Scholastic Inc./Point, 2010. 320p. $17.99.
ISBN 978 0 545 14031 7. [fiction] JS, G

Themes/Topics: The Beatles, identity, self-esteem, dating, high school, friendship, resilience, risk taking

Summary/Description

In chapters named after Beatles songs, 16-year-old Penny Lane Bloom describes her journey from exploitation to self-respect and true romance. After being two-timed by her latest boyfriend, Penny becomes the only member of her new club, *The Lonely Hearts Club*, a title inspired by her parents' devotion to the Beatles. Her idea not to date boys from her high school spreads to her best friend and her former best friend. Other girls with bad experiences join. Not worrying about pleasing boys, the girls form strong friendships, achieve personal goals, and gain self-esteem. The handsomest boy in the school pursues Penny. She finds the balance between her feelings and her promises to the club members. Revised rules allow all the members to develop healthy dating relationships, but stay loyal to the girlfriends who supported them.

Values: Penny Lane Bloom discovers how true friendship supports self-confidence and love.

Booktalk

Sixteen-year-old Penny Lane Bloom is fed up with men. The love of her life, that is since she was five years old, two-timed her. She crossed him off her romance list in a hurry. He wasn't the first. She fears that he won't be the last, so she is going solo. She has company. Her high school is filled with girls who have been lied to and taken for granted. They follow her lead and change their high school's girl-waits-for-boy culture. So what complication do you think will show up? (*Wait for answers.*) Right. Penny's true love comes along. Can she believe it or should she put her faith in something the Beatles, another culture-changing group, inspired, *The Lonely Hearts Club*. (*Show a picture of the book and a picture of the Sergeant Pepper's Lonely Hearts Club Band album cover.*)

Alternative booktalk available @ http://www.scholastic.com/teachers/article/lonely-hearts-club-booktalk

Book trailer available @ http://www.youtube.com/watch?v=0rYsaHXpP_k

Read Aloud/Talkback

1. Chapter 1, pages 5 to 7. Penny relates why she distrusts boys. *Talkback*: How would you describe the relationship between Penny and Nate?
2. Chapter 15, pages 106 to 108, beginning with "You really . . ." and ending with the chapter. At the first meeting, Diane reveals why she and Ryan broke up. *Talkback*: Do you agree with what Diane says about being forced?
3. Chapter 19, pages 135 to 137, beginning with "I really don't . . ." and ending with the chapter. Penny explains the club. *Talkback*: What is your opinion of the club?
4. Chapter 24, pages 167 to 168, beginning with "Pen . . ." and ending with "Big Dumb Idiot." This passage is the apologetic e-mail from

Nate to Penny. *Talkback*: On a scale of 1 to 10, how would you rate Nate's honesty?

5. Chapter 35, pages 263 to 264, "The New and Improved Rules of the Lonely Hearts Club." Tracy revises the rules. *Talkback*: Will the new rules ruin the club?

Author explanation available @ http://www.youtube.com/watch?v=iyJqHNdl0pM

Frequently asked question available @ http://www.eliz abetheulberg.com/faq.html

Author interviews available @

http://www.thecompulsivereader.com/2009/12/lonely-hearts-club-by-elizabeth-eulberg_29.html

http://www.motleypress.com/mpress/?p=67

http://www.mrsmagooreads.com/2010/08/interview-with-elizabeth-eulberg.html

http://iamareadernotawriter.blogspot.com/2010/12/bir2010-book-giveaway-lonely-hearts.html

http://stephsureads.blogspot.com/2009/12/review-and-interview-lonely-hearts-club.html

Related Works

1. **Green, John. *An Abundance of Katherines*.** New York: Dutton Books, 2006. 215p. $16.99. ISBN 0 525 47688 1. [fiction] JS, G (*Genre Talks for Teens*, 2009, pages 44 to 46.) Dumped by the 19th Katherine he has dated, Colin Singleton tries to develop a mathematical formula to predict the length of romantic relationships.

2. **Holbrook, Sara, and Allan Wolf. *More than Friends: Poems from Him and Her*.** Honesdale, PA: Wordsong, 2008. 64p. $16.95. ISBN 978 1 59078 587 4. [poetry] MJ, CG with high interest for girls. The voices of both a girl and a boy exploring their first "more than friends" relationship address the obstacles and distractions of giddy first love.

3. **Lockhart, E. *The Disreputable History of Frankie Landau-Banks*.** New York: Hyperion, 2008. 342p. $16.99. ISBN-13: 978 078683818 9. [fiction] JS, CG with high interest for girls (*Value-Packed Booktalks*, 2011, pages 51 to 53.) Frankie Landau-Banks, a member of the 2010 graduating class of a highly competitive boarding school, decides to be a power broker instead of a trophy date.

4. **Murdock, Catherine Gilbert.** *Dairy Queen*. Boston, MA: Houghton Mifflin Co., 2006. 275p. (Dairy Queen Trilogy) $16.00. ISBN-13: 978 0 618 68307 9. [fiction] JS, CG with high interest for girls (*Value-Packed Booktalks*, 2011, pages 63 to 64.) Hardworking 15-year-old D. J. Schwenk finds the complications of love when and where she least expects them.

5. **Zevin, Gabrielle.** *Memoirs of a Teenage Amnesiac*. New York: Farrar, Straus and Giroux, 2007. 271p. $17.00. ISBN-13: 978 0 374 34946 2. [fiction] JS, G (*Genre Talks for Teens*, 2009, pages 61 to 64.) High school junior, Naomi Paige Porter, hits her head in a fall, forgets her life from puberty on, and reevaluates her dating status in the popular crowd.

ⓒⓟ

Hautman, Pete. **The Big Crunch.**

New York: Scholastic Inc., 2011. 288p. $17.99.
ISBN 978 0 545 24075 8. [fiction] JS, CG

Themes/Topics: Dating, love, separation, family relationships

Summary/Description

Wes and June gradually become acquainted, and then fall in love after crashing into each other at a local store. Level-headed Wes has grown up in a stable home in the same neighborhood. Socially savvy June has highly anxious parents, who pull her from school to school as her father climbs the corporate ladder. When June's parents move, Wes and June deal with a long-distance and sometimes volatile relationship that pushes Wes to "borrow" a car and drive to Omaha to see June, a trip that results in arrest, grounding, and debt. By chance, June's father returns to the area with a new job. The two renew their relationship, but realize that life may pull them apart.

Values: June and Wes learn that responsibility, humor, patience, and persistence are part of interpersonal relationships.

Booktalk

Ask if anyone has heard of the Big Bang theory. Ask them to explain it. You may want to ask someone to read the explanation on page 55, beginning with "They were studying cosmology . . ." and ending with ". . . headed for nowhere."

Wes and June are each starting their junior years in the same town. Wes has lived there all of his life. June is the new girl. The girl in that passage that we just read feels as if she is racing through the universe. June's dad moves to new jobs more often than some people buy clothes. Her family's philosophy is "Next." June scopes out the in and out groups quickly, makes a few temporary friends, and notices a boy named Wes. And Wes notices the new girl. So what is going to happen? (*Wait for answers.*) You're right. It's a romance. But it has a twist. They don't meet, they collide. A little bruised and beaten, they're a couple. Then, they aren't. Then, they are, and maybe they won't be. It's a wild cosmic ride complicated by collisions with crazy friends, uncooperative parents, and high-tech miscommunication. Will they continue to collide and fly apart or finally come together in what June's science teacher calls *The Big Crunch*?

Author and book trailers available @

http://www.youtube.com/user/petehautman
http://www.petehautman.com/videos.html

Read Aloud/Talkback

1. Chapter 3, pages 22 to 25, beginning with "The garage was a . . ." and ending with the chapter. Wes cleans the garage. *Talkback*: What does the garage reveal about Wes and his family?

2. Chapter 9, page 55, beginning with "They were studying . . ." and ending with ". . . headed for nowhere." Big Bang theory discussion relates to pages 60 to 61, beginning with "Ordinarily, June . . ." and ending with ". . . through the door." June uses the Big Bang and Big Crunch theory, the book title, to frame her life. *Talkback*: Do the Big Bang and the Big Crunch relate to your lives?

3. Chapter 14, pages 86 to 87, beginning with "It was nearly midnight . . ." and ending with the chapter. June labels her mother an "attributer." *Talkback*: How does each member of June's family deal with life? Which method do you feel is most successful?

4. Chapter 42, pages 222 to 223, beginning with "When she went . . ." and ending with the chapter. June takes a personal inventory and distinguishes between her heart and head. *Talkback*: Use the house method to inventory your brain. Do you agree with June that matters of the heart are separate?

5. Chapter 52, pages 278 to 280, beginning with "June was falling . . ." and ending with the book. June positions their love in time, and refers again to the Big Bang and Big Crunch theories referred to in Read Aloud/Talkback 2. *Talkback*: Is the ending pessimistic, optimistic, or realistic?

Author interview available @ http://petehautman.blogspot
.com/2012/02/david-levithan-interviews-pete-hautman.html

Related Works

1. **Bagdasarian, Adam.** *First French Kiss and Other Traumas.*
   New York: Farrar, Straus and Giroux/Melanie Kroupa Books, 2002.
   134p. $16.00. ISBN 0 374 32338 0. [fiction] JS, CG (*Teen Genre
   Connections*, 2005, pages 73 to 74.) In five groups of essays, a fictional character tells his experiences in becoming a man.
2. **Holbrook, Sara, and Allan Wolf.** *More than Friends: Poems
   from Him and Her*. Honesdale, PA: Wordsong, 2008. 64p. $16.95.
   ISBN 978 1 59078 587 4. [poetry] MJ, CG with high interest for
   girls. A girl and a boy explore their "more than friends" relationship.
3. **Janeczko, Paul B. (compiler).** *Blushing: Expressions of Love
   in Poems & Letters*. New York: Orchard Books, 2004. 112p.
   $15.95. ISBN 0 439 53056 3. [poetry] CG with high interest for
   girls. Classic poems and letters trace relationships from first meeting through love, heartbreak, and healing.
4. **Spinelli, Jerry.** *Smiles to Go*. New York: Harper Collins/Joanna
   Cotler Books, 2008. 248p. $16.99. ISBN 978 0 06 028133 5. [fic-
   tion] JS, CG (*Value-Packed Booktalks*, 2011, pages 44 to 46.)
   Intellectually gifted ninth grader William Tuppence's life disinte-
   grates when he learns that an "unsmashable" proton is smashed.
5. **Zevin, Gabrielle.** *Memoirs of a Teenage Amnesiac*. New York:
   Farrar, Straus and Giroux, 2007. 271p. $17.00. ISBN-13: 978 0 374
   34946. [fiction] JS, G (*Genre Talks for Teens*, 2009, pages 61 to 64.)
   High School junior Naomi Page Porter hits her head, loses her memory,
   and rethinks her feelings about her love life, family, and friends.

༄༅

Koertge, Ron. Shakespeare Makes the Playoffs.

Somerville, MA: Candlewick Press, 2010. 170p. $15.99.

ISBN 978 0 7636 4435 2. [novel in verse] MJS, CG with high interest for boys

Themes/Topics: Interpersonal relationships, dating,
baseball, writing

Summary/Description

Fourteen-year-old Kevin Boland and his father attend a reading
together where Kevin meets Amy, a writer and musician. They share
writing ideas, and Kevin realizes that he may have more in common

with Amy than his trophy girlfriend, Mira. Amy, however, has a trophy boyfriend. Kevin is also coping with the pressure of baseball playoffs and his father's dating. Mira dumps Kevin because he attends a movie with Amy. Amy's boyfriend dumps Amy for another girl. Kevin and Amy become a couple as Kevin's father moves on to a new girlfriend.

Values: Kevin learns the importance of common interests, hard work, and moving forward.

Booktalk

Hold up a copy of Shakespeare Bats Cleanup. *Ask how many people remember this book.* If you know this book then you already know Kevin Bolton, the boy who loves writing and baseball. His nickname is Shakespeare. He has the girlfriend everyone else wants, the team is winning, and he is writing again. Life should be good, but it isn't. Writing and baseball require thinking, and he is thinking that Mira, (*Point to the name on the cover.*) his trophy girlfriend, might not be the girl he wants. What do you think happens? (*Wait for responses.*) Another girl shows up in his life, Amy. She writes too, and she gets what Kevin writes. Mira doesn't. Can Kevin and Amy collaborate just as friends? (*Wait for answers.*) Then, there is Dad. He is dating again. Kevin thinks that Dad should still be grieving the death of Kevin's mother. And shouldn't Kevin have a say about who is coming into their lives? (*Wait for responses.*) How do you play baseball with all that on your mind? So it will be a minor miracle if *Shakespeare Makes the Playoffs*.

Read Aloud/Talkback

1. "Poetry 101," pages 10 to 11. The poem compares the rhyme in poetry to a bully. *Talkback*: Check a book of poetry for the "mistakes" in rhyme and meter. Discuss how these mistakes contribute to the purpose of the poem. When he compares poetic forms to bullies, what is Kevin saying about difficult things in life?
2. "Love at First Bounce" and "Back to the Past," pages 12 to 14. Kevin explains his relationship with his baseman's mitt, emotions that Mira doesn't understand. *Talkback*: What do the poems tell you about Kevin, his mother, and Mira?
3. "Mr. B.," pages 40 to 41. Kevin describes his English teacher's view of poets and poetry. *Talkback*: Would you want Mr. B to be your teacher? Why or why not?

4. "A Haiku Just for Mira Because She Asked" and "Toxic Haiku Fallout," pages 62 to 64. Mira reacts to the poem Kevin writes for her. *Talkback*: Can this relationship be saved?

5. "That Night at Dinner," page 136. Kevin and his father put the game loss in perspective. *Talkback*: Do you agree with Kevin and his father about the lost game?

Discussion guide available @ http://www.candlewick.com/ book_files/0763644358.bdg.1.pdf

Author interviews available @

http://guyslitwire.blogspot.com/2010/03/interview-with-ron-koertge.html

http://lssarchives.homestead.com/poetscorner-ronkoertge.html

http://kidswriterjfox.blogspot.com/2010/03/interview-with-ron-koertge.html

http://yaauthorscafe.blogspot.com/2010/03/marlene-tell-us-about-your-book.html

http://californiareaders.org/interviews/koertge_ron.php

http://ronkoertge.com/about/videos/

Related Works

1. **Garfinkle, D.L. *Storky: How I Lost My Nickname and Won the Girl*.** New York: G. P. Putnam's Sons, 2005. 184p. $16.99. ISBN 0 399 24284 8. [fiction] MS (*Booktalks and Beyond*, 2009, pages 63 to 65.) High school freshman Michael "Storky" Pomerantz discovers that the popular girl is not the most compatible.

2. **Jeter, Derek with Jack Curry. *The Life You Imagine: Life Lessons for Achieving Your Dreams*.** New York: Scholastic Inc., 2000. 279p. $4.99pa. ISBN 0 439 35601 6. [nonfiction] JS, CG with high interest for boys (*Teen Genre Connections*, 2005, pages 61 to 63.) Derek Jeter talks about setting high goals in academics and athletics, dealing with setbacks, choosing role models, keeping a balance between focus and fun, being a team leader, thinking before acting, and greeting each day as a new challenge.

3. **Koertge, Ron. "Just a Couple of Girls Talking Haiku." In *Twice Told: Original Stories Inspired by Original Art*.** Drawings by Scott Hunt. New York: Dutton/Penguin Putnam, 2006. 320p. $19.99. ISBN 0 525 46818 8. [fiction] MJS, CG. A

haiku assignment brings people together for healing. The story appears on pages 59 to 69. The collection focuses on 9 images by 18 writers. A pair of writers reacts to each of the images.

4. **Koertge, Ron. *Shakespeare Bats Cleanup*.** Cambridge, MA: Candlewick Press, 2003. 116p. $15.99. ISBN 0 7636 2116 1. [fiction, poems] MJS, CG with high interest for boys (*Booktalks and Beyond*, 2007, pages 73 to 74.) Fourteen-year-old Kevin Boland, diagnosed with mono, writes poems about his mother's death, his father's writing career, and dating, while he is unable to play baseball.

5. **Zusak, Markus. *Getting the Girl*.** New York: Arthur A. Levine, 2003. 272p. $16.95. ISBN 0 439 38949 6. [fiction] S, CG with high interest for boys (*Teen Genre Connections*, 2005, pages 56 to 58.) Cameron, a thinker and a writer, gets the girl as he defines himself in relation to his older, tougher brothers who speak with their fists.

Action/Adventure/Survival

Unfortunately, action, adventure, and survival often center on man-made catastrophes, such as wars. Disaster traps the innocent who discover strength, heroism, and perhaps feelings or instincts they did not realize that they had. But survival in any crisis may depend not on physical strength or cunning, but trust. An especially interesting contrast in the "War" group occurs in *Purple Heart* and *Ghosts of War*, one fiction and one nonfiction, when two compassionate young men have very different experiences with trust.

War

Barrett, Tracy. **King of Ithaka.**

New York: Henry Holt and Co., 2010. 261p. $16.99.
ISBN 978 0 8050 8969 1. [fiction] JS, CG with high interest for boys

Themes/Topics: Rulers, Telemachos, Odysseus,
Greek mythology, Ithaca, bards, heroes

Summary/Description

When the people of Ithaca demand a new king, 16-year-old Telemachos seeks his father. With his companions, the centaur Brax and stowaway Polydora, Telemachos discovers that hero stories are usually false and that being king may require more than conquering nations. He meets brutal King Nestor and his duplicitous son who robs him and tries to kill him. Then, with the help of Polydora and Brax, who also flee Nestor, he travels to Sparta where he discovers the cruel truth about Helen of Troy. Eventually, a mysterious message from Athena in the form of Mentes sends him back home, where he discovers his father's treacherous and brutal character and his own personal strength.

Values: Telemachos learns that loyalty, love, industry, integrity, and compassion are necessary qualities for a good king, a successful personal life, and a stable kingdom.

Booktalk

Ask how many in the group have heard about Odysseus and Helen of Troy. Allow them to share what they know.

Odysseus is a great hero. You can read all about it in *The Illiad*. (*Hold up the book.*) Like other heroes before him, he had to battle gods, monsters, and mythical beasts. What would people expect from such a hero's son? (*Wait for responses.*) Telemachos is Odysseus's son and does not measure up. He sits by his mother, the queen, when she settles claims. Otherwise, he dodges work. The people are getting restless. They want a strong king, and one of the many men on this deteriorating island is willing to marry the queen and take the job. Telemachos decides to find his father, the rightful king, but Odysseus has been gone for 16 years, as long as Telemachos has lived. All he has to work with are stories, descriptions, and a mysterious prophecy from an island monster who eats raw eggs and sits in her own waste. Not a good start. But Telemachos takes on the task. He discovers a much different story of monsters, heroes, kings, and queens when he searches for the *King of Ithaca*.

Booktalk trailer available @ http://www.youtube.com/watch?v=nQk8gCWuSiE

Read Aloud/Talkback

1. Chapter 3, pages 27 to 28, beginning with "I glanced at Mentes . . ." and ending with ". . . same as mine." Telemachos encounters the mysticism of Mentes, and Penelope asks about Odysseus. *Talkback*: After reading the entire novel, do you react differently to this passage? What changes?
2. Chapter 4, pages 34 to 35, beginning with "You've got to feel . . ." and ending with the chapter. The sailors react to Telemachos, his home, and his father. *Talkback*: Do you agree with the sailors' reactions to Telemachos and Ithaca?

3. Chapter 9, pages 61 to 67. Telemachos confronts Daisy. *Talkback*: After reading this chapter, what do you think makes Daisy powerful? Intimidating?
4. Chapter 19, pages 143 to 145, beginning with "The bard . . ." and ending with the chapter. The bard sings for Nestor and guests. *Talkback*: How does this passage show the power and weakness of the bard?
5. Chapter 36, pages 256 to 258, beginning with "Eupeithes pushed his way . . ." and ending with ". . . know for sure." Eupeithes confronts Odysseus about his son's murder. *Talkback*: After reading this passage, how would you assess the fathers and Telemachos?

Reading activities available @

http://www.tracybarrett.com/files/king_of_ithaka_activities.doc
http://www.tracybarrett.com/newsletter.htm?newsletter=

Author interviews available @

http://thespectacleblog.wordpress.com/2010/09/10/interview-with-tracy-barrett-win-a-copy-of-king-of-ithaka/
http://authorturf.com/?p=1913

Related Works

1. **Gardner, John.** *Grendel*. New York: Vintage Books, 1989 (reissued edition). 192p. $10.95pa. ISBN 0 679 72311 0. [fiction] S/A. The "monster" from *Beowulf* tells his own story.
2. **McCarty, Nick.** *Troy: The Myth and Reality behind the Epic Legend*. New York: Rosen Publishing, 2008. 122p. (Prime Time History) $39.95. ISBN-13: 978 1 4042 1365 4. McCartny explains the Trojan War and the equally arrogant determination of Heinrich Schliemann to find evidence of its existence.
3. **Napoli, Donna Jo.** *Sirena*. New York: Scholastic Press, 1998. 210p. $15.95. ISBN 0 590 383 38388 4. [fiction] JS, G (*Booktalks Plus*, 2001, pages 91 to 93.) A siren attaches herself to a Trojan hero and experiences the pain of human love as she challenges his "heroism."
4. **Reeve, Philip.** *Here Lies Arthur*. New York: Scholastic Press, 2008. 339p. $16.99. ISBN-13: 978 0 545 09334 7. [fiction] JS, CG (*Value-Packed Booktalks*, 2011, pages 159 to 161.) Gwyna the Mouse, the daughter of a dead slave woman, is saved from death by a bard, Myriddin, and learns how words can turn a monster into a hero.
5. **Tennyson, Alfred Lord.** "Ulysses." @ http://www.victorianweb.org/authors/tennyson/ulyssestext.html (accessed on October 20, 2011). Ulysses defines the difference between himself and Telemachus, and strikes out to pursue new ideas and heroic plans.

ɞʡ

Bray, Libba. Beauty Queens.

New York: Scholastic Press, 2011. 400p. $18.99.
ISBN 978 0 439 89597 2. [fiction] S, G

Themes/Topics: Beauty contests, friendship, identity, conduct of life

Summary/Description

In this satirical look at modern public and private lives, a plane crash places the surviving teen beauty contestants on an island occupied by the forces of the pageant's sponsor, who is forging an illegal business relationship with a third world dictator and running for president. As the girls struggle to survive on the island, their secrets about sexual preferences, family backgrounds, and pageant motives emerge. Television pirates, carnivorous snakes, and eco-terrorists add to their physical and emotional conflicts and confusion. Their sponsor plans an island pageant ending in a beauty queen massacre to discredit the dictator. An epilogue explains the path each girl chooses. Footnotes explain the cultural references.

Value: The girls sort out society's expectations vs. their own identities and relationships.

Booktalk

Libba Bray introduces this book with "A Word from Your Sponsor." Ask two people to read it. Have the passage divided for reader one and two and the readers prepared. The first section starts with the beginning of the passage and ends with ". . . warning you about." Pages 1 and 2. The second section begins with "But let's not worry . . ." and ends with ". . . of black smoke." The second reader should communicate a growing disturbance about what is being read and stop reading. The first reader rescues the second reader by picking up at "And so our tale . . ." and ending with the passage. The second reader, now recovered, adds the footnote.

The sponsor doesn't mention the pirates, the third world dictator, the beauty product that can double as a bomb, eco-terrorists, and carnivorous snakes. The sponsor feels she can handle it all, and of course, so do her *Beauty Queens*. (*Show book cover.*)

Book trailers available @

http://www.youtube.com/watch?v=rwpJ7M1AcZM
http://www.youtube.com/watch?v=wSHDSuJZrAU
http://www.youtube.com/watch?v=2d8E7-uci7c

Read Aloud/Talkback

1. Chapter 2, pages 14 to 15, beginning with "Taylor sheathed . . ." and ending with ". . . wear gloves." Nicole reflects on her experience with the white world. *Talkback*: Are Nicole's feelings about reactions to her "otherness" only racial or universal?

2. "Commercial Break," pages 35 to 37. The commercial implies that everyone needs fixing. *Talkback*: What is your attitude toward fixing?

3. "Live on Barry Rex Live," pages 56 to 58. Ladybird Hope spins the crash. *Talkback*: How would you describe Ladybird's answers and her view of her audience?

4. Chapter 15, pages 176 to 177, beginning with "The girls had lost . . ." and ending with the chapter. Mary Lou and Adina compare their situation to *Lord of the Flies*. *Talkback*: Do girls need an island to find themselves?

5. Chapter 34, pages 332 to336. The girls' controversial answers make Agent Jones change his plan. *Talkback*: What is your opinion of the island pageant?

Discussion guide available @ http://wildgeeseguides.blogspot.com/2011/07/beauty-queens-by-libba-bray.html

Writing exercises available @ http://libbabray.com/writing exercises.html

Author interview available @ http://www.omnivoracious.com/2011/04/ya-wednesday-a-conversation-between-libba-bray-and-libba-bray.html

Related Works

1. **Anderson, Laurie Halse. *Prom*.** New York: Viking Press, 2005. 215p. $16.99. ISBN 0 670 05974 9. [fiction] JS, G (*Booktalks and Beyond*, 2007, pages 56 to 58.) Eighteen-year-old Ashley discovers her administrative talents when she agrees to help with the prom, an event she previously scorned.

2. **Bray, Libba. *Going Bovine*.** New York: Delacorte Press, 2009. 479p. $17.99. ISBN 978 0 385 73397 7. [fiction] S, CG with high

interest for boys (*Value-Packed Booktalks*, 2011, pages 4 to 5.) Dying 16-year-old Cameron takes a satirical world tour and learns to appreciate his family.

3. **Cabot, Meg.** *Airhead*. New York: Scholastic/Point, 2008. 352p. $16.99. ISBN-13: 978 0 545 04052 5. [fiction] JS, G (*Value-Packed Booktalks*, 2011, pages 47 to 49.) Seventeen-year-old intellectual tomboy Emerson Watts scorns appearance and worldly fame until she receives the brain of a famous model.

4. **Sandell, Lisa Ann.** *A Map of the Known World*. New York: Scholastic Press, 2009. 304p. $16.99. ISBN-13: 978 0 545 06970 0. [fiction] JS, G (*Value-Packed Booktalks*, 2011, pages 20 to 22.) After her brother's death, a high school freshman discovers new friends as well as her own strength, judgment, and talent.

5. **Zevin, Garielle.** *Memoirs of a Teenage Amnesiac*. New York: Farrar, Straus and Giroux, 2007. 271p. $17.00. ISBN-13: 978 0 374 34946 2. [fiction] JS, G (*Genre Talks for Teens*, 2007, pages 61 to 64.) After an amnesia-producing fall, high school junior Naomi Page Porter reevaluates her relationships with her family and friends.

గ్రఁ

de Graaf, Anne. Son of a Gun.

Grand Rapids, MI: Wm. B. Eerdmans Publishing Co., 2012. 125p. $8.00pa. ISBN 978 0 8028 5406 3. [nonfiction] MJS, CG

Themes/Topics: Liberia, Civil War (1989–1996), child soldiers, brothers and sisters

Summary/Description

Eight-year-old Lucky, his 10-year-old sister Nopi, and their school-mate James are kidnapped from their school and forced to become child soldiers. Both Lucky and his sister tell the story, which involves their initial kidnapping, escape, reunion with family, another kidnapping and escape, and the final reunion with their parents. Although they will never escape the horrors that they experienced and committed, they look forward to living in a more peaceful nation under guard of UN troops. The book includes an "Author's Note," descriptions of the Liberian Climate, education, daily life, and history. It also includes additional information about child soldiers and their writings and drawings from the UN "Save the Children" project. Web sites for further information and "Questions for Discussion" are also provided.

Values: Both brother and sister learn the importance
of family and peace.

Booktalk

Read Prologue aloud (pages 7 to 8) or ask someone in the group to read it.
How old do you think the speaker is? (*Wait for responses.*) He is
about 16. That is not too young for a soldier. Right? But he started being
a soldier when he was eight. An army (he did not know which one)
showed up at his school. They beat and killed his teachers. Then, they
took Lucky, the speaker, his 10-year-old sister Nopi, and his best friend
James along with all the other students. Any who protested or could not
keep pace died. To survive, the three became the people that they hated
and feared. They joined other wars. Can they change now? (*Wait for
responses.*) You can decide. When Lucky and his sister stopped walking,
when they found home again, they started to tell their stories. So here
they are, straight from the *Son of a Gun*.

Read Aloud/Talkback

1. Chapter 1, pages 11 to 12. Nopi introduces herself. *Talkback*: What
   surprises you about what Nopi says?
2. Chapter 4, pages 21 to 23, beginning with the chapter and ending
   with "I waited." *Talkback*: How does this passage affect you?
3. Chapter 5, pages 27 to 28, beginning with the chapter and ending with
   ". . . target practice." *Talkback*: How are the captors using their power?
4. Chapter 19, pages 68 to 70. Lucky reflects on his lost identity.
   Talkback: What parts of this passage show you hope? What parts
   show despair?
5. Chapter 24, pages 81 to 85. After they find home, Lucky and Nopi
   find that the present and past collide. *Talkback*: How does this passage communicate confusion? Hope?

Blog and slide show available @ http://www.annedegraaf.com/

Related Works

1. **Beah, Ishmael. *A Long Way Gone: Memoirs of a Boy Soldier*.**
   New York: Farrar, Straus and Giroux/Sarah Crichton Books, 2007.
   229p. $22.00. ISBN-13: 978 0 374 10523 5. [nonfiction] JS/A, CG
   with high interest for boys (*Genre Talks for Teens*, 2009, pages 98
   to 100.) After 12-year-old Ishmael's family dies in a rebel raid, he
   begins his physical, emotional, and intellectual journey for survival.

2. **Cooney, Caroline B. *Diamonds in the Shadow***. New York: Delacorte Press, 2007. 230p. $15.99. ISBN-13: 978 0 385 73261 1. [fiction] JS, CG with high interest for boys (*Genre Talks for Teens*, 2009, pages 272 to 275.) The Finch family agrees to sponsor four refugees from an African civil war.

3. **Lekuton, Joseph Lemasolai. *Facing the Lion: Growing up Maasai on the African Savanna***. Washington, DC: National Geographic, 2003. 123p. $15.95. ISBN 0 7922 5125 3. [nonfiction] MJS, CG with high interest for boys (*Booktalks and Beyond*, 2007, pages 234 to 236.) Joseph Lekuton describes his nomadic life as a Maasai and the life journey that led him to the United States.

4. **Mankell, Henning, and Anne Connie Stuksrud** (trans.). ***Secrets in the Fire***. Toronto, ON: Annick Press LATD, 2003. 166p. $16.00. ISBN 1 55037 801 5. [fiction] MJS, G. A young refugee from Mozambique, builds a new life after losing her sister and her legs in a land-mine explosion.

5. **Stassen, J. P., and Alexis Siegel** (trans.). ***Deogratias: A Tale of Rwanda***. New York: First Second, 2006. 78p. $16.95. ISBN-13: 978 1 59643 103 4. [graphic] S/A. Deogratias's descent into madness parallels his own country's insane descent into genocide.

ᘓᘔ

Kirby, Matthew J. Icefall.

New York: Scholastic Press, 2011. 336p. $17.99.
ISBN 978 0 545 27424 1. [fiction] M, CG with high interest for girls

Themes/Topics: Identity, war, storytelling, mystery, love, families, royalty, glaciers, Norse mythology

Summary/Description

Solveig, her brother the crown prince, and their older sister are hidden in a fortress protected by mountains and sea. The father sends Berserkers to protect them further while he battles the chieftain who wishes to marry Solveig's sister. As the winter wears on, the Berserkers become restless, and a poisoning makes it clear that they house a traitor. Solveig, the king's least favorite child, works with the father's skald. Her stories both inspire and calm the group. The skill gives her a new identity and growing confidence, but she becomes uncomfortable with the neutrality her role requires. The father's enemy arrives at the fortress, and the traitors are revealed. Solveig, takes advantage of a diversion created by her sister and saves the imprisoned household members. They all escape up the mountain. The skald who trained Solveig opens the glacier's lake, which drowns the chieftain and his army. When her father returns, Solveig is plotting her own life course independent of his will.

Values: Solveig learns that self-respect and identity are the basis of strength and power.

Booktalk

Ask how many know what an icefall is. Read a definition of icefall and show a picture of an icefall on a glacier.

Solveig lives next to a glacier in an isolated fortress. She hears it groan every day. She, her brother, and sister are there because their father is at war with a man who wants the hand of her beautiful sister. The man is old and cruel, and so the father said, "No." (*You might want to let them speak the answer.*) The three are in the safest place. But Dad didn't consider some things. (*Ask what they think those things are.*) A traitor is in the group he sent. The glacier could let loose. The chieftain could defeat the father and take the wife he wants. What can they do? Her brother is the crown prince. Her sister is beautiful. Solveig is the child with no special gifts or talents. Well, she has one talent. She can tell stories. TELL STORIES you say. How can stories make a difference? Solveig's stories are strong enough to shape people's lives. They may even be even strong enough to control an *Icefall*.

Alternative booktalk available @

http://www.scholastic.ca/bookfairs/teachers/pdfs/fall2011/bt_review_icefall.pdf

Read Aloud/Talkback

1. Chapter 2, page 17, beginning with "A moment later . . ." and ending with ". . . father's enemies." Solveig describes the Berserkers. *Talkback*: Draw a picture of the Berserkers.
2. Chapter 2, pages 22 to 23, beginning with "A crash causes . . ." and ending with ". . . all his layers?" Alric laughs with the Berserkers, and Sloveig comments on his ability to reshape himself. *Talkback*: Can a shaper have a shape?
3. Chapter 4, pages 47 to 48, beginning with "I am standing . . ." and ending with ". . . into the sea." Solveig has a dream of destruction. *Talkback*: List all the ways that this dream is important to the story. Compare your list with the list of others in the group.

4. Chapter 12, pages 158 to 161, beginning with "Then he exhales . . ." and ending with ". . . of us liars." Solveig realizes the power of her story, and Alric comments on the power and elusive quality of stories. *Talkback*: Is the story real or a fantasy?
5. Chapter 22, page 302, beginning with "Alric takes a step . . ." and ending with ". . . will become." Alric tells Solveig that her abilities go beyond the powers of a skald. *Talkback*: What is Alric telling Solveig about her talents?

Script available @

http://www.scholastic.ca/bookfairs/teachers/pdfs/fall2011/bt_script_icefall.pdf

Author interviews available @

http://www.crackingthecover.com/3249–2/
http://bookboxdaily.scholastic.com/2011/11/01/icefall/

Related Works

1. **Anderson, John David. *Standard Hero Behavior***. New York: Clarion Books, 2007. 273p. $16.00. ISBN-13: 978 0 618 75920 0. [fiction] JS, CG with high interest for boys. Thinking that he can never be a hero, 15-year-old Mason applies for a job as a bard and discovers that real heroism is far different from the kind in books.
2. **Farmer, Nancy. *The Land of the Silver Apples***. New York: Atheneum Books for young Readers/A Richard Jackson Book, 2007. 491p. $18.99. ISBN-13: 978 1 4169 0735 0. [fiction] MJ, CG with high interest for boys (*Genre Talks for Teens*, 2009, pages 202 to 205.) Jack embarks to save his sister from the hobgoblins, restores the Life Force to the land, and realizes that both beauty and fear are in the eye of the beholder.
3. **Farmer, Nancy. *The Sea of Trolls***. New York: Atheneum Books for Young Readers/A Richard Jackson Book, 2004. 459p. $17.95. ISBN 0 689 86744 1. [fiction] MJ, CG with strong interest for boys (*Booktalks and Beyond*, 2007, pages 160 to 162.) Eleven-year-old Jack, overworked and underappreciated by his father, apprentices to a local Bard, is captured by Berserkers, and watched over by a mysterious crow.
4. **Gardner, John. *Grendel***. New York: Vintage Books, 1989 (reissued edition). 192p. $10.95pa. ISBN 0 679 72311 0. [fiction] S/A. The monster from *Beowulf* tells his own story.
5. **Wooding, Chris. *Poison***. New York: Orchard Books, 2003. 273p. $16.99. ISBN 0 439 75570 0. [fiction] JS, CG with high

interest for girls (*Booktalks and Beyond*, 2007, pages 176 to 178.) Sixteen-year-old Azalia sets out to rescue her sister and discovers that she is the master writer who controls all life stories.

ෆ ෧

Klavan, Andrew. **The Last Thing I Remember.**
Nashville, TN: Thomas Nelson, 2009 (Book One). 346p.
(Homelanders, Book One) $14.99.
ISBN 978 1 59554 607 4. [fiction] MJS, CG with high interest for boys

Themes/Topics: Amnesia, terrorism, fugitives from justice

Summary/Description
Seventeen-year-old Charlie West wakes up strapped to a chair. He was tortured and is about to be killed. His story emerges in his survival journey as he recalls what brought him to this point. The last day he remembers happened more than a year ago when he was arrested and sentenced for the murder of his friend. When Charlie is captured again, an unknown person releases his handcuffs and charges him to save the life of the Head of Homeland Security. He completes the task, but discovers that the terrorist leading the attack recognizes him as a fellow terrorist. He, then, must flee the security guards who think he is part of the attack.

Values: Charlie's patriotism, religious beliefs, superior physical training, and the love and loyalty of his parents and girlfriend keep him positive and alive.

Booktalk
Charlie West is 17 years old, and he is in trouble. (*Read aloud chapter 1, pages 3 to 5.*) Who do you think Charlie West is? (*Wait for responses.*) The answer to that question is the reason that he is here. Charlie believes he knows who he is. He doesn't know what happened to him over the last year, why it happened, and who other people think he is because of what happened. As he tries to recover the when, where, why, and how, he may find a new answer to that who question, the most important part of *The Last Thing* (he) *Remember*(s).

Book trailer available @ http://www.youtube.com/watch?v=_pfVs0o9Loo

Read Aloud/Talkback

1. Chapter 4, pages 18 to 20, beginning with "I went back . . ." and ending with ". . . pink dust." Charlie describes his family by using his Word of the Day calendar. *Talkback*: Using the passage as a model, choose words that would explain your family members.

2. Chapter 5, pages 25 to 27, beginning with "My karate teacher . . ." and ending with ". . . this was it." Charlie recalls a quotation of Winston Churchill. *Talkback*: How is this quotation the center of the story? Do you have a favorite quotation that you live by?

3. Chapter 13, pages 136 to 138, beginning with "Sensei Mike . . ." and ending with ". . . into reality." Sensei Mike affirms that Charlie can become an Air Force pilot. *Talkback*: How do you react to Sensi Mike's vocational advice?

4. Chapter 24, pages 266 to 267, beginning with "You know who I . . ." and ending with the chapter. Charlie realizes how difficult it is to keep faith when things are against you. *Talkback*: How would you compare your own life preparation to Charlie's?

5. Chapter 31, pages 334 to 336, beginning with "The shooting from across . . ." and ending with the chapter. Charlie recalls all the voices that keep him strong. *Talkback*: What distinction does Charlie make among the person he is, the events that he can't remember, and the judgments of others?

Reading group guide available on pages 337 to 339 of this edition.

Discussion questions, related activities, and Web sites available @ http://www.cinemablend.com/new/An-Interview-With-Homelander-Series-Author-Andrew-Klavan-18146.html

Author interview available @ http://www.cinemablend.com/new/An-Interview-With-Homelander-Series-Author-Andrew-Klavan-18146.html

Related Works

1. **Brooks, Kevin. *Being*.** New York: Scholastic Inc./Chicken House, 2007. 336p. $16.99. ISBN 0 439 89973 7. [fiction] JS, CG with high interest for boys (*Genre Talks for Teens*, 2009, pages 85 to 87.) Sixteen-year-old Robert Smith, supposedly an orphan, undergoes a routine endoscopy, and is subsequently pursued by scientists and thugs when they discover that his body is a maze of wires and chemicals.

2. **Heneghan, James.** *Safe House*. Victoria, BC: Orca Book Publishers, 2006. 151p. $7.95pa. ISBN-13: 978 1 55143 640 1. [fiction] MJS, CG with high interest for boys (*Genre Talks for Teens*, 2009, pages 93 to 95.) When 12-year-old Liam Fogarty witnesses his defenseless parents gunned down by Protestant terrorists, he sees the face of the trigger man and must run and hide for his life.

3. **Klass, David.** *Firestorm: Book I*. New York: Farrar, Straus and Giroux/Frances Foster Books, 2006. 287p. (The Caretaker Trilogy) $17.00. ISBN 0 374 32307 0. [fiction] JS, CG with high interest for boys (*Genre Talks for Teens*, 2009, pages 119 to 120.) Jack Danielson, a brilliant, athletic, and handsome high school senior, discovers that his entire life has been a protective cover and that his real mission, as a visitor from the future, is to save the earth from ecological disaster.

4. **Klavan, Andrew.** *The Long Way Home:Book Two*. Nashville, TN: Thomas Nelson, 2010. 345p. (The Homelanders) $14.99. ISBN-13: 978 1 59554 713 2. [fiction] MJS, CG with high interest for boys. Charles West returns home to find answers about his lost year, including his friend's murder and his romance with Beth.

5. **Klavan, Andrew.** *The Truth of the Matter: Book Three*. Nashville, TN: Thomas Nelson, 2010. 346p. (The Homelanders) $14.99. ISBN-13: 978 1 59554 714 9. [fiction] MJS, CG with high interest for boys. Charles West's life becomes more dangerous as he tracks down Waterman as instructed in book one.

ॐ

McCormick, Patricia. **Purple Heart.**

New York: Harper Collins Publishers/Balzar & Bray, 2009. 199p. $16.99.
ISBN 978 0 06 173090 0. [fiction] JS, CG with high interest for boys

Themes/Topics: Iraq war, trauma, coming of age

Summary/Description

Eighteen-year-old Matt Duffy is awarded a Purple Heart when he wakes up in an army hospital. He never fully recalls an event that would merit a medal, but only bits and pieces of an incident that point to his killing a young Iraqi boy whom the unit befriended. Sent back to his unit, he lives with a heightened fear of danger and a growing suspicion that one of his fellow soldiers shares responsibility for the boy's death. After two people in his unit die in a suicide bombing, he learns that his best friend killed the boy after discovering he was a spotter. The soldier was traumatized by the shooting. The story's events illustrate the difficulty of building relationships, accepting honor, or assigning guilt in a modern war.

Values: Matt illustrates the importance of loyalty and reflection in a sanity-challenging situation.

Booktalk

Show a Purple Heart or a picture of a Purple Heart. Ask what it means.
    Eighteen-year-old Matt Duffy is a hero of the Iraqi War. He and his friend Justin were trapped in an alley by insurgents. Matt shot their way out. That's the story the authorities tell him. Is it true? If he did it, why would he ask that question? (*Wait for responses.*) Matt sees only parts of the event: an alley, a mangy dog, a boy who was kind of the unit mascot, and an explosion of bullets. Matt relives the incident almost every day. First, the boy is smiling. Then, with a terrified look on his face, he is flying through the air and suddenly dead. Did Matt's bullet kill him? Was it friendly fire? Did Matt take deadly aim? And, if Matt can't figure out what he did, why is someone handing him a *Purple Heart* (*Point to the book's* cover.) for doing it?

Book/author trailers available @
http://www.harpercollins.com/authors/33041/Patricia_McCormick/index.aspx

http://www.youtube.com/watch?v=3MxgBL2Q0rs

Read Aloud/Talkback

1. Pages 8 to 9, beginning with "The priest—the name . . ." and ending with ". . . always baseball." The priest introduces Matt to the concept of "*Be still. And know.*" *Talkback*: How would you interpret the priest's advice? Do you have a statement that guides your life? Share it.
2. Pages 54 to 55, beginning with "A shadow fell . . ." and ending with the chapter. Francis gives Matt a notebook to record what he remembers. *Talkback*: What does this exercise tell Matt and the reader?
3. Pages 56 to 60, beginning with "A letter from Caroline . . ." and ending with ". . . the worst." A letter from Caroline, who worries over normal teen issues, contrasts with the reality of Iraq. *Talkback*: How does American reality contrast to the soldiers' reality?
4. Pages 114 to 115, beginning with "He thought . . ." to the end of the chapter. Matt recalls his squad members' reaction to war. *Talkback*: How does this passage address protection?

5. Pages 161 to 162, beginning with "It was near . . ." and ending with ". . . and prayed." In turmoil, after returning to his unit, Matt turns to prayer. *Talkback*: What pushes Matt to pray?

Author interview available @ http://www.democrattribune.com/ blogs/1243/entry/31423/

Author interview and discussion guide available @ http:// www.teachervision.fen.com/tv/printables/harpercollins/purple- heart_rg.pdf

Related Works

1. **Aronson, Marc, and Patty Campbell (eds.).** *War Is: Soldiers, Survivors, and Storytellers Talk about War*. Cambridge, MA: Candlewick Press, 2008. 200p. $17.99. ISBN 978 0 7636 3625 8. [anthology: nonfiction and fiction] S, CG (*Value-Packed Booktalks*, 2011, pages 27 to 29.) Twenty selections explore war from the points of view of protestors, correspondents, soldiers, and military family members.

2. **Beah, Ishmael.** *A Long Way Gone: Memoirs of a Boy Soldier*. New York: Farrar, Straus and Giroux/Sarah Crichton Books, 2007. 229p. $22.00. ISBN-13: 978 0 374 10523 5. [nonfiction] JS/A, CG with high interest for boys (*Genre Talks for Teens*, 2009, pages 98 to 100.) Twelve-year-old Ishmael sees his family's village wiped out in a rebel raid and begins a physical, emotional, and intellec- tual survival journey that ends in a UN rehabilitation camp.

3. **Cormier, Robert.** *Heroes*. New York: Delacorte Press, 1998. 135p. $15.95. ISBN 0 385 32590 8. [fiction] JS, CG with high inter- est for boys (*Booktalks and More*, 2003, pages 118 to 120.) Francis Joseph Cassavant returns to his hometown with a silver medal and without a face. He won the medal for saving his company by falling on a grenade, but really meant to kill himself.

4. **Marston, Elsa.** *Santa Claus in Baghdad and Other Stories about Teens in the Arab World*. Bloomington, IN: Indiana University Press, 2008. 198p. $15.95. ISBN 978 0 253 22004 2. [short stories] JS, CG (*Value-Packed Booktalks*, 2011, pages 230 to 232.) Eight short sto- ries express the personal crises of Arab teens who live in societies with challenges different from ours, but universal coming of age choices.

5. **McCormick, Patricia.** *Sold*. New York: Hyperion, 2006. 263p. $15.99. ISBN 078685171 6. [fiction] JS, G (*Genre Talks for Teens*, 2009, pages 108 to 111.) Thirteen-year-old Lakshmi lives in Nepal. After the monsoons wash away the family crops, her stepfather sells her into prostitution.

ℭℨℨℨ

Neumeier, Rachel. **The Floating Islands.**

New York: Alfred A. Knopf, 2011. 388p. $16.99.
ISBN 978 0 375 84705 9. [fiction] MJ, CG

Themes/Topics: Magic, flight, cousins, responsibilities,
societal roles, loyalty, prejudice

Summary/Description

Trei's family dies in a volcanic eruption and his paternal Tolounnese uncle rejects him as a half-breed. He is welcomed by a maternal uncle on the Floating Islands. His uncle helps Trei enter training in the kajuraihi, a group of men who construct their own wings to soar over the island. He bonds with his classmates, which include an island prince. Trei's cousin, Araené, longs to be a chef but, because of her culture's attitudes, must masquerade as a boy to pursue her dream. She continues to present herself as a boy after her parents die suddenly and enters training for a mage. When Tolounn invades the islands, Trei, Araené, and the prince each helps defeat them. Trei is accepted as an Islander. The prince courts Araené, who is now permitted to pursue her personal magic.

Values: All three characters find new friends and family,
as they balance their talents and personal ambitions
with the common good.

Booktalk

Ask what statements like "He's a half-breed" and "She's just a girl" imply. How would you react to those statements? (*Wait for responses.*) When Trei's entire family dies in a volcanic eruption, he goes to his uncle's family. His uncle rejects Trei as a half-breed. Trei leaves Tolounn, his home, and travels to his mother's brother who lives on the mysterious Floating Islands. He is welcomed and sees men who build wings and soar in the sky. He decides to join them. Life is good for Trei, but his cousin Araené is not as happy. She has a dream, too. She wants to be a chef, an impossible task for an island girl. But a strange magic starts to surround her. She almost accepts its promises. Then, comes an attack from Tolounn's forces. Whose side would you be on if you were Trei? If you were Araené? (*Wait for responses.*) Their decisions could mean the end or a new future for them and for *The Floating Islands*.

Book trailer for educational purposes only available @
http://www.youtube.com/watch?v=Js_xTOyAiBw

Read Aloud/Talkback

1. Chapter 1, pages 4 to 5, beginning with "But Trei was . . ." and ending with ". . . he would die." Trei sees the Island wingmen for the first time. *Talkback*: Why do you think that Trei's attitude is so much different than the sailor's?
2. Chapter 1, pages 19 to 21, beginning with "Araené had made tiny crisp . . ." and ending with the chapter. Trei realizes that Araené's anger comes from her stifling position in society. *Talkback*: What does Trei's understanding of Araené reveal about Trei?
3. Chapter 6, pages 156 to 161, beginning with "Araené *was* horribly . . ." and ending with the chapter. Araené encounters the dragon and concludes that she has broken all the rules in one day. *Talkback*: Depict the scene in graphic format.
4. Chapter 10, pages 241 to 243, beginning with "In the west . . ." and ending with ". . . that might be." Araené encounters the ambiguous Cassameirin. *Talkback*: Why does Cassameirin make Araené so angry? Can you compare him to a person in your own life?
5. Chapter 14, pages 325 to 328, beginning with "Open me a door . . ." and ending with ". . . you had to be." The prince asks Araené to open a door and reveals that he shares her restrictions. *Talkback*: How are doors related to the cultural restrictions that Trei, Araené, and the prince face?

Related Works

1. **Colfer, Eoin. *Airman*.** New York: Hyperion Books for Children, 2008. 412p. $17.99. ISBN-13: 978 142310750 7. [fiction] MJS, CG with high interest for boys (*Genre Talks for Teens*, pages 116 to 119.) Intervening in a plot to kill the king, Conor is declared dead, but sent to the kingdom's prison island where he becomes a hero.
2. **Murdock, Catherine Gilbert. *Princess Ben*.** Boston, MA: Houghton Mifflin Co., 2008. 244p. $16.00. ISBN-13: 978 0 618 95971 6. [fiction] JS, G (*Value-Packed Booktalks*, 2011, pages 152 to 154.) Fifteen-year-old Princess Ben transforms from a difficult, overweight, and slothful girl to a worthy regent, who controls her magic, saves her country from war, helps slay a dragon, and finds love.
3. **Pierce, Tamora. *Melting Stones*.** New York: Scholastic Press, 2008. 320p. $17.99. ISBN-13: 978 0 545 05264 1. [fiction] JS, G (*Value-Packed Booktalks*, 2011, pages 168 to 170.) Fourteen-year-old Evvy, a

stone mage in training, and her wise rock companion Luvo discover that the birth of a volcano is disrupting an island's plant and water supply.

4. **Pierce, Tamora.** *The Will of the Empress*. New York: Scholastic Press, 2005. 320p. $17.99. ISBN 0 439 44171 4. [fiction] MJS, G (*Genre Talks for Teens*, 2009, pages 207 to 210.) Sandry's Discipline Cottage friends help her escape a forced marriage.

5. **Pratchett, Terry.** *Nation*. New York: HarperCollins Publishers, 2008. 367p. $17.89. ISBN-13: 978 0 06 143302 3. [fiction] MJS, CG with high interest for boys (*Value-Packed Booktalks*, 2011, pages 95 to 97.) A shipwreck and tidal wave place a girl and boy on the same island, where they build a community and examine their beliefs.

಄಄

Smithson, Ryan. **Ghosts of War: The True Story of a 19-Year-Old GI.**

New York: Collins, 2009. 320p. $16.99.
ISBN 978 0 06 166468 7. [nonfiction] JS, CG with high interest for boys

Themes/Topics: Iraq, 9/11, coming of age, Army life, post-traumatic stress, writing

Summary/Description

Ryan Smithson opts for the army rather than college after witnessing 9/11. He experiences the Army method of breaking soldiers down before building them up and devotes himself to the unit or team. He endures the stress of living under constant threat and feelings of isolation when leaving his family, his new wife, and finally his unit. In Iraq, he develops compassion for the people and a greater understanding of the meaning of dictatorship and the motivation behind the insurgent attacks. After his yearlong tour, he experiences post-traumatic stress and the release that writing and sharing his experiences affords him.

Values: Ryan's account demonstrates courage, patriotism, maturity, loyalty, risk taking, persistence, resilience, and compassion.

Booktalk

Ask what people in the group know about 9/11 and if anyone in the group knows someone who served in Iraq. Ask them to share what they learned.

Ryan Smithson was 16 when he saw the twin towers go down and thousands of Americans lose their lives. He visited the memorial and decided to honor those who died. He had the opportunity to go to college, but joined the U.S. Army. How do you think that decision changed his life? (*Wait for responses.*) He didn't become a hero as we think of a hero. He became a man who wrote a book to help himself and those of us who never went to Iraq. And, in his story, he tells us about facing something as dangerous as insurgents, the *Ghosts of War*.

Book trailers available @
http://www.youtube.com/watch?v=_53Rw_gQSDI

http://animoto.com/play/ph67JHqex1wAoG8Z32yUQg/

Read Aloud/Talkback

1. Part I, pages 3 to 5, beginning with the chapter and ending with ". . . so fake." Ryan describes his high school. *Talkback*: How does your perception of your school compare to Ryan's perception of his?
2. Part I, pages 16 to 17, beginning with "It was a nightmare . . ." and ending with the chapter. Ryan and Heather react to seeing the scene of 9/11. *Talkback*: When Ryan describes his reaction to the scene, what point is he making?
3. Part I, pages 75 to 79, beginning with "We cross the border . . ." and ending with "Their thumbs are up." Ryan describes crossing the border. *Talkback*: Does this passage surprise you?
4. Part II, pages 203 to 209. This chapter describes breaking the rules with the local children and the motivation for doing it. *Talkback*: How do you react to the GI Joe Schmo attitude about breaking the rules?
5. Part III, pages 307 to 310. In this chapter that shares the book's title, Ryan explains the significance of the *Ghosts of War*. *Talkback*: How does Ryan turn the war into a positive experience? How does this chapter contrast with Read Aloud 1?

Discussion guide, alternative booktalks, related works and links available @ http://www.yourlibrary.ws/ya_webpage/ritba/ritba11/ghostsofwar.html

Author statement and photo album available @ http://www.harpercollins.com/authors/34332/Ryan_Smithson/index.aspx

Read aloud and author statement available @ http://www.youtube.com/watch?v=Zo31upG8JAM

Related Works

1. **Aronson, Marc, and Patty Campbell (eds.).** *War Is: Soldiers, Survivors, and Storytellers Talk about War*. Cambridge,

MA: Candlewick Press, 2008. 200p. $17.99. ISBN-13: 978 0 7636 3625 8. [anthology: nonfiction and fiction] S, CG (*Value-Packed Booktalks*, 2011, pages 27 to 29.) Twenty selections divided into four sections explore war from the points of view of protestors, correspondents, soldiers, and family members.

2. **Beah, Ishamael. *A Long Way Gone: Memoirs of a Boy Soldier*.** New York: Farrar, Straus and Giroux/Sarah Crichton Books, 2007. 229p. $22.00. ISBN-13: 978 0 374 10523 5. [nonfiction] JS/A, CG with high interest for boys (*Genre Talks for Teens*, 2009, pages 98 to 100.) When Ishmael is 12, his family is killed in a rebel raid, and he begins his journey of physical, emotional, and intellectual survival.

3. **Keller, Julia.** *Back Home.* New York: Egmont, 2009. 194p. $15.99. ISBN 978 1 60681 005 4. [fiction] JS, CG (Issues/Courage, pages 12 to 15.) Thirteen-year-old Rachel Browning's father's war injury makes him a stranger to his family.

4. **Myers, Walter Dean. *Sunrise over Fallujah*.** New York: Scholastic Press, 2008. 304p. $17.99. ISBN-13: 978 0 439 91624 0. [fiction] JS, CG with high interest for boys (*Value-Packed Booktalks*, 2011, pages 93 to 95.) Private Robin Perry relates his experiences as a member of a Civil Affairs Unit in the Iraq invasion.

5. **Zenatti, Valérie, and Adriana Hunter (trans.). *When I Was a Soldier: A Memoir*.** New York: Bloomsbury Children's Books, 2005. 235p. $16.95. ISBN 1 58234 978 9. [nonfiction] JS, CG with high interest for girls (*Booktalks and Beyond*, 2007, pages 241 to 244.) Eighteen-year-old Valérie Zenatti enters the Israeli military service, experiences "rigorous training" and "harsh living conditions," and develops a questioning attitude toward her country's military mindset.

Trust

⟨ʒ⟩⟨ɛ⟩

Bacigalupi, Paolo. Ship Breaker.
New York: Little, Brown and Co., 2010. 326p. $17.99.
ISBN 978 0 316 05621 2. [fiction] JS, CG with high interest for boys

Themes/Topics: Conduct of life, recycling, abuse, father/son, social class

Summary/Description

In a grim futuristic society, Nailer scavenges old oil tankers for copper wiring. His abusive father has a feared and respected position in the scavenger community. When Nailer discovers a wrecked ship, he finds a girl, Nita, whom he can kill or return to her wealthy father. Nailer's father decides to hold Nita for ransom or sell her body parts. Nailer helps her escape to Orleans so that she can contact her father's firm, but a war within her clan makes her a valuable prize. Nailer's father, representing Nita's enemies, pursues them and captures her. Nailer joins her supporters to save her. In a sea battle, Nailer kills his father to save himself and Nita. Nailer returns home, but looks forward to more sea adventures and a closer relationship with Nita.

Value: Nailer learns to judge family by trust rather than blood.

Booktalk

Ask how many people recycle. Ask if they consider it a duty, a hobby, or a living.

Nailer lives in a future world full of shortages and poverty. He scavenges for copper from wrecked ships. Recycling means survival. He doesn't know how old he is, but he does know that soon he will be too large to fit in the small and dangerous spaces assigned to his crew. Then what? (*Wait for responses.*) His father is the toughest and most feared fighter around. He could protect and help Nailer, but he could also kill him. It depends on how high or how drunk Dad is on any given day. Then, Nailer gets a Lucky Strike. He finds a newly wrecked ship. The ship has a very rich, live girl covered in jewels. Should he kill or protect her? (*Wait for responses.*) His decision may be his key to leaving the life of the *Ship Breaker*.

Book trailer available @ http://www.youtube.com/
watch?v=kXa2ary4rSo&feature=g-vrec&context=G2abd0afRVAA
AAAAAAAQ

Read Aloud/Talkback

1. Chapter 5, page 51, beginning with "Yeah . . ." and ending with "Stood up." Pima reflects on luck and smarts. *Talkback*: Does Pima's advice apply today?
2. Chapter 8, page 92, beginning with "Nailer shivered . . ." and ending with ". . . and jewels." Nailer ponders pride and death. *Talkback*: Do you agree with Nailer's observation?

3. Chapter 10, pages 110 to 111, beginning with "The girl looked . . ." and ending with ". . . he understood." Nita begins to show her strength and cunning. *Talkback*: Nailer uses the words "soft," "clever," "smart," and "stupid." What are the distinctions? Do you agree?

4. Chapter 16, pages 194 to 197, beginning with "Sloth had been . . ." and ending with ". . . jolt of the train." Tool and Nita discuss a person's value. *Talkback*: How does each character judge a person's value? How do you judge a person's value?

5. Chapter 21, pages 273 to 274, beginning with "Family . . ." and ending with the chapter. Nailer ponders the meaning of family. *Talkback*: How does Nailer define family? Do you agree?

Study guides available @

http://www.hachettebookgroup.com/_assets/guides/
EG_9780316056212.pdf

http://www.viterbo.edu/uploadedFiles/academics/letters/english/
Ship%20Breaker%20by%20Paolo%20Bacigalupi.pdf

Author interviews available @

http://www.yalsa.ala.org/thehub/2011/03/25/author-interview-
paolo-bacigalupi/

http://www.publishersweekly.com/pw/by-topic/authors/interviews/
article/51699-q—a-with-paolo-bacigalupi.html

http://blog.schoollibraryjournal.com/teacozy/2010/12/06/interview-
paolo-bacigalupi/

http://www.youtube.com/watch?v=HPkawpVMOWk

http://www.youtube.com/watch?v=PpuuL3Op4cI&feature=relmfu

http://www.youtube.com/watch?v=CbDOHg01gnQ

http://www.sfwa.org/2011/11/nebula-awards-interview-paolo-
bacigalupi/

http://www.nationalbook.org/nba2010_ypl_bacigalupi_interv.html#
.UAwdf2HY9kk

Related Works

1. **Anderson, M. T. *Feed***. Cambridge, MA: Candlewick Press, 2003. 235p. $16.99. ISBN 0 7636 1726 1. [fiction] JS, CG (*Teen Genre Connections*, 2005, pages 201 to 203.) In a deteriorating society, teens party on the moon, respond to commercials from implanted feeds in their brains, and decorate dangerous skin lesions caused by a deteriorating environment.

2. **Farmer, Nancy. *The House of the Scorpion***. New York: Atheneum Books for Young Readers/A Richard Jackson Book, 2002.

380p. $17.95. ISBN 0 689 85222 3. [fiction] JS, CG with high interest for boys (*Teen Genre Connections*, 2005, pages 208 to 210.) In a futuristic society, clones produce body parts for the rich and the powerful.

3. **Lloyd, Saci. *The Carbon Diaries, 2015***. New York: Holiday House, 2008. 330p. $17.95. ISBN-13: 978 0 8234 2190 9. [fiction] JS, CG with high interest for girls (*Value-Packed Booktalks*, 2011, pages 166 to 168.) Laura and her family deal with climate change crises, as she faces questions of love and personal loyalty.

4. **O'Brian, Caragh M. *Birthmarked***. New York: Roaring Brook Press, 2010. 360p. $16.99. ISBN 978 1 59643 569 8. [fiction] JS, CG with high interest for girls (*Value-Packed Booktalks,* 2011, pages 157 to 159.) Sixteen-year-old midwife Gaia Stone lives outside the city wall and deals with pollution, water shortage, and genetic manipulation. When her parents are arrested, she enters the city illegally to find them.

5. **Pratchett, Terry. *Nation***. New York: HarperCollins Publishers, 2008. 367p. $17.89. ISBN 978 0 06 143302 3. [fiction] MJS, CG with high interest for boys (*Value-Packed Booktalks*, 2011, pages 95 to 97.) A shipwreck and a tidal wave place a young girl, from a British-style royal family, and an island boy, who has completed his manhood trials, on the same devastated island where they support and learn from each other.

ᘉᘓ

Brooks, Kevin. IBOY.

New York: Scholastic Inc./Chicken House, 2011. 304p. $17.99.

ISBN 978 0 545 31768 9. [fiction] S, CG with high interest for boys

Themes/Topics: Revenge, gangs, vigilante justice, cell phones, superheroes, love

Summary/Description

Sixteen-year-old Tom Harvey lives in a gang-run project. A hooded boy throws a cell phone at him from the high rise. It is imbedded in and interacts with his brain. He learns that on the day of his "accident" his girlfriend Lucy was gang raped. His anger supercharges him. He tries to comfort Lucy, gather information about the attack, and exact revenge on the attackers. His investigation leads him to the project gang boss who, with his gang, takes Tom and Lucy to a secluded place to kill them. As the boss taunts Tom about his family and Lucy, Tom finds a signal and generates enough power to blow up his attackers' via their cell phones. The violence and language may be controversial.

Value: Tom realizes the responsibility of using power positively.

Booktalk

Superheroes! What are they? Can you give me a superhero profile? (*Wait for responses.*) Tom Harvey knows about superheroes, and he knows he isn't one. In his gang-run neighborhood, he's a nerd or a wimp. Then, someone throws a cell phone at him from the high-rise project building. (*Read the opening paragraph, page 1.*) Seventeen days later, Tom wakes up in a hospital. The doctors explain how the cell phone opened his skull and stuck in his head. They can't get all the parts out. He may notice something unusual. He does. He receives more information than anyone can process. He is an iPhone. (*Ask how many people have iPhones or cell phones and what Tom might experience.*) One of the first messages in his head tells him that when the hooded kid threw the phone local gangsters were attacking Tom's girlfriend. He doesn't need a super brain to know that if he hunts down the attackers he'll be a victim. One nerd or wimp against the gang? Impossible. But as Tom thinks about the attack and what he wants to do to the attackers, he charges, just like a phone. He has information and the power to use it. Impossible is getting possible. Is mild-mannered Tom Harvey an out of control weapon? A freak? Or the superhero IBOY?

Book trailer available @ http://www.youtube.com/watch?v=YH5iHzTEkNE

Read Aloud/Talkback

1. Chapter 101, pages 38 to 42. Tom describes his brain power. *Talkback*: Answer the questions listed in the opening paragraph of the chapter. Compare your answers with Tom's. How does that paragraph and chapter draw you into Tom's transformation?
2. Chapter 111, page 57, quotation in italics. Aristotle's statement about the exceptional man introduces the chapter. *Talkback*: Do you agree with Aristotle's opening statement? Explain your opinion.
3. Chapter 1010, page 109, beginning with "I'm perfectly aware . . ." and ending with ". . . that it wasn't." Tom considers right and wrong. *Talkback*: What distinction does Tom make between getting factual information and knowing what to do with it?
4. Chapter 10100, pages 223 to 225, beginning with "As we sat . . ." and ending with ". . . *was* to want." Lucy and Tom ponder the idea

of two sides to everything. It connects to Tom's decision to reveal his identity in chapter 10101, pages 228 to 230, beginning with the chapter and ending with ". . . two sides to everything." *Talkback*: Restate ideas in this passage. Do you agree?

5. Chapter 10110, page 248, quotation in italics. Frederic Thrasher, in the introductory quotation, describes a gang. *Talkback*: If Thrasher is correct, should societies try to eliminate gangs? Why?

Author interviews @

http://dailyfig.figment.com/2011/11/03/kevin-brooks-on-peter-parker-and-boys-in-love/

Related Works

1. **Brooks, Kevin. *Being*.** New York: Scholastic Inc./Chicken House, 2007. 336p. $16.99. ISBN 0 439 89973 7. [fiction] JS, CG with high interest for boys (*Genre Talks for Teens*, 2009, pages 85 to 87.) Sixteen-year-old Robert Smith, supposedly an orphan, undergoes a routine endoscopy, discovers that his body is a maze of wires and chemicals, draws on new strength, escapes from the hospital, and seeks his identity.

2. **Northrop, Michael. *Gentlemen*.** New York: Scholastic Press, 2009. 234p. $16.99. ISBN-13: 978 0 545 09749 9. [fiction] JS, CG with high interest for boys (*Value-Packed Booktalks*, 2011, pages 116 to 118.) "Micheal" and his friends suspect that their remedial English teacher killed their fourth most troublesome group member and take action.

3. **Philbrick, Rodman. *The Last Book in the Universe*.** New York: The Blue Sky Press, 2000. 224p. $16.95. ISBN 0 439 08758 9. [fiction] MJ, CG with high interest for boys (*Booktalks and More*, 2003, pages 146 to 148.) Spaz, an epileptic who is unable to use the popular mind probes, discovers the power of books and family in a gang world.

4. **Sleator, William. *Hell Phone*.** New York: Amulet Books, 2006. 237p. $16.95. ISBN 0 8109 5479 6. [fiction] MJ, CG with high interest for boys (*Genre Talks for Teens*, 2009, pages 164 to 166.) Poverty-stricken 17-year-old Nick Gordon buys a cheap, used cell phone whose powers pull him into crime and hell.

5. **Voorhees, Coert. *The Brothers Torres*.** New York: Disney Book Group/Hyperion, 2008. 316p. $16.99. ISBN-13: 978 14310304 2. [fiction] S, CG with high interest for boys (*Value-Packed Booktalks*, 2011, pages 220 to 223.) Two brothers are almost killed as they sort out good and evil in a gang culture.

❧❧

Christopher, Lucy. Stolen.
New York: Scholastic Inc./Chicken House, 2010. 304p. $17.99.
ISBN 978 0 545 17093 2. [fiction] JS, CG with high interest for girls

Themes/Topics: Kidnapping, interpersonal relations, Australia

Summary/Description

Sixteen-year-old Gemma is abducted by Ty, a man who has stalked her since she was 10. He takes her to an isolated house in the Australian Outback where he plans to keep her perfect forever. After several futile escape attempts, she begins to love Ty. A snake bite threatens her life. Ty takes her for medical care and turns himself in. During her recovery and reunion with family, she disentangles herself from the relationship and prepares to testify at his trial.

Values: Gemma learns the difference between love and abusive control.

Booktalk

Sixteen-year-old Gemma is in an airport. Her family is on vacation. They argue. She walks away for some time alone. A man offers to get her a drink. He is handsome and somehow familiar. Would you take the drink? (*Wait for responses.*) Gemma does. Then, she is gone. Gone from everything she knows. Her new world is heat, sand, snakes, and scorpions—complete isolation. She can survive if she relies on this familiar stranger. He has waited six years to make her perfect. He planned a house for their happily forever after. What would you do? (*Wait for responses.*) At first, Gemma panics. Then, she learns how much he cares for her and how much he has suffered. He is a man, not a monster. As they grow closer each day, is her mind and heart being given, or, like her body, *Stolen*?

Alternative booktalk available @ http://www.scholastic.com/
teachers/article/stolen-booktalk
Book trailers available @
http://www.youtube.com/watch?v=JBt2_3Ui-Ek
http://www.youtube.com/watch?v=iF3xw_gHD00&feature=related

Read Aloud/Talkback

1. Pages 55 to 57, beginning with "You walked around . . ." and ending with ". . . saw it all." The passage communicates Gemma's terror. *Talkback*: What details build fear and horror?
2. Pages 90 to 92, beginning with "Catch you?" and ending with ". . . need saving." Gemma learns that Ty sees her as saved, not stolen. *Talkback*: What does this passage tell you about Ty?
3. Pages 137 to 140, beginning with "You were out . . ." and ending with ". . . sick on your head." The capture of the camel parallels Gemma's capture. *Talkback*: What does the passage about the camel add to the novel?
4. Pages 258 to 262, beginning with "There was water . . ." and ending with ". . . live, too." Ty tells the story of the rain. *Talkback*: How does this scene affect your opinion of Ty?
5. Pages 296 to 299, beginning with "My hands shake . . ." and ending with the novel. Gemma explains how she will testify. *Talkback*: Do you agree with Gemma's final words to Ty?

Author interviews available @

http://www.lucychristopher.com/questions
http://www.youtube.com/watch?v=Dp6VHn8OjtA
http://www.youtube.com/watch?v=IX1VjLL0itc&feature=related
http://www.youtube.com/watch?v=EssQmHJi8hw&feature=related

Related Works

1. **Dogar, Sharon.** *Waves*. New York: Scholastic Inc./Chicken House, 2007. 344p. $16.99. ISBN-13: 978 0 439 87180 8. [fiction] S, CG. Sixteen-year-old Charley, in a coma, sends her brother messages about the love and violence that caused her accident.
2. **Kasischke, Laura.** *Feathered*. New York: HarperTeen, 2008. 261p. $17.89. ISBN-13: 978 0 06 081318 5. [fiction] S, G (*Genre Talks for Teens*, 2009, pages 144 to 146.) Teenaged girls on a Mexican vacation become the victims of "normal" boys who drug, attack, and abandon them.
3. **McCaughrean, Geraldine.** *The White Darkness*. New York: HarperTempest, 2005. 373p. $17.89. ISBN-13: 978 0 06 089036 0. [fiction] JS, CG (*Genre Talks for Teens*, 2009, pages 105 to 108.) Fourteen-year-old Sym fights for survival after her Uncle Victor takes her on a "secret" vacation to the Antarctic, where he launches an expedition to a mythical city inside the earth.

4. **Pow, Tow. *Captives*.** New Milford, CT: Roaring Brook Press/A Neal Porter Book, 2007. 185p. $17.95. ISBN-13: 978 1 59643 201 7. [fiction] JS, CG (*Genre Talks for Teens*, 2009, pages 111 to 113.) While on a Caribbean vacation, two families are kidnapped by rebels. One father writes a bestseller about their captivity, and his son writes the truth.

5. **Vance, Susanna. *Deep*.** New York: Delacorte Press, 2003. 272p. $15.95. ISBN 0 385 73057 8. [fiction] MJS, G (*Teen Genre Connections*, 2005, pages 123 to 125.) An indulged 13-year-old girl and a street-wise 17-year-old girl cooperate to escape a serial killer and secure his arrest.

ʗʓʕʓ

Cohen, Joshua C. **Leverage.**

New York: Penguin Group/Dutton Books, 2011. 425p. $17.99.
ISBN 978 0 525 42306 5. [fiction] JS, CG with high interest for boys

Themes/Topics: Sports, steroids, football, gymnastics, bullies, rape, personal responsibility

Summary/Description

In alternating chapters, Danny, a gifted gymnast, and Kurt, a star football player, tell about overcoming fear and taking control of their lives. Danny's mother is dead. His father buries his grief in work. Kurt, abused in a juvenile home, is recruited by the football coach who pushes steroids. He now lives in a foster home and is haunted by the death of his abused smaller and weaker friend who died. Kurt and Danny witness the rape of a freshman gymnast by three drug-fueled football players. When Kurt, Danny, and the captain of the gymnastics team ignore what happened, the victim commits suicide. Their lives become chaotic and threatened by the same bullies. Together, with the help of a savvy girl from Kurt's juvenile home, they reveal the truth and survive. Violent situations and language could be considered controversial.

Values: Kurt and Danny overcome their fears as they trust each other and bring out the truth.

Booktalk

Have a dictionary available. Ask someone in the group to read the definition of leverage.

From that definition, we know that in physical, social, economic, or emotional situations, if we are going to come out on top, we need what? (*They should answer "leverage."*) Sophomore Danny is one of the smallest kids in the school. He is a star on the gymnastics team. His moves leave the crowds breathless, and he aims for a scholarship because his talent gives him . . . (*Let them fill in the blank with leverage.*) Kurt is a new student. He is on the football team, and he knows all about leverage. (*Read aloud the paragraph beginning* with *"Quarterback . . ." and ending with "Ooofff!" on page 36 in Chapter 6.*) Then, there are the school's three star football players. Their leverage comes in a bottle, compliments of their coaches who know they need . . . (*Let them fill in the blank with leverage.*) to win games. Danny and Kurt survive in two different worlds—split second timing and skill versus brute force and bullying. Then, a crime crashes those worlds together. Both Kurt and Danny are witnesses. If they tell what they saw, they could die, just like the victim. If they don't tell, being a hero on the bars or field won't mean much. And when anyone faces a decision that big, he or she needs . . . (*Let them fill in leverage.*)

Book trailer available @ http://www.youtube.com/ watch?v=TAK6xo_qMtc

Read Aloud/Talkback

1. Chapter 5, pages 28 to 29, beginning with the chapter and ending with ". . . hoping they're listening." Danny explains his power and ambition. *Talkback*: What does Danny reveal about himself?
2. Chapter 6, page 35, beginning with "Something I learned . . ." and ending with ". . . cruelty." Kurt reflects on what foster care taught him about life. *Talkback*: Do you agree with Kurt?
3. Chapter 11, pages 72 to 76. Coach Nelson delivers his "No man is an island" speech. *Talkback*: Find the original quotation that the coach uses and share the information that you find out about it with the group. How does this chapter tie to the rest of the novel?
4. Chapter 37, pages 286 to 288, beginning with the chapter and ending with "I ask." Danny explains his fear and the school's double standard. *Talkback*: Whose side were you on when you read the passage?
5. Chapter 61, pages 424 to 425. Danny watches Kurt score a final touchdown. *Talkback*: How have Danny and Kurt changed?

Author interviews available @

http://www.hopelessbibliophile.com/2011/03/chatting-with-joshua-cohen.html

http://booksobsession.blogspot.com/2011/08/interview-with-author-joshua-cohen.html

http://agoodaddiction.blogspot.com/2011/12/bir2011-leverage-by-joshua-c-cohen.html

http://www.patriciasparticularity.com/2011/06/author-interview-with-joshua-c-cohen.html

http://nataliewrightsya.blogspot.com/2012/07/writer-chat-wednesday-with-joshua-cohen.html

Guest post available @ http://www.reclusivebibliophile.com/guest-post-joshua-cohen

Related Works

1. **Coy, John. *Crackback*.** New York: Scholastic Press, 2005. 208p. $16.99. ISBN 0 439 69733 6. [fiction] JS, CG with high interest for boys. Pressured by his coach, teammates, and father to perform well in football, Miles Manning considers steroids.
2. **Deuker, Carl. *Gym Candy*.** New York: Houghton Mifflin Harcourt/Graphia, 2007. 313p. $8.99pa. ISBN-13: 978 0 547 07631 7. [fiction] JS, CG with high interest for boys (*Value-Packed Booktalks*, 2011, pages 61 to 63.) Mike Johnson, fueled by an ambitious father, takes steroids to excel in football.
3. **Freedman, Jeri. *Steroids: High-Risk Performance Drugs*.** New York: Rosen Publishing, 2009. 64p. $29.95. ISBN-13: 978 1 4358 5013 2. [nonfiction] MJS, CG. Freedman describes steroids and explains the legal uses and the dangers of abuse.
4. **Green, Tim. *Baseball Great*.** New York: HarperCollins Publishers, 2009. 250p. $16.99. ISBN-13: 978 0 06 162686 9. [fiction] MJ, B. A seventh grader, on an all-star baseball team, is offered gym candy to enhance his performance, and exposes the sources.
5. **Rhodes-Courter, Ashley. *Three Little Words: A Memoir*.** New York: Atheneum, 2008. 304p. $17.99. ISBN-13: 971 1 4169 4806 3. [nonfiction] S, CG with high interest for girls. Ashley Rhodes-Courter recalls her life with her dysfunctional biological family, her battles in the foster system, and her difficult adjustment to her stable adopted home.

☙❧

Henry, April. Girl, Stolen.

New York: Henry Holt and Co., 2010. 213p. $16.99.

ISBN 978 0 8050 9005 5. [fiction] JS, CG with high interest for girls

Themes/Topics: Kidnapping, blindness, disabilities, carjacking, fathers and sons

Summary/Description

Sixteen-year-old Cheyenne is accidentally kidnapped by Griffin, a 16-year-old car thief. Griffin's father discovers that Cheyenne's father is wealthy and plans a ransom. Griffin bonds with Cheyenne, who is blind and sick with pneumonia, and protects her from his father and two other car thieves. Believing that she will die when her father pays, Cheyenne knocks Griffin out with a wrench and escapes to the woods. He follows her, assures her that he will protect her, but breaks his ankle and finds himself at the mercy of his father's cohorts, who reveal that Griffin's father killed Griffin's mother. Cheyenne continues on, is captured by Griffin's father, fights him, and contacts the police. Griffin, now living with his aunt, calls Cheyenne after the trials.

Values: Self-reliance and her kidnapper's compassion save Cheyenne.

Booktalk

Sixteen-year-old Griffin steals cars. When he sees a big Cadillac filled with packages and the keys in the ignition, what does he do? (*Wait for the answer.*) But there is one item in the car he didn't count on—16-year-old Cheyenne. His luck holds. She is blind. Even better, she is rich. When he takes his mistake home, his father sees an opportunity. They can chop the car and ransom the girl for a double payoff. But Griffin has more in common with the girl than with his father. He suspects that she won't get out alive. Cheyenne can tell where people are, aim well, and hit hard, and she surely doesn't trust Griffin 100 percent. His father hits hard too, and Griffin knows that his father would kill him. What can he do? (*Wait for an answer. If there are no answers, start with "Griffin has the same trouble you are having . . ." and finish with the last two sentences in the booktalk. If there are several answers, you could say, "All of those suggestions have some pretty heavy consequences, and Griffin finds that out." Then, end with the last two sentences.*) Stealing and chopping cars is easy. It is much more complicated to return a *Girl, Stolen*.

Book trailers available @

http://us.macmillan.com/girlstolen/AprilHenry
http://www.youtube.com/watch?v=RhsbZUnup94

Read Aloud/Talkback

1. Chapter 7, pages 37 to 38, beginning with "Even three years . . ." and ending with ". . . at their eyes." Cheyenne's injury is explained. *Talkback*: In the passage, Cheyenne comments that turning away to see seemed like some kind of metaphor that she can't really describe. How would you explain the metaphor in relation to the story?

2. Chapter 8, page 42, beginning with the chapter and ending with ". . . with the results." Griffin reflects on Cheyenne's blindness, her beauty, and his stealing the car. *Talkback*: How has Cheyenne complicated Griffin's life? How do you react to his thought about the computer?

3. Chapter 15, pages 96 to 98, beginning with "At first when . . ." and ending with the chapter. Cheyenne recalls the school for the blind. *Talkback*: What has blindness taught Cheyenne about herself and survival?

4. Chapter 22, page 151, beginning with "Griffin realized . . ." and ending with the chapter. Griffin is conflicted about his situation. *Talkback*: How does this passage relate to blindness?

5. Chapter 32, pages 210 to 213, beginning with "Griffin's voice was . . ." and ending with the chapter. Griffin gives Cheyenne a Happy New Year call. *Talkback*: Will Cheyenne tell Griffin to call again? Should she? Use specific details from the story to support your opinion.

Reader's guide available @ http://media.us.macmillan.com/readersguides/9780312674755RG.pdf

Author interviews @

http://www.aprilhenrymysteries.com/teen_books/girlstolen.php

http://taysbookcorner.blogspot.com/2012/04/author-interview-april-henry-author-of.html

http://agoodaddiction.blogspot.com/2010/11/author-interview-april-henry.html

http://girlsofsummerlist.wordpress.com/author-interviews-2/author-interviews/april-henry/

http://www.publishersweekly.com/pw/by-topic/childrens/childrens-book-news/article/46981-meeting-the-inspiration-behind-girl-stolen-.html

Related Works

1. **Cameron, Ann. *Colibrí*.** New York: Farrar, Straus and Giroux/ Frances Foster Books, 2003. 240p. $17.00. ISBN 0 374 31519 1. [fiction] MJS, G (*Teen Genre Connections*, 2005, pages 269 to 271.)

Twelve-year-old Colibrí travels with the man who kidnapped her when she was four until a daykeeper counsels her to leave.

2. **McCormick, Patricia. *Sold*.** New York: Hyperion, 2006. 263p. $15.99. ISBN 078685171 6. [fiction] JS, G (*Genre Talks for Teens*, 2009, pages 108 to 111.) Thirteen-year-old Lakshmi is sold into prostitution by her stepfather and must eventually risk escape.

3. **Pow, Tom. *Captives*.** New Milford, CT: Roaring Brook Press/A Neal Porter Book, 2007. 185p. $17.95. ISBN-13 978 1 59643 201 7. [fiction] JS, CG (*Genre Talks for Teens*, 2009, pages 111 to 113.) While on a Caribbean vacation, two families are kidnapped by rebels. One father writes a best-selling version of their captivity. His son writes the truth.

4. **Sedgwick, Marcus. *Revolver*.** New York: Roaring Brook Press, 2010. 204p. $16.99. ISBN-13: 978 1 59643 592 6. [fiction] JS, CG with high interest for boys (*Value-Packed Booktalks*, 2011, pages 97 to 100.) In the gold rush of the Arctic wilderness, 14-year-old Sig is trapped by a man demanding money owed to him by Sig's dead father, and must choose either a Colt Revolver or his mother's religious advice to save himself.

5. **Vance, Susanna. *Deep*.** New York: Delacorte Press, 2003. 272p. $15.95. ISBN 0 385 73057 8. [fiction] MJS, G (*Teen Genre Connections*, 2005, pages 123 to 125.) An indulged 13-year-old and a brutally realistic 17-year-old are kidnapped by a serial killer and cooperate to escape.

Kephart, Beth. You Are My Only.

New York: Egmont/Laura Geringer Books, 2011. 256p. $16.99.
ISBN 978 1 60684 272 0. [fiction] JS, G

Themes/Topics: Kidnapping, family, mental hospitals, friendship, abusive relationships

Summary/Description

Emmy and Sophie, mother and daughter, tell their stories in alternating chapters. Emmy, a 19-year-old wife of an abusive husband, leaves her baby unguarded for a moment. The baby is kidnapped. She obsessively searches for her little girl and is saved from suicide by a stranger who finds her on the railroad tracks. Her husband has her arrested and committed. In the hospital, her hope is sustained by her roommate and the man who saved her.

Sophie begins her story at15. She has lived in 10 towns because her "mother" moves when any "No Goods" appear to ask questions. Living in poor rentals and eating what is left in the house or leftover from her waitress jobs, the mother homeschools Sophie and insists on perfection. Secretly, Sophie connects with the neighbors—Joey and his two aunts who are life partners. They provide a rich family support which inspires her to explore her past. The documents that she finds reveal the motive for the kidnapping, and one aunt notifies the police. The book ends with a coming reunion between Sophie and Emmy.

Values: Both Emmy and Sophie are saved by friends who inspire them to claim their identities.

Booktalk

Emmy is 19. She leaves her baby for a minute. When she comes back, the baby is gone. Sophie is about 15. She lives with her mother, learns through homeschooling, and never mixes with the "No Goods" who follow her and her mother from town to town and who ask questions. Sophie and her mother have lived in 10 different towns.(*How do you think these two stories connect? Wait for some answers*.) A reader might think, "Oh, it is another story about a mother and daughter being separated. Then they find each other, and they live happily ever after." But that isn't life, is it? Life is more "rough and tumble." In fact, Sophie's description of her house might be a description of any of our lives. (*Read the first two sentences on page 1*.) Emmy and her daughter each tell their stories of their lives in "huff-and-a-puff" houses. Each searches for something missing and finds something she doesn't expect. One day, each may be able to say *You Are My Only*.

Book trailer available @ http://www.youtube.com/watch?v=TwWkrWWG8VY

Read Aloud/Talkback

1. Pages 26 to 27, beginning with "I let the darkness . . ." and ending with the chapter. Emmy tells her story to the stranger. *Talkback*: What does Emmy reveal about herself?

2. Pages 28 to 32, beginning with the chapter and ending with ". . . already puddling the floor." Sophie describes the school session with her mother. *Talkback*: How do you react to Sophie's homeschooling?

3. Page 54, beginning with "*Perfection* . . ." and ending with ". . . supposed to be." Sophie questions her mother's goals. *Talkback*: What

does Sophie reveal about herself in this passage? Sophie wants to stay with Willa Cather's work. Find out more about Cather and discuss why Kephart made her a central figure.

4. Pages 124 to 126, beginning with "By the time . . ." and ending with the chapter. Sophie describes a safe place in the midst of trouble. *Talkback*: How does this home differ from Sophie's?

5. Pages 230 to 231, beginning with "Miss Helen's sick . . ." and ending with ". . . looking forward." Sophie describes living with Joey's family. *Talkback*: Rate the following statement on a scale of 1 to 5, with 1 as strongly disagree and 5 as strongly agree. This passage depicts a happily ever after conclusion.

Author read aloud available @ http://www.youtube.com/watch?v=j0qOZT-SVYA

Author read aloud as illustration of dialogue @ http://www.youtube.com/watch?v=jZPpFmmfZ1s&feature=relmfu

Author interviews and posts available @

http://savvyverseandwit.com/2011/11/interview-with-beth-kephart.html

http://www.melissacwalker.com/tag/beth-kephart/

http://cynthialeitichsmith.blogspot.com/2011/12/guest-post-beth-kephart-on-following.html

Related Works

1. **Cameron, Ann.** *Colibrí*. New York: Farrar, Straus and Giroux/Frances Foster Books, 2003. 240p. $17.00. ISBN 0 374 31519 1. [fiction] MJS, G (*Teen Genre Connections*, 2005, pages 269 to 271.) Twelve-year-old Colibrí travels with the man who kidnapped her when she was four until a daykeeper counsels her to leave the abusive relationship.

2. **Dessen, Sarah.** *Lock and Key*. New York: Viking, 2008. 422p. $18.99. ISBN-13: 978 0 670 01088 2. [fiction] JS, G (*Value-Packed Booktalks*, 2011, pages 13 to 15.) When the mother she has protected deserts her, Ruby moves to her sister's affluent home and learns how her mother constantly moved and lied to keep the sisters apart.

3. **Kidd, Sue Monk.** *The Secret Life of Bees*. New York: Penguin Books, 2002. 302p. $14.00. ISBN 0 14 200174 0. [fiction] S/A (*Booktalks and Beyond*, 2007, pages 196 to 199.) When 14-year-old Lily Owens leaves her abusive father and finds shelter with three women and their extended community, she finds the secrets of her past.

4. **McCormick, Patricia.** *Sold*. New York: Hyperion, 2006. 263p. $15.99. ISBN 078685171 6. [fiction] JS, G (*Value-Packed Booktalks*,

2011, pages 108 to 111.) Thirteen-year-old Lakshmi is sold into prostitution by her stepfather.

5. **Rapp, Adam, and Timothy Basil Ering (illus.). 33 *Snowfish*.** Cambridge, MA: Candlewick Press, 2003. 179p. $15.99. ISBN 0 7636 1874 8. [fiction] S (*Booktalks and Beyond*, 2009, pages 30 to 33.) Custis runs away from his "owner" who used him for sex and pornographic films and now may kill him.

ℭℨℬ

Northrop, Michael. Trapped.

New York: Scholastic Press, 2011. 240p. $16.99. ISBN 978 0 545 21012 6.

[fiction] JS, CG with high interest for boys

Themes/Topics: High school, blizzards, interpersonal relationships, crises management

Summary/Description

A killer New England blizzard traps sophomore Scotty Weems and six other teenagers, five boys and two girls, in their high school. As the snow piles up, and as the temperature drops, and as the power goes out, and as the pipes freeze, and as the roof collapses, Scotty throws away his high school stereotypes and realizes his friends and acquaintances are individuals. One of Scotty's best friends embarrasses himself by flirting with one of the girls and takes a homemade snow cart to find help and regain the group's respect. He crashes and disappears in the snow. Scotty tries to rescue him, finds him dead, pushes on to get help, collapses, and is rescued by the National Guard who also rescue the survivors in the high school.

Values: Scotty Weems learns that each person is a human rather than a stereotype.

Booktalk

A killer blizzard. What does that mean? (*Wait for an answer that probably involves school being closed.*) It doesn't get any better than that. But this snow is a nor'easter that buries people and houses, cuts power, and freezes water supplies. Where is sophomore Scotty Weems during the storm? In the high school with six other kids watching the snow pile up to the second floor. In other words, they are . . . (*Wait for the reply as you point to the title.*) The good news is that two of them are his best friends and two are among the hottest girls in school. The bad news is the other two: the student most likely to spend his life in jail and a gloom and doom library rat. Scotty and friends can control the situation until the plows get through the next day. Right? Wrong. One, anyone getting through that snow the next day or the day after that is impossible. Two, the good and the bad news makes a deadly mix that explodes when (*Wait for the reply as you point to the title.*) *Trapped*.

Book trailers available @

http://michaelnorthrop.net/?page_id=7
http://www.youtube.com/watch?v=bFCWH4oukdg&feature=related
http://michaelnorthrop.net/?p=5162

Read Aloud/Talkback

Because of the short chapters and building suspense, the entire book is an excellent read aloud.

1. Chapter 1, pages 1 to 3. Scotty Weems sets up the situation. *Talkback*: What details in this chapter make you want to read the story?
2. Chapter 8, pages 53 to 55, beginning with the chapter and ending with ". . . neck in the dark." The power goes off. *Talkback*: How does the description make the power going out super threatening?
3. Chapter 13, pages 82 to 85. Scotty sees life skills in a new light. *Talkback*: What does this chapter have to say about status and power?
4. Chapter 31, pages 186 to 189. The group is together in the room after the fight. *Talkback*: What does this chapter show about the personality of each character?
5. Chapter 37, page 218, beginning with "It's funny . . ." and ending with the chapter. Scotty moves on because he remembers his coach's words. *Talkback*: How is being a basketball player important?

Author interviews available @

http://michaelnorthrop.net/?page_id=5
http://www.hopelessbibliophile.com/2011/02/author-interview-michael-northrop.html
http://dailyfig.figment.com/2011/01/31/interview-with-michael-northrop/
http://martinwilsonwrites.com/2011/07/11/author-interview-michael-northrop/
http://www.theserpentinelibrary.com/2011/01/author-interview-michael-northrop.html

http://www.teenreads.com/authors/michael-northrop/news/
interview-030111

http://thebookscout.blogspot.com/2011/02/blog-tour-michael-
northrop-interview.html

Related Works

1. **Brooks, Kevin. *Black Rabbit Summer*.** New York: Scholastic Inc./Chicken House, 2008. 496p. $17.99. ISBN-13: 978 0 545 05752 3. [fiction] JS, CG with high interest for boys (*Value-Packed Booktalks*, 2011, pages 112 to 114.) After an alcohol- and drug-filled reunion with childhood friends, 16-year-old Pete Boland unravels the mystery of two missing persons and reevaluates his friendships.

2. **McCaughrean, Geraldine. *The White Darkness*.** New York: HarperTempest, 2005. 373p. $17.89. ISBN-13: 978 0 06 089036 0. [fiction] JS, CG (*Genre Talks for Teens*, 2009, pages 105 to 108.) Fourteen-year-old Sym becomes part of a deadly Antarctic journey with her mentally ill uncle.

3. **Murphy, Jim. *Blizzard!*** New York: Scholastic Press, 2000. 136p. $18.95. ISBN 0 590 67309 2. [nonfiction] MJS, CG (*Teen Genre Connections*, 2005, pages 97 to 99.) Murphy traces the 1888 blizzard's destruction, duration, and results through human interest stories of its powerful and humble participants and victims.

4. **Naylor, Phyllis Reynolds. *Blizzard's Wake*.** New York: Atheneum Books for Young Readers, 2002. 212p. $16.95. ISBN 0 689 85220 7. [fiction] MJS, CG with high interest for girls. In March 1941, 15-year-old Katie Sterling saves her mother's killer during a blizzard, and then shelters him in her home.

5. **Northrop, Michael. *Gentlemen*.** New York: Scholastic Press, 2009. 234p. $16.99. ISBN-13: 978 0 545 09749 9. [fiction] JS, CG with high interest for boys (*Value-Packed Booktalks*, 2011, pages 116 to 118.) Three remedial students suspect their English teacher of murder, and their inferences lead to violence.

☙❧

Price, Charlie. Desert Angel.
New York: Farrar, Straus and Giroux, 2011. 236p. $16.99.
ISBN 978 0 374 31775 1. [fiction] JS, CG with high interest for girls

Themes/Topics: Mexican Americans, illegal aliens, California, abuse, murder, trust

Summary/Discussion

Physically and sexually abused, 14-year-old Angel wakes up in her California desert home and discovers that her mother has been murdered. Angel runs from her mother's boyfriend and killer who hunts her. She finds help in a desert Mexican community inhabited by legal and illegal immigrants. As the killer closes in, Angel's background tells her that she should trust no one even though the people support her. She pursues and confronts the killer alone. Her new friends follow her, rescue her, apprehend the killer, and give her a new home.

Values: Angel learns the meaning of friendship, family, and love.

Booktalk

Fourteen-year-old Angel and her mother lived with Scotty, one more man her mother let pick them up on the road. He took them to their new home, a trailer in the middle of the California desert. One morning, Angel woke up to find her mother dead. Angel knows she's next. What should she do? (*Wait for the answers.*) She runs, without food or water. Scotty is a hunter, a tracker. He can find her anywhere. Angel does what her mother did. She attaches herself to strangers. She won't trust them, just use them—for cover, for survival. Good idea? (*Wait for the answers.*) They listen to her past, her troubles. They ask her to stay. Are they sincere or will they give her up for a reward? Send her to a nightmare foster care? Call the police? Lock her up as crazy? If Scotty thinks that they know her story, he could kill them too. Angel needs to think through how to become the hunter, not the hunted in her new life as a *Desert Angel*.

Book trailer available @ http://www.youtube.com/watch?v=qXEaPQCsDRI

Read Aloud/Talkback

1. Chapter 3, pages 11 to 13. Scotty tries to kill Angel, but she escapes. *Talkback*: What does this murder attempt show about Scotty and Angel?
2. Chapter 4, page 15, beginning with "She knew . . ." and ending with ". . . you is you." Angel reflects on what she knows about life. *Talkback*: What do you think Angel might say she knew by the end of the novel?
3. Chapter 10, pages 41 to 42, beginning with "Angel was distracted . . ." and ending with ". . . and drama." Angel compares

the Mexican women to her mother. *Talkback*: What impresses you about Angel's comparison?

4. Chapter 13, page 68, beginning with "Rita went . . ." and ending with ". . . herself stop." Angel reacts to Rita's reference to love. *Talkback*: From what you know about Angel's experiences, how would she define love at this point?

5. Chapter 15, pages 86 to 87, beginning with "And there's another thing . . ." and ending with ". . . wouldn't butt her." Rita confronts Angel about the danger she poses to others. *Talkback*: Is Rita right?

Author explanation of story background available @ http://bestbooks1.blogspot.com/2012/02/inspiration-behind-desert-angel.html

Author interview available @ http://www.cosy-books.com/2012/02/author-interview-charlie-price-desert.html

Related Works

1. **Cameron, Ann. *Colibrí*.** New York: Farrar, Straus and Giroux/Frances Foster Books, 2003. 240p. $17.00. ISBN 0 374 31519 1. [fiction] MJS, G (*Teen Genre Connections*, 2005, pages 269 to 271.) Twelve-year-old Colibrí tavels with the man who kidnapped her when she was four until a daykeeper counsels her to leave the abusive relationship.

2. **Haas, Jessie. *Chase*.** New York: HarperCollins Publishers, 2007. 250p. $17.89. ISBN-13: 978 0 06 112851 6. [fiction] MJS, CG with high interest for boys (*Genre Talks for Teens*, 2009, pages 90 to 93.) Fifteen-year-old Phin, an orphan, witnesses a murder by the Irish underground "Sleepers," escapes, and is pursued by an undercover Pinkerton man and an underground member who failed to kill Phin.

3. **Heneghan, James. *Safe House*.** Victoria, BC: Orca Book Publishers, 2006. 151p. $7.95pa. ISBN-13: 978 1 55143 640 1. [fiction] MJS, CG with high interest for boys (*Genre Talks for Teens*, 2009, pages 93 to 95.) Twelve-year-old Liam Fogarty flees after he sees Protestant terrorists gun down his parents and can identify the killer.

4. **Mikaelsen, Ben. *Tree Girl*.** New York: HarperCollins Children's Books, 2004. 240p.$16.99. ISBN 0 06 009004 9. [fiction] JS, CG with high interest for girls (*Teen Genre Connections*, 2005, pages 94 to 96.) Fifteen-year-old Gabriela Flores sees her teacher, friends, and most of her family gunned down in her small Guatemalan village and flees to survive.

5. **Monninger, Joseph.** *Baby*. Asheville, NC: Front Street, 2007. 173p. $16.95. ISBN-13: 978 159078 502 7. [fiction] JS, CG with high interest for girls (*Value-Packed Booktalks*, 2011, pages 31 to 33.) Assigned to her last chance for foster care, 15-year-old Baby fights the people who can help her the most.

Mystery/Suspense

Mystery and suspense books plunge the protagonists into danger by surprise, entanglements, or magic. *Bomb*, a nonfiction account of the race to get the atom bomb, has all the action and suspense of a fiction selection. Even though the modern characters in *White Crow* lack any magic or unusual power, they become tragically connected to the thinking of deranged men from the past who sought powerful magic from the secrets of life after death.

Surprise

Almond, David. **Raven Summer.**

New York: Delacorte Press, 2008. 198p. $16.99.
ISBN 978 0 385 73806 4. [fiction] JS, CG

Themes/ Topics: Terrorism, refugees, foundlings, interpersonal relations, conduct of life, fate, England, stories

Summary/Description

Fourteen-year-old Liam Lynch and his friend Max find an abandoned baby, a crude note, and a jar of money in a field. The baby goes to foster care, and the boys become news. The two friends grow apart. Liam focuses on local adventure games led by Nattrass, a sadistic former friend. Max ponders girls and a career. When Liam and his family visit the foster family, Liam's mother wants to adopt the baby, and Liam connects with two other foster children, Crystal and Oliver. Crystal lost her family in a fire and cuts herself. Oliver, a Liberian refugee, claims political asylum.

Crystal and Oliver are separated when the foster home dissolves. They reconnect, run to Liam's home, and Liam wanders with them. Crystal tells about her fragmented life in foster care and Oliver reveals that he is really the 17-year-old Henry Meadows who was drafted as a soldier at 8. Nattrass tracks and threatens them. Liam defends Henry, and soldiers training in the area intervene. Henry tells his story to Liam's father, a professional writer, and Henry and Crystal may join the family.

Values: Liam's experiences lead him to compassion and integrity.

Booktalk

A raven leads 14-year-old Liam and his friend Max to a beautiful abandoned baby, a foundling. A note declares her a "CHILDE OF GOD." The two boys save her and make national T.V. They are heroes. So they are nationally known good guys. Right? That baby leads Liam to her foster home where he meets Oliver, a mysterious boy from Liberia, and Crystal, a girl who lost her family in a fire. A girl who cuts herself. They aren't so innocent. Are they, too, foundlings that Liam should save? (*Wait for responses.*) Liam already has a friend who could be saved. He loves to play at blood and violence. The violent games give Liam a rush, sometimes. A hero rush. Is good guy Liam becoming a bad guy? Doesn't a hero need a bad guy to be a hero? Isn't a hero, then, part of that evil too? (*Wait for responses.*) A single raven and Liam's "friends" (*Make quotation marks with your hands when you say this.*) force him to answer those questions, one *Raven Summer*.

Read Aloud/Talkback

1. Chapter 3, pages 75 to 77. The parents argue about christening Alison. *Talkback*: Will christening save Alison? Consider Read Aloud 2.
2. Chapter 4, pages 78 to 80. This chapter describes the christening in which the vicar declares that all of us are foundlings. *Talkback*: Why is a ceremony like this significant?
3. Chapter 8, pages 94 to 98. Liam describes the Spotlight game. *Talkback*: Do you agree with Nattrass's view of humanity? Why or why not?
4. Chapter 11, pages 150 to 151, beginning with "We sit on . . ." and ending with ". . . absolutely gorgeous!" Liam, Crystal, and Oliver ponder ancient rocks. *Talkback*: Is there any connection between Oliver's reaction and Crystal's reaction?
5. Chapter 18, pages 177 to 185. In this chapter, Nattrass catches them. Oliver tells his story. *Talkback*: How is Oliver's story central to the novel?

Discussion guide available @ http://www.randomhouse.com/
catalog/teachers_guides/9780385738064.pdf

Author interviews available @

http://www.youtube.com/watch?v=ggFLVAxgfK0&feature=relmfu
http://www.youtube.com/watch?v=LxGUWmMnJ2M&feature=
related
http://www.youtube.com/watch?v=Dz4aTpL0BtM&feature=relmfu
http://www.youtube.com/watch?v=2F0XL0EXG_8&feature=relmfu
http://www.youtube.com/watch?v=NZvmbPFUXo4&feature=related

Related Works

1. **Almond, David. *Kit's Wilderness*.** New York: Delacorte Press, 2000. 229p. $15.95. ISBN 0 385 52665 3. [fiction] JS, CG (*Booktalks and More*, 2003, pages 209 to 211.) Thirteen-year-old Kit Watson and his parents move to a legend-filled coal mining town where he is drawn into a game of Death and discovers his own creativity.

2. **Almond, David. *Skellig*.** New York: Delacorte Press, 1999. 182p. $15.95. ISBN 0 385 32653 X. [fiction] MJS, CG (*Booktalks and More*, 2003, pages 99 to 101.) A new baby ties her brother Michael to the magical Skellig who saves her from death.

3. **Beah, Ishmael. *A Long Way Gone: Memoirs of a Boy Soldier*.** New York: Farrar, Straus and Giroux/Sarah Crichton Books, 2007. 229p. $22.00. ISBN-13: 978 0 374 10523 5. [nonfiction] JS/A, CG with high interest for boys (*Genre Talks for Teens*, 2009, pages 98 to 100.) Twelve-year-old Ishmael loses his family and begins a journey of physical, emotional and intellectual survival that takes him to a UN rehabilitation camp, and eventually the United States where he tells his story.

4. **Cooney, Caroline B. *Diamonds in the Shadow*.** New York: Delacorte Press, 2007. 230p. $15.99. ISBN-13: 978 0 385 73261 1. [fiction] JS, CG with high interest for boys (*Genre Talks for Teens*, 2009, pages 272 to 275.) The Finch family sponsors an African family fleeing civil war and becomes the center of diamond smuggling plot.

5. **Hautman, Pete. *Godless*.** New York: Simon & Schuster Books for Young Readers, 2004. 198p. $15.95. ISBN 0 689 86278 4. [fiction] JS, CG (*Genre Talks for Teens*, 2009, pages 27 to 29.) Jason Brock, disillusioned by his parents' religion, starts a new one centered on the town water tower and unleashes violence and mental illness.

CℛꙂↃ

Cadnum, Michael. Flash.

New York: Farrar, Straus and Giroux, 2010. 235p. $17.99.
ISBN 978 0 374 39911 5. [fiction] JS, CG with high interest for boys

Themes/Topics: Robbers and outlaws; interpersonal relationships; San Francisco Bay Area, CA

Summary/Description

Eighteen-year-old Milton and 16-year-old Bruce, brothers, botch a bank robbery. Terrence, a legally blind teenager, happens upon them when they are covering up the crime. Terrence tells his girlfriend Nina and her older brother, a wounded military policeman recently returned from Iraq, about the encounter. Nina moves to protect Terrence from the robbers and keep her brother from hurting Milton and Bruce. Because of Milton's distrust for Bruce, their attempt to kill Terrence results in Milton shooting his brother and Bruce starting a fire that threatens their own home. Milton attempts escape through the flames. The events renew Nina's relationship with her brother.

Values: The characters illustrate the importance of trust, truth, and integrity.

Booktalk

Ask the group how long they think it takes to change a person's life completely.

In this story, one day changes five people's lives. The two Borchard brothers have a plan. They'll rob a bank and solve their mother's money problems. Good plan? (*Wait for a response.*) They botch it. While they are covering up their mistakes, Terrence, their blind neighbor, shows up. At first, they think he's no problem. Later, they decide to kill him—no witness, no crime. Good plan? (*Wait for a response.*) But Terrence tells Nina, the girl he loves, and her brother about his encounter with the brothers. Nina's brother is a military policeman back from Iraq. He thinks he can get the reward money. Good plan? (*Wait for a response.*) Nina is afraid. Her brother is different now, quiet and dangerous. Maybe she should take action before he does. Good plan? (*Wait for a response.*) Bombs and guns can change life in a *Flash*.

Read Aloud/Talkback

1. Chapter 4, page 19, beginning with "But Nina . . ." and ending with ". . . life's cold secrets." Carraway answers Nina's question about the explosion. *Talkback*: How does this passage set the stage for the rest of the story?

2. Chapter 7, pages 36 to 37, beginning with "When she had . . ." and ending with the chapter. Nina assesses her brother's new demeanor. *Talkback*: What is your assessment of Nina's brother from this passage?

3. Chapter 17, pages 88 to 92, beginning with "The two of them . . ." and ending with the chapter. The brothers encounter the town vagrant. *Talkback*: Can you believe them? Why or why not?

4. Chapter 31, pages 148 to 150, beginning with the chapter and ending with ". . . who has the gun." Terrence and Nina discuss the head of the gallery. *Talkback*: What does the conversation reveal about both characters and their relationship?

5. Chapter 51, pages 234 to 235. In this concluding chapter, Terrence reflects on the evening and Nina's response. *Talkback*: Why is Nina's response significant?

Author interview available @ http://www.michaelcadnum
.com/index.php?option=com_content&
task=view&id=14&itemid=54

Related Works

1. **Dowd, Siobhan.** *Bog Child*. New York: Random House/A David Fickling Book, 2008. 322p. $16.99. ISBN 978 0 285 75169 8. [fiction] S, CG with high interest for boys (*Value-Packed Booktalks*, 2011, pages 114 to 116.) Eighteen-year-old Fergus must decide between a peaceful life of healing and the subtle pressures of Sinn Fein.

2. **Herrick, Steven.** *Cold Skin*. Honesdale, PA: Front Street, 2007. 279p. $18.95. ISBN 978 1 59078 572 0. [fiction in verse] S, CG (*Value-Packed Booktalks*, 2011, pages 123 to 125.) In this post–World War II mystery set in an Australian mining town, nine voices react to the murder of a beautiful, talented teenage daughter of a war hero.

3. **Myers, Walter Dean.** *Sunrise over Fallujah*. New York: Scholastic Press, 2008. 304p. $17.99. ISBN-13: 978 0 439 91624 0. [fiction] JS, CG with high interest for boys (*Value-Packed Booktalks*, 2011, pages 93 to 95.) Private Robin Perry (aka Birdy) relates his experiences as a member of a Civil Affairs Unit in the Iraq invasion.

4. **Northrop, Michael.** *Gentlemen*. New York: Scholastic Press, 2009. 234p. $16.99. ISBN-13: 978 0 545 09749 9. [fiction] JS, CG

with high interest for boys (*Value-Packed Booktalks*, 2011, pages 116 to 118.) "Micheal" suspects his remedial English teacher of murdering his friend, and participates in a revenge plot that teaches him about judgment and personal responsibility.

5. **Sedgwick, Marcus. *Revolver*.** New York: Roaring Brook Press, 2010. 204p. $16.99. ISBN 978 1 59643 592 6. [fiction] JS, CG with high interest for boys (*Value-Packed Booktalks*, 2011, pages 97 to 100.) When a menacing stranger appears to claim his dead father's money, 14-year-old Sig chooses between the Bible and the gun.

ⓒⓈⓉⓄ

Coben, Harlan. Shelter.

New York: G. P. Putnam's Sons, 2011. 304p. $18.99.
ISBN 978 0 399 25650 9. [fiction] JS, CG with high i nterest for boys

Themes/Topics: Family history, white slavery, child rescue, drug addiction, holocaust, choices

Summary/Description

Mickey Bolitar's father is dead and his mother is in rehab. He lives with his Uncle Myron. When he walks by the house of the legendary "Bat Lady," she appears and tells him that his father is not dead. His girlfriend of three weeks, a new student just like Mickey, is missing. Spoon, the janitor's son, and Ema, an overweight Goth girl, are both school outcasts and agree to help him find her. They trace Ashley to a seedy strip club which holds girls and women in white slavery. Popular and sophisticated Rachel Caldwell formerly sheltered Ashley in her home and joins the trio. They discover a butterfly symbol common to Mickey's father, the Bat Lady, Ema, and the father's former employer. Mickey learns that the Bat Lady, with roots in the Holocaust, is part of a child rescue organization for which his father worked. With the help of his team and his father's former boss, Mickey defeats the slavers and discovers that Bat Lady meant that his father's heroic spirit lives in Mickey.

Values: Mickey's widening sense of responsibility develops from his loyalty to family and friends, as well as respect for others.

Booktalk

Mickey Bolitar is in a tight spot. His father is dead, his mother is in rehab, and his girlfriend has disappeared. Then, when he walks by the

broken-down house of the town's legendary "Bat Lady," the bent and an-
cient woman appears with her long white hair and in a long white dress.
She calls him Mickey and tells him that his father is alive. What do you
think happens next? (*Wait for responses.*) Mickey is going after the girl.
He is definitely going to find out more about what that lady had to say.
And those two decisions give him anything but *Shelter*.

Book trailers available @ http://www.mickeybolitar.com/

Read Aloud/Talkback

1. Chapter 1, pages 1 to 3, beginning with the chapter and ending
    with ". . . my father die." Mickey sees the Bat Lady. The passage
    would make an excellent booktalk. *Talkback*: What do you think
    Coben accomplishes with this passage?
2. Chapter 5, pages 66 to 70, beginning with "Do you know . . ." and
    ending with the chapter. Myron describes his brother's life-changing
    encounter with the Bat Lady. *Talkback*: Why do you think Mickey's
    father would not share what happened?
3. Chapter 12, pages 144 to 145, beginning with "I smiled . . ." and
    ending with the chapter. Mickey meets Agent. *Talkback*: After read-
    ing the entire novel, how do you react to this passage?
4. Chapter 16, pages 198 to 203, beginning with "I shrugged . . ." and
    ending with the chapter. Ema and Mickey tie the Bat Lady to Lizzy
    Sobek and refer to the quotation containing the title cited on page
    176. *Talkback*: How does this passage move beyond exposition for
    the story?
5. Chapter 27, pages 296 to 304, beginning with "Bat Lady . . ." and
    ending with the chapter. Bat Lady. Lizzy Sobek explains her involve-
    ment, her perception of life, and the choices it brings. *Talkback*: Do
    you agree or disagree with the Bat Lady? Why?

Author interviews available @

http://www.mickeybolitar.com/
http://www.youtube.com/watch?v=shL_Su9uO9Q

Related Works

1. **Coben, Harlan.** *Seconds Away*. New York: Penguin Young
    Readers Group, 2012. 352p. $18.99. ISBN-13: 978 0 399 25651 6.
    [fiction] JS, CG. In this second Mickey Bolitar book, Mickey, Ema,
    and Spoon find increasing danger as information about the father's
    death unfolds.

2. **Konigsburg, E. L. *The Mysterious Edge of the Heroic World*.** New York: Atheneum Books for Young Readers/Ginee Seo Books, 2007. 244p. $16.99. ISBN-13: 978 1 4169 4972 5. [fiction] M, CG (*Genre Talks for Teens*, 2009, pages 146 to 149.) Two boys help a homeowner downsize, and discover how a homosexual gives his own life so that his orphaned younger brother could leave Germany during the Holocaust.

3. **Nir, Yeluda. *The Lost Childhood: A World War II Memoir*.** New York: Scholastic Press, 2002. 288p. $16.95. ISBN 0 439 16389 7. [nonfiction] JS, CG. This memoir of a Polish Jew explains the massacre of the Jews by the Nazis and Ukrainians, his own disguise as a Catholic, and life in German work camps.

4. **Opdyke, Irene Gut, and Jennifer Armstrong. *In My Hands: Memories of a Holocaust Rescuer*.** New York: Alfred A. Knopf, 1999. 276p. $18.00. ISBN 0 679 89181 1. [nonfiction] JS, CG (*Booktalks and More*, 2003, pages 255 to 257.) Opdyke describes how her family life and personal beliefs led her to help and hide Jews persecuted during the German occupation of Poland.

5. **Spinelli, Jerry. *Milkweed*.** New York: Alfred A. Knopf, 2003. 208p. $15.95. ISBN 0 375 81374 8. [fiction] JS, CG (*Teen Genre Connections*, 2005, pages 240 to 243.) The approximately eight-year-old gypsy narrator lives on the streets, steals to survive, and tries to follow his Jewish friends to the ovens.

இஇ

Lane, Andrew. Death Cloud.

New York: Farrar, Straus and Giroux, 2010. 311p.
(Sherlock Holmes: The Legend Begins, #1) $16.99.
ISBN 978 0 374 38767 9. [fiction] MJS, CG with high interest for boys

Themes/Topics: Murder, Great Britain, Victorian period, coming of age, conduct of life

Summary/Description

In this first book of the series, 14-year-old Sherlock Holmes spends the summer holiday with an aunt and uncle he has never met. His brother, Mycroft, arranges for a tutor, Amyus Crowe, who challenges Sherlock to think. Two deaths linked to a mysterious cloud and boil-covered bodies draw Sherlock, his new street friend, Mathew Arnatt, Crowe, and Crowe's daughter, Virginia into an investigation. With his keen mind and supportive friends, Sherlock thwarts a plan to massacre the British army with killer bees. Acknowledgements list the author's references. An Afterword explains Lane's process and lists further reading suggestions.

Values: Holmes learns the importance of friends and the power of knowledge.

Booktalk

Ask the group to explain what they know about Sherlock Holmes.

We know about the middle-aged genius who solves Victorian England's most tangled crimes. Andrew Lane shows us how the genius began. Fourteen-year-old boarding school student Sherlock spends his summer with an eccentric aunt and uncle, whom he has never met, and his own private tutor. It looks like a long and boring holiday. (*Right?*) Then he meets a street boy named Matty Arnatt, who tells him about a dead man covered in boils and a mysterious cloud that left the body. And of course, what happens? (*Wait for a response.*) They wonder. Is it the plague, a new mysterious disease? Or something more sinister? Something that Sherlock could die investigating. A boring summer turns into a life-threatening thriller, when young Sherlock Holmes and friends follow the *Death Cloud*.

Book trailer available @ http://www.youngsherlock.com/trailers/death-cloud-trailer/

Read Aloud/Talkback

1. Chapter 2, pages 32 to 34, beginning with "The alley doglegged . . ." and ending with ". . . pale and quiet." Matty describes the dead man being removed from the house. *Talkback*: What does the discussion of death tell you about Matty, Sherlock, and the death itself?
2. Chapter 3, pages 44 to 48, beginning with "There was a single . . ." and ending with ". . . obvious dislike for him." Sherlock receives a letter from Mycroft. *Talkback*: List the issues that the letter raises. Describe the relationship between Sherlock and Mycroft?
3. Chapter 3, pages 52 to 53, beginning with "Sherlock scanned . . ." and ending with ". . . he said, nodding." Crowe demonstrates his respect for knowledge and Sherlock. *Talkback*: After reading this passage, what is your opinion of Mr. Crowe?
4. Chapter 7, pages 120 to 122, beginning with "Amyus Crowe . . ." and ending with ". . . solve it." Crowe instructs Sherlock to phrase

each problem himself. *Talkback*: How does Crowe's advice about phrasing the problem apply to everyday life?

5. Chapter 17, pages 305 to 306, beginning with "Sherlock gazed out . . ." and ending with the novel. Sherlock realizes how his life has changed. *Talkback*: Has Sherlock changed? If so, in what way?

Read aloud available @ http://www.youtube.com/watch?v=kgbU9ycxx9Y

Author interviews available @

http://www.youngsherlock.com/uncategorized/qa-with-andy/
http://bookzone4boys.blogspot.com/2010/06/interview-with-andrew-lane-author-of.html
http://thebookbase.com/906/author-interview-andrew-lane
http://www.youtube.com/watch?v=oIYfY73TyJk

Related Works

1. **Altman, Steen-Elliot, Michael Reaves (text) and Bong Dazo (illus.).** *The Irregulars . . . in the Service of Sherlock Holmes*. Milwaukee, OR: Dark Horse Books, 2005. 126p. $12.95. ISBN 1 59307 303 8. [graphic] MJS, CG with high interest for boys. Street children penetrate an underground other world and help clear Mr. Watson.

2. **Lane, Andrew.** *Black Ice*. New York: Farrar, Straus and Giroux, 2013. 288p. (The Legend Begins, #3.) $17.99. ISBN-13: 978 0 374 38769 3. [fiction] MJ, CG with high interest for boys. Sherlock visits Mycroft in London where he is accused of a vicious murder.

3. **Lane, Andrew.** *Rebel Fire*. New York: Farrar, Straus and Giroux, 2012. 352p. (The Legend Begins, #2.) $16.99. ISBN 978 0 374 38768 6. [fiction] MJ, CG with high interest for boys. Involved in the dark secrets of his friend and tutor, Sherlock goes to America where the defeated Rebel forces may rise again.

4. **Mack, Tracy, Michael Citrin (text) and Greg Ruth (illus.).** *Sherlock Holmes and the Baker Street Irregulars: The Fall of the Amazing Zalindas, Casebook No. 1*. New York: Orchard Books, 2006. 259p. $16.99. ISBN 0 439 82836 8. [fiction] M, CG with high interest for boys. Sherlock Holmes and street urchins investigate deaths tied to royal treasure.

5. **Peacock, Shane.** *The Eye of the Crow*. Toronto, ON: Tundra Books, 2007. 251p. (The Boy Sherlock Holmes) $21.99. ISBN-13: 978 0 88776 850 7. [fiction] MJ, CG with high interest for boys (*Value-Packed Booktalks*, 2011, pages 130 to 132.) Thirteen-year-old Holmes, called "Jew-boy," prefers London's street life to school.

Ↄↄ

Whaley, John Corey. **Where Things Come Back.**

New York: Atheneum, 2011. 228p. $19.99.
ISBN 978 1 4424 1333 7. [fiction] S, CG

Themes/Topics: Missing persons, interpersonal relations, best friends, extinct birds, family life, Arkansas, hope, choice

Summary/Description

Seventeen-year-old Cullen Witter tells about the summer that his 15-year-old brother, Gabriel, disappears. Their story entwines with the story of a young Cabot Searcy, who sees his life controlled by divine purpose. The catalyst is Alma Ember, a girl who left the small Arkansas town for college and married Cabot who is obsessed with *The Book of Enoch*. After they marry because Alma thinks she is pregnant, Cabot refuses to work. Alma returns home and dates Cullen. Cabot Searcy comes to town to reclaim Alma and take revenge on Cullen. Instead, he attacks and kidnaps Gabriel. As Cabot searches for meaning, the Witter family grieves Gabriel's possible death, and Cullen loses another girl he truly loves to the critically injured bully he hates. The town focuses on a charlatan who sees his destiny as discovering an extinct woodpecker that will bring them fame. At the conclusion, the narrator warns the reader to cope with each event instead of obsessing about the grand meaning.

Values: Cullen learns the importance of stable family and friendship.

Booktalk

Ask how many in the group have experienced strange coincidences? Ask them to share them. Now, ask how many in the group saw those coincidences as having a greater meaning. Ask them to explain.

Seventeen-year-old Cullen Witter has a whole summer of why did that happen? The biggest why is the disappearance of his 15-year-old brother Gabriel. But instead of focusing on what could be a murder, his small town of Lily, Arkansas, focuses on an extinct woodpecker whose rediscovery could bring them fame and fortune. Wouldn't that make you mad? (*You might signal for a nodding response.*) But Cullen is a little distracted, too. Suddenly, Cullen, the most undatable boy in Lily, has two attractive possibilities. One is a divorced older woman and the other is his worst enemy's girlfriend. Mystery, fame, love, and maybe divine intervention converge *Where Things Come Back*.

Book trailer available @ http://www.johncoreywhaley .com/news/

Read Aloud/Talkback

1. Chapter 1, pages 6 to 7, beginning with "Like most teenage . . ." and ending with ". . . of the world." Cullen explains Ada Taylor's reputation as a "black widow." *Talkback*: How is this passage ironic in relation to the rest of the novel?
2. Chapter 1, pages 7 to 9, beginning with "Dr. Webb says . . ." and ending with ". . . choose the latter." Cullen explains Dr. Webb's bubble theory. *Talkback*: How do you react to Dr. Webb's bubble theory?
3. Chapter 13, page 121, beginning with "Before Lucas Cader . . ." and ending with "That's genius." Cullen describes Gabriel. *Talkback*: What is your impression of Gabriel? How does his vision of God differ from Cabot Searcy's?
4. Chapter 17, page 181, beginning with "In those days . . ." and ending with ". . . *God Knows What*." Cullen reflects on "what if" and second chances. *Talkback*: How are "what if" and second chances related? Do you agree with Gabriel?
5. Chapter 21, pages 226 to 228, beginning with "Dr. Webb says . . ." and ending with the novel. Dr. Webb talks about coping and the meaning of life. *Talkback*: Do you agree with Dr. Webb? Is Gabriel's return real or another of Cullen's ways of coping through imagination?

Reading group guide available @ http://books .simonandschuster.net/Where-Things-Come-Back/ John-Corey-Whaley/9781442413337/reading_group_ guide/?mcd=enkl110718&cp_type=enkl&md=epaa&cp_ date=110718&custd=568127

Author interviews available @

http://www.thetkreview.com/2011/11/03/the-5-under-35-interview-series-john-corey-whaley/

http://bookbridges.wordpress.com/2012/07/17/author-interview-john-corey-whaley-where-things-come-back/

http://latimesblogs.latimes.com/jacketcopy/2012/01/201printz-john-corey-whaley.html

http://www.yalsa.ala.org/thehub/2012/01/12/author-interview-john-corey-whaley/

Author accepts the Printz Award @ http://www.youtube.com/watch?v=8aOj_ir2SOY&feature=related

Related Works

1. **Bray, Libba. *Going Bovine*.** New York: Delacorte Press, 2009. 479p. $17.99. ISBN 978 0 385 73397 7. [fiction] S, CG with high interest for boys (*Value-Packed Booktalks*, 2011, pages 4 to 5.) In a coma journey, a dying teen realizes the joy of life.
2. **Hoose, Phillip. *The Race to Save the Lord God Bird*.** New York: Farrar, Straus and Giroux/Melanie Kroupa Books, 2004. 196p. $20.00. ISBN 0 374 36173 8. [nonfiction] JS, CG (*Booktalks and Beyond*, 2007, pages 100 to 102.) This narrative about the Lord God Bird traces its history of extinction from 1809.
3. **Salinger, J.D. *The Catcher in the Rye*.** Boston, MA: Little, Brown & Co., 1991. 224p. $6.99pa. ISBN 0316769487. [fiction] S/A. Set in 1949 and first published in 1951, the book records the thoughts of a young man who tells his psychiatrist about his alienation from the world.
4. **Weaver, Will. *Full Service*.** New York: Farrar, Straus and Giroux, 2005. 232p. $17.00. ISBN 0 374 32485 9. [fiction] JS, CG (*Booktalks and Beyond*, 2007, pages 257 to 259.) Fifteen-year-old Paul Sutton, who belongs to a strict religious community, takes a town job and develops his own faith.
5. **Zusak, Markus. *I Am the Messenger*.** New York: Alfred A. Knopf, 2002. 357p. $20.50. ISBN 0 375 93099 X. [fiction] S, CG (*Booktalks and Beyond*, 2007, pages 143 to 146.) Average 19-year-old Ed becomes a hero and receives Aces that direct him to help people.

Entanglements

Blundell, Judy. Strings Attached.

New York: Scholastic Press, 2011. 320p. $17.99.
ISBN 978 0 545 22126 9. [fiction] JS, CG with high interest for girls

Themes/Topics: Coming of age, organized crime, 1945 to 1950, conduct of life

Summary/Description

Seventeen-year-old Kit Corrigan leaves her Providence, Rhode Island, home to test her talent in New York night clubs. Nate Benedict, a lawyer for the mob, follows her and sets her up in an apartment. He hopes that Kit will give his son Billy, her former boyfriend, who has enlisted in the Korean War, incentive to stay alive and return home. The story moves back and forth from the New York present to the complicated relationships with her family, the angry Billy Benedict, and his controlling father. When Nate uses Kit to set up a mob hit, all the family secrets come together. Kit becomes front page news as Nate's alleged girlfriend. A furious and jealous Billy dies trying to secure evidence against his father from Kit's aunt, Nate's former mistress. Nate blames the Corrigan family for Billy's death. The father's hit man mistakenly kills the aunt instead of Kit, and evidence arrives from the aunt posthumously to convict Nate.

Values: Kit's journey demonstrates the importance of honesty, family, and commitment.

Booktalk

Seventeen-year-old Kit drops out of school and heads for New York. She leaves her angry and poor Providence, Rhode Island, home behind. Or does she? The fixer, gangster lawyer, Nate Benedict, who gives her and her family favors, follows her. He gives her an apartment, new clothes, a chance at the big time, a chance to be a professional dancer, and a Lido doll. It's 1950, and in New York City, the Lido is the club. Do you think this is a free gift? (*Wait for responses.*) What will she have to give back? She is supposed to keep his son, the angry, violent, and exciting Billy, alive and bring him back from Korea. But there are some complications—unwanted phone calls, FBI agents who watch her, and Communists who share her building. Nate's gifts tangle her in lies and murder along with romance. Is she, or anyone around her, safe with *Strings Attached*?

Book trailer available @ http://www.youtube.com/watch?v=aIc82VNaJPg

Read Aloud/Talkback

1. Chapter 2, pages 14 to 15, beginning with "*Luck doesn't last . . .*" and ending with "*. . . who I was.*" Kit reflects on her family roots. *Talkback*: How would you react to Kit's assessment of her own situation in relation to her family's decisions?

2. Chapter 4, page 36, beginning with "When I walked out . . ." and ending with the chapter. Kit becomes a Lido girl. *Talkback*: Kit agonizes about using Nate Benedict's influence to become a Lido girl. Do you think she should? Why or why not?

3. Chapter 19, pages 156 to 161. Kit recalls the period after Billy's angry blowup. *Talkback*: What outside pressures are affecting Kit and Billy? Are their plans realistic?

4. Chapter 22, pages 188 and 189, beginning with "The director and the . . ." and ending with the chapter. Kit is late to her call back. *Talkback*: In the exchange, who is right? Why?

5. Chapter 35, pages 308 to 310, beginning with "The second time. . ." and ending with the novel. Kit reflects on what has happened and looks forward to her future. *Talkback*: How has Kit changed? Consider Read Alouds 1 through 4.

Reading guide available @ http://www.scholastic.com/content/ collateral_resources/pdf/s/StringsAttachedReadingGroupGuide .pdf?cid=TRADE/nl/060111/sljteen/paid/newsletter/// librarian/336X280

Author interviews available @

http://www.youtube.com/watch?v=UBhbCGU5IXg
http://www.teenreads.com/authors/judy-blundell/news/interview-033111

Related Works

1. **Blundell, Judy.** *What I Saw and How I Lied*. New York: Scholastic Press, 2008. 288p. $16.99. ISBN-13: 978 0 439 90346 2. [fiction] JS, G (*Value-Packed Booktalks*, 2011, pages 109 to 110.) In this mystery set in 1947, 15-year-old Evie finds herself entangled in her parents' deceit and theft as well as a questionable romance.

2. **Cushman, Karen.** *The Loud Silence of Francine Green*. New York: Clarion Books, 2006. 225p. $16.00. ISBN-13: 978 0 618 50455 8. [fiction] MJ, G (*Genre Talks for Teens*, 2009, pages 21 to 24.) Thirteen-year-old Francine Green confronts the bullies in her life after witnessing the purges of McCarthyism.

3. **Lisle, Janet Taylor.** *Black Duck*. New York: Philomel/Sleuth, 2006. 252p. $15.99. ISBN 0 399 23963 4. [fiction] MJS, CG with high interest for boys (*Genre Talks for Teens*, 2009, pages 149 to 152.) Two 14-year-olds find a man's body on the beach and become embroiled in a conflict between rival Prohibition bootleggers.

4. **Myers, Walter Dean.** *Harlem Summer*. New York: Scholastic Press, 2007. 176p. $16.99. ISBN-13: 978 0 439 36843 8. [fiction] MJ, CG with high interest for boys (*Genre Talks for Teens*, 2009, pages 267 to 269.) During a 1920s Harlem summer, 16-year-old Mark Purvis learns about the sunny and shady side of his community.

5. **Newton, Robert.** *Runner*. New York: Alfred A. Knopf, 2007. 201p. $18.99. ISBN-13: 978 0 375 93744 6. [fiction] MJ, CG with high interest for boys (*Genre Talks for Teens*, 2009, pages 230 to 233.) In 1919, 15-year-old Charlie Feehan works for a crime boss and must reconcile the bad results of his choice.

රැ⁣ඩ

Cooney, Caroline B. **They Never Came Back.**

New York: Delacorte Press, 2010. 200p.
ISBN 978 0 385 73808 8. [fiction] MJ, G

Themes/Topics: Identity, abandoned children, foster care, fugitives from justice, embezzlement, Connecticut

Summary/Description

Fifteen-year-old Cathy studies Latin in summer school and confronts her past. When Cathy was 10, her name was Murielle. Her parents, wanted for embezzlement, fled the country and intended Cathy's aunt to get her on the same plane. The aunt did not cooperate, and Murielle was placed in foster care. She changed her name to Cathy. In summer school, Cathy/Murielle is confronted by her cousin, the aunt's son, who recognizes her. Cathy claims that she is a double. Her fellow students, especially a girl whose mother was prosecuted in the same embezzlement case, pressure her to help the FBI lure her parents back to the United States for prosecution. A student puts Murielle's picture on the Web. It draws a message from the parents. Murielle claims her identity, tells the parents to run, and joins her aunt's family.

Values: Murielle values forgiveness, family, loyalty, and justice.

Booktalk

Fifteen-year-old Cathy lives with a foster family and decides to study Latin in an intense summer school session. But life outside the classroom gets more intense than life in it. Another student confronts her. He says that she looks just like his cousin whom social services took away from his family five years ago. This cousin, Murielle, was abandoned by her parents who fled the country. They were accused of embezzling millions of dollars. Mistaken identity? The boy's parents come to see her. They think she is their niece. Her fellow students research the case on the Web. The FBI shows up. If you were Cathy, what would you do? (*Wait for responses.*) Cathy wants just to study Latin. But maybe she should explore her old life instead of an old language. And, maybe, she will find her identity, her parents' identity, and most important, why *They Never Came Back*.

Book trailer available @ http://www.youtube.com/ watch?v=_CD0YiLTZI0&feature=related

Alternative booktalk available @ http://bcbooktalk.blogspot .com/2010/01/they-never-came-back-by-caroline-b.html

Read Aloud/Talkback

1. Chapter 1, pages 1 to 3, beginning with the chapter and ending with ". . . seeing Murielle." Tommy recognizes Cathy as Murielle. *Talkback*: Why does Cooney open with this scene?
2. Chapter 7, pages 49 to 53, beginning with "A floor above . . ." and ending with ". . . what you're doing." Julianna's family is the family that suffered. *Talkback*: Why is this passage important?
3. Chapter 9, page 82, beginning with "Love was interesting . . ." and ending with ". . . start with anything." Cathy reflects on love. *Talkback*: Do you agree with Cathy? Why?
4. Chapter 15, page 141, beginning with "At what point . . ." and ending with ". . . stops hoping." Cathy reacts to her parents returning. *Talkback*: Do children always hope for a parent's return? Why?
5. Chapter 17, pages 154 to 158, beginning with the chapter and ending with ". . . them to pay." Cathy ponders four questions. *Talkback*: Are these questions that you think about?

Reading guide available @ http://www.juniorlibraryguild.com/ images/9781936129171/StudyguideTeacher/They NvrCameBa_TE_JLGG.pdf

Author answers available @ http://www.caroline bcooneybooks.com/author/answers.html

Author interviews available @ http://www.cmlibrary.org/readers_club/meetAuthor.asp? author=111

http://www.movparent.com/page/content.detail/id/500144/
Interview-with-author-Caroline-B--Cooney.html?nav=5014
http://blog.sanriotown.com/cathyziqinxie:hellokitty.com/2010/
04/04/interview-with-caroline-b-cooney/

Related Works

1. **Cooney, Caroline B. *A Friend at Midnight***. Colorado Springs, CO: Waterbrook Press, 2006. 183p. $15.95. ISBN 1 4000 7208 5. [fiction] J, CG with high interest for girls (*Genre Talks for Teens*, 2009, pages 6 to 9.) Eight-year-old Michael's father abandons him at the airport and raises questions about family loyalty and forgiveness.

2. **Fleischman, Paul. *Seek***. Chicago, IL: Cricket Books/A Marcato Book, 2001. 167p. $16.95. ISBN 0 8126 4900 1. [fiction] JS, CG with high interest for boys. Senior Robert Radkovitz finds his sense of worth as he seeks his biological father on the airways.

3. **Garfinkle, D.L. *Storky: How I Lost My Nickname and Won the Girl***. New York: G. P. Putnam's Sons, 2005. 184p. $16.99. ISBN 0 399 24284 8. [fiction] MJ, CG (*Booktalks and Beyond*, 2007, pages 63 to 65.) A high school freshman finds happiness with down-to-earth people instead of glitzy, demanding ones.

4. **Ryan, Pam Muñoz. *Becoming Naomi León***. New York: Scholastic Press, 2004. 256p. $16.95. ISBN 0 439 26969 5. [fiction] MJS, CG with high interest for girls (*Booktalks and Beyond*, 2007, pages 249 to 251.) Naomi and her physically challenged brother deal with the return of their abusive mother who abandoned them.

5. **Simmons, Michael. *Pool Boy***. Brookfield, CT: Roaring Brook Press/A Neal Porter Book, 2003. 164p. $23.90. ISBN 0 7613 1914 2. [fiction] JS, CG with high interest for boys (*Booktalks and Beyond*, 2007, pages 54 to 56.) After his father is convicted of insider trading, 15-year-old Brett works for the family's former pool man, and learns the satisfaction of hard work and good personal relationships.

ദ്ധ

Deuker, Carl. Payback Time.

New York: Houghton Mifflin Harcourt, 2010. 298p. $16.00.
ISBN 978 0 547 27981 7. [fiction] JS, CG with high interest for boys

Themes/Topics: Reporting, football, obesity, secrets, high school, conduct of life

Summary/Description

The 5 foot 4, 200 pound senior, Daniel True, is nicknamed Mitch because of his Michelin Man appearance. He is passed over for editor of the school newspaper and assigned sports where he makes friends with Kimi, a beautiful North Korean refugee, an outstanding member of his class, and the newspaper's photographer. Mitch decides to shed weight and hopes to date Kimi. They notice a new football player, 6 foot 3, 220 pound Angel, who works to stay out of the limelight. They suspect he is an undercover policeman or an illegal player. They confront hostility from drug dealers, police, the editor of the city paper, the high school coach, and Angel. Finally, the coach reveals that Angel is hiding from a gang he testified against in the death of a child. Mitch's investigation leads a national gang network to Angel and himself. He protects Angel, ditches his possibly outstanding story, makes a good friend in Kimi, and resolves to start over as a more confident Daniel True in college.

Values: When timid Mitch develops self-discipline and confidence, he finds courage.

Booktalk

Meet Mitch, short for Michelin Man. The 5 foot 4, 200 pound senior, looks like a stack of tires. He is too fat for sports or girls. He is a social zero. But Mitch can write. He knows that he will be the editor of the school paper. Wrong. The pretty girl who can't write gets it. She assigns Mitch sports. His dreams of scoring a big story or a great college resume disappear. What should he do? (*Wait for responses.*) When one door closes, another opens. Right? As high school sports writer, he will be the city paper stringer. He notices a story, a 6 foot 3, 220 pound mountain of muscle named Angel. At football practice, Angel stars. At games, he pushes the team to victory. The coach ignores him. If Mitch mentions him in any articles, CUT! What do you think is the story? (*Wait for responses.*) Will Mitch follow his hunch or hide behind his milkshake? Angel's story doesn't stop at high school. Mitch is stirring up some mean guys whose fists go with the nicknames. Is Mitch ready for *Payback Time*?

Book trailer available @ http://www.youtube.com/watch?v=pcYi72OGXr8

Booktalk/review available @ http://www.youtube.com/watch?v=2txoX2Vy03g

Read Aloud/Talkback

1. Part One, Chapter 1, pages 3 to 5. Daniel introduces himself. *Talkback*: What is your impression of Mitch?
2. Part One, Chapter 6, pages 14 to 18. Mitch loses his best friend. *Talkback*: Is Horst a traitor or an exploiter? Explain with specifics.
3. Part One, Chapter 9, pages 27 to 29, beginning with "Kids who don't like . . ." and ending with ". . . was the problem." Mitch describes Kimi. *Talkback*: What does Mitch's description tell you about both Kimi and Mitch?
4. Part Two, Chapter 10, pages 96 to 97, beginning with "She was right . . ." and ending with the chapter. Mitch admits that Alyssa is the better choice for editor. *Talkback*: How do you react to Mitch's assessment of Alyssa?
5. Part Five, Chapter 14, pages 292 to 294, beginning with *"We'll never know . . ."* and ending with the chapter. Mitch describes the gang attack and his feelings about it. *Talkback*: Does Mitch's reaction to the attack make sense?

Discussion questions available @ https://sites.google.com/site/jornyalitsum2011/payback-time

Author interviews available @

http://www.whohub.com/carldeuker
http://5678princessreviews.blogspot.com/2010/07/carl-deuker-interview.html

Author answers questions @ http://www.members.authorsguild.net/carldeuker/disc.htm

Related Works

1. **Carter, Alden. *Love, Football, and Other Contact Sports*.** New York: Holiday House, 2006. 261p. $16.95. ISBN 0 8234 1975 4. [short stories] JS, CG with high interest for boys (*Genre Talks for Teens*, pages 64 to 66.) This short story collection looks into the private lives of the high school football team.
2. **Deuker, Carl. *Gym Candy*.** New York: Houghton Mifflin Harcourt/Graphia, 2007. 313p. $8.99pa. ISBN-13: 978 0 547 07631 7. [fiction] JS, CG with high interest for boys (*Value-Packed Booktalks*, 2011, pages 61 to 63.) Mick Johnson, pushed by his father to be a football star, turns to nonaddictive steroids.
3. **Deuker, Carl. *Runner*.** New York: Houghton Mifflin Co., 2005. 216p. $16.00. ISBN 0 618 54298 1 [fiction] JS, CG with high interest for boys (*Booktalks and Beyond*, 2007, pages 70 to 73.) High school

senior Chance Taylor is offered a job because of his running ability and becomes entangled with terrorists.

4. **Going, K. L. *Fat Kid Rules the World***. New York: G. P. Putnam's Sons, 2003. 183p. $17.99. ISBN 0 399 23990 1. [fiction] JS, CG with high interest for boys (*Teen Genre Connections,* 2005, pages 4 to 6.) The unlikely friendship between an outcast and a popular student makes both stronger.

5. **Schwartz, John. *Short: Walking Tall When You're Not Tall at All***. New York: Roaring Brook Press/Flash Point, 2010. 132p. $16.99. ISBN 978 1 59643 323 6. [nonfiction] JS, CG. Schwartz uses his own experiences as a short person to warn "abnormal," "below-average" people that difference is good and that negative labels are often a part of commercial hype.

ᘓᘔ

Haines, Kathryn Miller. **The Girl Is Murder.**

New York: Roaring Brook Press, 2011. 342p. $16.99.
ISBN 978 1 59643 609 1. [fiction] JS, G

Themes/Topics: Friendship, disabilities, identity, family, religion, ethnicity, lies, World War II, Harlem, 1940s

Summary/Description

When Iris Anderson's mother commits suicide and her detective father returns from Pearl Harbor as an amputee, 15-year-old Iris and her father move to the Lower East Side where Iris enters public school. Suze, a member of the Rainbows, a neighborhood gang, befriends her. A boy in her school, Tom Barney, disappears. Iris decides to help her father, whom the Barney's employ. In pursuing the case, Iris lies to her father and friends, discovers Harlem life, learns about prejudice, and realizes the shallowness of her former private school friend. The father learns that Tom died during an army training exercise and proves to Iris that he is competent in spite of his handicaps. Iris sees her mistakes, reconciles with her friends, and persuades her father to trust her and teach her investigation techniques.

Booktalk

Fifteen-year-old Iris used to go to a private school. She used to have a wealthy mother and an absentee father. World War II changes all that. Her mother commits suicide. Her father loses his leg at Pearl Harbor and, after five years, is returning home as a full time dad. He is just starting his detective agency, so there is no money for private school or a fancy home. They move to New York's Lower East Side, and Iris goes to a public school. How do you think Iris is feeling? (*Work with the responses you receive, but you probably will get confused, lost, and sad among them.*) Iris is no quitter. She isn't going to let her or her father wind up on the street. She decides to help out. A missing person's case, a possible murder, shows up in her new school. Her dad is hired to solve it. He doesn't want Iris involved. If you were Iris, what would you do? (*Wait for responses.*) Dad hasn't told Iris what to do for five years. He isn't going to start now. She'll find out what happened to the missing boy and prove to her father that *The Girl Is Murder*.

Book trailer available @ http://www.youtube.com/
watch?v=sk-w4tCzkk0

Read Aloud/Talkback

1. Chapter 3, pages 33 to 34, beginning with "Oh really?" and ending with ". . . Pearl Harbor." Iris meets former classmates and reflects on how her life has changed. *Talkback*: What details in this passage reveal how Iris is changing? Is the change good?
2. Chapter 4, pages 57 to 58, beginning with "He was being . . ." and ending with ". . . right thing." Iris and her father conflict over her detective work and his authority. *Talkback*: Who is right?
3. Chapter 5, pages 72 to 73, beginning with "Despite my promise . . ." and ending with ". . . no longer available." Iris reflects on belonging. *Talkback*: Does this passage relate to any high school experience or just Iris's?
4. Chapter 12, pages 193 to 196, beginning with "Mama killed herself." and ending with the chapter. Iris talks about her relationship with her mother. *Talkback*: What does the passage reveal about Iris?
5. Chapter 21, pages 329 to 331, beginning with "I felt like I was . . ." and ending with ". . . one who's changed." Iris confronts Grace about her treatment of Tom Barney. *Talkback*: How does the passage affect your feelings about Grace and Iris?

Study guide available @ http://media.us.macmillan.com/
teachersguides/9781596436091TG.pdf

Author interview available @
http://agoodaddiction.blogspot.com/2011/12/author-interview-
contest-kathryn-miller.html
http://www.fictionenthusiast.com/2012/07/author-interview-
kathryn-miller-haines.html

http://shusky20.blogspot.com/2012/07/girl-is-trouble-blog-tour-
interview.html

http://www.teensreadandwrite.com/2011/12/blog-tour-and-contest-
kathryn-miller.html

http://bethanyhensel.com/?p=453

Related Works

1. **Blundell, Judy.** *What I Saw and How I Lied*. New York: Scholastic
    Press, 2008. 288p. $16.99. ISBN-13: 978 0 439 90346 2. [fiction]
    JS, G (*Value-Packed Booktalks*, 2011, pages 109 to 111.) In 1947,
    15-year-old Evie enjoys her glamorous mother, new stepfather, and
    comfortable life until she discovers that her family's wealth comes
    from money stolen from Jews.

2. **Haines, Kathryn Miller.** *The Girl Is Trouble*. New York: Roaring
    Brook Press, 2012. 325p. $17.99. ISBN 978 1 59643 610 7. [fiction]
    JS, G. In this sequel to *The Girl Is Murder*, Iris works with her
    father and confronts big trouble when she investigates her mother's
    "suicide."

3. **Kerr, M. E.** *Slap Your Sides*. New York: HarperCollins Publishers,
    2001. 198p. $15.95. ISBN 0 06 029481 7. [fiction] MJS, CG (*Teen
    Genre Connections*, 2005, pages 233 to 235.) Kerr presents views
    of World War II that range from conscientious objection to jin-
    goism.

4. **Myers, Walter Dean (poem), and Christopher Myers (illus.).**
    Harlem. New York: Scholastic Press, 1997. 30p. $16.95. ISBN 0
    590 54340 7. [nonfiction] MJS, CG (*Booktalks Plus*, 2001, pages 241
    to 243.) This illustrated poem gives the feel of Iris's Harlem.

5. **Whelan, Gloria.** *Summer of the War*. New York: HarperCollins
    Children's Books, 2006. 176p. $15.99. ISBN-13: 978 06 008072 3.
    [fiction] MJ, G (*Genre Talks for Teens*, 2009, pages 238 to 240.)
    During her 1942 summer, 14-year-old Mirabelle conflicts with her
    cousin who has grown up in Europe.

☙❧

Price, Charlie. The Interrogation of
Gabriel James.

New York: Farrar, Straus and Giroux, 2010. 170p. $16.99.
ISBN 978 0 374 33545 8. JS, CG with high interest for boys

Themes/Topics: Murder, crime, Montana, communes, mental
illness, choices

Summary/Description

During an interrogation, illuminated by flashbacks, Gabriel James pieces together the events that led to the murder of the mentally ill son of a commune founder and the son's criminal cohort. Dead pets, street drugs, his would-be girlfriend's abusive home life, and racial attacks motivate Gabe to investigate. He discovers that the homeschooled son of the commune leader leads a gang that sells drugs, terrorizes the community by stealing the pets, and attacks any racial or belief group different than its own. Gabe's mother and father were once part of the commune and Gabe may be the former leader's son.

Values: Gabe realizes that seemingly personal decisions have lifelong consequences.

Booktalk

This story starts with two funerals. We don't know who died and we don't know who killed the people getting buried. That is a mystery. But there is even a bigger mystery in this story and Gabriel James is at the center of it. He just doesn't know it. Gabe's journey starts with trying to get a date. How do you figure out if somebody likes you? (*Wait for answers.*) Gabe has a friend who is his personal radar. Gabe is sure that a quiet girl he never noticed before is interested, but suddenly she isn't. Pets disappear. The new angry Native American runner on their track team isn't welcome. Gabe's street friend suddenly wants to go to a mental hospital. How does that all add up to murder? Even Gabe can't do the math until all the factors are on the table in *The Interrogation of Gabriel James*.

Read Aloud/Talkback

1. Chapter 2, pages 11 to 12, beginning with "I had done . . ." and ending with ". . . about the rest." Gabe describes himself. *Talkback*: Do you agree that Gabe is an average guy? Is he detached?
2. Chapter 8, pages 48 to 51, beginning with ". . . Raelene was the . . ." and ending with "Yeah, that's it." Gabe assesses Raelene. *Talkback*: What impresses Gabe about Raelene? What does his description tell about him?
3. Chapter 17, pages 123 to 124, beginning with "You're like Typhoid . . ." and ending with the chapter. Gabe reflects on Emily's accusation that he is a Typhoid Mary. *Talkback*: Do you think that Emily is correct? Why?

4. Chapter 24, pages 162 to 163, beginning with "I waited her out . . ." and ending with ". . . how that felt." Gabe confronts his mother. *Talkback*: Whose side are you on? Why?

5. Chapter 25, pages 167 to 168. This is the concluding chapter. *Talkback*: Was Gabe right to intervene? What happens next?

Author interviews available @

http://blog.printsasia.com/2011/12/15/author-interview-charlie-
    price-the-interrogation-gabriel-james/
http://anewscafe.com/2011/05/03/donis-dish-a-conversation-with-
    charlie-price-edgar-award-winner/

Charlie Price acceptance of the Edgar Award @ http:// www.youtube.com/watch?v=xNtm8CsRYFI

Related Works

1. **Brooks, Martha. *Mistik Lake***. New York: Farrar, Straus and Giroux/Melanie Kroupa Books, 2007. 207p. $16.00. ISBN-13: 978 0 374 34985 1. [fiction] S, G (*Genre Talks for Teens*, 2009, pages 4 to 6.) At the family's summer retreat, 17-year-old Odella falls in love while unraveling the family secrets that include her parentage.

2. **Cormier, Robert. *The Rag and Bone Shop***. New York: Delacorte Press, 2001. 154p. $15.95. ISBN 0 385 72962 6. [fiction] MJS, CG with high interest for boys (*Teen Genre Connections*, 2005, pages 129 to 131.) A young boy decides to use a knife against a bully after a vicious police interrogation.

3. **Marchetta, Melina. *Jellicoe Road***. New York: HarperCollins/ Harper Teen, 2006. 419p. $17.99. ISBN-13: 978 0 06 143183 8. [fiction] S, CG with high interest for girls (*Value-Packed Booktalks*, 2009, pages 125 to 127.) Taylor Markham faces her past and learns about her mother's "family" and the traditions it created.

4. **Myers, Walter Dean. *Monster***. New York: HarperCollins Publishers, 1999. 281p. $15.95. ISBN 0 06 028077 8. [fiction] JS, CG with high interest for boys (*Booktalks and More*, 2003, pages 13 to 15.) Naïve 16-year-old Steve Harmon, on trial for murder, creates a play about his trial and his experiences before the trial. By the end of the novel, both Steve and the reader question his innocence.

5. **Zusak, Markus. *I Am the Messenger***. New York: Alfred A. Knopf, 2002. 357p. $20.50. ISBN 0 375 93099 X. [fiction] S, CG with high interest for boys (*Booktalks and Beyond*, 2007, pages 143 to 146.) Average 19-year-old Ed Kennedy, an underage cabdriver, drifts

through life until he becomes a hero in a bank robbery and receives Aces directing him to help people.

✿✿

Sheinkin, Steve. **Bomb: The Race to Build and Steal the World's Most Dangerous Weapon.**

New York: Roaring Brook Press, 2012. 266p. $19.99.
ISBN 978 1 59643 487 5. [nonfiction] MJS,
CG with high interest for boys

Themes/Topics: Atomic bomb, World War (1939–1945), Secret Service, Soviet Union, Great Britain, commando operation, Norway, Vemork, Operation Freshman (1942), Germany

Summary/Description

The United States works to build the atom bomb and prevent the Germans from building it first, while the Soviets organize to steal the atomic weapon secrets from the United States. Sheinkin's account is both a spy mystery and a world survival story, as he relates the efforts of world famous scientists, skilled spies, and "military commandos," who struggled to give their governments the edge in world domination. He emphasizes the necessity of the race and the problems it gave to subsequent generations. Photos supplement the text. Source Notes are divided into "Bomb Race Sources," "Character Sources," and "Primary Sources." Quotation Notes are included for each chapter and an index allows for easy access of information.

Values: Sheinkin's account emphasizes the importance of loyalty, integrity, and wisdom.

Booktalk

How many here like mysteries? Thrillers? (*Indicate that you want a show of hands.*) Your history book holds an incredible one. You just never have the time in class to get the full story. How many people here have heard of the atom bomb? (*Wait for responses.*) To win World War II, the United States not only had to build the most dangerous bomb in the world, but it also had to prevent Germany from developing it first. Both operations were secret, but the Soviet Union had a secret operation in progress, too.

They wanted to know about the weapons their "friends" (*Make quotation marks around friends with your hands.*) had. And they were especially interested in a very dangerous secret weapon called "The Gadget." That was the code name for what? (*Wait for response atom bomb.*) They decided to steal the plans from the United States. So the world faced the possibility of two of the most dangerous dictators in history, Hitler and Stalin, controlling the most destructive weapon. And this is the story of how the most brilliant scientists, the most highly skilled spies, and the most daring commandos cooperated and competed in a cutthroat race to get the *Bomb*.

Read Aloud/Talkback

1. "Prologue: May 22, 1950," pages 1 to 3. Harry Gold breaks down when confronted by the FBI. *Talkback*: Why does the author begin with this incident?
2. "Glider's Down," pages 58 to 59, beginning with "On a drizzly afternoon . . ." and ending with the chapter. Sheinkin describes the disastrous glider attempt by British commandos. *Talkback*: Why is this incident central?
3. "Operation Gunnerside," pages 76 to 77, beginning with "On the night of . . ." and ending with ". . . for all I know." Haukelid and his men are dropped to raid the Vemork plant. *Talkback*: What does this brief description tell you about the men in the mission?
4. "Test Shot," pages 184 to 185, beginning with "Naturally, we were . . ." and ending with the chapter. The scientists react to the successful test. *Talkback*: Why is this a moment of victory and defeat?
5. "Race to Trinity," pages 238 to 239. Albert Einstein's letter to President Roosevelt. *Talkback*: What does this letter tell us about Albert Einstein?

Author read aloud available @ http://www.teachingbooks.net/ book_reading.cgi?id=8116&a=1

Author interview available @ http://www.slj.com/2012/09/ books-media/author-interview/cc_september2012_interview/

Related Works

1. **Burnett, Betty, Ph.D.** *The Trial of Julius and Ethel Rosenberg: A Primary Source Account*. New York: Rosen Central Primary Source, 2004. 64p. (Great Trials of the Twentieth Century.) $31.95. ISBN: 0 8239 3976 6. [nonfiction] MJS, CG. The account explains

the background, context, and trial of the infamous and controversial Rosenbergs.

2. **Grant, R. G. *Why did Hiroshima Happen?*** New York: Gareth Stevens Publishing, 2011. 48p. (Moments in History.) $31.95. ISBN: 978 1 4339 4163 4. [nonfiction] MJS, CG. Grant traces the attitudes and conflicts that led to dropping the bomb. He presents a different view than Sheinkin.

3. **Hersey, John. *Hiroshima*.** New York: Vintage Books, 1985. 152p. $6.50pa. ISBN 0 679 72103 7. [nonfiction] JS/A, CG. Written in 1946, this journalistic account of the atom bomb compiles memories of the survivors. In the final chapter, written four decades after the original, Hersey tries to revisit the people he originally interviewed.

4. **Janeczko, Paul B. *Top Secret: A Handbook of Codes, Ciphers, and Secret Writing*.** Cambridge, MA: Candlewick Press, 2004. 144p. $16.99. ISBN 0 7636 0971 4. [nonfiction] MJ, CG with high interest for boys. This how-to guide and history of spy communication leads the user through codes, ciphers, and secret language. A short exercise follows each system presented.

5. **Zindel, Paul. *The Gadget*.** New York: HarperCollins Publishers, 2001. 184p. $15.99. ISBN 0 06 028255 X. [fiction] MJ, CG (*Teen Genre Connections*, 2005, pages 151 to 154.) Thirteen-year-old Stephen Orr, living in a new and strange Los Alamos home and frustrated by his father's distance and secrecy, unwittingly befriends a Russian spy who seeks information about the atom bomb project.

ᘓᘔ

Strasser, Todd. Kill You Last.
New York: Egmont, 2011. 223p. $16.99.
ISBN 978 1 60684 024 5. [fiction] JS, CG with high interest for girls

Themes/Topics: Modeling, murder, infidelity, sexual
exploitation, conduct of life

Summary/Description

In this third book of Strasser's Thrilogy, 18-year-old Shelby's family comes under police investigation, when three girls connected to her father's photography studio are found dead. Convinced he is innocent, she investigates and discovers that he has been scamming young girls for money and sex by promising them modeling careers. Her former best friend is one of his victims. Shelby and her friend sort out harassing emails sent to Shelby. The trail leads to Shelby's mother, who blamed the girls for her husband's infidelity and killed them.

Values: Shelby distinguishes family loyalty from community responsibility.

Booktalk

Ask the following questions and wait for responses:

Do you like mysteries with nonstop action? Piles of dead bodies? Multiple killer possibilities?

If you answered yes to all those questions, this is your story.

Eighteen-year-old Shelby goes where she wants, buys what she wants, and drives the hot sports cars that everyone wants. Then, things go wrong. Three of her dad's photography clients are missing. Then, they are dead. Shelby is sure that her dad did not murder those girls. But other accusations surface. Was her father running a scam? Did he exploit the girls? If the answers are yes, did he kill the girls to shut them up? She has to find the truth, even if the murderer is promising to *Kill You Last*.

Read Aloud/Talkback

1. "Prologue," unnumbered page before page 1. The prologue introduces us to Shelby's problem and support. *Talkback*: Why does Strasser start with this prologue when the same passage appears on pages 138 to 139, beginning with ". . . a text showed up"?
2. "Chapter 7," pages 35 to 36, beginning with "When we finished . . ." and ending with ". . . wanted to believe." Shelby talks about her ambiguous feelings about her father. *Talkback*: Do you think that Shelby could have changed her father's behavior?
3. Chapter 11, pages 54 to 57. The news story about the modeling scam shakes Shelby's faith in her father. *Talkback*: What was your reaction to the story?
4. Chapter 40, pages 205 to 206, beginning with "Mercedes's eyes were . . ." and ending with the chapter. Shelby asks Mercedes about her father's guilt. *Talkback*: What clues does Mercedes give Shelby?
5. Chapter 45, page 223, beginning with "It's not easy . . ." and ending with the chapter. Shelby talks about her future plans. *Talkback*: How do you react to Shelby and her plans?

Author interview available @ http://www.youtube.com/watch?v=apJrK6rDe2o&feature=related

Related Works

1. **Blundell, Judy. *What I Saw and How I Lied***. New York: Scholastic Press, 2008. 288p. $16.99. ISBN-13: 978 0 439 90346 2. [fiction] JS, G (*Value-Packed Booktalks*, 2011, pages 109 to 111.) Fifteen-year-old Evie discovers that her stepfather's crimes support her comfortable life.
2. **Haddon, Mark. *The Curious Incident of the Dog in the Night-Time***. New York: Vintage Contemporaries, 2003. 226p. $12.00. ISBN 1 4000 327 7. [fiction] S/A, CG with high interest for boys (*Booktalks and Beyond*, pages 119 to 121.) A brilliant, autistic teenager investigates the murder of his neighbor's dead dog and uncovers the murderer and family secrets.
3. **Harrison, Michael. *Facing the Dark***. New York: Holiday House, 2000. 128p. $15.95. ISBN 0 8234 1491 4. [fiction] MJS, CG (*Teen Genre Connections*, 2005, pages 135 to 137.) An accused murderer's son, Simon, and the victim's daughter, Charley, give their perceptions of the crime and its solution in alternating chapters.
4. **Oates, Joyce Carol. *Freaky Green Eyes***. New York: Harper Tempest, 2003. 341p. $17.89. ISBN 0 06 623757 2. [fiction] MJS, CG (*Teen Genre Connections*, 2005, pages 140 to 141.) Fourteen-year-old Franky Pierson discovers that her celebrity father murdered her mother.
5. **Simmons, Michael. *Pool Boy***. Brookfield, CT: Roaring Brook Press/A Neal Porter Book, 2003. 164p. $23.90. ISBN 0 7613 2924 2. [fiction] JS, CG with high interest for boys (*Booktalks and Beyond*, 2007, pages 54 to 56.) After his father is convicted of insider trading, 15-year-old Brett works for Alfie More, the family's former pool man and learns about himself and life.

Magic

Black, Holly. White Cat.

New York: Margaret K. McElderry Books, 2010. 310p. (The Curse Workers) $17.99.
ISBN: 978 1 469 6396 7. [fiction] JS, CG with high interest for boys

Themes/Topics: Memories, swindlers and swindling, brothers

Summary/Description

Cassel Sharpe believes he is the only non-magic member of his "worker" family. Workers can change memories, emotions, or luck with the touch of their hands. Their power is automatically illegal, so many become con artists like Cassel's mother or members of organized crime like Cassel's grandfather and brothers.

After sleepwalking on a roof while dreaming about a white cat, Cassel Sharpe is no longer permitted to attend his upper-class school. His life-threatening dream comes from Lila, his childhood friend and daughter of a major crime boss. His two older brothers have manipulated his memories. Four years ago, his brothers tried to force him to kill Lila in a mob takeover. Cassel transformed her into a cat and told her to run, but she was caught and kept in a cage. Now, she wants revenge. Cassel discovers his superior powers as a transformation worker, brings Lila back to human form, turns his brothers' deception against them, and returns to school

> **Values:** Cassel demonstrates friendship and love even
> as he uses his criminal skills to fight the brothers
> who manipulated and betrayed him.

Booktalk

Cassel Sharpe comes from a worker family. Not hard worker or blue collar, but magic worker. Workers can change a person's emotions, memories, or luck. They can kill with the touch of a hand. The government is so afraid that they make curse working a crime and force workers to wear gloves. So what do the outcasts do? They go underground and form mobs. Cassel's family is in one of those mobs. His mother is a con, his brothers are rising in the ranks, and grandpa has been a hit man for years. Should he trust them? (*Wait for responses.*) Cassel is the only family member without superhuman powers. Do you believe that? (*Wait for responses.*) He killed a girl four years ago, his best friend. Her dad is a mob boss. His family kept the secret, or he would be dead. But Cassel is starting to dream. One dream almost made him sleepwalk off a roof. He wonders if someone found out about what he did, like his friend's mob boss father. The answer seems related to a scary creature that keeps showing up in the dreams—a strange, familiar, talking *White Cat*.

> **Trailer available @** http://www.youtube.com/
> watch?v=CB8Zr9BA3ng
> **Series book trailer available @** http://www.simonandschuster
> .com/multimedia?video=1431765717001

Read Aloud/Talkback

1. Chapter 4, pages 56 to 59, beginning with "That night . . ." and ending with the chapter. Cassel relates the cat dream. *Talkback*: How is the cat dream both humorous and horrible? Point out the details that support your answer.

2. Chapter 5, pages 68 to 69, beginning with "The first time . . ." and ending with ". . . about the cat." Cassel becomes a criminal. *Talkback*: What does this experience say about Cassel? Support your answer with details from the passage.

3. Chapter 6, pages 91 to 93, beginning with "I'm not good . . ." and ending with "Friendships suck." Cassel gives his interpretation of friendship. *Talkback*: Do you agree?

4. Chapter 19, pages 302 to 303, beginning with "The thing is . . ." and ending with ". . . all magic." A freshman worker gives her impression of the worker gift. *Talkback*: Does the freshman statement apply just to magic or is there a bigger message?

5. Chapter 19, page 309, beginning with "The most important . . ." and ending with the chapter. Cassel describes the mark. *Talkback*: According to the description, who is the mark?

Reading group guide available @ http://books .simonandschuster.com/White-Cat/Holly-Black/Curse -Workers-The/9781416963967/reading_group_guide

Author interview available @ http://www.ask.blinkx.com/ watch-video/holly-black-describes-the-inspiration-behind- white-cat/4aA-vPHG36qi3W3aFJJNEQ

Related Works

1. **Black, Holly. *Black Hand*.** New York: Margaret McElderry Books, 2012. 296p. (The Curse Workers Trilogy) $17.99. ISBN-13: 9781442403468. [fiction] JS, CG with high interest for boys. Cassel is balancing training for the Fed and pursuing a girl who is taking her place in her own crime family.

2. **Black, Holly. *Red Glove*.** New York: Margaret McElderry Books, 2011. 325p. (The Curse Workers Trilogy) $17. 99. ISBN 9781442403390. [fiction] JS, CG with high interest for boys. Two government agents offer Cassel an opportunity to work for the government and avenge his older brother's death which they blame on Zacharov, the mob boss Cassel's brother

3. **Haddix, Margaret Peterson. *Escape from Memory*.** New York: Simon & Schuster Books for Young Readers, 2003. 220p. $16.95. ISBN 0 689 85421 8. [fiction] MJS, CG with high interest for girls

(*Teen Genre Connections*, 2005, pages 144 to 147.) Strange memories lead 15-year-old Kira to her real mother and death.

4. **Meyer, Marissa. *Cinder: Book One*.** New York: Feiwel and Friends, 2012. 390p. (The Lunar Chronicles) $17.99. ISBN 978 0 312 64189 4. [fiction] JS, G (Fantasy/New Worlds, pages 171 to 173.) A young cyborg discovers her royal blood and exceptional powers.

5. **Zevin, Gabrielle. *All These Things I've Done*.** New York: Farrar Straus Giroux, 2011. 354p. (Birthright: Book the First) $16.99. ISBN: 978 0 374 30210 8. [fiction] JS, G (Fantasy/New Powers, pages 198 to 201.) Sixteen-year-old Anya Balanchine is the reluctant "heir apparent" of a New York crime family, in a future where chocolate, caffeine, and teenage cell phone use are illegal.

෴

Bunce, Elizabeth C. Star Crossed.

New York: Scholastic Inc./Arthur A. Levine Books, 2010. 368p. $17.99.
ISBN 978 0 545 13605 1. [fiction] JS, CG with high interest for girls

Themes/Topics: Renaissance life, street life, magic,
persecution, loyalty, family

Summary/Description

Under the name Celyn Contrare, Digger is a lady-in-waiting to the shy Merista Nemair. Digger, a street thief since she was 10, hides from the king's Inquisition that persecutes magic. Blackmailed by the evil Lord Daul, she spies on the Nemair family and their contacts who are planning a rebellion against the king. Her feelings for Merista and her parents overcome her fear of Daul, and eventually, with the help of a prince and a flock of magicians, she defends them against Daul and the Inquisition which Digger's brother leads.

Values: Digger learns the true meaning of family and the
importance of loyalty to one's core beliefs.

Booktalk

Ask someone to read the definition of star crossed.

Star-crossed people have the good news in their lives overshadowed by bad news. In this fantasy/mystery, a teenage street thief named Digger gets plenty of that combination. She has special magic. Good news. The convent where she lives wants to "cure" that magic. Bad news. Her brother, a high church official, is willing even to kill her to make her pure. Really (*Wait for the audience to fill in the response.*) bad news. She escapes. (*Draw audience response of the good news.*) But big brother could be around every corner. (*Draw audience response of the bad news.*) She spends each day running and stealing to prepare for the next. Then, she meets the shy Lady Merista. Digger becomes her lady-in-waiting. (*Draw audience response of the good news.*) We know that there has to be some bad news. (*Draw audience response of bad news.*) Merista is hiding secrets of her own. The castle walls hold danger and treachery. Magic that Digger doesn't understand sizzles in the air. The evil Lord Daul arrives and blackmails Digger into becoming his private spy. What she finds could bring death to everyone in the castle, even herself. There may not be any more good news for anyone when a simple street thief is *Star Crossed*.

Book trailer available @ http://www.youtube.com/ watch?v=y9L4uH3f0b8

Read Aloud/Talkback

1. Chapter 12, page 115, beginning with "Well, then . . ." and ending with ". . . one of my own." Daul compares his status to Digger's. *Talkback*: Could the same kind of threat be made today? After reading the full story, how would you react to this passage?

2. Chapter 12, pages 117 to 118, beginning with "I had worked . . ." and ending with the chapter. Digger knows that she has magic and recognizes it in others. *Talkback*: Is Digger as innocent as she claims? Why does she talk to herself about the issue for so long?

3. Chapter 16, pages 148 to 151, beginning with "Cwalo had . . ." and ending with the chapter. Cwalo and Digger discuss the castle as they play chess. *Talkback*: What does this passage reveal about both Cwalo and Digger? Why is the discussion valuable to both parties?

4. Chapter 18, page 165, beginning with "Why are you . . ." and ending with ". . . Goddess's justice." Daul reveals his motivation. *Talkback*: Who do you think motivates Daul? How does his explanation tie to the rest of the story?

5. Chapter 32, pages 309 to 311, beginning with "A strong hand . . ." and ending with the chapter. Digger confronts Werne to save Merista and reveals her identity. *Talkback*: What does this scene reveal about both Digger and Werne? Are they alike?

Author interviews available @

http://enchantedinkpot.livejournal.com/71080.html
http://smallreview.blogspot.com/2011/11/author-interview-elizabeth-c-bunce.html

http://chavelaque.blogspot.com/2010/10/q-elizabeth-c-bunce-author-of.html

http://www.ekristinanderson.com/?p=2381

Author's background resources available @ http://www.elizabethcbunce.com/resources.html

Related Works

1. **Bunce, Elizabeth C. *A Curse Dark as Gold*.** New York: Scholastic/ Arthur A. Levine Books, 2008. 422p. $17.99. ISBN-13: 978 0 439 89576 7. [fiction] JS, G (*Value-Packed Booktalks*, 2011, pages 137 to 139.) In this retelling of Rumpelstiltskin, secrets and witch hunts almost cause a young woman to lose her livelihood and family.

2. **Bunce, Elizabeth C. *Liar's Moon*.** New York: Scholastic Inc./ Arthur A. Levine Books, 2011. 368p. $17.99. ISBN-13: 978 0 545 13608 2. [fiction] JS, CG with high interest for girls. In this sequel to *Star Crossed*, Digger, back in Gerse, discovers her friend Lord Durrell facing a murder charge and decides to prove him innocent.

3. **Murdock, Catherine Gilbert. *Princess Ben*.** Boston, MA: Houghton Mifflin Co., 2008. 344p $16.00. ISBN-13: 978 0 618 95971 6. [fiction] JS, G (*Value-Packed Booktalks*, 2011, pages 152 to 154.) Fifteen-year-old Princess Ben emerges from a difficult, over-weight, and slothful little girl to a worthy regent, saves the kingdom, and finds personal happiness.

4. **Pierce, Tamora. *Melting Stones*.** New York: Scholastic Press, 2008. 320p. $17.99. ISBN-13: 978 0 545 05264 1. [fiction] JS, G (*Value-Packed Booktalks*, 2011, pages 168 to 170.) Fourteen-year-old Evvy, a stone mage in training, helps Rosethorn and Myrrhtide investigate a mysterious disruption in an island's plant and water supply.

5. **Pierce, Tamora. *The Will of the Empress*.** New York: Scholastic Press, 2005. 320p. $17.99. ISBN 0 439 44171 4. [fiction] MJS, G (*Genre Talks for Teens*, 2009, pages 207 to 210.) Sixteen-year-old Sandry from *Magic Steps* of *The Circle Opens Quartet*, with the help of her three magically gifted friends, eludes unwanted suitors and defeats an evil Empress who wishes to control the kingdom.

ॐ

Johnson, Maureen. The Name of the Star.

New York: Penguin Group Inc./Putnam's Sons, 2011. 372p. $16.99. ISBN 978 0 399 25660 8. [fiction] JS, CG with high interest for girls

Themes/Topics: Boarding schools, murder, witnesses, ghosts, London

Summary/Description

Rory leaves Louisiana and arrives at her new London boarding school on the day that a series of brutal Jack-the-Ripper copycat murders breaks out. Rory is the only witness to the prime suspect, even though a girl was with her at the time. A new undercover policewoman becomes their roommate. She is part of a special police unit. Each unit member, due to a near-death experience, can see ghosts. They realize that Rory has the same gift, and reveal their purpose. She bonds with the group, learns about their "ghostbusting" equipment which blows up hostile ghosts, and joins in the search for the ghostly Ripper. In a final confrontation, Rory risks her life to save her friends, is saved by a hostile ghost, and discovers that she has become part of the team, and a replacement for the "ghostbusting" machines which "The Ripper" destroyed.

Values: Rory learns the relationship between courage and friendship.

Booktalk

Ask how many people in the group have heard of Jack the Ripper. Ask them to share what they know.

Rory Deveaux leaves Louisiana and arrives in London on the day that a series of brutal murders begins. The murders mimic the work of the notorious Jack the Ripper, but even people who see the murders occur can't see the murderer. That is, all but one witness. Guess who that is. (*Wait for responses.*) Right. The girl from Louisiana. Is she lying? Hysterical? Or in possession of special powers? (*Wait for responses.*) The police want to find out. They plant a roommate with Rory. A roommate from a secret unit. She can see ghosts. She shadows Rory and knows that Rory can too. The murderer knows also knows that Rory has the gift. Witness Rory becomes the hunted Rory. And when the media hypes the crime spree into a "Rippermania" event, Rory and the ghostbusters unit of the London police follow a twisting trail of death and betrayal to find *The* (real) *Name of the Star*.

Book trailers available @

http://www.youtube.com/watch?v=dMXtrGNN9rw
http://www.youtube.com/watch?v=raFedaKpOFA

Read Aloud/Talkback

1. Chapter 13, page 113, beginning with "There's something witnesses . . ." and ending with ". . . but the facts." Rory explains the problem with witnesses. *Talkback*: What is your reaction to Rory's explanation?

2. "BBC Television Centre," pages 134 to 138. Shepherd Bush broadcasts the letter and picture he receives from "The Ripper." *Talkback*: Why does Johnson include this incident?

3. Chapter 21, pages 183 to 185, beginning with the chapter and ending with ". . . told me to adapt." Rory uses Uncle Bick's story to explain how she feels about adapting. *Talkback*: Why is this story effective in making Rory's point?

4. Chapter 22, pages 197 to 200, beginning with "Who is Jack . . ." and ending with ". . . got away with it." Jerome explains the Ripper mystique. *Talkback*: How does this explanation affect your reaction to the story and to Jack the Ripper?

5. Chapter 26, page 260, beginning with "Fear can't hurt . . ." and ending with ". . . can save you." Jo reacts to Rory's admission of fear. *Talkback*: How is Jo's advice critical to the story's conclusion?

Author interviews available @

http://www.youtube.com/watch?NR=1&feature=endscreen&v=rW
  8oW6FdSW8
http://www.youtube.com/watch?v=hGhnztT56g0&feature=related
http://www.maureenjohnsonbooks.com/faq/
http://bookpage.com/interview/a-ghostly-jack-the-ripper-returns
http://www.youtube.com/watch?v=XewewM1VXyA

Discussion questions available @ http://libraryladyhylary
  .blogspot.com/2012/02/name-of-star-book-review.html

Related Works

1. **Beagle, Peter S. *Tamsin*.** New York: ROC, 1999. 275p. $21.95. ISBN 0 451 45763 3. [fiction] JS/A, G. Nineteen-year-old Jennifer moves into a haunted estate and helps Tamsin, a ghost from the Bloody Assizes, reunite with her lover.

2. **Bunce, Elizabeth C. *A Curse Dark as Gold*.** New York: Scholastic/ Arthur A. Levine Books, 2008. 422p. $17.99. ISBN-13: 978 0 439 89576 7. [fiction] JS, G (*Value-Packed Booktalks*, 2011, pages 137 to 139.) This supernatural mystery, based on the Rumpelstiltskin story, involves sisters who inherit a haunted woolen mill.

3. **Bunting, Eve. *The Presence: A Ghost Story*.** New York: Clarion Books, 2003. 195p. $15.00. ISBN 0 618 26919 3. [nonfiction] JS, CG (*Teen Genre Connections*, 2005, pages 156 to 158.) Noah Vanderhost died 120 years ago at 17, and now haunts the church where he commits murders.

4. **Dowd, Siobhan. *Bog Child*.** New York: Random House/A David Fickling Book, 2008. 322p. $16.99. ISBN-13: 978 0 285 75169 8. [fiction] S, CG with high interest for boys (*Value-Packed Booktalks*, 2011, pages 114 to 116.) As 18-year-old Fergus studies for medical school entrance exams, he is distracted by his imprisoned brother's hunger strike, his dangerous job as a courier for Sinn Fein, and strange dreams sent to him by an ancient murdered girl.

5. **Gaiman, Neil, and Dave McKean (illus). *The Graveyard Book*.** New York: Harper Collins, 2008. 312p. $17.99. ISBN-13: 978 0 06 05 3092 1. [fiction] MJS, CG with high interest for boys (*Value-Packed Booktalks*, pages 161 to 163.) Raised by graveyard ghosts, Bod transitions to the real world and faces the forces that killed his family.

ℭ℘

Reese, James. The Strange Case of Doctor Jekyll & Mademoiselle Odile.

New York: Roaring Brook Press, 2012. 357p. (Shadow Sisters) $17.99.
ISBN 978 1 59643 684 8. [fiction] JS, CG with high interest for girls.

Themes/Topics: Witchcraft, shape shifting, orphans, Paris siege of 1870 to 1871, double personalities

Summary/Description

After seeing her mother and father murdered for the mother's witchcraft, 16-year-old Odile and her younger brother flee to Paris, now on the brink of war, where they live in the catacombs. She meets Dr. Jekyll while testing her witch skills in the zoo. He offers shelter and help for her brother, but wants the formula for her magical salts which transform the doctor into the nefarious Mr. Hyde and her brother into a notorious killing machine. Odile learns the secret of the salts, but hides it from Dr. Jekyll until he threatens to kill both her and Julian, a young man who has helped her since she arrived in Paris and whom she loves. Odile and Julian turn Jekyll's threat into a positive. They give the money from their negotiations with Jekyll to the housemaid who has helped Odile. Then, Odile and Julian escape together. The still wealthy Dr. Jekyll is doomed by his choices.

Values: Odile realizes the importance of consequences.

Booktalk

Ask if anyone in the group has heard of Dr. Jekyll and Mr. Hyde. Hold up the book. Ask them to share what they know with the group. Then, hold up The Strange Case of Doctor Jekyll & Mr. Hyde.

How did the well-educated, gentlemanly Dr. Jekyll transform himself into the notoriously evil Mr. Hyde? In Stevenson's work, (*Point to or hold up the book.*) the doctor says that he did it all himself. Reese (*Point to or hold up the book.*) tells a different story. He reveals that 16-year-old Odile, a mysterious street girl, is the source of Dr. Jekyll's magic. Odile is a witch. So was her mother. Odile brings her brother to Paris after her parents are killed. A chance meeting at the zoo brings Odile and Jekyll together, and together they can control the world. Who is more evil? You be the judge when you read *The Strange Case of Doctor Jekyll & Mademoiselle Odile*.

Book trailer available @ http://jamesreesebooks.com/

Read Aloud/Talkback

1. Chapter 5, pages 98 to 101, beginning with "I'd turned away from . . ." and ending with ". . . I stepped aside?" Odile gives her brother the salts. *Talkback*: Should Odile have taken the risk?
2. Chapter 6, pages 128 to 135, beginning with "It was hollow . . ." and ending with the chapter. Odile explores Poole's suit of armor. *Talkback*: What does Odile find out about Poole?
3. Chapter 9, pages 200 to 202, beginning with "All my life . . ." and ending with ". . . would surely pounce." Odile reacts to Jekyll's explanation of why Hyde is important. *Talkback*: How would you react to Jekyll's explanation? Why?
4. Chapter 15, pages 335 to 338, beginning with "I saw it too . . ." and ending with "Ascended." Odile takes the remaining salts. *Talkback*: What does Odile realize?
5. Chapter 16, pages 349 to 353, beginning with "I looked at . . ." and ending with the novel. Odile bargains with Poole and the doctor. *Talkback*: Who wins? Explain your answer.

Related Works

1. **Bray, Libba. *A Great and Terrible Beauty***. New York: Delacorte Press, 2003. 405p. $18.99. ISBN 0 385 90161 5. [fiction] S, G

(*Booktalks and Beyond*, 2009, pages 157 to 159.) Sixteen-year-old Gemma decides that her supernatural powers bring evil.

2. **Hautman, Pete. *Invisible*.** New York: Simon & Schuster Books for Young Readers, 2005. 149p. $15.95. ISBN 0 689 86800 6. [fiction] JS, CG (*Genre Talks for Teens*, 2009, pages 29 to 32.) Seventeen-year-old Doug Hanson, a brilliant loner, lives a vicarious life through his "best friend," a popular football star.

3. **Leavitt, Martine. *Heck Superhero*.** Asheville, NC: Front Street, 2004. 144p. $16.95. ISBN 1 886910 94 4. [fiction] MJ, CG with high interest for boys (*Booktalks and Beyond*, pages 28 to 30.) Thirteen-year-old Heck deals with survival on the street by moving back and forth between real and comic book worlds.

4. **Shelly, Mary. *Frankenstein*.** New York: Pocket Books, 2004. 352p. $3.95pa. ISBN 0 7434 8758 3. [fiction] S/A CG. Written in the first half of the 19th century, the novel traces a monster's creation and his fight for acceptance from his creator.

5. **Stevenson, Robert Louis. *The Strange Case of Doctor Jekyll & Mr. Hyde*.** Lincoln, NE: University of Nebraska Press, 1990. 158p. $15.00. ISBN 0 8032 4212 3. [fiction] JS/A, CG with high interest for boys. Originally published in 1886, the story focuses on Dr. Jekyll whose potion transforms him in to the evil Mr. Hyde.

ʊʒʊ

Sedgwick, Marcus. White Crow.
New York: Roaring Brook Press, 2011. 234p. $16.99.
ISBN 978 1 59643 594 0. [fiction] JS, CG with high interest for girls

Themes/Topics: Horror stories, good and evil, friendship, village life, suicide, East Anglia (England)

Summary/Description

The novel intertwines the 18th-century world of Dr. Barrieux and the village cleric and the 21st-century world of Rebecca, a summer visitor, and Ferelith, an abandoned and isolated teen resident of Winterfold. Dr. Barrieux and the cleric want to find what follows death. They lure victims into Barrieux's home, conduct a bizarre ceremony, behead them with a guillotine, and ask the remaining head what it sees. In the 20th-century story, Rebecca comes to Winterfold because her police inspector father, from whom she is emotionally estranged, is being investigated in the death of a girl involved in one of his cases. Ferelith develops a love/hate relationship with her, involves her in a series of "dare do" situations, and shackles her in crumbling Winterfold Hall. She releases Rebecca, who then returns to recover her locket, her father's gift to her. Ferelith follows her. They explore the house, which continues to crumble during a storm. The girls are trapped in the doctor's final grave. Ferelith commits suicide, but Rebecca is rescued by her father and they reconcile.

Value: Rebecca learns the importance of family trust and love.

Booktalk

Point to the cover and the question. Ask them to read it aloud. "What's on the other side of Death?" That is a question that people have explored for centuries. (*Ask for any answers to the question.*) In this story, an 18th-century doctor and cleric conduct some gory research, but never find the answer. In the 21st century, two girls take up where the doctor and cleric leave off. The first girl lives in the town of Winterfold. Her mother is insane. Her father deserted her. The second girl just moved to Winterfold. She has no friends, her boyfriend just dropped her, and her father is implicated in the death of a young girl. Two girls, nothing to lose. They start a game of "dare ya." The game becomes deadly serious when they dare to seek something that no one has ever seen, something like (*Point to the title and have them read it as they did the question.*) *The White Crow.*

Book trailers available @ http://www.youtube.com/
watch?v=zWokSDWlZAo

Read Aloud/Talkback

1. "1798, 8m, 26d.," pages 28 to 29. The cleric relates his vision of hell. *Talkback*: What does this passage reveal about the cleric?
2. "1798, 9m, 15d.," page 55. The cleric describes his journey to "Truth." *Talkback*: How does the cleric's story impact the novel?
3. "Catholic Day," page 57. Ferelith ponders choices. *Talkback*: What does Ferelith reveal about herself?
4. "The Warning," pages 77 to 80, beginning with "Then I told her . . ." and ending with the chapter. Ferelith tells the story of Winterfold Hall. *Talkback*: What, to you, is the most interesting part of Ferelith's story?
5. "Bones of You," pages 224 to 226. Ferelith and Rebecca climb into the chamber, and Ferelith commits suicide. *Talkback*: What was your reaction when you read this chapter? How did the author lead you to that reaction?

Author read aloud available @ http://www.youtube.com/watc h?feature=endscreen&v=9tRLcefm9II&NR=1

Study guide available @ http://www.orionbooks.co.uk/ media/files/marcus-sedgwick-teachers-notes-for-white-crow-and-revolver

Author interviews available @

http://www.youtube.com/watch?v=N0v-NWW8W0s&feature= endscreen&NR=1

http://www.youtube.com/watch?v=LbaaIkgehUs&feature=related

Related Works

1. **Bunce, Elizabeth C. *A Curse Dark as Gold*.** New York: Scholastic/ Arthur A. Levine Books, 2008. 422p. $17.99. ISBN-13: 978 0 439 89576 7. [fiction] JS, G (*Value-Packed Booktalks*, 2011, pages 137 to 139.) Two sisters inherit their father's supposedly haunted woolen mill and uncover a history of witch hunts, lies, and treachery.

2. **Gantos, Jack. *The Love Curse of the Rumbaughs*.** New York: Farrar, Straus and Giroux, 2006. 185p. $17.00. ISBN 0 374 33690 3. [fiction] JS, CG with high interest for girls (*Booktalks and Beyond*, 2007, pages 133 to 136.) The novel recounts Ivy's 7th to 17th year in which she discovers the family curse which she plans to pass on.

3. **Poe, Edgar Allan, and Michael McCurdy (illus.). *Tales of Terror*.** New York: Alfred A. Knopf, 2005. 89p. $15.95. ISBN 0 375 83305 6. [fiction] S/A, CG. This Poe collection, accompanied by a CD and illustrated with stark black-and-white pictures, includes "The Masque of the Red Death," "The Black Cat," "The Pit and the Pendulum," "The Tell-Tale Heart," "The Cask of Amontillado," and "The Fall of the House of Usher."

4. **Sedgwick, Marcus. *Revolver*.** New York: Roaring Brook Press, 2010. 204p. $16.99. ISBN-13: 978 1 59643 592 6. [fiction] JS, CG with high interest for boys (*Value-Packed Booktalks*, 2011, pages 97 to 100.) In this survival mystery that combines 3 time periods, 14-year-old Sig confronts terror and saves his sister and himself.

5. **Zevin, Gabrielle. *Elsewhere*.** New York: Farrar, Straus and Giroux, 2005. 277p. $19.95. ISBN 0 374 32091 8. [fiction] MJS, G (*Booktalks and Beyond*, 2007, pages 188 to 190.) Liz dies in a traffic accident shortly before her 16th birthday, begins her new life in Elsewhere, a world where she becomes younger each day, learns about her spirit, and has the option of returning to earth.

Fantasy

Fantasy books often pull characters into strange and different worlds that force them to discover new aspects of themselves. Sometimes, new traits or powers emerge and transform a person within his or her familiar world. As Ilsa Bick, the author of *Ashes*, points out, teenagers also must find new talents and powers as they experience the constant pressures of new experiences in the real world, and that is why teens so identify with and enjoy this genre.

New Worlds

Bick, Ilsa J. Ashes.

New York:Egmont, 2011. 465p. $17.99.
ISBN-13: 978 1 60684 175 4. [fiction] JS, CG with high interest for girls

Themes/Topics: Apocalyptic events, cancer, family, appreciation for life

Summary/Description

Seventeen-year-old Alex, whose parents died in an accident, is dying from a malignant brain tumor. While she is hiking in the Michigan woods, a nuclear explosion creates an electromagnetic pulse which wipes out every electronic device, kills millions of people, changes teenagers into flesh-eating zombies, and awakens Alzheimer patients. Alex begins a survival journey with Tom, a young army veteran, and eight-year-old Ellie, whose grandfather was killed by the pulse. As supplies dwindle and desperation grows, they need to figure out whom they can trust. After Ellie is stolen and Tom is wounded, Alex seeks help in the town of Rule, a male-dominated survival community with rigid rules and rationing. Although Alex values the safety and the feelings that she has for Chris, a member of one of Rule's old families, she leaves and discovers a horrific truth about the community.

Values: Alex, dealing with her imminent death and a cataclysmic event that changes humanity, learns the value of life and the meaning of family.

Booktalk

Seventeen-year-old Alex has nothing to lose. Her parents are dead. She has a malignant brain tumor. It isn't a question of if her life will end shortly but how. She takes her father's gun into the Michigan woods to decide. (*Ask what kind of story the group thinks this is. Wait for responses.*) She meets an old man and a little girl. Then the real story starts. An atomic explosion sets off an electromagnetic pulse that destroys every electronic device and billions of people. The old man dies immediately. Now, it is just Alex and the little girl, Ellie. Most teenagers turn into flesh-eating zombies. Some seem saved. Alex is one of them. But old people are panicked and want to kill any young person they see. Survivors steal from and kill other survivors. Alex and Ellie come very close to being victims, but Tom, a young veteran from Afghanistan, rescues them. The three form a family. (*Ask what kind of story the group expects now.*) The question of course is: "Will they all survive or end in *Ashes*?"

Book trailers available @

http://www.youtube.com/watch?v=2A8aLLRos9o
http://www.youtube.com/watch?v=mymXnUswLtc&feature= related

Read Aloud/Talkback

1. Chapter 12, pages 65 to 66. Ellie discovers Alex's possessions. *Talkback*: What does this chapter reveal about Alex?
2. Chapter 21, pages 120 to 125. Tom saves Alex. *Talkback*: Why is a confrontation like this important to the novel?
3. Chapter 27, pages 172 to 173, beginning with "I don't care . . ." and ending with "Wh-where?" Tom explains his belief in fate. *Talkback*: Do you agree with Tom? Why or why not?
4. Chapter 43, pages 289 to 295. Alex and Chris talk about survival. *Talkback*: What survival rules do you think the community makes? What rules would you make?

5. Chapter 69, pages 459 to 465. After her "escape," Alex realizes another Rule survival tactic. *Talkback*: What is your reaction to this conclusion?

Author interviews @

http://www.youtube.com/watch?v=CkPLp1n1AzA&feature=related

http://www.youtube.com/watch?v=0NSSLbwdPq0

http://www.youtube.com/watch?v=8y8ZEq06FZY

http://www.youtube.com/watch?v=4fuYfA011pg&feature=related

http://thebooksisterhood.blogspot.com/2011/12/interview-ilsajbick.html

Discussion guide @ http://www.egmontusa.com/files/2011/08/Ashes-Discussion-Guide.pdf

Related Works

1. **Armstrong, Jennifer, and Nancy Butcher. *Fire Us Trilogy*.** New York: HarperCollins. [fiction] MJS, CG (*Teen Genre Connections*, 2005, pages 204 to 210.)

    a. ***The Kindling: Book One***. 2002. 224p. $15.89. ISBN 0 06 029411 6. After an adult-killing virus sweeps the United States, seven orphans become a family.

    b. ***The Keepers of the Flame: Book Two***. 2002. 231p. $17.89. ISBN 0 06 029412 4. The 10 travelers from Book One discover a cult-like community.

    c. ***The Kiln: Book Three***. 2003. 193p. $15.99. ISBN 0 06 008050 7. The group discovers that the father of one of their members started the virus to purify the country.

2. **Collins, Suzanne. *Hunger Games Trilogy*.** New York: Scholastic Press. [fiction] JS, CG (*Value-Packed Booktalks*, 2011, pages 78 to 84.)

    a. ***The Hunger Games***. 2008. 374p. $17.99. ISBN-13: 978 0 439 02348 1. In this dystopian society, representatives from each conquered district send one girl and one boy between the ages of 12 and 18 to fight to the death.

    b. ***Catching Fire***. 2009. 400p. $17.99. ISBN-13: 978 0 439 02349 8. As the face of rebellion, Katniss and Peeta are put back in the games.

    c. ***Mockingjay***. 2010. 390p. $17.99. ISBN-13: 978 0 439 02351. Katniss joins the rebels and must choose the man she loves.

ᘓᘔ

Bodeen, S. A. The Gardener.

New York: Feiwel and Friends, 2010. 232p. $16.99.
ISBN 978 0 312 37016 9. [fiction] MJS, CG with high interest for boys

Themes/Topics: Experiments, single parent families, fathers

Summary/Description

Oversized, superintelligent high school junior, Mason, lives with his mother who works at a rest home for the mysterious TroDyn company. His missing father left a bedtime story on a DVD to remember him by. At the home, Mason discovers catatonic teenagers. The DVD story awakens one—a beautiful, fearful girl. Mason falls in love with her and helps her escape from a person she calls the gardener. The girl, Laila, is part of a TroDyn experiment that creates people who need only light to live, and Mason accepts that Laila needs the lab to live. The gardener, his father, conceived the experiment. Mason and his mother foil a plot to use the garden people as soldiers. Mother and son save the gardener's life. In the spring, Mason encounters an uprooted Laila on his college campus tour.

Values: Mason demonstrates loyalty, persistence, and responsibility.

Booktalk

Sixteen-year-old Mason has a football star size body and a mangled face. Does he feel sorry for himself? No, he scares away the bullies from the little guys. But this hero has some emotional baggage. Mom drinks too much. Dad left years ago. His only connection with Dad is a DVD in which a headless man reads a bedtime story called *The Blue Bunny*. Obviously, Dad wasn't too gifted in audio visuals. Mason watches the DVD again and again. What is the point? (*Wait for responses.*) One night, Mason thinks Mom is too drunk to do her job. He follows her to work. He expects old people, but meets four catatonic teenagers. One is gorgeous. When Mason plays his DVD, just to pass the time, she wakes up and runs. Now, what do you expect to happen? (*Wait for responses.*) Mason follows, and so do people who could kill them. Mason is in a new world full of superbullies. He has a beautiful stranger to save from enemies he doesn't know, in a place he doesn't understand, and ruled by a man he never met called *The Gardener*.

Book trailer available @ http://www.youtube.com/
watch?v=rLFYdCeEyPU

Read Aloud/Talkback

1. Chapter 9, pages 111 to 112, beginning with "Her expression . . ."
   and ending with "She stopped speaking . . ." Laila repeats her lab
   education. *Talkback*: What mood does Bodeen create in this passage?
2. Chapter 10, page 125, beginning with "Laila looked . . ." and ending
   with ". . . before she fell." Laila responds to Dr. Emerson. *Talkback*:
   How does this passage work with Read Aloud 1?
3. Chapter 11, page 133, beginning with the chapter and ending with
   ". . . who she is." Mason reacts to Laila's identity. *Talkback*: How do
   you feel about each of the three reactions?
4. Chapter 14, pages 169 to 171, beginning with "As the door
   opened . . ." and ending with "The Greenhouse." Eve shows Mason
   the Greenhouse. *Talkback*: Depict the scene in graphic art.
5. Chapter 16, pages 186 to 194. In this chapter, Mason's father explains
   his motivation for the experiment. *Talkback*: Is Mason's father a mad
   scientist or a wise future planner?

Author interview available @ http://www.youtube.com/
watch?v=EkjFiMCgkhU

Related Works

1. **Brooks, Kevin. *Being*.** New York: Scholastic Inc./Chicken House,
   2007. 336p. $16.99. ISBN 0 439 89973 7. [fiction] JS, CG with high
   interest for boys (*Genre Talks for Teens*, 2009, pages 85 to 87.) Sixteen-
   year-old Robert Smith, supposedly an orphan, undergoes a routine
   endoscopy, and is pursued by scientists and thugs when they discover
   that his body is not human, but a maze of wires and chemicals.
2. **Klass, David. *The Caretaker Trilogy*.** New York: Farrar, Straus
   and Giroux/Frances Foster Books, 2006. [fiction] JS, CG with high
   interest for boys

   a. ***Firestorm: Book I*.** 2006. 287p. $17.00. ISBN 0 374 32307 0.
      (*Genre Talks for Teens*, 2009, pages 119 to 120.) Jack Danielson, a
      brilliant, athletic, and good looking high school senior, discovers that
      he is a visitor from the future who is destined to save the planet.
   b. ***Whirlwind: Book II*.** 2008. 295p. $17.95. ISBN-13: 978 0 374 32308
      0. (*Genre Talks for Teens*, 2009, pages 120 to 123.) Jack and Gisco flee
      to the Amazon rain forest to rescue P.J. from the Dark Lord.

c. *Timelock: Book III*. 2009. 246p. $17.99. ISBN 978 0 374 32309 7. (*Value-Packed Booktalks*, 2011, pages 163 to 166.) Spirited away to the deserts of the future, Jack helps rescue his father from public execution and the earth from its final destruction.

3. **Patterson, James. *Maximum Ride: The Angel Experiment*.** New York: Little Brown and Co., 2005. 421p. $16.99. ISBN 0 316 15556 X. [fiction] JS, CG (*Booktalks and Beyond*, 2007, pages 181 to 183.) Fourteen-year-old Maximum Ride (Max) leads a six-member "family" made up of children genetically altered with Bird DNA and raised in cages

ʕ ʔ

Cabot, Meg. Abandon.

New York: Scholastic/Point, 2011. 320p. (The Abandon Trilogy) $17.99. ISBN 978 0 545 28410 3. [fiction] JS, G

Themes/Topics: Afterlife, Hades, Persephone myth, Florida Keys, high school, family secrets, coming of age

Summary/Description

Seventeen-year-old Pierce and her mother move back to Isla Huesos, the Island of Bones, in Key West, Florida. When Pierce was 15, she died for an hour after falling into the family swimming pool to rescue a bird. In the afterlife, she encountered John, a death deity, whom she had first met at her grandfather's funeral when she was seven. He tried to keep her with him, to protect her, but she escaped. She keeps his gift, a precious colored diamond that will protect her from the Furies. John appears periodically to keep Pierce from any trouble. As Pierce tries to adjust to the high school customs and pecking order as well as her eccentric family, she discovers that the island is the entrance to the Underworld and that her grandmother is a Fury trying to destroy her and John. John reappears and returns her to the underworld for protection. Pierce is determined to warn her family of their danger.

Value: Pierce is motivated by a concern for others and a sense of justice.

Booktalk

Ask someone to read pages 1 to 2 aloud. You just met Pierce Oliviera. Her father is one of the richest and most powerful men in the world.

Can his money and power help her? (*Wait for responses.*) No. She is facing Death, literally. He is handsome, caring, moody, and frightening. He pulls her to him and pushes her away at the same time. He is both the good and the bad boy. She is the modern day Persephone. Should she escape from Death and deal with the horrible secrets that can destroy her family or should she give in with *Abandon*?

Book trailers available @ http://www.youtube.com/watch?v=tl MLDeAl3Us&list=PL34028333C3E22F96&feature=plcp

Read Aloud/Talkback

1. Pages 16 to 21, beginning with the chapter and ending with ". . . bright blue sky." Pierce describes meeting John for the first time. *Talkback*: How does John represent what is waiting on the other side?
2. Pages 30 to 35, beginning with the chapter and ending with ". . . moment between us." Pierce meets John in the cemetery when she returns to the island. *Talkback*: Does John have a right to be angry? Why or why not?
3. Pages 60 to 63, beginning with "While I'd been speaking . . ." and ending with ". . . my clothes were." John gives Pierce the diamond. *Talkback*: How do you react to the gift?
4. Page 116, beginning with "By the time . . ." and ending with the chapter. Pierce realizes that each person must act to prevent evil. *Talkback*: Does this passage mark a change?
5. Pages 200 to 203, beginning with "Uncle Chris seemed to . . ." and ending with ". . . than I'd thought." Uncle Chris reacts to Pierce putting herself down. *Talkback*: Do you agree with Uncle Chris? Why is "Check yourself before you wreck yourself" important here?

Discussion guides available @

http://www.megcabot.com/abandon/discussion-guide.php
http://teacher.scholastic.com/products/tradebooks/discguide/ Abandon_DiscussionGuide.pdf

Author interviews available @

http://www.megcabot.com/abandon/faq.php
http://www.seventeen.com/entertainment/features/author-meg-cabot-abandon-interview
http://novelnovice.com/2011/04/27/exclusive-qa-with-abandon-author-meg-cabot/
http://www.youtube.com/watch?v=4QYyshDhx-Y

http://www.youtube.com/watch?v=5bknqOG6tJE

Playlist available @ http://www.megcabot.com/abandon/
playlist.php

Related Works

1. **Cabot, Meg.** *Underworld*. New York: Scholastic Inc., 2012. 336p. $17.99. ISBN-13: 978 0 545 28411 0. [fiction] JS, G. In this second book of the series, John Hayden holds Pierce in the underworld to "protect" her, in what may be her most serious threat.

2. **Creagh, Kelly.** *Nevermore*. New York: Simon & Schuster Children's Publishing/Atheneum Books for Young Readers, 2010. 560p. $17.99. ISBN 1 4424 0200 8. [fiction] JS, CG with high interest for girls. A popular cheerleader is paired in an English project with a moody reject and is drawn into a supernatural dream world.

3. **Leavitt, Martine.** *Keturah and Lord Death*. Asheville, NC: Front Street, 2006. 216p. $16.95. ISBN-13: 978 1 932425 29 1. [fiction] JS, G (*Genre Talks for Teens*, 2009, pages 178 to 180.) Sixteen-year-old Keturah Reeve slowly falls in love with Lord Death, because he gives her reprieves from death so that she can help others.

4. **O'Connor, George.** *Hades: Lord of the Dead*. New York: First Second/A Neal Porter Book, 2012. 77p. (Olympians) $9.99pa. ISBN 978 1 59643 434 9. [graphic] MJS, CG. In this retelling of Persephone's story, O'Connor raises the question about whether or not Persephone wanted to stay in the underworld or return to earth. The volume includes an Author's Note, "Greek Notes" which explain the panels, character profiles of the main characters, discussion questions, bibliography, and recommended reading list for young and old readers. *Abandon* appears on the list for older readers.

5. **Stoker, Bram.** *Dracula*. New York: Barnes and Noble Classics, 1992. 404p. $6.98pa. ISBN 0 88029 901 0. JS/A, CG with high interest for boys. Originally published in 1897, this gothic horror story tells of Count Dracula's search for new blood.

❧❧

Hinwood, Christine. The Returning.
New York: Dial Books/Penguin Group, 2011. 302p. $17.99.
ISBN 978 0 8037 3528 6. [fiction] JS, CG with high interest for girls

Themes/Topics: War, village life, prejudice, interpersonal relations, coming of age

Summary/Description

After six years of war between the Uplanders and Downlanders, 19-year-old Cam returns to his village. Since he is the only survivor from this tiny town, the citizens suspect him of treason. Cam leaves and seeks the Uplander lord who maimed him in battle but spared his life. Cam becomes an advisor to the lord and helps him marry the girl to whom Cam was once betrothed. In Cam's journey, he meets and falls in love with the war orphan Diido who has been abused and enslaved. By the end of the story, the Uplander and Downlander populations are joined by the young lord's marriage. Cam, a valued advisor to the royal family of a new united kingdom, is accepted by the town and promises to be welcomed back to his family.

Values: Cam, Graceful, Lord Gyaar, Pin, and Diido discover that friendship and love grow from generosity and personal choices rather than traditions, nationality, or blood.

Booktalk

"After" is an interesting word, what does it mean? (*Wait for responses. Point out that it usually marks time or status. It might be used in "happily ever after."*) This story is not a "happily ever after" story. It's an after the war story. Nineteen-year-old Cam spent six years in war between the Downlanders and the Uplanders. His Downlander town thinks he is a traitor. He is the only fighter from his village to return home. Cam looks more like an Uplander than a Downlander, and he does have a haunting secret. The Uplander who took his arm saved his life. Cam thinks about him all the time. Does he feel a special bond? Does he want to find out why the man saved him? He isn't sure, but his questions begin his journey to return to the people he fought, the people he never really knew. Return is an interesting word too. What do you associate with it? (*Wait for responses.*) Will Cam be going forward or back? And which arrival—coming home after the war or the journey to his enemy—will prove to be *The Returning*?

Read Aloud/Talkback

1. "Cam's War," pages 109 to 111, beginning with ". . . When Layne Golrance . . ." and ending with ". . . as far as he could." Cam remembers his first war kill. *Talkback*: What does this experience reveal about Cam?

2. "Diido's Revenge," pages 121 to 123, beginning with the chapter and ending with ". . . especially to her." Diido is thrown out of her

home, and the wise woman questions her. *Talkback*: What does this passage show you about Diido's situation?

3. "Diido's Revenge," pages 133 to 134, beginning with "Yah! . . . " and ending with the chapter. *Talkback*: How does this passage tie to Read Aloud 2? Does your opinion of her change?

4. "Gyaar's War," pages 152 to 153, beginning with "As Gyaar grew out . . ." and ending with ". . . same bloody battlefield" *Talkback*: How do the father, Gyodan, and Gyaar differ in their views of war? How does this event put Gyaar in conflict with himself?

5. "Handfast," pages 239 to 240, beginning with "It might have been . . ." and ending with ". . . that it was real." *Talkback*: How is this scene a turning point in the story?

Discussion guide and author interview available @
http://us.penguingroup.com/static/images/yr/pdf/
TheReturningDG.pdf

Related Works

1. **Bell, Hilari. *The Goblin Wood*.** New York: HarperCollins Publishers, 2003. 294p. $17.99. ISBN 0 06 051372 1. [fiction] MJS, CG (*Booktalks and Beyond*, 2007, pages 150 to 152.) Two enemies find love and save the goblins from extinction.

2. **Blackman, Malorie. *Naughts & Crosses*.** New York: Simon & Schuster Books for Young Readers, 2005. 387p. $15.95. ISBN 1 4169 0016 0. [fiction] JS, CG (*Booktalks and Beyond*, 2007, pages 16 to 19.) In a fantasy world torn by conflict, a light-skinned naught and dark-skinned cross become friends and fall tragically in love.

3. **Hale, Shannon. *Book of a Thousand Days*.** New York: Bloomsbury, 2007. 306p. $17.95. ISBN-13: 978 1 599990 051 3. [fiction] JS, G (*Genre Talks for Teens*, 2009, pages 194 to 197.) Fifteen-year-old Dashti and her 16-year-old mistress are walled into a tower for 7 years because the mistress wants to choose her own suitor. Dashti proves to be the more competent and loyal of the two.

4. **Murdock, Catherine Gilbert. *Princess Ben*.** Boston, MA: Houghton Mifflin Co., 2008. 344p. $16.00. ISBN-13: 978 0 618 95971 6. [fiction] JS, G (*Value-Packed Booktalks*, 2011, pages 152 to 154.) Fifteen-year-old Princess Ben transforms from a difficult, overweight, and slothful little girl to a worthy regent who saves her country from war and finds personal happiness.

5. **Reeve, Philip. *Here Lies Arthur*.** New York: Scholastic Press, 2008. 339p. $16.99. ISBN-13: 978 0 545 09334 7. [fiction] JS, CG (*Value-Packed Booktalks*, 2011, pages 159 to 161.) The daughter of

a dead slave woman is saved from death by King Arthur's Bard and learns that storytellers define heroism.

✂✂

Meyer, Marissa. **Cinder.**

New York: Feiwel and Friends, 2012. 390p. (The Lunar Chronicles) $17.99.
ISBN 978 0 312 64189 4. [fiction] JS, G

Themes/Topics: Dysfunctional families, fairy tales, futuristic societies, humanity, romance, mystery

Summary/Description

In this futuristic "Cinderella," Cinder, a teen cyborg and outstanding mechanic, financially supports her stepmother and two stepsisters. Prince Kaito asks her to repair an android which contains information about Princess Selene, a lunar princess supposedly killed in childhood. A plague has infested the kingdom. The king dies. The evil Lunar queen, who has an antidote for the disease, is forcing the prince into marriage. Cinder's stepmother accuses Cinder of causing her stepsister to contract the plague and volunteers Cinder for vaccine research. The doctor discovers that Cinder is Lunar and immune. The prince invites Cinder to the ball where the Lunar queen recognizes her as Princess Selene whom she tried to kill. The prince is forced to turn Cinder over to the queen, but the doctor visits Cinder in jail, helps her escape, and invites her to join him in Africa where he hopes to develop an antidote for the plague.

Values: Cinder acts with courage, loyalty, and love in the face of cowardice and rejection.

Booktalk

How many here know the story of Cinderella? (*Ask someone to tell it. Then, hold up the book.*) This is a Cinderella story with an attitude. (*Point to the cover.*) Cinder doesn't sweep and clean. She is a super mechanic. She isn't blond and wispy. She is a cyborg, and considered a "technological mistake" stocked with wires and interfaces instead of organs. And the prince? He needs Cinder to repair an android before the big ball. There *is* a cruel stepmother. After her real daughter is stricken by a mysterious plague, she blames Cinder and volunteers her for plague research. Is there room for romance and adventure? (*Wait for responses.*) Yes, the prince is interested in Cinder, but an evil Lunar queen tells him "me first." There is plenty of adventure. The laboratory doctor discovers that this "technological mistake" (*Point to the Cover.*) is someone people will kill for. Is he her godfather? Since the prince is busy saving himself and his kingdom, Cinder's "happily ever after" seems all up to *Cinder.*

Alternate booktalk and trailer available @ http://asuen .wordpress.com/2012/01/26/cinder-book-giveaway/

Alternate booktalk available @ http://www.geneva.lib.il.us/ teen/node/258

Read Aloud/Talkback

1. Chapter 4, pages 43 to 44, beginning with "The lingering moon . . ." and ending with ". . . in the ashes." Cinder reflects on the lunar culture and the royal family. *Talkback*: What details characterize Queen Levana as evil and what details set the stage for Cinder's identity reveal?

2. Chapter 8, pages 76 to 82, beginning with the chapter and ending with "Ratio: 36.28%." Cinder experiences her recurring nightmare and the scan which assesses her humanity. *Talkbalk*: What do both the nightmare and the scan reveal?

3. Chapter 19, page 172, beginning with "The lines around . . ." and ending with ". . . telling the truth." The doctor explains Lunar beauty. *Talkback*: Does this science fiction beauty have any relationship to Cinder and to our world today?

4. Chapter 22, pages 204 to 205, beginning with "The chanting stopped . . ." and ending with ". . . brainwashed *her.*" Cinder experiences the queen's ability to brainwash. *Talkback*: Is this scene simply a fantasy event or does it apply in today's world?

5. Chapter 25, pages 237 to 240, beginning with "I've been doing . . ." and ending with ". . . losing your mind." The doctor explains the invention of Cinder's adopted father. *Talkback*: How is controlling personal power critical to growing up or moving into a culture?

Discussion questions available @ http://marissameyer.live journal.com/tag/discussion

Background information available @ http://www.mariss ameyer.com/blog/

Related art available @ http://thelunarchronicles .deviantart.com/

Author interviews and guest posts available @ http://www.marissameyer.com/media-type/interviews/ http://www.voya.com/2013/01/13/wouldnt-you-like-to-know- marissa-meyer/

Related Works

1. **Bunce, Elizabeth C. *A Curse Dark as Gold*.** New York: Scholastic/ Arthur A. Levine Books, 2008. 422p. $17.99. ISBN-13: 978 0 439 89576 7. [fiction] JS, G (*Value-Packed Booktalks*, 2011, pages 137 to 139.) In this "Rumpelstiltskin mystery" two sisters inherit the family woolen mill entangled with ghosts, debt, and family guilt.

2. **Haddix, Margaret Peterson. *Just Ella*.** New York: Simon & Schuster Books for Young Children, 1999. 185p. $17.00. ISBN 0 689 82186 7. [fiction] MJS, G. In this feminist retelling of "Cinderella," 15-year-old Ella decides to control her own life after realizing that the court centers on appearance and empty ceremony.

3. **Murdock, Catherine Gilbert. *Princess Ben*.** Boston, MA: Houghton Mifflin Co., 2008. 344p. $16.00. ISBN-13: 978 0 618 95971 6. [fiction] JS, G (*Value-Packed Booktalks*, 2011, pages 152 to 154.) Fifteen-year-old Princess Ben transforms from a difficult, overweight, and slothful little girl to a worthy regent who controls her personal magic, saves her country from war, and finds happiness.

4. **Napoli, Donna Jo. *Beast*.** New York: Atheneum Books for Young Readers, 2000. 260p. $17.00. ISBN 0 689 83589 2. [fiction] JS, CG (*Teen Genre Connections*, 2005, pages 171 to 173.) In this retelling of "The Beauty and the Beast," a young Persian prince offends the gods, is turned into a lion, and makes his way back to humanity through love.

5. **Napoli, Donna Jo. *Crazy Jack*.** New York: Delacorte Press, 1999. 134p. $15.95. ISBN 0 385 32627 0. [fiction] MJS, CG (*Booktalks and More*, 2003, pages 107 to 109.) Jack, a visionary, lives by the advice for a full life that his father forgot.

ℭℨℨ

Napoli, Donna Jo. The Wager.

New York: Henry Holt and Co., 2010. 259p. $16.99.
ISBN 978 0 8050 8781 9. [fiction] JS, CG

Themes/Topics: Conduct of life, wagers, aristocracy, pride and vanity, devil, Don Juan, Sicily (1016–1194)

Summary/Description

Vain and selfish 19-year-old Don Giovanni loses his estate when a tidal wave devastates Messina. Having squandered his money on luxuries, he now wanders as a menial laborer and beggar. The devil, presenting himself as a mysterious stranger, offers him a magic bag that produces unlimited wealth if Giovanni will not change his clothes or bathe for three years, three months, and three days. Losing the wager means forfeiting his soul. Giovanni accepts. His appearance deteriorates. He confronts social isolation, depression, and disease. The street beggars whom he employs help him overcome the devil's tricks. Giovanni eventually buys a villa, but shares his lands and money with his servants and the poor. His example inspires others to do the same. He wins the bet and the hand of a princess who, in the persona of a young, male artist, recognizes his inner strength. Her portrait of Giovanni shows that he has learned about suffering, and her yellow wedding dress symbolizes their hope.

Values: Don Giovanni learns the power of love, cleanliness, and generosity.

Booktalk

Show a bottle of shampoo and a bar of soap. Ask the group how important they think those two items are.

Don Giovanni is 19, handsome, and rich. Everyone works for him and obeys him.

Then, a tidal wave washes away his world. He must start over. When times are good, he is a menial worker. When times are bad, he is a beggar. Always, he is friendless. A mysterious stranger makes him an offer of unlimited wealth under one condition—Don Giovanni cannot change his clothes or bathe for three years, three months, and three days. If he does change clothes or bathe, he loses his soul. Of course, the stranger is the devil. Don Giovanni believes that he is smarter than the devil. How hard can it be to give up soap and new clothes for such a short time? (*Wait for responses.*) Giovanni discovers filth's power when he dares to take on *The Wager*.

Read Aloud/Talkback

1. Chapter 7, pages 66 to 69, beginning with "He laughed again." and ending with "Your soul." The devil presents the wager. *Talkback:* What is the Devil's trap?
2. Chapter 11, pages 118 to 123, beginning with the chapter and ending with ". . . could find." Don Giovanni reflects on the world from which he is isolated. *Talkback:* What has Giovanni learned? How has he changed?
3. Chapter 14, pages 167 to 169, beginning with "A bark came." and ending with the chapter. Giovanni ponders the significance of cleanliness. *Talkback:* Do you agree with Giovanni's conclusions?

4. Chapter 15, pages 175 to 183, beginning with "Don Giovanni . . ." and ending with "Shall we begin?" Giovanni meets the princess disguised as an artist. *Talkback*: What does the conversation reveal about both speakers?

5. Chapter 18, page 226, beginning with "A hair ball . . ." and ending with ". . . eye of a man." Giovanni sees his humanity in the portrait that the artist presents. *Talkback*: Why is Giovanni grateful for this portrait?

Author interviews available @ http://www.donnajonapoli.com/

Related Works

1. **Alexander, Lloyd. *The Golden Dream of Carlo Chuchio*.** New York: Henry Holt and Co., 2007. 320p. $16.95. ISBN-13: 978 0 8050 8333 0. [fiction] JS, CG with high interest for boys (*Genre Talks for Teens*, 2009, pages 123 to 126.) Orphaned and romantic Carlo Chuchio seeks a treasure, but finds true value in his journey and love of a slave girl.

2. **Aronson, Marc. *Race: A History Beyond Black and White*.** New York: Atheneum Books for Young Readers/Ginee Seo books, 2007. 322p. $18.99. ISBN-13: 978 0 689 86554 1. [nonfiction] S, CG. Explaining race through the "us" versus "strangers" thinking of the ancient world, Aronson traces the history of man-persecuting-man from the survival instincts of primitive tribes to a multicultural modern day world in which the them/us phenomena is experienced through possessions.

3. **Coelho, Paulo, and Alan R. Clarke (trans.). *The Alchemist*.** San Francisco, CA: HarperSanFrancisco, 1998. 174p. $13.00pa. ISBN 0 06 250218 2 [fiction] JS/A, CG. In this fairy tale-like novel, Santiago, a young shepherd, seeks his personal calling, learns about the world and himself, finds love, and discovers his riches and treasure at home.

4. **García, Laura Gallego. *The Legend of the Wandering King*.** New York: Arthur A. Levine Books, 2005. 213p. $16.95. ISBN 0 439 58556 2. [fiction] JS, CG. A proud prince learns to be a great poet and a responsible adult by making up for an injustice driven by his jealousy of another poet.

5. **Napoli, Donna Jo. *Beast*.** New York: Atheneum Books for Young Readers, 2000. 260p. $17.00. ISBN 0 689 83589 2 [fiction] JS (*Teen Genre Connections*, 2005, pages 171 to 173.) In this retelling of "The Beauty and the Beast," Orasmyn, a young Persian prince who offends the gods, is turned into a lion so that he may learn suffering and make his way back to humanity through love.

ℭ℥℩

Scott, Inara. **Delcroix Academy: The Candidates.**

New York: Hyperion, 2010. 293p. $16.99.
ISBN 978 142311636 1. [fiction] J, G
(Previously published as *The Candidates*)

Themes/Topics: Private school, special talent, covert
organizations, super power, friendship, trust

Summary/Description

Fourteen-year-old Dancia, who tries not to be noticed, reveals her
supernatural power when she saves her grandmother from a shooter
and is offered a scholarship to the Delcroix Academy for the exception-
ally talented. She becomes torn between two conflicting student friends:
Cameron, a charismatic establishment student, and Jack, a rebel. Jack
claims he is being followed and shows Dancia evidence that Cameron is
a Watcher assigned to her. Cameron explains his role in a world organization and the powers that Dancia and Jack hold. Jack steals books from the
school's secret library and pleads with Dancia to flee with him. Dancia saves
Jack from his pursuers, but stays at Delcroix with Cameron who persuades
her that he cares for her and that his organization works for the good.

Value: Dancia learns to value her talent and trust her
judgments about people.

Booktalk

Fourteen-year-old Dancia lives under the radar. She gets Bs and wears
beige. Any friends she makes, she hurts, big time, so she doesn't make
any. One day, she can't hide. (*Ask a member of the group to read the
Prologue on page 1.*) That familiar tingle enables Dancia to save Grandma
and everyone else. So what do you think happens? (*Wait for responses.*)
Right! Dancia is noticed. Delcroix Academy, the most exclusive school in
town, recruits her with full scholarship, an opportunity that she and her
grandmother never could afford. She attends classes with the talented
children of the most powerful people in the world. Dancia is no stand
out at Delcroix. But she does draw the attention of two other students:
one is the most popular and gorgeous boy in school and the other is a
moody, homeless rebel who could destroy it. Who do you think is the
more dangerous? (*Wait for responses.*) That is what Dancia is trying to

figure out. Is Delcroix an academy or something much more powerful and sinister? Dancia is learning the answers the hard way as one of *The Candidates*.

Book trailers available @

http://www.youtube.com/watch?v=ZIpkhaQ5fkU&feature=related

http://www.youtube.com/watch?v=l_N5OqP-lPg

Read Aloud/Talkback

1. Chapter 7, pages 61 to 62, beginning with "I'm not sure . . ." and ending with the chapter. Dancia reflects on reasons not to make friends. *Talkback*: Dancia has two reasons not to make friends. Do you agree with her? Why?

2. Chapter 16, pages 145 to 147, beginning with "Grandma turned . . ." and ending with the chapter. Grandmother gives Dancia advice about not trusting appearances and following her instincts. *Talkback*: Is the talk with Grandma valuable?

3. Chapter 22, pages 201 to 203, beginning with "Jack sat back . . ." and ending with ". . . could I control that?" Jack and Dancia discuss her powers. *Talkback*: What challenge does this passage present to all teenagers?

4. Chapter 23, pages 213 to 214, beginning with "I just couldn't . . ." and ending with the chapter. Grandma reacts to Dancia wanting to save Jack. *Talkback*: How would you interpret Grandma's reaction?

5. Chapter 27, pages 253 to 259, beginning with "He began to pace . . ." and ending with ". . . would have smiled." Cameron explains Dancia's talent in relation to the usual human talent. *Talkback*: What are the implications of Cam's power explanation?

Discussion guide available @ http://novelnovice .com/2010/12/22/study-guide-for-delcroix-academy-the-candidates-by-inara-scott/

Author interviews available @

http://www.inarascott.com/about-inara/faqs/

http://blkosiner.blogspot.com/2010/12/author-interview-monday-inara-scott.html

http://thebookbutterfly.com/2010/08/ten-tantalizing-questions-for-inara.html

http://foreveryoungadult.com/2010/08/18/between-two-lockers-with-inara-scott/

http://www.authorsnow.com/author-spotlight-inara-scott-
delcroix-academy-the-candidates-giveaway-alert-now-
%E2%80%93–083110/

http://chickloveslit.com/2012/05/sophomore-reading-challenge-
feature-inara-scott.html

http://www.ourtimeinjuvie.com/author-spotlight/author-spotlight-
interview-with-inara-scott-2

http://www.yareads.com/author-interview-inara-scott/author-
interviews/3240

http://fayeflamereviews.blogspot.com/2010/08/author-interview-
inara-scott-giveaway.html

http://cynthialeitichsmith.blogspot.com/2010/09/new-voice-inara-
scott-on-delcroix.html

Related Works

1. **Kim, Susan, Laurence Klavan, Faith Erin Hicks (art) and Hilary Sycamore (color).** *Brain Camp*. New York: First Second, 2010. 151p. $16.99. ISBN 978 1 59643 366 3. [graphic] MJ, CG. Two "losers" are sent to a camp that promises to improve their achievement and attitudes, but they discover a lethal breeding ground for space aliens.

2. **Klass, David.** *Firestorm: Book I*. New York: Farrar, Straus and Giroux/Frances Foster Books, 2006, 287p. (The Caretaker Trilogy) $17.00. ISBN 0 374 32307 0. [fiction] JS, CG with high interest for boys (*Genre Talks for Teens*, 2009, pages 119 to 120.) Jack Danielson, a brilliant, athletic, and good-looking high school senior, discovers that he is a visitor from the future charged to save the earth.

3. **Lubar, David.** *Hidden Talents*. New York: Tom Doherty Associates, 1999. 213p. $16.95. ISBN 0 312 86646 1. MJ, CG with high interest for boys (*Booktalks and More*, 2003, pages 63 to 65.) Thirteen-year-old Martin Anderson channels his classmates' paranormal talents to positive efforts and defeats the school bullies.

4. **Sala, Richard.** *Cat Burglar Black*. New York: First Second, 2009. 126p. $16.99. ISBN-13: 978 1 59643 144 7. [graphic] MJS, G. When K. Westree is sent to a mysterious boarding school owned by an aunt she never knew, she is drawn into a secret society and mysteries surrounding her father.

5. **Scott, Inara.** *The Marked*. New York: Hyperion Books for Children, 2012. 320p. (Delcroix Academy Series #2) $10.40. ISBN-13: 978 142311637 0. [fiction] J, G. Dedicated to using her powers for good, Dancia continues to question the Academy.

✿✿

Wooding, Chris. Malice.

New York: Scholastic Press, 2009. 384p. $14.99.
ISBN-13: 978 0 545 16043 8. [fiction/graphic]
MJS, CG with high interest for boys

Themes/Topics for Both Volumes: Friendship,
coming of age, real world versus literary world

Summary/Description

In a combination of text and graphics, Wooding relates the adventures of Kady and Seth in the dark fantasy world of Malice. When their friend Luke disappears, Seth follows him to Malice and aligns himself with Justin. Kady follows Seth. Tall Jake oversees the traps and threats in Malice where people die by having time sucked out of them. Their essence is preserved in a crystal form and used to create mechanical monsters. Although white tickets allow them to escape Malice, some choose to stay in the challenges of their new world. The disjointed experiences of teens trapped in Malice appear in graphic novels which then become blank. If the teens return to the real world, they cannot remember their experiences.

Values: Seth and Kady illustrate the importance of friendship, heroism, and selflessness.

Booktalk

Luke, Seth, and Kady are best friends. Luke disappears after he performs a ritual and repeats the command: "Tall Jake take me away." He reappears, his picture anyway, in a graphic. (*Show the first graphic section as you are speaking.*) The pictures form chaotic scenes, not stories. Is Luke dead? Then, both the pictures and words disappear. The proprietor of Black Dice Comics, Icarus Scratch, may know where Luke is, but he refuses to tell. Seth performs the ritual. He disappears too. Kady follows the strange and threatening Icarus Scratch to find them. Scratch is linked to danger, deceit, the mysterious voice of Tall Jake, and a monstrous woman named Miss Benjamin. He seems to be the doorman for this treacherous graphic world (*Quickly leaf through some of the graphic sections that follow the first section.*) full of horrible creatures and unpredictable consequences—the world of (*Point to the cover and encourage a group response.*) *Malice.*

Book trailer, character, and author information @
http://www.scholastic.com/malice/
http://www.scholastic.com/browse/video.jsp?pID=164014
    9541&bcpid=1640149541&bclid=57826465001&bct
    id=57906331001
Book trailers for the duology available @ http://www.you
    tube.com/watch?v=x-wT7vl_0lE

Read Aloud/ Talkback

1. "Drawing Blanks," page 37, beginning with "They didn't seem . . ."
    and ending with ". . . one of them." The passage explains how Seth
    sees his adults. *Talkback*: Do you agree with Seth?
2. "London," pages 56 to 60, beginning and ending with Section 2.
    Seth and Kady meet the proprietor of Black Dice Comics. *Talkback*:
    How does Wooding make the proprietor sinister? Create your own
    sinister character with words and drawings.
3. "A Name for the Cat," pages 152 to 159, beginning with Section
    3 and ending with the chapter. Kady views the meeting between
    Icarus Scratch and Miss Benjamin. *Talkback*: What fairy tale plots
    and characters does this section remind you of?
4. "Into the Dark," pages 231 to 232, beginning with "You know
    there's . . ." and ending with Section 2. Seth explains the basis
    of Malice. *Talkback*: According to Seth, what is the power of the
    writer?
5. "Three Are Divided," page 362, beginning with "Malice was terrify-
    ing . . ." and ending with Section 2. Seth reflects on why he wants to
    stay in Malice. *Talkback*: What is your reaction to Seth's decision and
    his reasons for it?

Author explanation available @ http://www.chriswooding
    .com/the-books/malice/
Author interviews available @ http://www.youtube.com/
    watch?v=Ru6cqCfReGE

ஜ

Wooding, Chris. Havoc.
New York: Scholastic Press, 2010. 400p. $16.99.
ISBN 978 0 545 16045 2. [fiction, graphic]
MJS, CG with high interest for boys

Summary/Description

Retrieving the Shard from the real world, Seth involves high-achieving Alicia, who knows about Malice but is too timid to join Seth in his search for reentry. Kady and Justin, still in Malice, contact Havoc and discover that Kady was Havoc's organizer. Kady challenges the new leader's plans, and with the returning Seth's help escapes death. Reacting to a message from Seth, Alicia follows Scratch and discovers Grendel, the misshapen author of Malice. Kady, Justin, and Seth find the Queen of Cats and align themselves with an army to defeat Tall Jake who hopes to take over the real world. He escapes. Kady, Justin, and Seth follow him to the Scratch estate and the final confrontation. To defend Alicia, Grendel destroys his characters and pulls Scratch into Malice with him. Kady returns to the real world. Justin and Seth return to Malice.

Values: Kady, Justin, and Seth illustrate the values of *Malice* with the addition of independence.

Booktalk

Hold up "Malice." In this crazy and dangerous world with all new rules, Seth, Kady, and Justin have managed to stay alive. Seth has returned to the real world to retrieve The Shard, the weapon that can destroy Tall Jake. Do you think that Tall Jake will let that happen? (*Wait for responses.*) No Way. He controls *Malice*, and now he has bigger plans. The real world. He has more and more readers every day. What does that mean? (*Wait for responses.*) The adults can't figure out why their children are missing or why their returning children can't tell where they have been. They can never learn about *Malice*. Tall Jake has a clear shot at world dominance. But Seth, Justin, Kady, and a new but reluctant ally, the beautiful and brainy Alicia, are against him. What can four teenagers do against a supernatural power? They can create (*Point to the cover and encourage a group response.*) *Havoc*.

Read Aloud/Talkback

1. "Number 6," Section 3, pages 138 to 139. Seth leaves a message for Alicia. *Talkback*: If you were Alicia, how would you view Seth's message?
2. "Crouch Hollow," Section 3, pages 220 to 222. Alicia hears the conversation of Tall Jake, Scratch, and Miss Benjamin. *Talkback*: What parts of this passage produce horror? What parts produce humor? Is there a real-life message?

3. "Three of Six," Section 2, pages 284 to 292. The Queen of Cats and Lack discuss the power of belief. *Talkback*: Do you agree with the statements concerning faith? Why or why not?

4. "The Dark Before the Dawn," Section 2, pages 310 to 311, beginning with "You're asking me . . ." and ending with ". . . friends were waiting." Seth decides to accept pain. *Talkback*: Why is Seth's decision an important one?

5. "Back to the Attic," Section1, page 363, beginning with "What if . . ." and ending with ". . . waiting for him." Seth ponders the effects of destroying Tall Jake. *Talkback*: How do you view Seth's doubts? Is he a Peter Pan?

Author explanation @ http://www.chriswooding.com/
the-books/havoc/

Related Works

1. **Funke, Cornelia. *Inkheart Trilogy*.** New York: Scholastic Press/ The Chicken House, 2003. [fiction] MJS, CG.

    a. ***Inkheart***. 2003. 544p. $19.95. ISBN 0 439 53164 0. The mysterious Dustfinger arrives and pulls Meggie and her family into Inkheart.

    b. ***Inkspell***. 2005. 672p. $19.99. ISBN 0 439 55400 4. Dustfinger returns to Inkheart through Orpheus who both reads and writes characters into different worlds and Fenoglio, the original writer, has lost control of his characters.

    c. ***Inkdeath***. 2008. 704p. $24.99. ISBN-13: 978 0 439 86628 6. This final volume sees the deciding battle of good and evil and Meggie's new love.

2. **Smith, Alexander Gordon. *Lockdown: Escape from Furnace*.** New York: Farrar, Straus and Giroux, 2009. 273p. $14.99. ISBN 978 0 374 32491 9. [fiction] MJS, CG with high interest for boys (*Value-Packed Booktalks*, 2011, pages 86 to 88.) Alex Sawyer is sentenced to Furnace Penitentiary, a mile below the earth's surface, and confronts a demonic warden, human-like creatures in gas masks, and giants in black suits who use terror, guns, hard labor, gang violence, howling beasts, and syringes to terrify and subdue the inmates.

3. **Wooding, Chris. *Poison*.** New York: Orchard Books, 2003. 273p. $16.99. ISBN 0 439 75570 0. [fiction] JS, CG with high interest for girls (*Booktalks and Beyond*, 2007, pages 176 to 178.) When the phaeries steal her baby sister, Azalia, 16-year-old Poison sets out to bring her back and experiences a conflict-fraught journey that culminates in her becoming the master writer of the future.

New Powers

ഗ‌ഇ

Billingsley, Franny. Chime.

New York: Penguin Group Inc./Dial Books, 2011. 361p. $17.99.
ISBN 978 0 8037 3552 1. [fiction] JS, G

Themes/Topics: Twins, sisters, fiction, guilt, self-perception, stepmothers, witches, supernatural

Summary/Description

Seventeen-year-old Briony Larkin believes she is an evil witch responsible for her twin sister's strange behavior, her minister father's absence from the house, the flood and fire in their home, and her stepmother's illness and death. Twenty-two-year-old Eldric comes to the town with his father who plans to drain the swamp. As revenge against the project, Boggy Mun, the swamp spirit, launches the swamp cough on the town. In this early 20th-century supernatural setting, Briony, who has second sight and receives messages from the swamp voices, can save her sister from the disease if she prevents the swamp project by Halloween night. As she proceeds with her mission, she and Eldric fall in love, and she protects him from her rival, a Dark Muse, who is draining his talent and life. Briony finally recalls that she poisoned her stepmother, but Eldric, in the witchcraft trial that ensues, establishes, with the help of Briony's sister and father, that the stepmother was a Dark Muse who was feeding on the father and the twins. The trial evidence establishes that Briony is not a witch but the town's new Chime Child, a good person, who with second sight protects them from evil spirits.

Values: The twins and Eldric learn to trust each other, themselves, and their talents.

Booktalk

Do you think that a witch would get along with a minister's daughter? (*Wait for responses.*) Seventeen-year-old Briony is both a minister's daughter and a witch. She hates herself. She has seen her jealousy and anger produce floods, fire, and death. She has the second sight and hears the swamp voices. Staying away from the people whom she loves is the best gift she can give them. Her stepmother promises to keep

Briony's secret. She helps her gain self-control, but the stepmother dies. No one will guide and protect her now. Briony knows what will happen to someone even suspected of being a witch. She sees an innocent girl hanged. But if Briony is evil, shouldn't she die? A handsome stranger comes to town. Can he save her, or is he a spy who will expose her secret? Unfortunately, she may love him. What does that mean? (*Wait for responses*.) Then, a rival for his affections appears. Will Briony's powers destroy them both? The answer is in the sounds of the *Chime*.

Alternative booktalk @ http://www.youtube.com/watch?v=mNZau-rZ8Z0

Read Aloud/Talkback

1. Chapter 1, pages 1 and 2. Briony believes she is evil. *Talkback*: Does Briony's plea reveal her to be evil?
2. Chapter 7, pages 63 to 64, beginning with "Father had prepared . . ." and ending with ". . . his job." Briony reflects on his father's sermon. *Talkback*: Do you agree with Briony? Why or why not?
3. Chapter 10, page 113, beginning with "The day had turned . . ." and ending with the chapter. Briony longs for someone to care for her. *Talkback*: What is your reaction to Briony's reflection on life and caring?
4. Chapter 14, pages 151 to 153, beginning with "Then a marvelous . . ." and ending with ". . . a girl with red hair." Briony reacts to the hanging. *Talkback*: Based on this passage, what kind of Chime Child will Briony be?
5. Chapter 32, pages 359 to 361, beginning with "I lay my hand . . ." and ending with the novel. Briony and Eldric express their love, and Briony believes she is loveable. *Talkback*: Describe the relationship between Briony and Eldric. Compare this Read Aloud to Read Aloud 1.

Author read aloud available @ http://www.youtube.com/watch?v=mIhjAiewI9Y&feature=related

Author acceptance speech for Horn Book Award available @ http://www.youtube.com/watch?v=58TVdAorhHs&feature=related

Author interviews available @

http://www.publishersweekly.com/pw/by-topic/authors/interviews/article/46266-q—a-with-franny-billingsley.html

http://thebrokenplaces.wordpress.com/2011/08/08/interview-with-franny-billingsley-author-of-chime/

http://enchantedinkpot.livejournal.com/85871.html
http://www.goodreads.com/author_blog_posts/1048863-an-
interview-with-the-amazing-franny-billingsley

Related Works

1. **Dowd, Siobhan.** *Bog Child*. New York: Random House/A David Fickling Book, 2008. 322p. $16.99. ISBN-13:978 0 285 75169 8. [fiction] S, CG with high interest for boys (*Value-Packed Booktalks*, 2011, pages 114 to 116.) Eighteen-year-old Fergus is recruited with false promises by a terrorist group and learns from the voice of an ancient corpse that her people faced similar prejudice and violence.

2. **Hearn, Julie.** *The Minister's Daughter*. New York: Atheneum Books for Young Readers, 2005. 263p. $16.95. ISBN 0 689 87690 4. [fiction] JS, G (*Booktalks and Beyond*, 2007, pages 136 to 138.) To hide her own disgrace, a minister's daughter accuses a young girl and her grandmother of witchcraft, and then is herself denounced as a witch in the New World.

3. **Jordon, Sherryl.** *The Raging Quiet*. New York: Simon &Schuster, 1999. 266p. $17.00. ISBN 0 689 82140 9. [fiction] JS, G (*Booktalks and More*, 2003, pages 15 to 17.) When 16-year-old Marnie falls in love with and calms a deaf man, the village forces her into a witch-craft trial.

4. **Napoli, Donna J.** *Breath*. New York: Atheneum Books for Young Readers, 2003. 260p. $16.95. ISBN 0 689 86174 5. [fiction] JS, CG (*Teen Genre Connections*, 2005, pages 173 to 174.) Twelve-year-old Salz's cystic fibrosis symptoms make the village suspicious of him.

5. **Wooding, Chris.** *Poison*. New York: Orchard Books, 2003. 273p. $16.99. ISBN 0 439 75570 0. [fiction] JS, G (*Booktalks and Beyond*, 2007, pages 176 to 178.) Sixteen-year-old rebellious Poison travels to rescue her baby sister from the phaeries and discovers her role as the master writer who controls the world.

ぐぢ

Larbalestier, Justine. **How to Ditch Your Fairy.**

New York: Bloomsburg, 2008. 304p. $16.99.
ISBN-13: 978 1 59990 301 9. [fiction] MJ, G

Themes/Topics: Fairies, magic, interpersonal relations

Summary/Description

In New Avalon, everyone has a personal fairy that ensures success in the fairy's specialty, such as shopping, love, or sports. Fourteen-year-old Charlie has a parking fairy. She doesn't drive, but is pressured to ride with anyone who needs a parking space. The school bully, who is involved in a gambling scheme, considers her his private parking pass. She makes a disastrous fairy trade with Fiorenze, the classmate she hates, who is burdened with the all-the-boys-like-you fairy. They become friends and cooperate to lose their fairies completely. Fiorenze's mother, a fairy specialist, helps them attract more positive fairies. The girls build a strong friendship and gain a better understanding of themselves, their peers, and their parents. A list of Demerits and Suspensions, a List of Known Fairies, and a Glossary of New Avalon terms appear at the end of the novel.

Values: The girls work to find their strengths and learn appreciation of others.

Booktalk

In New Avalon, everyone has a personal fairy, kind of a personal servant. Some people have a clothes shopping fairy. The stores practically give them things. That one could never be bad, but let's read some of the other possibilities. (*Turn to pages 301 to 303. Ask a member of the audience to read some of the best or worst choices from the List of Known Fairies.*) Fourteen-year-old Charlie has a parking fairy. Every driver wants Charlie. Parking spaces magically open in the most crowded situations. (*Is that good or bad?*) Charlie can't drive and doesn't want to ride around in someone's car for the rest of her life. For her, it's bad. Charlie wants the fairy of her archenemy, Fiorenze. Fiorenze has the all-the-boys-like-you fairy. Every boy in the school is at her feet, including the boy that Charlie likes. How could having that fairy be bad? (*Wait for responses.*) Both girls take extreme measures with extreme consequences to solve the sometimes life-threatening problem of *How to Ditch Your Fairy*.

Alternative booktalk available @ http://www.yalibrariantales .com/2009_09_01_archive.html

Book trailer available @ http://www.youtube.com/ watch?v=aRnKUsqhOXo

Read Aloud/Talkback

1. Chapter 4, pages 21 to 23, beginning with "You people are . . ." and ending with ". . . don't even think about New Avalon." Steffie talks about being the new kid in New Avalon. *Talkback*: How would you describe Charlie's view of New Avalon? Do you have those kinds of views about your social group or community?
2. Chapter 13, pages 85 to 88, beginning with "Yeah, Steffie said . . ." and ending with "Fairy honor." Charlie discovers Steffi's fairy. *Talkback*: Do you know someone who seems to have a getting-out-of-trouble fairy?
3. Chapter 23, pages 152 to 153, beginning with "Sometimes the whole point . . ." and ending with ". . . so many centuries later?" Charlie questions the point of reading history. *Talkback*: Do you agree that history writers are liars?
4. Chapter 30, pages 198 to 200, beginning with "I did . . ." and ending with the chapter. Charlie is thrilled with her new fairy. Her friends are not. *Talkback*: Are the girlfriends just jealous?
5. Chapter 41, pages 270 to 275. In this chapter, Charlie and Steffi renew their friendship via fairies. *Talkback*: Are fairies a good or bad thing?

Author blog about the writing process @
http://justinelarbalestier.com/books/how-to-ditch-your-fairy/
Author interviews available @
http://justinelarbalestier.com/books/how-to-ditch-your-fairy/how-to-ditch-your-fairy-faq/
http://justinelarbalestier.com/interviews/   http://justinelarbalestier.com/interviews/

Related Works

1. **Ferris, Jean. *Once upon a Marigold*.** New York: Harcourt Brace and Co., 2002. 275p. $5.95pa. ISBN 0 15 205084 1. [fiction] MJS, G (*Booktalks and Beyond*, 2007, pages 173 to 176.) A troll defeats an evil queen and brings a trendsetting couple together.
2. **Hearn, Julie. *The Minister's Daughter*.** New York: Atheneum Books for Young Readers, 2005. 263p. $16.95. ISBN 0 689 87690 4. [fiction] JS, G (*Booktalks and Beyond*, 2007, pages 136 to 138.) A story about witchcraft and vicious lies combines the worlds of fairies and Puritans.

3. **Lubar, David. *Hidden Talents***. New York: Tom Doherty Associates, 1999. 213p. $16.95. ISBN 0 312 86646 1. [fiction] MJ, CG with high interest for boys (*Booktalks and More*, 2003, pages 63 to 65.) Thirteen-year-old Martin Anderson enrolls in an alternative school and bonds with other boys who have paranormal talents.

4. **Lubar, David. *Sleeping Freshmen Never Lie***. New York: Penguin Group/Speak, 2005. 279p. $6.99pa. ISBN-13: 978 0 14 240780 6. [fiction] MJ, CG with high interest for boys (*Genre Talks for Teens*, 2009, pages 49 to 51.) Freshman Scott Hudson discovers his skills, true friends, and a new appreciation for his family.

5. **McCaughrean, Geraldine. *The Stones Are Hatching***. New York: HarperCollins Publishers, 1999. 230p. $15.95. ISBN 0 06 028765 9. [fiction] MJ, CG with high interest for boys. Creatures from the Old Magic guide 11-year-old Phelim on his hero's journey.

ʕ﹏ʔ

McBride, Lish. **Hold Me Closer, Necromancer.**
New York: Henry Holt, 2010. 343p. $16.99.
ISBN 978 0 8050 9098 7. [fiction] S, CG with high interest for boys

Themes/Topics: Magic, death, werewolves, identity

Summary/Description

Aimless college dropout Sam is a threat to Douglas Montgomery, a powerful necromancer. Douglas gives Sam one week to submit or face the destruction of friends and family. Trying to protect himself and his loved ones, Sam discovers his own necromancer heritage and his family's efforts to hide it. The predatory necromancer becomes impatient and imprisons Sam with Brid, the successor to a werewolf pack ruler. Sam faces torture and death, until a Harbinger finds him and facilitates contacts to Sam's family and Brid's pack. Friends, family, and the pack converge on Douglas's household in an epic battle, just as Douglas is trying to murder Sam and rob him of his powers. Sam kills Douglas instead, becomes part of the werewolf family as well as his own, and inherits Douglas's possessions and powers which he uses to benefit those he loves. Violence and sex make this a choice for older readers.

Values: Sam keeps loyalty to friends and family as well as his appreciation for life as he discovers the power and danger of his personal magic.

Booktalk

Sam is a big man in fast food. During a game of potato hockey, he puts a potato through a classic car's taillight. The car owner wants to know who is going to pay. But when he sees Sam hiding under a table, he forgets about the taillight. He grabs Sam by the throat and wants to know why he is living in Seattle without permission. Without permission?!!! Who is this guy? (*Wait for responses.*) His name is Douglas Montgomery, and he sends a superhuman muscleman after Sam and friends. He gives Sam an undead friend, and finally a cage complete with a female werewolf who can rip out Sam's throat. Montgomery knows that clueless Sam is a necromancer with life and death powers. Mr. Montgomery will cut, kill, and drain anyone's blood, including Sam's, to get them. Does Sam have options? (*Wait for answers.*) Can he trust the werewolf maiden? Or is it another Montgomery trap when she beckons *Hold Me Closer, Necromancer*?

Book trailers available @

http://us.macmillan.com/BookCustomPage.aspx?isbn=978080
     5090987&m_type=2#video
http://www.lishmcbride.com/hold-me-closer-necromancer

Read Aloud/Talkback

1. Chapter 6, pages 72 to 73, beginning with "Brannoc let go . . ." and ending with ". . . hurt you." Brannoc explains the value of mistakes. *Talkback*: Does this advice transfer to real life?

2. Chapter 8, pages 90 to 91, beginning with "The animals now . . ." and ending with ". . . take me for a threat." Sam prepares to confront Douglas. *Talkback*: How does this passage combine comedy and horror?

3. Chapter 11, pages 128 to 129, beginning with the chapter and ending with ". . . center yourself." Sam explains how the path to his mother's house illustrates her views on living. *Talkback*: What does the passage reveal about Sam and his home?

4. Chapter 14, pages 162 to 163, beginning with "Most surprising was . . ." and ending with ". . . inside me." Sam's mother explains why she fears his powers. *Talkback*: What does Sam conclude about his powers? Do you agree?

5. Chapter 31, pages 334 to 340, beginning with "Are you ready?" and ending with ". . . in my wake." Frank and Sam bury Brooke and confront Dunaway. *Talkback*: Why do you think McBride includes this scene?

Author interviews available @

http://enchantedinkpot.livejournal.com/89902.html

http://www.lishmcbride.com/blog/which-i-answer-questions
http://ibteens.blogspot.com/2011/02/hold-me-closer-necromancer-
    review.html

Related Works

1. **Gaiman, Neil, and Dave McKean (illus.)** *The Graveyard Book*.
   New York: Harper Collins, 2008. 312p. $17.99. ISBN-13: 978 0 06
   05 3092. [fiction] MJS, CG with high interest for boys (*Value-Packed
   Booktalks*, 2011, pages 161 to 163.) Bod, raised in a cemetery, is
   guided into the real world by his undead guardian and prepared
   for his final confrontation with the secret society that destroyed his
   family.

2. **Horowitz, Anthony.** *Raven's Gate*. New York: Scholastic Press,
   2005. 256p. (The Gatekeepers) $17.95. ISBN 0 439 67995 8. [fic-
   tion] MJ, CG with high interest for boys (*Booktalks and Beyond*,
   2007, pages 138 to 141.) A juvenile delinquent discovers that his
   supernatural powers can permit the evil Old Ones to enter the
   modern world.

3. **McBride, Lish.** *Necromancing the Stone*. New York: Henry Holt &
   Co., 2012. 352p. $16.99. ISBN-13: 978 0 8050 9099 4. [fiction] S,
   CG with high interest for boys. In this sequel, Sam concentrates on
   controlling his powers and verifying he is alive.

4. **Sleator, William.** *Hell Phone*. New York: Amulet Books, 2006.
   237p. $16.95. ISBN 0 8109 5479 6. [fiction] MJ, CG with high inter-
   est for boys (*Genre Talks for Teens*, 2009, pages 164 to 166.) Poverty-
   stricken seventeen-year-old Nick Gordon buys a cheap used cell
   phone and is pulled into the world of death and hell.

5. **Waters, Daniel.** *Generation Dead*. New York: Hyperion Books,
   2008. 392p. $8.99pa. ISBN-13: 978 142 310 922 8. [fiction] JS, CG
   with high interest for girls (*Value-Packed Booktalks*, 2011, pages 176 to
   178.) When Oakdale High establishes a program for students who die
   but come back to life, fully living students face acceptance challenges.

☙❧

Stiefvater, Maggie. The Scorpio Races.

New York: Scholastic Press, 2011. 416p. $17.99.
ISBN 978 0 545 22490 1. [fiction] JS, CG with high interest for girls

Themes/Topics: Water horses, racing, coming of age, orphans,
revenge, happiness

Summary/Description

Nineteen-year-old Sean Kendrick and his horse Corr are the returning champions of the Scorpio Races, which are run with the mystical water horses from the ocean. Puck Connolly is the first woman ever to compete, and she will ride a land horse. Sean's winnings will purchase the horse from his boss, Mr. Malvern. Puck's prize money will pay off her family's home which Malvern owns. Sean and Puck fall in love. Malvern's jealous son tries to destroy Sean's horse and harm Puck, the two things that mean the most to Sean. Sean protects Puck and loses the race. She wins, pays off the house, and buys Sean's horse. Sean's horse, which broke its leg in a struggle with Malvern's son, can no longer race, but stays with Sean rather than return to the sea.

Values: Both Puck and Sean discover that loving and being loved is true winning.

Booktalk

November heralds winter, nature's death. On the island of Thisby, November marks the race of the killer water horses. In that race, someone will die. What are these horses? Listen to how Sean, a racer, describes them. (*Ask someone in the group to read the description on page 2, beginning with "These are not . . ." and ending with ". . . hating us."*) They killed his father, but at 19, Sean is a four-time champion. He can't wait for the races to begin. Puck Connolly is younger, and a girl. Water horses killed both her parents. She hates the horses. But racing is the only way to keep her older brother from leaving home, and winning is the only way to save their house. Will it be a legendary champion or the first girl to ever enter who wins or dies? (*Wait for answers.*) But there is a third choice, a man who can easily kill both of them. Mystery, love, and survival each has a stake in *The Scorpio Races*.

Alternative booktalk available @ http://www.youtube.com/watch?v=emwNdZFYEic&feature=related

Book trailers available @

http://www.youtube.com/watch?v=IvO8S-a9-Vo&feature=related
http://www.youtube.com/watch?v=05IugPzB9uQ&feature=related

http://teacher.scholastic.com/products/tradebooks/videocenter/
index.htm?bcpid=326025746001&bckey=AQ~,AAAAAFv
844g~,BASb5BU03X_snhKHxBqPjQh5fJeKd4Q2&bclid=
322133292001&bctid=1105623165001

Read Aloud/Talkback

1. "Prologue," pages 1 to 5. A 10-year-old Sean watches his father die. *Talkback*: How do the details of the prologue tie to the rest of the novel?
2. Chapter 11, "Sean," pages 72 to 75. Sean describes the Malvern Stables. *Talkback*: After reading this passage, how would you describe the difference between Malvern and Sean?
3. Chapter 26, "Puck," page 149, beginning with "I see a lone . . ." and ending with ". . . about him, too." Puck sees Sean riding. *Talkback*: What does this passage tell you about Sean and Puck's feelings for him?
4. Chapter 29, "Puck," pages 169 to 170, beginning with "What's going on . . ." and ending with ". . . after all." Puck discovers the sea wishes. *Talkback*: Would you describe Puck as wild?
5. Chapter 56, "Sean," pages 359 to 361, beginning with "I draw myself . . ." and ending with the chapter. Sean decides on his "wishing shell." *Talkback*: What did you think of Sean's wish?

Read alouds and background music available @

http://maggiestiefvater.com/the-scorpio-races/extras/
http://www.youtube.com/watch?v=YC1Hw6-q3yM&feature=
related

Discussion guide available @ http://mediaroom.scholastic .com/files/discussion-guide-scorpio-races-2012.pdf

Author interviews available @

http://www.teachingbooks.net/book_reading.cgi?id=7408&a=1
http://m-stiefvater.livejournal.com/tag/how%20i%20write
http://maggiestiefvater.com/tag/how-i-write/
http://mediaroom.scholastic.com/maggiestiefvater
http://soundcloud.com/scholasticaudio/the-scorpio-races-interview

Name pronunciation available @ http://www.teachingbooks .net/pronounce.cgi?aid=11591

Related Works

1. **Bruchac, Joseph. *Wabi: A Hero's Tale*.** New York: Dial Books, 2006. 198p. $16.99. ISBN 0 8037 3098 5. [fiction] MJS, CG (*Genre Talks for Teens*, 2009, pages 189 to 191.) In this retelling

of an Abenaki hero's tale, Wabi traces his life from his hatching to his heroic human deeds that involve a race for and a rescue of his love.

2. **Collins, Suzanne. *Hunger Games Trilogy***. New York: Scholastic Press. [fiction] JS, CG (*Value-Packed Booktalks*, 2011, pages 79 to 84.)

   a. ***The Hunger Games***, 2008. 374p. $17.99. ISBN-13: 978 0 439 02348 1. Katniss and Peeta are chosen for the Hunger Games of survival and come to epitomize the power of love over personal interest.

   b. ***Catching Fire***, 2009. 400p. ISBN-13: 978 0 439 02349 8. Katniss and Peeta are placed back in the games and demonstrate that they value love, loyalty, and duty over material gain.

   c. ***Mockingjay***, 2010. 390p. $17.99. ISBN-13: 978 0 439 02351. In a propaganda war, Katniss learns about government manipulation and chooses Peeta over Gale as she commits to peace.

3. **Spinner, Stephanie. *Quiver***. New York: Alfred A. Knopf, 2002. 176p. $15.95. ISBN 0 375 81489 2. [fiction] JS, G (*Teen Genre Connections*, 2005, pages 177 to 170.) Combining the boar hunt, the race with the golden apples, and the transformation of Atlanta and her husband Hippomanes into lions, Spinner explains the why behind Atlanta's cruel marriage conditions and her resulting capitulation to a suitor.

Tan, Shaun. Lost & Found: Three.

New York: Scholastic Inc./Arthur A. Levine Books, 2011. 128p. $21.99.
ISBN 978 0 545 22924 1. [illustrated fiction] MJS, CG

Themes/Topics: Hope, difference, invasion

Summary/Description

Simple narrative and powerful illustrations tell three stories. "The Red Tree" shows a young girl, overwhelmed by life, finding hope and confirmation in beauty. "The Lost Thing" tells how one sensitive observer finds a home for a very different creature. "The Rabbits" by John Marsden is a parable about the damage done by "invaders and colonists."

Values: The three stories highlight the importance of faith, empathy, and cultural difference. Notes from Shaun Tan and John Marsden explain the roots of the stories.

Booktalk

Hold up copies of The Arrival *and* Tales from Outer Suburbia. *Ask if anyone in the group is familiar with the books. You may want to take a few minutes and circulate them. Share people's reactions.*

Turn the pages of Lost and Found *as you are talking. You may pause and wait for reactions.*

Shaun Tan is a man of few words and many beautiful pictures. He uses both to tell his stories. You can read his books very quickly, very slowly, once, or hundreds of times. Each time you will see something new. His newest book tells just three stories. The first talks about how overwhelming life can be. The second tells about strange out-of-place creatures that pop up in life. And the third, by John Marsden, tells about rabbits that no one can trust. In fact, you may be one of them. But all three stories are about what is (*Hold up the book.*) Lost and Found.

Alternative booktalk available @ http://blog.scholastic.com/ ink_splot_26/2011/03/shaun-tan-lost-and-found.html

The Lost Thing film available @ http://www.youtube.com/wat ch?v=f7kEXUN68HU&feature=related

Book trailer and process information available @ http:// www.thelostthing.com/

Read Aloud/Talkback

Each story is a life-parable Read Aloud in which the pictures are as important as the words. *Talkback*: What does each story say about life? How do the pictures support each message?

Author interview without words available @ http://www .spiegel.de/international/zeitgeist/an-interview-without-words- illustrator-shaun-tan-draws-conclusions-a-769089.html

Other author interviews available @

http://www.bookslut.com/features/2009_07_014748.php

http://www.thevine.com.au/entertainment/movies/shaun-tan- interview/

http://www.youtube.com/watch?v=h3kYyXWmY0w&feature= related

http://motionographer.com/2011/01/19/the-lost-thing-interview- with-shaun-tan/

http://forbiddenplanet.co.uk/blog/2012/shaun-tan-interviewed/

http://www.guardian.co.uk/books/2011/dec/02/neil-gaiman-shaun- tan-interview

Related Works

1. **Selznick, Brian. *The Invention of Hugo Cabret***. New York: Scholastic Press, 2007. 544p. $22.99. ISBN-13: 978 0 439 81378 5. [illustrated fiction] MJS, CG (*Genre Talks for Teens*, 2009, pages 152 to 154.) A combination of words and pictures tells the story of the orphan who maintains the train station clocks and becomes friends with George Méliès, a pioneer French filmmaker.

2. **Selznick, Brian. *Wonder Struck***. New York: Scholastic Press, 2011. 640p. $29.99. ISBN 978 0 545 02789 2. [fiction] MJS, CG with high interest for boys (*Multiple Cultures/Roots*, pages 279 to 282.) Two stories, one in text and one in illustration, unfold and merge as a deaf young boy discovers his long-lost deaf grandmother.

3. **Sís, Peter. *The Wall: Growing up behind the Iron Curtain***. New York: Farrar, Straus and Giroux/Frances Foster Books, 2007. 56p. $18.00. ISBN-13: 978 0 374 34701 7. [graphic, nonfiction] MJS, CG (*Genre Talks for Teens*, 2009, pages 255 to 257.) In this illustrated memoir, Sís describes childhood in Soviet-controlled Czechoslovakia and the brief glimpses of Western life that changed him.

4. **Tan, Shaun. *The Arrival***. New York: Scholastic/Arthur A. Levine Books, 2007. 128p. $19.99. ISBN-13: 978 0 439 89529 3. [wordless graphic] The story, told completely in pictures, communicates the joy of arrival to a new country and how that joy is passed to others.

5. **Tan, Shaun. *Tales from Outer Suburbia***. New York: Scholastic/Arthur A. Levine Books, 2009. 96p. $19.99. ISBN-13: 978 0 545 05587 1. [illustrated stories and poems] MJS/A, CG with high interest for boys (*Value-Packed Booktalks*, 2011, pages 174 to 176.) Fifteen very short off-the-wall tales explore the mystery and magic of cryptic advice, multiple cultures, creativity, nature, love, bullies, government, pets, and exploration.

෴

Tomlinson, Heather. **Toads and Diamonds.**

New York: Henry Holt and Co., 2010. 278p. $16.99.
ISBN 978 0 8050 896 4. [nonfiction] JS, G

Themes/Topics: Fairy tales, stepsisters, blessing and curse, history of India, prejudice

Summary/Description

When fetching water, stepsisters 15-year-old Diribani and 16-year-old Tana each meets a goddess. The goddess decrees that flowers and jewels will fall from Diribani's mouth each time she speaks.

Toads and snakes will fall from Tana's. Diribani's gift draws envy, greed, and superstition. Tana's gift draws fear and gratitude. Each girl finds love. Diribani is drawn to the prince who takes her to the palace for protection. Tana is attracted to the son of a jewel merchant, her late father's main competition. Each girl seeks her gift's purpose. Diribani designs wells for the mine workers. Tana embarks on a pilgrimage and discovers gem workers, including her love, imprisoned by the greedy mayor. Like others in the area, the workers are dying of plague. Tana helps the boy she loves escape, travels the countryside, and leaves snakes to eat plague-carrying rats. She stops to clean a fountain and encounters Diribani and the evil mayor who has kidnapped her. The sisters kill him. The rains come. The goddess appears and takes away their dubious gifts so that they can live normal lives with the men they love. Chapters alternate between Diribani and Tana. An Author's Note separates fact from fiction and suggests names to research from Indian culture.

Values: Tana and Diribani use love and family strength to develop identity and integrity.

Booktalk

Two stepsisters live in poverty. Both meet a goddess. Both receive gifts. Fifteen-year-old Diribani is the more beautiful and so is her gift. Each time she speaks, flowers and precious gems fall from her mouth. One conversation could ensure her family's future. Did she receive a blessing or a curse? (*Wait for responses.*) Sixteen-year-old Tana is more practical, the family decision maker. Each time she speaks, toads and snakes fall from her mouth. Is her gift a blessing or a curse? (*Wait for responses.*) The gifts may separate the sisters from each other and the real world forever. But is there a bigger question? Is any present really bad or good until the gifted make it that way, even *Toads and Diamonds*?

Book trailer available @ http://www.youtube.com/watch?v=5zWH79aa6Js

Read Aloud/Talkback

1. Chapter 3, pages 20 to 21, beginning with the chapter and ending with ". . . she had one." Facing a poisonous snake, Diribani evaluates her life. *Talkback*: What does Diribani's reaction to the snake reveal about her and her beliefs?

2. Chapter 6, pages 30 to 31, beginning with "Tana couldn't . . ." and ending with ". . . could happen." Tana ponders Diribani's gift in relation to her own life. *Talkback*: After reading Read Alouds 1 and 2, how would you compare the two sisters?

3. Chapter 13, pages 113 to 114, beginning with "As Lady Yisha . . ." and ending with ". . . path of violence." Diribani reflects on the princess's hunting gift and the goddess's will. *Talkback*: How does Diribani perceive her own beliefs in relation to the princess's?

4. Chapter 23, pages 200 to 203, beginning with the chapter and ending with ". . . didn't comment." Diribani reacts to the Believers' prayer hall. *Talkback*: Do you feel that Diribani enters the prayer hall by accident? How does the experience affect her?

5. Chapter 29, pages 259 to 270. In this chapter, the girls cooperate to defeat Alwar, the evil mayor *Talkback*: What part does magic play? What part does personal action play?

Author interviews available @

http://enchantedinkpot.livejournal.com/53869.html

http://www.macteenbooks.com/featured-authors/#.UButQfaPVpA

http://www.tor.com/blogs/2010/03/adventure-calling

http://whatever.scalzi.com/2010/04/08/the-big-idea-heather-tomlinson/

http://mackids.squarespace.com/mackidssquarespacecom/2010/3/29/title-post-heather-tomlinson-on-toads-and-diamonds.html

http://mackids.squarespace.com/mackidssquarespacecom/2011/3/17/toads-and-snakes-what-do-you-know.html

http://mackids.squarespace.com/mackidssquarespacecom/2011/3/7/x-marks-the-spot.html

http://www.tor.com/blogs/2010/03/irritation-the-step-mother-of-invention

http://www.tor.com/blogs/2010/02/ya-fairy-tale-fiction

http://snifflykitty.blogspot.com/2011/02/interview-with-heather-tomlinson.html

Links to research sources available @ http://www.heathertomlinson.com/toads-and-diamonds-links/

Related Works

1. **Alexander, Lloyd. *The Golden Dream of Carlo Chuchio*.** New York: Henry Holt and Co., 2007. 320p. $16.95. ISBN-13: 978 0 8050 8333 0. [fiction] JS, CG with high interest for boys (*Genre Talks for Teens*, 2009, pages 123 to 126.) Orphaned and romantic

Carlo Chuchio seeks a treasure and discovers it in the journey itself.

2. **Napoli, Donna Jo. *Beast*.** New York: Atheneum Books for Young Readers, 2000. 260p. $17.00. ISBN 0 689 83589 2. [fiction] JS, CG (*Teen Genre Connections*, 2005, pages 171 to 173.) A Persian prince turned into a lion learns about being human.

3. **Ramen, Fred. *Indian Mythology*.** New York: Rosen Central, 2008. 64p. (Mythology Around the World) $29.25. ISBN-13: 978 1 4042 0735 6. [nonfiction] MJ, CG. Ramen gives an overall view of Indian mythology and emphasizes that it is still developing.

4. **Ram-Prasad, Chakravarthi. *Exploring the Life, Myth, and Art of India*.** New York: Rosen Publishing, 2010. 143p. (Civilizations of the World) $39.95. ISBN-13: 978 1 4358 5615 8. [nonfiction] JS, CG. Although Tomlinson created new religions for the novel, many ideas and practices find matches in this explanation of how religious beliefs blend with everyday life and art in Indian culture.

5. **Spinner, Stephanie. *Quiver*.** New York: Alfred A. Knopf, 2002. 176p. $15.95. ISBN 0 375 81489 2. [fiction] JS, G (*Teen Genre Connections*, 2005, pages 177 to 179.) Spinner explains Atlanta's challenge to prospective suitors and the powerful gods.

CÇD

Zevin, Gabrielle. All These Things I've Done.
New York: Farrar, Straus and Giroux, 2011. 354p.
(Birthright: Book the First) $16.99.
ISBN 978 0 374 30210 8. [fiction] JS, G

Themes/Topics: Organized crime, celebrities, high schools, family life, New York City

Summary/Description

In this first book of the Birthright series, 16-year-old Anya Balanchine is the reluctant "heir apparent" of a New York crime family, in a future where chocolate, caffeine, and teenage cell phone use are illegal. She cares for her dying grandmother, her older mentally challenged brother, and her younger sister. Both parents died in gang hits. When her ex-boyfriend is poisoned by contraband chocolate, she is arrested for the crime. The new district attorney, Charles Delacroix, helps her, but asks her to end her relationship with his son, Win. The most powerful Asian chocolate dealer pressures her to lead the family. Her grandmother dies questionably and her older brother is manipulated into an assassination attempt of the crime family leader. She smuggles her brother out of the country and shoots the hit man hired to kill him. Her cousin offers her co-leadership of the family. Anya is sentenced to detention facility, but continues her relationship with Win.

Value: Anya learns to respect her own power as she takes responsibility for others.

Booktalk

Hold up a chocolate candy bar. Ask if anyone can tell you what Prohibition was and when it occurred. The first right answer gets the chocolate bar. If we were in 16-year-old Anya's world of the future, we would both be criminals. Selling, distributing, and possessing chocolate or caffeine, not liquor, is a crime. Anya's father headed the Balanchine family, one of the biggest chocolate producers. Anya's mother and father were both killed by hit men. Anya cares for her dying grandmother, her little sister, and her older brain-damaged brother. She doesn't have time for the mob. (*Wait for a reaction to any of the following questions.*) But does she have choices? Can she choose her friends, even boyfriends? Can she ignore the suspicions that surround her? She hopes so, but when she looks at the laws and her life she doubts it. You will see why when she admits *All These Things I've Done.*

Book trailer and writing process information available @
http://www.memoirsofa.com/

Read Aloud/Talkback

1. Chapter 2, pages 35 to 37, beginning with "On the board . . ." and ending with ". . . about recidivists." Anya confronts her history teacher. *Talkback*: After reading the passage, define recidivism. Compare your definition to a dictionary definition. What is your opinion of Mr. Beery?
2. Chapter 3, page 54, beginning with "I smiled at him . . ." and ending with ". . . forensic science." Anya explains why she likes forensic science. *Talkback*: What does Anya's reaction to her forensic assignment reveal about her?
3. Chapter 10, page 161, beginning with "Daddy always said . . ." and ending with the chapter. Anya recalls her father's advice about options.*Talkback*: Do you agree with the advice? Why?
4. Chapter 15, pages 280 to 282, beginning with "I'm here . . ." and ending with "As is mine." Yuji visits Anya to convince her of her

responsibilities. *Talkback*: What challenges does Yuji present to Anya? Why does the author choose "internecine" rather than bloody?

5.   Chapter 16, pages 292 to 293. Yuji's note is printed in italics. *Talkback*: Is Yuji's note an apology or another challenge?

Author interviews and blog selections available @

http://wamc.org/post/gabrielle-zevin-all-these-things-ive-done

http://www.youtube.com/watch?v=WXtjfwp-V0w

http://wamc.org/post/gabrielle-zevin-all-these-things-ive-done

http://gabriellezevin.tumblr.com/tagged/all-these-things-i%27ve-done

http://www.bookpage.com/the-book-case/2012/01/09/behind-a-books-makeover-part-1-from-the-author/

http://bookprobereviews.com/?p=897

http://macteenbooks.com/allthesethingsivedone/pdf/WhyGabrielleZevinLovesBooks.pdf

Related Works

1.   **Farmer, Nancy. *The House of the Scorpion*.** New York: Atheneum Books for Young Readers/A Richard Jackson Book, 2002. 380p. $17.95. ISBN 0 689 85222 3. [fiction] JS, CG with high interest for boys (*Teen Genre Connections*, 2005, pages 208 to 210.) A clone realizes his relationship with his drug lord "father," escapes, and vows to fight him.

2.   **Lisle, Janet Taylor. *Black Duck*.** New York: Philomel/Sleuth, 2006. 252p. $15.99. ISBN 0 399 23963 4. [fiction] MJS, CG with high interest for boys (*Genre Talks for Teens*, 2009, pages 149 to 152.) Two 14-year-old boys find a man's body on the beach and become embroiled in a conflict between rival bootleggers.

3.   **Lloyd, Saci. *The Carbon Diaries*, 2015.** New York: Holiday House, 2008. 330p. $17.95. ISBN-13: 978 0 8234 2190 9. [fiction] JS, CG (*Value-Packed Booktalks*, 2011, pages 166 to 168.) The futuristic United Kingdom sets a carbon ration. Laura, her family, and community deal with blackouts, fuel shortages, and looting.

4.   **Myers, Walter Dean. *Harlem Summer*.** New York: Scholastic Press, 2007. 176p. $16.99. ISBN-13: 978 0 439 36843 8. [fiction] MJ, CG with high interest for boys (*Genre Talks for Teens*, 2009, pages 267 to 269.) Sixteen-year-old Mark Purvis learns about the shady and sunny sides of Harlem and life in the 1925 summer.

5. **Zevin, Gabrielle. *Because It Is My Blood*.** New York: Farrar, Straus and Giroux, 2012. 368p. (Birthright: Book the Second) $16.99. ISBN-13: 978 0 374 38074 8. [fiction] JS, G. After being released from detention and vowing to go straight, Anya is pulled back into the criminal world

Heritage

Our heritage or history shows us how human beings relate to their times and each other. In all corners of the world throughout time, we see determination driving dreams. Unfortunately, there are always people who would step on those dreams, and many times the only answer to that repression is revolution.

Determination

Atkins, Jeannine. **Borrowed Names.**

New York: Henry Holt &a Co., 2010. 209p. $19.99.
ISBN 978 0 8050 8934 9. [poetry] JS, G

Themes/Topics: Laura Ingalls Wilder, C. J. Walker, Marie Curie, mothers and daughters

Summary/Description

Three poem narratives follow the lives of Laura Ingalls Wilder, C. J. Walker, and Marie Curie in relation to their daughters. Born two years after the Civil War, the three mothers pass a legacy of achievement to their daughters. When the younger women open themselves to a world made freer by new legislation, transportation, and art, they enhance their mothers' legacies. The Introduction explains the time period, Time Line shows the six women's lives in relation to each other, and Selected Biography suggests further reading about each mother and daughter. Photos of the mothers and daughters introduce each section.

Values: Each story emphasizes hard work, faith, and love.

Booktalk

Ask how many girls in the group have heard of Laura Ingalls Wilder, Madam C. J. Walker, and Marie Curie. These three women were very different. Wilder built her home in the wilderness, lived her life in a log cabin, and wrote the *Little House on the Prairie* books. Madam C. J. Walker went from doing white people's laundry to building a million-dollar beauty empire. Marie Curie, a controversial scientist, discovered radium and was the first person, not the first woman, to win two Nobel Prizes. What did these three women have in common? All were born two years after the Civil War. All believed in work. Each had a daughter who helped and inspired her to achieve. What do you wonder about the daughters? (*Wait for responses. The following are possible questions: Did these girls live their lives in their mothers' shadows? Did they get along with their ambitious mothers?*) Jeannine Atkins explores some of the complicated answers by probing and shaping the stories of a few *Borrowed Names*.

Book trailer available @ http://jeannineatkins.livejournal
.com/125019.html

Read Aloud/Talkback

Each set of poems is appropriate for dramatic reading. The following poems may be of special interest:

1. "Broken Reflections," pages 70 to 71. Rose helps her mother Laura Ingalls Wilder move from facts to the truth of fiction. *Talkback*: What does this poem say about the mother/daughter relationship? About the relationship between fact and fiction?
2. "River View," pages 124 to 125. Madam Walker chooses a New York home. *Talkback*: What does the poem reveal about Madam Walker, A'Lelia, and their new life?
3. "Circles," pages 131 to 132. When Madam Walker dies, A'Lelia realizes her importance. *Talkback*: What does this poem reveal about A'Lelia?
4. "Gold," pages 168 to 169. Marie Curie is awarded her second Nobel Prize. *Talkback*: How does Mé's work relate to her life?
5. "Seeing Inside Soldiers," pages 177 to 178. As war rages, 18-year-old Iréne uses the X-ray to help surgeons operate on soldiers. *Talkback*: What is Iréne's revelation about her life?

**Suggested activities, description of the writing process,
and FAQ available @** http://www.jeannineatkins.com/
books/borrowed.htm

Author interviews available @

http://www.simandan.com/?p=4088

http://authoramok.blogspot.com/2010/07/poetry-friday-5-
    questions-for-jeannine.html

http://www.hungermtn.org/scrap-by-scrap-turning-history-into-
    poems/

http://hipwritermama.blogspot.com/2010/04/shining-light-on-
    borrowed-names-by.html

http://bethanyhegedus.livejournal.com/5318.html

http://joycemoyerhostetter.blogspot.com/2010/04/meeting-
    jeannine-atkins.html

Related Works

1. **Fradin, Judith Bloom, and Dennis Brindell Fradin.** *Jane Addams: Champion of Democracy*. New York: Clarion Books, 2006. 216p. $21.00. ISBN-13: 978 0 618 50436 7. [nonfiction] MJS, CG with high interest for girls (*Genre Talks for Girls*, 2009, pages 246 to 249.) The authors trace Addams's life that included a tragedy-marked childhood, as well as dedication to social causes and social change to her death in 1935.

2. **Fradin, Dennis Brindell, and Judith Bloom Fradin.** *Ida B. Wells: Mother of the Civil Rights Movement*. New York: Clarion Books, 2000. 178p. $18.00. ISBN 0 395 89898 6. [nonfiction] MJS, CG with high interest for girls (*Booktalks and More*, 2003, pages 249 to 252.) Born a slave in 1862, Wells came of age during Reconstruction and became a reporter, civil rights activist, and cofounder of the NAACP.

3. **McClafferty, Carla Killough.** *Something Out of Nothing: Marie Curie and Radium*. New York: Farrar, Straus and Giroux, 2006. 134p. $18.00. ISBN 0 374 38036 6. [nonfiction] MJS, CG (*Booktalks and Beyond*, 2007, pages 223 to 225.) McClafferty chronicles the obstacles that Curie overcame in her path to success.

4. **Peiss, Kathy.** *Hope in a Jar: The Making of America's Beauty Culture*. New York: Metropolitan Books, 1998. 334p. $25.00. ISBN 0 8050 5550 9. [nonfiction] JS, G (*Booktalks and More*, 2003, pages 5 to 7.) This history parallels the development of cosmetics to the growing role of feminism and civil rights.

5. **Weatherford, Carole Boston, and Floyd Cooper (art).** *Becoming Billie Holiday*. Honesdale, PA: Boyd Mills Press/Wordsong, 2008. 117p. $19.95. ISBN-13: 978 1 59078 507 2. [fictional verse memoir] JS, CG with high interest for girls (*Value-Packed Booktalks*, 2011,

pages 210 to 212.) Using Billie Holiday song titles for each poem, Weatherford creates a fictional memoir of Holiday's childhood and young adulthood.

ᘓᘔ

Brooks, Martha. Queen of Hearts.

New York: Farrar, Straus and Giroux, 2010. 211p. $17.99.
ISBN 978 0 374 34229 6. [fiction] JS, G

Themes/Topics: Tuberculosis, hospitals, coming of age, friendship, family, Manitoba (Canada), 20th century, World War II

Summary/Description

In 1941, shortly before her 16th birthday, Marie Claire and her younger brother and sister are sent to a tuberculosis sanatorium near their farm in Manitoba, Canada. Bitter and grieving over her own illness, her brother's death, and her parents' detachment, Marie withdraws, but eventually opens to the supportive staff and Signy, her wealthier, 17-year-old, city-bred, annoyingly optimistic roommate who has suffered numerous setbacks for 5 years. Marie also bonds with Jack Hawkings, a young musician recovering from tuberculosis. When she is no longer contagious, Marie transfers to a cottage and learns that she has been Signy's major support and inspiration. She tries to forget the ward, but reluctantly visits the failing Signy whose parents substitute gifts for love. With Jack's support, Marie plans a Christmas trip home, but at the last minute returns to her former roommate who faces the holiday alone.

Values: Marie Claire learns from the staff and her friends in the hospital that healing involves being generous to others.

Booktalk

Ask if anyone can describe tuberculosis. If not, briefly describe the disease. In the summer of 1940, 15-year-old Marie Claire sees tuberculosis as a disease someone else gets. By 1941, Marie and her younger brother and sister are patients in a tuberculosis sanatorium. Marie is a small town farm girl. Her roommate Signy is a rich city girl. Are they going to get along? (*Wait for a response.*) Tuberculosis forces both girls into the same freezing balcony treatments, the always antiseptic surroundings, and the strangling coughs. And part of facing tuberculosis for everyone is facing death. Your own death, your family's, and your friends'. (*What else might two teenage girls trapped in this situation think about?*) What many of us think about—love. Signy, the rich girl, has beautiful clothes and free time to dream about romance. Milking and mucking cows, helping her brother and sister, and going to school to the stern Catholic sisters, Marie hasn't had time for love. But this killer disease helps her not only find it, but also makes her (*Show the Cover.*) the *Queen of Hearts*.

Read Aloud/Talkback

1. Chapter 2, pages 10 to 13, beginning with "But by fall . . ." and ending with ". . . pulls out of the yard." Oncle Gérard is diagnosed and leaves. *Talkback*: What details make this scene touching? Ominous?
2. Chapter 5, pages 40 to 43, beginning with "In the hallway . . ." and ending with ". . . has just ended." Marie, and her younger brother and sister are admitted. *Talkback*: What do the details of the scene tell about Marie, her family, and the sanitarium?
3. Chapter 10, pages 76 to 79, beginning with the chapter and ending with ". . . the work for now." Marie's lung has collapsed. *Talkback*: What surprised you in this passage?
4. Chapter 11, pages 81 to 90. This chapter includes Marie's 16th birthday and Luc's death. *Talkback*: What does each section of this chapter tell about the person with whom Marie interacts and Marie herself?
5. Chapter 25, pages 203 to 204, beginning with the chapter and ending with ". . . walking into his arms." *Talkback*: What does this passage say about love?

Discussion guide available @ https://sites.google.com/a/harwood.org/2012–2013-dcf/home/queen-of-hearts

Related Works

1. **Bray, Libba. *Going Bovine***. New York: Delacorte Press, 2009. 479p. $17.99. ISBN 978 0 385 73397 7. [fiction] S, CG with high interest for boys (*Value-Packed Booktalks*, 2011, pages 4 to 5.) Sixteen-year-old Cameron contracts mad cow disease, is given four to five months to live, and begins a coma journey that helps him realize life's joys.
2. **Brooks, Martha. *True Confessions of a Heartless Girl***. New York: Farrar, Straus and Giroux/Melanie Kroupa Books, 2003. 181p. $16.00. ISBN 0 374 37. [fiction] JS, G (*Booktalks and Beyond*, 2007, pages 47 to 49.) Pregnant 17-year-old Noreen Stall steals her boyfriend's truck and drives to the small community of Pembina Lake where she learns the power of love and personal responsibility.

3. **Ellis, Deborah.** *The Heaven Shop*. Narkham, ON: Fitzhenry &a Whiteside, 2004. 192p. $16.95. ISBN 1 55041 908 0. [fiction] MJ, CG (*Booktalks and Beyond*, pages 229 to 231.) Thirteen-year-old Binti Phiri and her family learn to survive in the AIDS epidemic after their father dies of the disease.

4. **Giff, Patricia Reilly.** *All the Way Home*. New York: Dell Yearling, 2001. 169p. $5.99pa. ISBN 0 440 41182 3. [fiction] MJ, G. Eleven-year-old Muriel, a polio victim during World War II, seeks the mother she remembers from the polio hospital and is surprised at what she finds.

5. **Hostetter, Joyce Moyer.** *Blue*. Honesdale, PA: Calkins Creek Books, 2006. 193p. $16.95. ISBN-13: 978 1 59078 389 4. [fiction] MJS, G (*Genre Talks for Teens*, 2009, pages 225 to 227.) Thirteen-year-old Ann Fay Honeycutt becomes the man of the house when her father leaves for World War II, but she and her brother are stricken with polio.

ଔଔ

Gantos, Jack. Dead End in Norvelt.

New York: Farrar, Straus and Giroux, 2011. 341p. $15.99.
ISBN 978 0 374 37993 3. [fiction] MJS, CG
with high interest for boys

Themes/Topics: Behavior, old age, Norvelt (Pennsylvania), Eleanor Roosevelt

Summary/Description

Soon to be 12-year-old Jack Gantos, whose nose bleeds with every shock he gets, lives in Norvelt, a New Deal town named for Elea*nor* Roose*velt*. He is grounded for the summer when he fires his father's World War II souvenir and mows down his mother's corn field so that his father can build a runway for a military surplus airplane. Then Jack's mother sends Jack to help arthritic Miss Volker who writes the town's obituaries. Through her personalized narratives, which she ties to historic events, Jack improves his typing and learns the town's history. The deaths of the original founders escalate, and Jack discovers a murder plot based on Miss Volker's promise not to marry until all the original residents are dead.

Value: Jack learns that good personal decisions produce positive consequences and poor ones bring negative consequences.

Booktalk

Ask how many people have read stories by Jack Gantos. Give time to listen to the titles and their reactions. Sometimes he writes fiction. Hold up one of his fiction books. Sometimes fact. Hold up Hole in My Life. *Hold up* Dead End in Norvelt. *This story is a little of each.*

Jack Gantos was 12 in the summer of 1962, and he looked forward to two exciting months of freedom. Instead, he was grounded for life. He shot his father's World War II souvenir gun and dug up his mother's corn field. Neither of those things was his fault. Ask him. You may not want to read about how an 11-year-old in denial spends his summer, especially when he winds up writing obituaries about the town founders. Am I right? (*Wait for responses.*) But then, there are the Hells Angels, his father's plan to fly, his best friend's determination to make him like dead people, and Jack's nose. It spurts blood at each crisis. And crises and bodies pile up by the minute. Jack is tracking down a killer. Blood, death, and mystery. Does that get you interested? It did Jack, even when he thought he was stuck at a *Dead End in Norvelt.*

Book trailer available @ http://www.youtube.com/
watch?v=OefX-U-VqiM

Book trailers, interviews, and read alouds available @
http://us.macmillan.com/deadendinnorvelt/JackGantos

Read Aloud/Talkback

1. Chapter 6, pages 85 to 88, beginning with "I was thinking . . ." and ending with the chapter. *Talkback*: What details give the passage a balance of seriousness and humor?

2. Chapter 7, pages 90 to 91, beginning with "Because of Miss Volker's . . ." and ending with ". . . back to its past." Jack sees a dying town and knows that his mother sees it too. *Talkback*: How does the passage reveal the town and Jack's mother? After touring your own town, write a description that reveals what you feel about it.

3. Chapter 13, pages 182 to 184, beginning with "For me, heaven . . ." and ending with the chapter. Jack gives his vision of heaven as well as his mother's and father's. *Talkback*: Using Jack's vision as a model, write your own vision of heaven.

4. Chapter 14, pages 185 to 186, beginning with the chapter and ending with ". . . deeper in debt." Jack's family plays monopoly. *Talkback*: Choose a game that you or your family plays. Explain what you think it teaches.

5. Chapter 21, pages 259 to 262, beginning with "Better sharpen . . ." and ending with ". . . that terrible time." Miss Volker writes Mrs. Hamsby's obituary. *Talkback*: Miss Volker sees Mrs. Hamsby as a significant historian. Do you agree?

Read aloud available @ http://www.bobedwardsradio.com/ blog/2012/5/5/jack-gantos-dead-end-in-norvelt.html

Author interviews available @

http://www.youtube.com/watch?v=wuqa6IWQxZQ&afeature=related
http://audiobooker.booklistonline.com/2012/02/02/interview-with-jack-gantos/
http://authorturf.com/?p=2936
http://www.jackgantos.com/jacks-secret-tips-for-aspiring-authors/
http://www.teachingbooks.net/tb.cgi?aid=2500#AuthorInterviews
http://www.readingrockets.org/books/interviews/gantos/

Reading guide available @ http://www.jackgantos.com/ wp-content/uploads/2011/06/Dead-End-in-Norvelt-Teachers-Guide.pdf

Related Works

1. **Freedman, Russell.** *Eleanor Roosevelt: A Life of Discovery*. New York: Clarion Books, 1993. 198p. $17.95. ISBN 0 89919 862 7. [nonfiction] MJS, CG with high interest for girls. Freedman relates the challenges and victories in Eleanor Roosevelt's personal and professional lives.

2. **Gantos, Jack.** *Hole in My Life*. New York: Farrar, Straus and Giroux, 2002. 200p. $16.00. ISBN 0 374 39988 3. [nonfiction] JS, CG with high interest for boys (*Teen Genre Connections*, 2005, pages 1 to 3.) Gantos tells about the consequences of selling and delivering drugs for a 10,000-dollar payoff.

3. **Gantos, Jack.** *The Love Curse of the Rumbaughs*. New York: Farrar, Straus and Giroux, 2006. 185p. $17.00. ISBN: 0 374 33690 3. [fiction] JS, CG (*Booktalks and Beyond*, 2007, pages 133 to 136.) The Rumbaughs are cursed with an unhealthy love of mothers. The Rumbaugh pharmacy is mentioned in *Dead End in Norvelt*.

4. **Laskas, Gretchen Moran.** *The Miner's Daughter*. New York: Simon &a Schuster, 2007. 256p. $15.99. ISBN 978 1 4169 1262 0. [fiction] JS, G. Sixteen-year-old Willa Lowell lives in Arthurdale, a New Deal homestead, like Norvelt.

5. **Levin, Betty.** *The Unmaking of Duncan Veerick*. Asheville, NC: Front Street, 2007. 212p. $16.95. ISBN-13: 978 1 932425 96 3.

[fiction] MJ, CG with high interest for boys (*Genre Talks for Teens*, 2009, pages 135 to 138.) Thirteen-year-old Duncan, sent by his parents to help an elderly neighbor, discovers old bones, mummies, theft, and fraud.

❦

Morpurgo, Michael. **An Elephant in the Garden.**

New York: Feiwel and Friends, 2010. 199p. $16.99.
ISBN 978 0 312 59369 8. [fiction] MJ, CG
with high interest for boys

Themes/Topics: War, World War II, Dresden (Germany), zoos, flight, trust, love

Summary/Description

Lizzie, a nursing home resident, shares her World War II story with nine-year-old Karl and his mother. The child Lizzie lives with her little brother Karl and their mother in Dresden, Germany. Her mother is a zookeeper. If England and Canada bomb Dresden, the zoo animals will be killed. The mother brings an elephant she has raised into their garden each night and takes her back to the zoo each day. When Dresden is bombed, the family and the elephant flee to a relative's home in the country. They find a Canadian soldier whose plane has crashed. The soldier saves Lizzie's little brother from drowning, and gains the mother's trust. They overcome hunger, cold, and sickness, and come close to being arrested but eventually find the American forces. The tanks scare the elephant, who runs away. Lizzie and the Canadian soldier fall in love. He returns for her. They marry, and the rest of the family, including Lizzie's father who was captured by the Russians, move to Canada. Lizzie and the elephant reunite at a Toronto circus performance.

Values: The family values life, trust, and friendship even in dangerous times.

Booktalk

Lizzie lives in Dresden, Germany, during World War II. Her mother is a zookeeper. Soon, the American and British forces bomb Dresden. When the raid begins, the zookeepers have to shoot the zoo animals and protect the town. Lizzie's mother takes care of a very special elephant,

Marlene. Lizzie's mother saw Marlene born, named her, and cares for her every day. She is determined that Marlene will live. How can she protect her? (*Wait for responses.*) She keeps Marlene in their garden each night and takes her back to the zoo during the day. Dresden is soon bombed. The garden is burned with the city, and they flee—everybody, even Marlene. And soon the family learns if they are going to survive freezing temperatures, starvation, and hostile forces, it is a good idea to keep *An Elephant in the Garden*.

Book trailer available @ http://sakuramedal.wordpress.com/ 2011/10/03/an-elephant-in-the-garden-by-michael-morpurgo/

Read Aloud/Talkback

1. Part 1, Chapter 2, pages 24 to 28, beginning with "At home . . ." and ending with the chapter. Lizzie relates the argument her parents have with the aunt and uncle. *Talkback*: What does the passage reveal about Germany at the time? How does this passage prepare the reader for the rest of the story?
2. Part 1, Chapter 3, pages 36 to 38, beginning with "Mutti had taken . . ." and ending with ". . . so terrible?" Lizzie and her mother clash about Marlene. *Talkback*: Who has the better attitude, Lizzie or her mother?
3. Part 2, Chapter 3, pages 71 to 75, beginning with "The bombers were . . ." and ending with ". . . was sure of it." Dresden is bombed. *Talkback*: Is the reaction to Marlene silly?
4. Part 4, Chapter 1, pages 136 to 140, beginning with "Without this compass . . ." and ending with ". . . drink as well." Peter guides them to safety. *Talkback*: What makes this unlikely group successful?
5. Part 4, Chapter 3, pages 174 to 176, beginning with "When at last . . ." and ending with ". . . in spirit." The countess relates what she said to the German major. *Talkback*: What does the countess reveal about herself when she protects Lizzie and her companions?

Related activities available @ http://clubs-kids.scholastic .co.uk/products/78447

Author presentation available @ http://www.youtube.com/wat ch?v=0bwVmDHyPGQ&afeature=related

Author interview available @ https://encinolibrary.wordpress .com/2011/11/23/an-elephant-in-the-garden-by-michael-morpurgo/

Discussion questions available @ http://sweetonbooks.com/
all-titles/781-an-elephant-in-the-garden.html

Related Works

1. **Gleitzman, Morris.** *Once*. New York: Henry Holt &a Co., 2010.
   163p. $16.99. ISBN-13: 978 0 8050 9026 0. [fiction] MJS, CG
   (*Value-Packed Booktalks*, 2011, pages 91 to 93.) When told Hitler
   is his savior, Felix leaves the Catholic orphanage, seeks his Jewish
   parents, and discovers the horrors of the war and prejudices.

2. **Konigsburg, E. L.** *The Mysterious Edge of the Heroic World*.
   New York: Atheneum Books for Young Readers/Ginee Seo Books,
   2007. 244p. $16.99. ISBN-13: 978 1 4169 4972 5. [fiction] M, CG
   (*Genre Talks for Teens*, 2009, pages 146 to 149.) Amedeo discovers
   valuable art and a World War II sacrifice when helping a wealthy
   woman downsize her home.

3. **Lawrence, Iain.** *B for Buster*. New York: Laurel-Leaf, 2004.
   317p. $5.99pa. ISBN 0 440 23810 2. [fiction] MJS, CG with high
   interest for boys (*Booktalks and Beyond*, 2007, pages 102 to 105.)
   Sixteen-year-old Kak enlists in the Canadian Air Force during
   World War II and becomes the wireless operator on a bomber. The
   pigeons trained by a man labeled a coward save Kak's life.

4. **Morpurgo, Michael.** *War Horse*. New York: Scholastic Inc.,
   2010. 176p. $6.99pa. ISBN 978 0439796644. [fiction] MJ, CG with
   high interest for boys. In 1914, a foal is sold and sent to the Western
   Front, experiences the horrors of war, inspires those around him,
   and longs for the farmer's son he left behind.

5. **Zusak, Markus.** *The Book Thief*. New York: Alfred A. Knopf,
   2006. 552p. $21.90. ISBN 0 375 93100 7. [fiction] JS, CG with
   high interest for girls (*Genre Talks for Teens*, 2009, pages 241 to
   243.) Death tells the story of Liesel Meminger, the daughter of a
   Communist who survives the war in a German foster home.

☙❧

Seiple, Samantha. **Ghosts in the Fog: The Untold Story of Alaska's WWII Invasion.**
New York: Scholastic Press, 2011. 224p. $16.99.
ISBN 978 0 545 29654 0. [nonfiction] MJS, CG with high interest for boys

Themes/Topics: World War II, Aleutian Islands, Japanese culture, prejudice, spying

Summary/Description

Shortly after Pearl Harbor, the Japanese launched offensives on Midway and the Aleutian islands to crush the United States. The U.S. government kept the Aleutian battles secret to avoid a panic. The account, which includes personal details and stories, shows the critical effects of leadership and weather in fighting the Aleutian battles. It highlights the differences in Japanese and American cultures, and reveals the mistreatment of the Aleuts by the U.S. Government. The narrative includes photographs, source notes, image credits, and an index.

Values: The narrative highlights the necessity for compassion, planning, discipline, and courage.

Booktalk

Ask how many people in the group have heard of World War II. Establish who was fighting. Ask how many people have heard about Pearl Harbor.

Pearl Harbor, the sneak attack on Hawaii by the Japanese, is one of the most famous battles in history. After Pearl Harbor, the Japanese planned to destroy the U.S. Navy. They attacked Midway Island in the South Pacific and the Aleutian Islands in Alaska. (*Show the locations on a map as you speak.*) Midway was a turning point for the United States. It is a prominent part of our history books, but almost no one knows about the Aleutians. Midway was a victory. The Aleutians was a mistake that was too close to the mainland. The U.S. government didn't want America to panic. Poorly prepared and ill-equipped American soldiers were sent to fight the well-prepared, superbly supplied Japanese who vowed never to surrender. What would be the third threat? (*Wait for responses.*) Neither side counted on the weather. In the cold, the ice, and the low-lying clouds, neither the Japanese nor the Americans knew whether they were shooting at other soldiers or *Ghosts in the Fog*.

Alternative booktalk and official government documentary of the Aleutian Battle available @ http://www.samanthaseiple.com/ghosts-in-the-fog/

Alternative booktalk trailer @ http://jeanvnaggarliteraryagency.blogspot.com/2011/10/ghosts-in-fog-reviews-videos-and-wwii.html

Read Aloud/Talkback

1. Chapter 2, pages 27 to 30, beginning with "Before the canoe-like . . ." and ending with ". . . drift ashore." Seiple describes how

the Aleuts fish and hunt. *Talkback*: Why does Seiple include this description in a war story?

2. Chapter 4, pages 67 to 69, beginning with the chapter and ending with ". . . the American navy." Seventeen-year-old Larry Dirks discovers that the American Navy destroyed his home. *Talkback*: Why was this event important to include?

3. Chapter 4, pages 77 to 81, beginning with "Even though the U.S . . . ." and ending with ". . . no time for that." Seiple outlines the dangers of weather and limited training for the pilots. *Talkback*: How does this passage affect your feelings about the battle and the soldiers fighting them?

4. Chapter 6, pages 110 to 114, beginning with "On August 28. . ." and ending with ". . . all-out war." Seiple describes Castner's Cutthroats and their mission. *Talkback*: If you were casting this mission for a movie, whom would you choose to play each man described?

5. Chapter 7, pages 121 to 142, beginning with "It was about noon . . ." and ending with the chapter. Seiple recounts the suicidal battle of Attu. *Talkback*: What does this battle reveal about the Japanese?

Author interview available @ http://www.samanthaseiple.com/ audio/1040WHO-Samantha-Interview-Clip.wav

Additional WWII books suggested for teens available @ http://www.samanthaseiple.com/wwii-books-for-teens/

Related Works

1. **Bastedo, Jamie. *On Thin Ice*.** Calgary, AB: Fitzhenry &a Whiteside Co./Red Deer Press, 2006. 348p. $10.95pa. ISBN 0 88995 337 6. [fiction] JS, CG with high interest for girls (*Genre Talks for Teens*, 2009, pages 262 to 264.) Sixteen-year-old Ashley accepts her Inuk powers and helps her family preserve their culture.

2. **Bruchac, Joseph. *Code Talker: A Novel about the Navajo Marines of World War Two*.** New York: Dial Books, 2005. 231p. $16.99. ISBN 0 8037 2921 9. [fiction] MJS, CG with high interest for boys. In this novel about the heroic Navajos of World War II, Bruchac includes the prejudice encountered at the white man's school.

3. **Edwardson, Debby Dahl. *Blessing's Bead*.** New York: Farrar, Straus and Giroux/Melanie Kroupa Books, 2009. 178p. $16.99. ISBN-13: 978 0 374 30805 6. [fiction] JS, CG with high interest for girls (*Value-Packed Booktalks*, 2011, pages 236 to 239.) Blessing

learns about her Eskimo heritage even though her family has been upended by epidemic, white men, and war.

4. **Hesse, Karen. *Aleutian Sparrow*.** New York: Aladdin Paperbacks, 2003. 156p. $5.99pa. ISBN-13: 1 4169 0327 5. [novel in verse] MJ, G. A young Aleut girl experiences war, encampment, and destruction of World War II. Her experiences closely follow the events of *Ghosts in the Fog*.

5. **Sullivan, Paul. *Maata's Journal*.** New York: Atheneum Books for Young Readers, 2003. 240p. $16.95. ISBN 0 689 83463 2. [fiction] JS, G. Seventeen-year-old Maata, an Inuit, records her survival in an Arctic expedition from April to July of 1924.

ॐॐ

Ryan, Pam Muñoz (text), and Peter Sís (illus.). **The Dreamer.**

New York: Scholastic Press, 2010. 384p. $17.99.
ISBN 978 0 439-26970 4. [fiction] MJ, CG

Themes/Topics: Creativity, oppression, coming of age

Summary/Description

Biography, fiction, personal fantasy, and sensory illustrations tell the story of Neftalí Reyes, who becomes one of the most famous poets of Chile by following the calls of nature's beauty, his gift of words, and the demands of social responsibility. The chapter names are elements of nature, such as "Wind," "Mud," "Forest," "Tree," and "Pinecone." The final two chapters which express his coming of age are "Passion" and "Fire." Throughout his childhood, Neftalí and his brother struggle against their tyrannical and abusive father who denies their talents. Inspired by his uncle, a newspaper reporter and editor, Neftalí expresses his own ideas. When he goes to the university, he adopts the pen name Pablo Neruda to protect himself from his father.

Values: Pablo Neruda shows his persistent pursuit of creativity, beauty, and nature, which eventually brings him contentment and recognition.

Booktalk

Neftalí Reyes lives in Chile. He's a zero in sports. He's not that good looking, and numbers just jumble in his head. But he is a saver. When he finds a word that he likes to hear, he writes it on a piece of paper and keeps it in the drawer in his bedroom. When he walks to school, he picks up the things that others throw away—an old shoe, a pinecone, maybe a piece of glass. (*You may want to show these things as you talk about them or speak.*) He thinks of words to match all of them. How would you describe him? (*Wait for responses.*) His father wants a son who is a successful businessman or a brilliant doctor, a rich man who will make the family proud. He will do anything to change a losing son that people laugh at into a winning son. How do you think Neftalí reacts? (*Wait for responses.*) He becomes a fighter. He knows that to live the life that he wants, he must leave. And when he pursues his dream, he changes his country and the world with his words. Later, another dictator like his father calls him a loser, a traitor. But the world knows different. Neftalí, who has renamed himself Pablo Neruda, wins a Nobel Prize, one of the greatest awards it can give, for words. (*You may want to show a picture of the Nobel Medal.*) Neftalí, the winner, gives new eyes and hope. He is *The Dreamer*.

Alternative booktalk available @ http://www.scholastic.com/browse/video.jsp?pID=1640149541&abcpid=1640149541&abclid=57826465001&abctid=86953451001

Book trailer available @

http://www.youtube.com/watch?v=rkent3K8lLo
http://www.youtube.com/watch?v=aPLZaipsMNQ&afeature=related

Read Aloud/Talkback

The entire book, with illustrations, will make a wonderful read aloud, reader response experience. Below are a few specific suggestions:

1. "Poems and Odes" by Pablo Neruda, pages 359 to 370. These pages present a small collection of Neruda's poems. *Talkback*: Choose your favorite poem. Read it aloud or illustrate it.

2. "Mud," pages 42 to 44, beginning, with "For a month . . ." and ending with ". . . you will see." Rodolfo warns Neftalí about their abusive father. *Talkback*: How do you account for the two conflicting ways the brothers view the father?

3. "Forest," pages 99 to 103, beginning with "Neftalí looked around . . ." and ending with ". . . black and shiny armor." Neftalí encounters the rhinoceros beetle. *Talkback*: What is real and what is fantasy? What do you think that the question and illustration on pages 102 and 103 communicate?

4. "Forest," pages 104 to 105, beginning with "At lunch . . ." and ending with the chapter. The father speaks for Neftalí and his future. *Talkback*: Is this the good father?

5. "Fire," pages 343 to 353, beginning with "There, in the . . ." and ending with the novel. This passage explains how poetry directs the poet's life. *Talkback*: How does poetry direct his life? What do you think directs your life?

Author interviews available @

http://oomscholasticblog.com/2010/06/summer-book-dreamer-by-pam-munoz-ryan.html

http://bwibooks.com/articles/pam-munoz-ryan.php

http://elizabethvaradansfourthwish.blogspot.com/2010/09/interview-with-pam-munoz-ryan.html

http://www.pammunozryan.com/pages/novels/interviewDreamer.pdf

http://www.youtube.com/watch?v=LovauoreX_k&afeature=related

Discussion guides and suggested activities available @

http://www.scholastic.com/teachers/lesson-plan/dreamer-discussion-guide

http://scholarworks.gvsu.edu/cgi/viewcontent.cgi?article=1079&acontext=lajm

Author interviews, read alouds, and supplementary material available @ http://www.teachingbooks.net/tb.cgi?tid=18032&a=1

Related Works

1. **Bryant, Jen (text), and Melissa Sweet (illus).** *A River of Words: The Story of William Carlos Williams.* Grand Rapids, MI: Eerdmans Books for Young Readers, 2008. 34p. $17.00. ISBN 978 0 8028 5302 8. [illustrated biography] Simple text and a collage of illustrations and graphics explain Williams's life. The timeline of his life, the Author's Note, Illustrator's Note, and For Further Reading provide information for readers from middle grades and up.

2. **Janeczko, Paul B. (compiler).** *Seeing the Blue between: Advice and Inspiration for Young Poets.* Cambridge, MA: Candlewick Press, 2002. 132p. $17.99. ISBN 0 7636 0881 5. [nonfiction] MJS, CG. Thirty-two poets give examples of their work and advice to young writers.

3. **Selznick, Brian.** *The Invention of Hugo Cabret.* New York: Scholastic Press, 2007. 544p. $22.99. ISBN-13: 978 0 439 81378 5. [fiction] M, CG (*Genre Talks for Teens*, 2009, pages 152 to 154.) In

this story, told with a combination of text and illustrations, 12-year-old orphan Hugo Cabret maintains the train station clocks. Trying to rejuvenate a damaged automaton found by his deceased father, he meets Georges Méliès, a pioneer French movie maker thought to be dead.

4. **Sís, Peter.** *The Wall: Growing up behind the Iron Curtain*. New York: Farrar, Straus and Giroux/Frances Foster Books, 2007. 56p. $18.00. ISBN-13: 978 0 374 34701 7. [graphic, nonfiction] MJS, CG (*Genre Talks for Teens*, 2007, pages 255 to 257.) Sís explains how brief glimpses of Western life changed his thinking and his own life.

5. **Spires, Elizabeth.** *I Heard God Talking to Me: William Edmondson and His Stone Carvings*. New York: Farrar, Straus and Giroux, 2009. 56p. $17.95. ISBN-13: 978 0 374 33528 1. [biography in verse] JS, CG (*Value-Packed Booktalks*, 2011, pages 241 to 243.) In 23 poems, Elizabeth Spires personifies the creations and expresses the vision of William Edmondson who was inspired by God to carve and set spirits free within pieces of limestone.

Repression

ʕ·ᴥ·ʔ

Bartoletti, Susan Campbell. They Called Themselves the K.K.K.: The Birth of an American Terrorist Group.

Houghton Mifflin Books for Children, 2010. 168p. $19.00.
ISBN 978 0 618 44033 7. [nonfiction] JS, CG

Themes/Topics: Ku Klux Klan, racism, hate groups, Reconstruction, prejudice

Summary/Description

Bartoletti documents the development of the Ku Klux Klan from its Reconstruction origins as a self-righteous, prankster social club to its present day resolve to survive. When members discover that their dress and language intimidate former slaves, they fashion the K.K.K. into an enforcement organization, led by Nathan Bedford Forrest, a former Confederate general, to revive pre-Civil War conditions. President Andrew Johnson complements their efforts by supporting policies that deny fair working conditions, voting rights, and legal protection for freed-men. The Republican Party resists and Johnson's successor, President Ulysses S. Grant, helps reverse the Johnson policies, but the K.K.K. becomes firmly entrenched. The book includes a Civil Rights Time Line, Quote Attributions, and an extensive Bibliography and Source Notes section presented in essay form. It describes the content and the relevance of sources used and the personal travel involved in information gathering.

Values: This historical account illustrates the need for honesty, equality, and fair government.

Booktalk

Ask how many people have heard about the Taliban. Ask them to share their information.

When we invaded Iraq, we were told that we were protecting ourselves from terrorism. When we invaded Afghanistan, we were told that we were protecting ourselves from terrorism. Someday, we may invade Pakistan to protect ourselves from . . . (*Signal the group to fill in the blank with an oral response.*) All that protection seems to be taking a long time and to be far away, but we have a homegrown terrorist organization. It started after the Civil War as a kind of a joke. It escalated into a torture and killing machine that claimed to protect white Americans from anyone who was black, anyone who supported black people's rights, and soon from anyone who was different from its white members. You don't need profiling to find them. Just look under the hood (*Point to the picture on the cover.*) or read this guidebook. *They Called Themselves the K.K.K.: The Birth of an American Terrorist Group.*

Book trailer available @ http://www.youtube.com/watch?v=m Lis3yglxlQ&afeature=related

Read Aloud/Talkback

1. Copyright page, quotation by W.E.B. Du Bois. Du Bois comments on the power of a secret force. *Talkback*: Do you agree with DuBois? Use examples to support your opinion.
2. Chapter 2, pages 19 to 21, beginning with "As the former . . ." and ending with ". . . freed people to slavery." This passage explains the Black Codes of the Johnson Reconstruction. *Talkback*: What does this passage say about laws and lawmakers in general?
3. Chapter 4, page 58, beginning with "Today, psychologists . . ." and ending with the chapter. The paragraph comments on why people

join groups like the K.K.K. *Talkback*: How does this passage relate to Read Aloud 1? What does it imply about terrorism?

4. Chapter 6, pages 85 to 88, beginning with "In some parts . . ." and ending with the chapter. This is the story of Hannah Tutson who was attacked by the K.K.K. *Talkback*: What is your reaction to this attack?

5. "Bibliography and Source Notes," pages 167 to 168, beginning with "In the midst of . . ." and ending with the chapter. Bartoletti describes attending a modern day K.K.K. meeting. *Talkback*: What is your reaction to Bartoletti's account?

Author interviews available @

http://www.youtube.com/watch?v=d23buy5aHc4

http://www.chasingray.com/archives/2010/12/wbbt_interview_do_ justice_to_t.html

http://www.kirkusreviews.com/blog/young-adult/They-Called- Themselves-the-KKK-Bartoletti/#continue_reading_post

http://cynthialeitichsmith.blogspot.com/2010/08/guest-post-susan- campbell-bartoletti-on.html

Author background information and read aloud @ http:// www.teachingbooks.net/book_reading.cgi?id=4614&a=1

Teaching guide available @ http://www.civiced-ri.org/kkk.pdf

Related Works

1. **Aronson, Marc. *Race: A History beyond Black and White*.** New York: Atheneum Books for Young Readers/Ginee Seo Books, 2007. 322p. $18.99. ISBN-13: 978 0 689 86554 1. [nonfiction] S, CG. Aronson traces the history of persecution from the primitive to modern-day worlds.

2. **Fradin, Dennis Brindell, and Judith Bloom Fradin. *Ida B. Wells: Mother of the Civil Rights Movement*.** New York: Clarion Books, 2000. 178p. $18.00. ISBN 0 395 89898 6. [nonfiction] JS, CG (*Booktalks and More*, 2003, pages 249 to 252.) Wells used the media and equal rights organizations to fight prejudice and the lynching associated with the instrument.

3. **Hesse, Karen. *Witness*.** New York: Scholastic Press, 2001. 176p. $16.95. ISBN 0 439 27199 1. [fiction] JS, CG (*Booktalks and More*, 2003, pages 180 to 183.) Hesse describes the K.K.K. invasion of a small Vermont town through the eyes of 11 citizens.

4. **Stockett, Kathryn. *The Help*.** New York: G. P. Putnam's Sons/Amy Einhorn Books, 2009. 444p. $24.95. ISBN 978 0 399 15534 5. [fiction]

G, S/A. Told in the voices of three Southern women, the story explores the volatile relationship between whites and blacks in the 1960s.

5. **Taylor, Mildred D. *The Land: Prequel to Roll of Thunder, Hear My Cry*.** New York: Phyllis Fogelman Books, 2001. 275p. $17.99. ISBN 0 8037 1950 7. [fiction] JS, CG (*Teen Genre Connections*, 2005, pages 267 to 269.) As the son of a slave and plantation owner, Paul Logan struggles to find his own identity as a free man.

೮ॢ೮ॢ

Chapman, Fern Schumer. **Is It Night or Day?**

New York: Farrar, Straus and Giroux, 2010. 205p. $17.99.
ISBN 978 0 374 17744 7. [fiction based on true events] MJS, CG
with high interest for girls

Themes/Topics: Refugees, Jews, Jewish Holocaust, World War II, Chicago

Summary/Description

Twelve-year-old Edith's family, who has lived prosperous and respected lives in a small German town, becomes the object of anti-Semitism. The mother and father cannot leave, but send Edith to her aunt and uncle in Chicago, Illinois. Edith recounts the wrenching separation and her subsequent adjustment as she makes and loses friends, encounters cruelty and coldness in her new home, and faces new labels of "alien" and "enemy." She grieves alone when she learns that her mother, father, and grandmother died in concentration camps. But remembering Jewish teachings, vows to live her life fully even if she can't determine whether she is at the end or the beginning of it.

Values: Edith learns the value of self-reliance, integrity, and generosity.

Booktalk

We read much about the World War II and Hitler's Holocaust. But what about the people who got out of Germany, the lucky ones? Twelve-year-old Edith is supposed to be a lucky one. Her parents send her to the wonderful United States of America to live with her aunt and uncle—a family. But the aunt and uncle have a daughter. They need a servant. Edith gets that job. Is Edith lucky? (*Wait for the responses.*) Speaking German makes Edith the enemy in this new country. Being Jewish is no asset for social acceptance in the 1940s America either. Is Edith lucky? (*Wait for responses.*) She wonders if this is the land her father promised. She can't sort out that question. She is so confused that she can't even answer *Is It Night or Day?*

Book trailer available @ http://www.youtube.com/ watch?v=UvEBHX0brkc

Values: The story demonstrates the importance of fortitude, honesty, and acceptance.

Read Aloud/Talkback

1. Chapter 2, pages 34 to 35, beginning with "I clutched the heavy . . ." and ending with the chapter. Edith leaves Germany and her family. *Talkback*: How does this passage affect you?
2. Chapter 3, pages 46 to 47, beginning with "I tried to breathe . . ." and ending with the chapter. Edith experiences abandonment. *Talkback*: What does Edith's reaction tell you about her family?
3. Chapter 4, pages 64 to 67, beginning with "At the dance there was . . ." and ending with the chapter. Edith's encounter with a colored doctor reveals many layers of prejudice. *Talkback*: What prejudices are presented in this incident?
4. Chapter 11, pages 149 to 152, beginning with "When I found . . ." and ending with the chapter. Edith goes to watch Hank Greenberg play baseball. *Talkback*: What does Edith learn from Hank Greenburg?
5. Chapter 16, pages 200 to 201, beginning with "Here on the beach . . ." and ending with the chapter. Edith contemplates her life. *Talkback*: Why is this last passage so important to Edith and to the reader?

Discussion guide available @ http://fernschumerchapman .com/wp-content/uploads/2012/06/Night_or_Day_Questions.pdf

Author interviews available @

http://fernschumerchapman.com/?page_id=5075

Author article available @ http://fernschumerchapman .com/?page_id=5144

Related Works

1. **Baer, Edith. *Walk the Dark Streets*.** New York: Farrar, Straus and Giroux/Frances Foster Books, 1998. 280p. $18.00. ISBN 0 374 38229 8. [fiction] JS, CG (*Booktalks Plus*, 2001, pages 153 to 155.) Telling Germany's and Eva Bentheim's story during the Nazi rise to

power, the novel opens in 1933 and ends in 1940, when Eva leaves Germany for America.

2. **Chotjewitz, David, and Doris Orgel (trans.). *Daniel Half Human***. New York: Simon Pulse, 2004. 325p. $5.99pa. ISBN 9 780689 857485. [fiction] JS, CG with high interest for boys (*Booktalks and Beyond*, 2007, pages 191 to 194.) As an interpreter for the U.S. Army in 1945, Daniel returns to the now bombed-out Hamburg, Germany, where he grew up and lost his best friend when Daniel was revealed to be a Jew.

3. **Denenberg, Barry. *One Eye Laughing, the Other Weeping: The Diary of Julie Weiss***. New York, NY: Scholastic Inc., 2000. 256p. (Dear America) $12.95. ISBN 0 439 09518 2. [fiction] MJ, G. When Julie Weiss is12, Hitler invades Austria. Her family is targeted by the Nazis. Her mother commits suicide, her brother leaves for Palestine, and her father arranges for Julie to emigrate and live with her aunt and uncle in the United States.

4. **Gleitzman, Morris. *Once***. New York: Henry Holt &a Co., 2010. 163p. $16.99. ISBN 978 0 8050 9026 0. [fiction] MJS, CG (*Value-Packed Bookalks*, 2011, pages 91 to 93.) Sheltered in a Polish Catholic orphanage, a naïve Felix runs away to find his parents and confronts the horrors of Hilter's Germany.

5. **Konigsburg, E. L. *The Mysterious Edge of the Heroic World***. New York: Atheneum Books for Young Readers/Ginee Seo Books, 2007. 244p. $16.99. ISBN-13: 978 1 4169 4972 5. [fiction] M, CG (*Genre Talks for Teens*, 2009, pages 146 to 149.) Two boys discover a piece of art that ensured a safe passage from Germany for a Jewish child.

۞

Marrin, Albert. Flesh and Blood So Cheap: The Triangle Fire and Its Legacy.

New York: Alfred A. Knopf, 2011. 182p. $19.99.
ISBN 978 0 375 86889 4. [nonfiction] JS, CG

Themes/Topics: Triangle Shirtwaist Company, clothing factories, New York City, safety measures, immigrants, early 20th century

Summary/Description

Marrin describes the immigration, industrialization, fashion changes, greed, and union organization which culminated in the Triangle Factory Fire. He, then, relates the gains and the abuses of both management and labor which followed the fire, and similar conditions existing today in developing countries. He incorporates poetry and interviews from the time as well as charts, sidebars, and pictures, which depict the conditions and people central to the period. A Bibliography and Source Notes provide additional sources. An index allows easy access to the information.

> **Values:** While Marrin sees sweatshop conditions as a natural part of developing countries, he also reinforces the need for honesty and fairness from both management and labor.

Booktalk

Ask the group how many of them have jobs. Ask them to describe how long they work, their benefits, and the rules under which they work.

Show the pictures of workers on pages 60, 63, and 64. Briefly describe their jobs. Ask why they think such conditions existed.

At the end of the 19th century and the beginning of the 20th, hundreds of thousands of people, in this case primarily Jews and Italians, came to this country and stayed in New York. Like other immigrants, they came for jobs and better futures. They found something different: long hours of slave labor to feed their starving families, their children working in factories instead of going to school, and a government that allowed it all to happen. (*What would you have done?*) Some women, some thirteen and fourteen, started to speak out. They ignited a spark that changed the entire country. Unfortunately, that spark of protest grew into one of the worst industrial fires in our history—The Triangle Fire. Did they stop? No. They resolved that never again would this country see *Flesh and Blood So Cheap*.

Book trailer available @ http://www.youtube.com/watch?v= O-kB2g7CAao

Read Aloud/Talkback

1. "Prelude," page 6, beginning with "The Triangle Fire . . ." and ending with ". . . know today." Marrin suggests the significance of the fire. *Talkback*: What does this passage suggest to you about the place of labor and women in U.S. history?
2. Chapter 3, page 74, "In the Factory." The poem by Morris Rosenfeld emphasizes the worker's dehumanization. *Talkback*: What images do you think are most important?

3. Chapter 4, pages 94 to 95, "Why?" The feminist poem drives home the need to vote. *Talkback*: What is your reaction to the poem?
4. Chapter 6, page 128. On this page are a picture of the memorial procession and an excerpt of Morris Rosenfeld's poem which mourns the victims. *Talkback*: Is Rosenfeld's poem simply a memorial?
5. "Never Again!," pages 130 to 133. This section includes Rose Schneiderman's "Bread and Roses" speech and the context in which it was given. *Talkback*: What made this speech effective?

Teacher's guide for The Triangle Fire available @ http://labor-studies.org/featured-resources/triangle-factory-fire/#
Author interviews available @

http://www.albertmarrin.com/awards-honors.html
http://www.albertmarrin.com/biography-marrin.html

Related Works

1. **Gratz, Alan. *The Brooklyn Nine: A Novel in Nine Innings*.** New York: Dial Books, 2009. 299p. $16.99. ISBN-13: 978 0 8037 3224 7. [fiction] JS, CG (*Value-Packed Booktalks*, 2011, pages 195 to 198.) Nine short stories, ranging from 1845 to 2002, chronicle the lives of the Schneider/Snider/Flint family from immigration to integration.
2. **Hesse, Karen. *Brooklyn Bridge*.** New York: Feiwel and Friends, 2008. 229p. $17.95. ISBN-13: 978 0 312 37886 8. [fiction] MJS, CG (*Value-Packed Booktalks*, 2011, pages 198 to 200.) Fourteen-year-old Joseph Michtom lives in Brooklyn, New York, in the early 20th century. His prosperous Russian immigrant family's life contrasts with the bleak lives of homeless children under the Brooklyn Bridge.
3. **Hood, Thomas. "The Song of the Shirt."** The Victorian Web. Available: http://www.victorianweb.org/authors/hood/shirt.html (accessed on May 2012). [poem] S/A, CG. The poem protests the brutal working conditions for women in Victorian England.
4. **Hopkinson, Deborah. *Shutting Out the Sky: Life in the Tenements of New York 1880–1924*.** New York: Scholastic Inc./Orchard Books, 2003. 134p. $17.95. ISBN 0 439 37590 8. [nonfiction] MJS, CG. Hopkinson illustrates the New York tenement living conditions.
5. **Siegel, Robert. "Jacob Riis: Shedding Light on NYC's 'Other Half.'"** NPR Books. Available: http://www.npr.org/templates/story/story.php?storyId=91981589 (accessed on May 2012). [nonfiction] JS/A, CG. The site provides 11 of Riis's photographs and a written and oral discussion of his work.

CRO

Metselaar, Menno, Ruud van der Rol and Arnold J. Pomerans (trans.). **Anne Frank: Her Life in Words and Pictures.**

New York: Roaring Brook Press/Flash Point, 2009. $12.99.
ISBN-13: 978 1 59643 547 6. [nonfiction] MJS, CG

Themes/Topics: World War II, Anne Frank, holocaust, Netherlands, Nazi occupation

Summary/Description

Using narrative describing the Frank's home life and the progression of the war, family and holocaust pictures, passages from Anne Frank's diary as well as maps and diagrams, the book tells and illustrates the Franks's story within the context of the Nazi rise to and fall from power. The sections begin with the period from "1925 to 1933" and ends with "1945 and after," to give a picture of the world into which Anne was born and the effect of her legacy. A glossary provides additional information about Germany and the Netherlands during World War II.

Value: Anne's story illustrates faith and hope within a world of hate and destruction.

Booktalk

Ask how many in the group have heard of Anne Frank and how many have read her diary. Invite them to share their impressions. This scrapbook lets us see as well as hear her. As you speak, turn the pages toward the audience. She was a little girl, and then a teenager who loved parties, writing, and family. She fled from her home country to another, and then left her new home for a cramped and dangerous hiding place. In that two years, she kept a journal. (*Show pages 116 to 137.*) It was a birthday present that gave her immortality. It inspired people to make the building where Anne hid a museum. (*Show pages 78 to 91.*) Now, you can see her world as well as hear her voice in *Anne Frank: Her Life in Words and Pictures*.

Read Aloud/Talkback

The entire book provides appropriate passages and pictures to use with the *Diary of Anne Frank* and any other literature about the holocaust. Below are five specific suggestions:

1. "1940–1942," page 57. Anne's diary describes living within Nazi rules. *Talkback*: If you had been a Jew, living at this time, how would you have reacted?
2. "1942–1944," pages 72 to 75, beginning with "The mailman . . ." and ending with ". . . was yet to happen." The Franks go into hiding. *Talkback*: After reading Anne's words and the narrative, how do you feel about the Franks?
3. "1942–1944," page 140, beginning with "Anne discovered . . ." and ending with ". . . completely independent of others." Anne sees her internal changes. *Talkback*: Do you think that Anne's feelings are unusual for her age?
4. "1942–1944," pages 158 to 159, beginning with "In the weeks . . ." and ending with ". . . came to pass." Anne continues to see herself as independent. This reading includes the famous diary passage in which she clings to the hope that ". . . people are truly good at heart." *Talkback*: What does Anne expect from people? Do you agree with her?
5. "1944–1945," page 177, beginning with "One evening . . ." and ending with ". . . for a few hours." The passage describes the party that Margot and Anne shared with the other prisoners at Bergen-Belsen. *Talkback*: What does this passage say about celebration?

Discussion guide available @ http://media.us.macmillan.com/ teachersguides/9781596435476TG.pdf

Author interview available @ http://barbarabbookblog.blogspot .com/2010/03/welcome-meeno-metselaar-anne-frank.html

Related Works

1. **Frank, Anne. *The Diary of a Young Girl: The Definitive Edition*.** Edited by Otto H. Frank and Mirjam Pressler. Translated by Susan Massotty. New York: Doubleday, 1991. 340p. $25.00. ISBN 0 385 47378 8. [nonfiction] JSA/CG. The edition contains approximately 30 percent more material and is based on the scholarship of *The Diary of Anne Frank: The Critical Edition*.
2. **Müller, Melissa, Rita Limber and Robert Kimber (trans.). *Anne Frank: The Biography*.** New York: Henry Holt and Co., 1998. 330p. $14.00pa. ISBN 0 8050 5997 0. [nonfiction] JSA/CG. This work places Anne Frank in a family, social, and political context.
3. **Opdyke, Irene Gut, with Jennifer Armstrong. *In My Hands: Memories of a Holocaust Rescuer*.** New York: Alfred A. Knopf, 1999. $18.00. ISBN 0 679 89181 1. [nonfiction] JS, CG (*Booktalks and More*, pages 255 to 258.) Opdyke's family life and personal

beliefs led her to help and hide Jews during the German occupation of Poland.

4. **Sawyer, Kem Knapp.** *Anne Frank: A Photographic Story of a Life*. New York: DK Publishing Inc., 2004. 127p. $4.99pa. ISBN 0 7566 0341 2. [nonfiction] MJ, CG. Using narrative and pictures, Sawyer tells about Anne's life in the annex and the reactions of those around her. The book includes timelines, a Bibliography, a list of relevant organizations, and an index.

5. **Schloss, Eva, and Evelyn Julia Kent.** *Eva's Story: A Survivor's Tale by the Stepsister of Anne Frank*. Grand Rapids, MI: William B. Eerdmans Publishing Co., 1988, 2010. 226p. $14.99pa. ISBN 978 0 8028 6495 6. [nonfiction] JS, CG. Schloss's mother married Otto Frank after the war. Her story of survival in a concentration camp completes Anne's story of her life in hiding.

ꙮ

Perkins, Mitali. **Bamboo People.**

Watertown, MA: Charlesbridge, 2010. 272p. $16.95.
ISBN 978 1 58089 328 2. [fiction] JS, CG with high interest for boys

Themes/Topics: Burma, coming of age, survival, friendship, family

Summary/Description

Studious Chiko responds to an advertisement for a teaching position and is inducted into the army under a sadistic captain. He bonds with Tai, an orphaned street boy tricked by an advertisement for street sweepers. Tai teaches Chiko to survive. Chiko teaches Tai to read and write. When offered a city office assignment, Chiko recommends Tai for the job, so that Tai can find the sister from whom he was separated on the day he was taken. Chiko takes Tai's place on a suicide mission against the Karenni where he loses his leg. Tu Reh and his father of the "enemy" Karenni find him. Tu Reh saves Chiko's life, befriends him, defends him from other Karenni, and helps him get an artificial leg. Chiko is released from the army to his home where Tai and his sister now live. Tai tells Chiko that his father, a political prisoner, will soon return home.

Values: The stories of Chiko, Tai, and Tu Reh show the importance of trust, integrity, loyalty, and love within a violent and sometimes sadistic world.

Booktalk

Ask how many in the group have ever answered an advertisement for a job. Ask a few to share their experiences.

In this story, two teenage boys answer job advertisements. One applies to be a street sweeper, the other to be a teacher. Both are inducted into the Burmese army and taken away from their families to train in a jungle. One trusts street smarts. The other trusts books. Neither knows how to escape. Then, there is a third boy, their Karenni enemy. According to the Burmese authorities, the Karenni minority causes all the country's problems. This Karenni boy remembers Burmese soldiers burning his home and bamboo fields. He knows Burmese soldiers will try to kill him, so he will strike first. But wild animals, land mines, enemies, and even fellow soldiers can destroy all three boys, instantly. Who should they believe and trust? Are their people the Burmese? The Karenni? Or the *Bamboo People*?

Book trailer available @ http://www.youtube.com/watch?v=sx1fskadcHQ&afeature=related

Book trailers, discussion guides, and background information available @ http://www.bamboopeople.org/2009/01/reader-book-trailer.html

Read Aloud/Talkback

1. Part 1, Chapter 1, pages 4 to 6, beginning with "She's right . . ." to the end of the chapter. Chiko reflects on his father's legacy of learning. *Talkback*: What does this passage tell you about life in Burma?
2. Part 1, Chapter 14, pages 69 to 73. This chapter shows Tai's intelligence and street smarts when given an impossible task by the sadistic captain. *Talkback*: What does this passage have to say about education?
3. Part 1, Chapter 22, pages 105 to 108. This chapter shows Tai's dedication to his family and his acceptance of Chiko as his brother. *Talkback*: After reading this chapter, how would you define family?
4. Part 2, Chapter 3, pages 147 to 149, beginning with "When we reach . . ." and ending with the chapter. Tu Reh and his father find Chiko, and the father offers his son a choice. *Talkback*: What is Tu Reh's point in his comparison to bamboo?
5. Part 2, Chapter 24, pages 241 to 246. In this chapter, Tu Reh defends Chiko in the community meeting. *Talkback*: How do the Karenni define themselves in this chapter?

Author interviews available @

http://www.teachingbooks.net/tb.cgi?aid=3369&a=1
http://www.yabookshelf.com/2010/08/interview-with-mitali-
     perkins-author-of-bamboo-people/
http://www.bookbundlz.com/bbarticle.aspx?articleid=64
http://www.youtube.com/watch?v=JnsfjzszkpU
http://www.bamboopeople.org/
http://thesecretadventuresofwritergirl.blogspot.com/2010/10/
     interview-mitali-perkins-author-of.html

Related Works

1. **Beah, Ishmael. *A Long Way Gone: Memoirs of a Boy Soldier*.** New York: Farrar, Straus and Giroux/Sarah Crichton Books, 2007. 229p. $22.00. ISBN-13: 978 0 374 10523 5. [nonfiction] JS/A, CG with high interest for boys (*Genre Talks for Teens*, 2009, pages 98 to 100.) When Ishmael is 12, his family's village is wiped out in a rebel raid, and he begins his journey of physical, emotional, and intellectual survival that ends in a UN rehabilitation camp, and eventually the United States.

2. **Ellis, Deborah. *Sacred Leaf*.** Toronto, ON: House of Anansi Press/Groundwood Books, 2007. 206p. (The Cocalero Novels) $16.95. ISBN-13: 978 088899 751 7. [fiction] MJ, CG with high interest for boys (*Genre Talks for Teens*, pages 287 to 289.) In this second Cocalero novel, Diego joins the coca farmers against the army who are destroying the coca crops.

3. **Engle, Margarita. *The Surrender Tree: Poems of Cuba's Struggle for Freedom*.** New York: Henry Holt &a Co., 2008. 169p. $16.95. ISBN-13: 978 0 8050 8674 4. [novel in verse] JS, CG (*Value-Packed Booktalks*, 2011, pages 184 to 186.) Rosa, the healer, tends the sick and the wounded, regardless of their loyalties in the Cuban wars for freedom.

4. **Nanji, Shenaaz. *Child of Dandelions*.** Asheville, NC: Front Street, 2008. 214p. $17.95. ISBN-13: 978 1 932425 93 2. [fiction] JS, G (*Genre Talks for Teens*, pages 289 to 292.) Fifteen-year-old Sabine and her family, declared "foreign Indians" in Uganda, are discriminated against and forced to leave the country.

5. **Pow, Tom. *Captives*.** New Milford, CT: Roaring Brook Press/A Neal Porter Book, 2007. 185p. $17.95. ISBN 978 1 59643 201 7. [fiction] JS, CG (*Genre Talks for Teens*, 2009, pages 111 to 113.) Two families are kidnapped by rebels. The father of one family

writes a bestselling book that portrays the rebels full of bitterness and hate. The son's version expands on the reasons behind the rebellion fought against a dictator backed by American greed.

Revolution

Anderson, Laurie Halse. **Forge.**
New York: Atheneum Books for Young Readers, 2010. 297p.
(Seeds of America) $16.99.
ISBN: 978 1 4169 6144 4. [fiction] MJS, CG

Themes/Topics: Pennsylvania history, American Revolution, Valley Forge, 18th century, soldiers, African Americans, freedmen, slavery

Summary/Description

In this sequel to *Chains*, Isabel leaves Curzon to find her sister Ruth. Curzon saves a rebel boy in a fight with British soldiers, becomes his friend, and enlists in the army. In spite of the rudeness and prejudice of a "bigoted bully," Curzon becomes a vital part of the company that eventually winters in Valley Forge. Bellingham, his former master, visits Valley Forge and forces Curzon back into slavery. Bellingham has also purchased Isabel. He notes their affection and promises to hurt Isabel if Curzon rebels or runs away. Isabel and Curzon plan to escape when Bellingham sells Isabel, but must fight Bellingham who guesses their plan. Once again, Isabel rescues Curzon. They flee under the cover of Curzon's Valley Forge comrades. In an Appendix, Anderson answers questions about the book and includes suggestions for Further Reading. A Glossary defines words related to that period.

Values: With resilience, risk-taking, and persistence, Curzon and Isabel clarify their loyalties and love.

Booktalk

Hold up Chains. *Ask if anyone in the group has read the book. If they have, ask them to give a brief summary.* In *Chains*, Curzon helps Isabel cope with a cruel mistress. Isabel saves Curzon's life and they escape.

In this story, they separate. Isabel is determined to find her sister, but Curzon predicts she will lose her own liberty in a lost cause. He joins the rebels again and finds himself at Valley Forge without enough food, shelter, or clothing. (*Ask members of the group to share what they know about Valley Forge.*) Is his choice a lost cause also? A bigoted bully and a former master want him dead or in chains. Then, Isabel returns. Do you think she was successful? (*Wait for responses.*) No, she is a slave. Isabel saved Curzon's life. Now, can he save hers—and his—after being tempered like steel in the *Forge*?

Author interview/booktalk available @ http://books.sim onandschuster.com/Forge/Laurie-Halse-Anderson/9781416961444

Read Aloud/Talkback

1. "Prelude," pages 3 to 5. Curzon realizes that Isabel has made them free. *Talkback*: Why isn't this passage completely happy?
2. Chapter 5, pages 22 to 25. Curzon joins the battle. *Talkback*: What is your impression of the battle?
3. "Before," page 46. Curzon explains his feelings for Isabel after Ebenezer asks him about the seeds and the ribbon that he carries. *Talkback*: How do you react to Curzon's description of his feelings or relationship with Isabel?
4. Chapter 10, pages 48 to 51, beginning with "The officers ordered . . ." and ending with ". . . powerful silence." The British surrender. *Talkback*: What details in this passage are the most significant to you?
5. "Before," pages 146 to 147. Curzon describes his treatment as a slave of the Bellinghams. *Talkback*: What is your impression of each father and son?

Reading group guide and curriculum connections available@

http://books.simonandschuster.com/Forge/Laurie-Halse-Anderson/ 9781416961444/reading_group_guide

Author interviews available @

http://www.youtube.com/watch?v=r-bnxxEHSIQ
http://www.facebook.com/video/video.php?v=1666048486408
http://birthofanovel.wordpress.com/2010/02/22/laurie-halse- anderson-talks-to-gretchen-haertsch/
http://www.readingrockets.org/books/interviews/anderson/ transcript/
http://madwomanintheforest.com/forge-questions/

Related Works

1. **Allen, Thomas B.** *George Washington, Spymaster: How the Americans Outspied the British and Won the Revolutionary War*. Washington, DC: National Geographic, 2004. 184p. $16.95. ISBN 0 7922 5126 1. [nonfiction] MJS, CG (*Booktalks and Beyond*, 2007, pages 215 to 218.) Beginning with Washington's early life, Allen portrays Washington as a spymaster who eventually defeats the British with wit rather than might.

2. **Anderson, Laurie Halse. *Chains***. New York: Simon &a Schuster Books for Young Readers, 2008. 316p. (Seeds of America) $16.99. ISBN-13: 978 1 4169 0585 1. [fiction] JS, CG with high interest for girls (*Value-Packed Booktalks*, 2011, pages 179 to 181.) In this first book, Isabel and her younger sister Ruth are sold to a British family in Boston even though their mistress freed them in her will. Curzon recruits her as a spy.

3. **Anderson, M. T.** *The Astonishing Life of Octavian Nothing Traitor to the Nation; Volume II: The Kingdom on the Waves*. Cambridge, MA: Candlewick Press, 2008. 561p. $22.99. ISBN 978 0 7636 2950 2. [fiction] JS, CG with high interest for boys (*Value-Packed Booktalks*, 2011, pages 181 to 183.) With Dr. Tefusis, Octavian joins Lord Dunmore's Ethiopian Regiment in Norfolk, reunites with Pro Bono, faces prejudice from the British and his fellow soldiers, and learns about his heritage.

4. **Anderson, M. T.** *The Astonishing Life of Octavian Nothing: Traitor to the Nation; Volume I: The Pox Party*. Cambridge, MA: Candlewick Press, 2006. 351p. $17.99. ISBN 0 7636 2402 0. [fiction] JS, CG (*Genre Talks for Teens*, 2009, pages 217 to 220.) Octavian and his mother Cassiopeia are pampered and studied by Boston scholars.

5. **Freedman, Russell.** *Washington at Valley Forge*. New York: Holiday House, 2008. 112p. $24.95. ISBN 978 0 8234 0069 8. [nonfiction] JS, CG. At Valley Forge, Washington transforms his troops from a cold, starving, and hopeless group of would-be soldiers to a disciplined and optimistic army that can defeat the British.

వ్ఁ

Bartoletti, Susan Campbell. The Boy Who Dared.
New York: Scholastic Press, 2008. 202p. $16.99.
ISBN-13: 978 0 439 68013 4. [fiction] MJS, CG with high interest for boys

Themes/Topics: World War II, Hitler, the Resistance Movement, Mormons

Summary/Description

Seventeen-year-old Mormon Helmuth, reviews events that lead him to the death row in a World War II German prison. He watches Hitler take on a god-like quality, and witnesses government torture and discrimination. He suspects that his school lessons are biased and distorted. His older brother buys a radio on the black market. Helmuth accesses forbidden British broadcasts and learns the government's lies. He writes and circulates antigovernment pamphlets. The Gestapo arrests and tortures him until he reveals his fellow resisters. He targets himself to save his friends. They receive prison sentences. He receives a death sentence. Helmuth's thoughts and experiences in his death row cell are in italics, interspersed with the memories of life before prison. The book includes pictures of Helmuth, his family, and friends, the poster announcing his execution, a map of 1936 Europe, a Third Reich Time Line, a Bibliography, a brief discussion of sources, and a teaching guide Web site where Bartoletti discusses her writing process.

Values: Helmuth demonstrates courage, patriotism, loyalty, and faith.

Booktalk

Ask someone in the group to read aloud the italicized passage on page 3. This is the way that 17-year-old Helmuth starts his day. He is a prisoner in World War II Germany. He is a full-blooded Aryan. (*Ask if the group knows what Aryan means. Wait for answers or explain.*) He is not a Jew, a Communist, a gypsy, or any other person the government has labeled defective. He lives this nightmare by choice. His family takes the path of good Germans. They commit to the Fatherland or remain silent. Helmuth reads, writes, and listens. He sees atrocities around him. (*Show pictures of the rioting in German cities and the abuse of Jews.*) As a Mormon, he believes that no man can put himself above God. Hitler does that. Helmuth speaks out. At first, he challenges his family, maybe a teacher, but he has to tell other Germans that Hitler lies, not just about Jews and Communists, but also about German victories. He knows that the leadership's lies will topple the Reich. Who are Germany's true patriots? Those who commit, those who keep silent, or *The Boy Who Dared*?

Book trailers available @

http://www.scholastic.com/teachers/book/boy-who-dared
http://www.youtube.com/watch?v=eDPxeFTrbHo
http://www.youtube.com/watch?v=t7jWslKUqmY

http://www.scholastic.com/browse/video.jsp?pID=1640149541&
abcpid=1640149541&abckey=AQ~,AAAAAFv844g~,BASb5B
U03X-iSxP2xnUo82nI3lwCMiDm&abclid=1557820329&abct
id=14273522001

Read Aloud/Talkback

1. Page 3, the italicized passage. The novel begins by revealing Helmuth's greatest fear. *Talkback*: Why do you think that the author starts with the execution?
2. Pages 23 to 25, beginning with "It's the end . . ." and ending with ". . . destroy the government." Helmuth trusts the simple answers of his mother and the government. *Talkback*: Why does the author include this incident?
3. Pages 42 to 45, beginning with "Suddenly the classroom door . . ." and ending with ". . . with a pulse all their own." Helmuth questions the romantic heroism of the new curriculum. *Talkback*: Is Helmuth's question a good one? What is your impression of the teacher?
4. Pages 70 to 73, beginning with "Two nights later . . ." and ending with ". . . stares back at him." Helmuth reacts to his family's participation in anti-Semitism. *Talkback*: What is Helmuth discovering about his family?
5. Pages 153 to 154, the italicized passage. Helmuth decides that he has done the right thing. *Talkback*: Do you agree with Helmuth's conclusion?

Teaching guides available @

http://www.scholastic.com/teachers/lesson-plan/discussion-guide-boy-who-dared

http://www.ilfonline.org/clientuploads/YHBA/10–11%20YHBA%20Resources/BoyWhoDared.pdf

http://www.focusonthefamily.com/parenting/protecting_your_family/book-reviews/b/boy-who-dared.aspx

http://nvholocausteducation.org/yahoo_site_admin/assets/docs/Literature_and_the_Holocaust_Colleen_Moriarty_MS_ELA.340143759.pdf

Author interview available @ http://www.youtube.com/watch?v=jr-lp7CNI1Q

Related Works

1. **Giblin, James Cross. *The Life and Death of Adolf Hitler*.** New York: Clarion Books, 2002. 246p. $21.00. ISBN 0 395 90371.

[nonfiction] MJS, CG (*Teen Genre Connections*, pages 250 to 252.) Giblin portrays a disturbed, talented, and dedicated Hitler appealing to the prejudices and fears of the Germans after World War I.

2. **Hughes, Dean. *Soldier Boys***. New York: Atheneum Publishers, 2001. 162p. $16.00. ISBN 0 689 81748 7. [fiction] MJS, CG with high interest for boys (*Booktalks and More*, 2003, pages 51 to 54.) Dieter Hedrick, a decorated member of Hitler's Youth, and Spencer Morgan, an American Mormon, want to prove their manhood by fighting in a war.

3. **Opdyke, Irene Gut, with Jennifer Armstrong. *In My Hands: Memories of a Holocaust Rescuer***. New York: Alfred A. Knopf, 1999. 276p. $18.00. ISBN 0 679 89181 1. [nonfiction] JS, CG (*Booktalks and More*, 2003, pages 255 to 257.) Opdyke's family life and personal beliefs led her to aid Jews during the German occupation of Poland.

4. **Tunnell, Michael O. *Brothers in Valor: A Story of Resistance***. New York: Holiday House, 2001. 260p. $16.95. ISBN 0 8234 1541 4. [fiction] JS, CG. Cited by Bartoletti in her bibliography as an alternate version of the same events, this novel tells about the Helmuth Hübener Group that resisted Hitler's claim to be God.

5. **Zusak, Markus. *The Book Thief***. New York: Alfred A. Knopf, 2006. 552p. $21.90. ISBN 0 375 93100 7. [fiction] JS, CG with high interest for girls (*Genre Talks for Teens*, pages 241 to 243.) Death tells the story of Liesel Meminger, the daughter of a Communist in Hitler's Germany.

❦

Paulsen, Gary. Woods Runner.
New York: Wendy Lamb Books, 2010. 164p. $7,99pa.
ISBN 978 0 375 85908 3. [fiction] MJ, CG with high interest for boys

Themes/Topics: Kidnapping, frontier and pioneer life, Pennsylvania, soldiers, espionage, Indians of North America, American Revolution, 18th century

Summary/Description

Alternating fiction chapters and historical segments tell the story of 13-year-old Samuel's journey to save his parents and the historical context in which it occurred. Part I describes his frontier life and his realization that his family has been attacked by the British and the Iroquois Indians. Part II relates his journey to New York to find his parents. In

Part III, spies help him rescue his parents. The Epilogue describes the family's life in Philadelphia 3 years later and 16-year-old Samuel's decision to join Morgon's Rifles. An Afterword explains Paulsen's purpose in writing the story.

Values: Samuel demonstrates his loyalty, generosity, and fairness.

Booktalk

Ask the group who fought in the American Revolution. Ask about slaves, Native Americans, and wilderness settlers.

Thirteen-year-old Samuel doesn't know anything about war. The Pennsylvania woods is his world. Civilization in the East promises to change that. The city and plantation people are brewing the revolution against the British. Samuel and his family hear about it. Then, British troops and the Iroquois attack their settlement, burn the houses, massacre some people, and capture others. Ask why the settlement would not know. (*Wait for responses.*) Samuel is in the woods during the attack. His parents are captured and herded to New York. (*What would you do?*) Samuel follows. He knows how to track the party and hide from the troops, but then what? What does he know about a city? The British? The patriots? Or a revolution? What can one boy do against a trained army, when he has lived his life as a *Woods Runner*?

Book trailers available @

http://www.youtube.com/watch?v=h0WOQsp69RI&afeature=related

Read Aloud/Talkback

1. Chapter 1, pages 3 to 9, beginning with "And he pictured . . ." and ending with ". . . London and Paris." Samuel reflects on the two worlds to which he belongs. *Talkback*: How do both worlds strengthen Samuel? How does Samuel represent the rising nation?
2. Chapter 4, pages 27 to 29, beginning with the chapter and ending with ". . . in savage rage." Samuel surveys the massacre. *Talkback*: How is this scene both devastating and hopeful?
3. Chapter 5, pages 34 to 35, beginning with the chapter and ending with ". . . what others could not." Paulsen describes Samuel's knowledge. *Talkback*: Does Samuel surprise you? If so, in what way?
4. Chapter 14, pages 106 to 109, beginning with "The thought of his parents . . ." and ending with the chapter. Abner explains his good deeds. *Talkback*: What is your impression of Abner?

5. Chapter 18, pages 149 to 150, beginning with "She was studying . . ." and ending with the chapter. Samuel's mother sees a difference in him. *Talkback*: Has Samuel changed?

Read aloud available @ http://www.teachingbooks.net/book_ reading.cgi?id=4005&a=1

Teacher's guide available @ http://www.randomhouse.com/ catalog/teachers_guides/9780375859083.pdf

Author interviews available @

http://www.randomhouse.com/book/196874/woods-runner-by-gary-paulsen#blurb_tabs

http://www.thechildrensbookreview.com/weblog/2010/01/author-interview-gary-paulsen.html

http://blogcritics.org/books/article/conversation-with-a-master-an-interview/

http://www.bookotron.com/agony/audio/2010/2010-interviews/ gary_paulsen-2010.mp3

http://www.randomhouse.com/features/garypaulsen/book-report-corner.html

Survival tips available @ http://www.randomhouse.com/features/ garypaulsen/newadventures.html

Related Works

1. **Allen, Thomas B. *George Washington, Spymaster: How the Americans Outspied the British and Won the Revolutionary War***. Washington, DC: National Geographic, 2004. 184p. $16.95. ISBN 0 7922 5126 1. [nonfiction] MJS, CG (*Booktalks and Beyond*, 2007, pages 215 to 218.) Allen portrays Washington as a spymaster who eventually defeats the British with wit rather than might.

2. **Anderson, Laurie Halse. *Chains***. New York: Simon &a Schuster Books for Young Readers, 2008. 316p. (Seeds of America) $16.99. ISBN 13: 978 1 4169 0585 1. [fiction] JS, CG with high interest for girls (*Value-Packed Booktalks*, 2011, pages 179 to 181.) A falsely held slave spies for the rebels and saves her friend from a British prison.

3. **Anderson, M.T. *The Astonishing Life of Octavian Nothing: Traitor to the Nation; Volume I: The Pox Party***. Cambridge, MA: Candlewick Press, 2006. 351p. (The Astonishing Life of Octavian Nothing: Traitor to the Nation) $17.99. ISBN 0 7636 2402 0. [fiction] JS, CG (*Genre Talks for Teens*, 2009, pages 217 to 220.) Octavian discovers that his sheltered life with scholars is really slavery.

4. **Anderson, M. T.** *The Astonishing Life of Octavian Nothing: Traitor to the Nation; Volume II: The Kingdom on the Waves*. Cambridge, MA: Candlewick Press, 2008. 595p. (The Astonishing Life of Octavian Nothing: Traitor to the Nation) $22.99. ISBN-13: 978 0 76 3629502. [fiction] JS, CG (*Value-Packed Booktalks*, 2011, pages 181 to 183.) Octavian escapes to Boston and finds a freedom offer from counterrevolutionary forces.

5. **Paulsen, Gary.** *Soldier's Heart: Being the Story of the Enlistment and Due Service of the Boy Charley Goddard in the First Minnesota Volunteers*. New York: Delacorte Press, 1998. 106p. $15.95. ISBN 0 385 32498 7. [fiction] JS, CG with high interest for boys. Paulsen shows, this time in the Civil War, how war destroys.

✿✿

Sheinkin, Steve. **The Notorious Benedict Arnold.**

New York: Roaring Brook Press/Flashpoint, 2010. 337p. $19.99.
ISBN 978 1 59643 486 8. [nonfiction] JS, CG with high interest for boys

Themes/Topics: American Revolution, conduct of life, Benedict Arnold, heroism, treason

Summary/Description

Sheinkin traces Benedict Arnold's tumultuous life from his difficult childhood to his decision to ally himself with the English. Haunted by family disgrace and poverty, he becomes a successful businessman and is drawn into the American Revolution. His bravery, flamboyance, and abrasiveness make him a hero in battle and a disaster in politics. Encouraged by his second wife, Peggy Shippen, and angry with the congress, the public, and fellow officers, he arranges with the British to expose West Point. The plot's failure, seen as a divine gift to the revolution, unifies the colonies. Sheinkin also recounts the path of John André, the British officer, who hanged as a spy for arranging Arnold's treachery. Source Notes includes an extensive bibliography and Quotations Notes for each chapter. Maps appear throughout the book.

Values: Vanity and arrogance overshadow Arnold's work ethic.

Booktalk

Ask how many people have heard of Benedict Arnold.

If you call someone a Benedict Arnold today, what are you saying? (*Wait for responses.*) Right, you are calling that person a traitor, a backstabber. Arnold not only sold out his country, but he was also one of the most recognized heroes of the American Revolution. (*Ask how many people knew that.*) He was George Washington's most trusted general and the man that the British most wanted to kill. Neither side thought he could be bribed. They were wrong. Arnold wanted an American Revolution that included huge homes, a trophy wife, and endless personal praise. Why was luxury more important than his country? How did he almost accomplish the most history-changing betrayal the world has ever seen? Brains, cunning, stealth, daring, and bitterness produced *The Notorious Benedict Arnold.*

American Stories Through Song trailer available @ http://www.youtube.com/watch?v=YTHgxBvhaFo&afeature=related

Read Aloud/Talkback

The brief and detailed chapters make the entire book an excellent read aloud. The following chapters are especially appealing:

1. "Arnold's War," pages 24 to 31. Arnold joins the revolution and meets the Green Mountain Boys. *Talkback*: Why do Arnold and Ethan Allen conflict? Be specific.

2. "To the Dead River," pages 60 to 62, beginning with "The cheering didn't . . ." and ending with "Two drowned." This description of the first part of the March to Quebec shows the hardships Arnold and his men face. *Talkback*: List a soldier's enemies?

3. "Battle of Valcour Island," pages 126 to 128. The passage describes the overwhelming forces faced by the rebels. *Talkback*: What does the passage reveal about Arnold?

4. "Conquer or Die," pages 175 to 177. This chapter describes the Paoli Massacre. *Talkback*: Why was this described as a "Massacre" rather than a battle?

5. "Papers of a Dangerous Tendency," pages 269 to 272, beginning with the chapter and ending with ". . . you stopped me." André is captured. *Talkback*: How is the capture ironic?

Read aloud available @ http://www.randomhouse.com/audio/listeninglibrary/catalog/author.php?authorid=162089

Author interviews available @

http://stevesheinkin.com/
http://us.macmillan.com/author/stevesheinkin
http://www.hbook.com/2011/12/news/boston-globe-horn-book-
    awards/the-notorious-benedict-arnold-acceptance-speech/
http://storytellershistory.com/meet-the-author.php
http://www.stevesheinkin.com/bio.html

Lesson plans available @

http://classroombookshelf.blogspot.com/2012/02/2012-yalsa-award-
    for-excellence-in.html
http://ci454.wikispaces.com/The+Notorious+Benedict+Arnold

Discussion and teaching guide, author interviews, and read alouds available @ http://www.teachingbooks.net/ tb.cgi?tid=21656&a=1

Related Works

1. **Allen, Thomas B. *George Washington, Spymaster: How the Americans Outspied the British and Won the Revolutionary War*.** Washington, DC: National Geographic, 2004. 184p. $16.95. ISBN 0 7922 5126 1. [nonfiction] MJS, CG with high interest for boys (*Booktalks and Beyond*, 2007, pages 215 to 218.) Washington defeats the British with wit rather than might.

2. **Aronson, Marc. *The Real Revolution: The Global Story of American Independence*.** New York: Clarion Books, 2005. 238p. $21.00. ISBN 0 618 18179 2. [nonfiction] JS, CG (*Booktalks and Beyond*, 2007, pages 218 to 221.) Aronson begins with the stories of three soldiers: Robert Clive, George Washington, and James Wolfe, then moves to the challenges to the 18th-century British expansionism that led to developing the American character and revolution

3. **Blackwood, Gary. *The Year of the Hangman*.** New York: Dutton Books, 2002. 261p. $16.99. ISBN 0 525 46921 4. [fiction] MJS, CG with high interest for boys (*Teen Genre Connections*, 2005, pages 142 to 144.) The alternate history novel speculates what America would have been like if the British had won. Benedict Arnold leads pirates.

4. **Freedman, Russell. *Washington at Valley Forge*.** New York: Holiday House, 2008. 112p. $24.95. ISBN 978 0 8234 0069 8. [nonfiction] JS, CG. Washington transforms his troops from a hopeless group of would-be soldiers to a disciplined and optimistic army.

5. **Murphy, Jim. *The Real Benedict Arnold*.** New York: Clarion Books, 2007. 264p. $20.00. ISBN-13: 978 0 395 77609 4. [nonfiction]

JS, CG with high interest for boys (*Genre Talks for Teens*, 2009, pages 249 to 252.) Murphy examines the family background, social status, vicious rumors, political upheaval, jealousy, brilliant military sense, and personal relationships that shape Arnold's decisions.

☙❧

Schröder, Monika. **My Brother's Shadow.**
New York: Farrar, Straus and Giroux/Frances Foster Books, 2011. 217p. $17.99.
ISBN 978 0 374 35122 9. [fiction] JS, CG with high interest for boys

Themes/Topics: Germany (1918–1933), World War I (1914–1918), family life, prejudice, journalism, political activism, conduct of life

Summary/Description

Sixteen-year-old Moritz, too young to serve in the German army, helps support his family by working in a print shop. His older brother Hans fights on the Western Front. Their father was killed in battle. Their mother and sister are political activists who are trying to overthrow the Kaiser. Moritz wants to be a journalist. His interest in writing and reading help him learn about his mother's resistance work and build a relationship with Rebecca, a Jewish resistance worker. Hans arranges for Moritz to take his place in a neighborhood gang that steals from the merchants and the wealthy. Hans returns home maimed, bitter, and addicted. Hans joins a hate campaign against Jews and Communists, and the gang pressures Moritz to betray his employer, his family, and Rebecca. After a confrontation between the brothers, Hans leaves home and pursues the path that will lead Germany to World War II. Moritz's mother wins an election which will tie her to the Communist movement. Moritz is promoted to a journalist.

Values: Moritz rejects hate and violence as he tries to help his family and country survive.

Booktalk

It is 1918. Germany has been at war for four years. The people are starving, and the fractured country is full of rebellion, gangs, and lies. Sixteen-year-old Moritz is too young to fight. His father died in the war. His brother is in the trenches on the Western Front. His mother and sister are working to throw the Kaiser, the leader of Germany, out of office.

Moritz works as a printer, but he wants to be a journalist. That means that he has to see different points of view. What are they? (*Wait for answers.*) Right now, two points are most important. How will the loyal soldiers, like his brother, see the war and the defeat that is coming? How will the social reformers, like his mother and sister, see the country's transformation and its new beginning? World War I may be ending, but a new war is starting. It will split families and target Communists and Jews. And this war will change the world even more. If you were to ask Moritz what he fears most, he would probably reply, *My Brother's Shadow*.

Book trailer available @ http://www.youtube.com/ watch?v=46jLWcswcfk

Read Aloud/Talkback

1. Chapter 9, pages 44 to 46. In this chapter, Moritz visits his mother who is hiding with his aunt. *Talkback*: What is Moritz learning about his mother and aunt? What is your feeling about each of the characters in the chapter?
2. Chapter 11, pages 55 to 58, beginning with "I am relieved . . ." and ending with the chapter. As he picks food for his family, Moritz reflects on his brother's situation in the trenches and then loses the food to the police. *Talkback*: How does this passage reveal Moritz as both sensitive and naïve?
3. Chapter 20, pages 102 to 103, beginning with "I stare . . ." and ending with the chapter. Moritz visits Hans. *Talkback*: Why do you think that the author includes this scene?
4. Chapter 29, pages 136 to 137, beginning with the chapter and ending with ". . . extraordinary Mama is." Goldmann compliments Moritz's mother. *Talkback*: Should Moritz be embarrassed?
5. Chapter 40, pages 188 to 190, beginning with "Von Ewald wants to . . ." and ending with the chapter. Moritz confronts Hans. *Talkback*: What does this scene reveal about both brothers?

Discussion guide available @ http://media.us.macmillan.com/ discussionguides/9780374351229DG.pdf

Author interviews available @

http://www.monikaschroeder.com/about
http://www.hungermtn.org/what-my-last-book-taught-me-learn-to-drive-in-the-dark/
http://www.historicalnovels.info/Monika-Schroder.html
http://www.mangamaniaccafe.com/?p=5645

http://bethanyhegedus.blogspot.com/2011/09/inside-writers-studio-with-monika.html

http://www.teachingbooks.net/tb.cgi?aid=13705

Related Works

1. **Frost, Helen. *Crossing Stones***. New York: Farrar, Straus and Giroux, 2009. 184p. $16.99. ISBN-13: 978 0 374 31653 2. [novel in verse] JS, CG with high interest for girls (*Value-Packed Booktalks*, 2011, pages 193 to 195.) Four friends react to events from April 1917 to January 1918 that include World War I and women's rights.

2. **Morpurgo, Michael. *Private Peaceful***. New York: Scholastic Press, 2003. 202p. $16.95. ISBN 0 439 63648 5. [fiction] JS, CG with high interest for boys. Private Peaceful waits for his older brother to be executed and reviews how they came to this point.

3. **Murphy, Jim. *Truce***. New York: Scholastic Press, 2009. 128p. $19.99. ISBN-13: 978 0 545 13049 3. [nonfiction] MJS, CG. Murphy explains the lies and ambitions that launched World War I and the 1914 Christmas truce that illustrates the humanity of European troops.

4. **Remarque, Erich Maria. *All Quiet on the Western Front***. New York: Fawcett Crest, 1975. 296p. $4.95pa. ISBN 0 449 21394 3. [fiction] S/A. A young German soldier, pressured to go to war and disillusioned by what he sees, tells this anti-war World War I story originally published in 1928.

5. **Spillebeen, Geert (text), and Terese Edelstein (trans.). *Kipling's Choice***. Boston, MA: Houghton Mifflin Co., 2005. 160p. $16.00. ISBN 0 618 43124 1. [fiction] JS, CG (*Booktalks and Beyond*, 2007, pages 213 to 215.) As 18-year-old John Kipling dies, he and the reader review his privileged but demanding life as the son of Rudyard Kipling, England's poet laureate whose work extolled risk and patriotism.

Multiple Cultures

Multiple Cultures books open our eyes to other worlds that sometimes are next door. Characters tell us about the communities or countries that they come from and the new ones they enter. In the happiest accounts, traditions and attitudes from old cultures and experiences in new cultures find a balance. And even though these books talk about cultures from around the world, each addresses what author Gary Schmidt calls, in his VOYA interview (October, 2012) "the great American question: How do you live side by side with someone who isn't like you?" He calls it "the question that unites" Americans, but as the world grows smaller, it must become the question that unites the world and allows it to survive.

Conflict

Abdel-Fattah, Randa. **Where the Streets Had a Name.**

New York: Scholastic Press, 2010. 304p. $17.99.
ISBN 978 0 545 17292 9. [fiction] JS, CG with high interest for girls

Theme/Topics: Palestinian/Israeli conflict, family, coming of age, friendship

Summary/Description

Thirteen-year-old Hayaat lived on the West Bank of Jerusalem in 2004. Having been driven from their land by the Israelis, her extended family skirts the violence perpetrated by both sides of the Israeli/Palestinian conflict. Hayaat's face is deformed by an Israeli bullet that killed her friend,

Maysaa. Her friend Samy, a Christian, has lost both parents. His mother is dead and his father is in prison. Hayaat and Samy sneak into Jerusalem to fulfill the wish of Hayaat's aged grandmother who longs to touch the soil of her home before she dies. Endangered by checkpoints, barriers, and demonstrations, they do not reach the land that the family owned, but return safely with a jar of Jerusalem soil. In the midst of this desolation and loss, the family plans the oldest daughter's wedding. Hayaat concludes that the past can "torment and heal," and based on her relationships with family and friends she looks forward to a future with love.

Values: Hayaat relies on family, friendship, tradition,
and hope.

Booktalk

Display a map which shows Palestine and Israel. Ask if anyone knows about the conflict between Israel and Palestine. Ask them to share what they know. Be prepared with headlines or pictures of the conflict.

Thirteen-year-old Hayaat's shattered face proves she knows about that conflict first hand. Her best friend, Samy, saw his mother die and his father go to prison. It is 2004. Hayaat and Samy are Palestinians who live in the West Bank of Bethlehem. (*Point out the West Bank on the map.*) Every day, they fight the Israelis. Are these struggles for survival, honor, or both? They don't know. They just know that even simple tasks mean confrontation and humiliation. But these two plan more than a simple task. Hayaat wants her grandmother to touch her lost land once more. What will they have to do? (*Wait for responses.*) The journey may take their lives or give them back, all because they wish to reconnect to a place *Where the Streets Had a Name.*

Alternative booktalk/review available @ http://www.youtube.com/
watch?v=LT7XqB7BMGw

Read Aloud/Talkback

1. Chapter 2, pages 19 to 27, beginning with the chapter and ending with ". . . coffee shop only." Hayaat describes their former happy life and her father's depression after losing the land. *Talkback*: What details in Hayaat's narrative communicate the family's hardship? Why do you think that the father is most affected?
2. Chapter 6, pages 66 to 67, beginning with "I don't bother . . ." and ending with the chapter. The grandmother reflects on the people who took her home. *Talkback*: What is the grandmother's message? Why is it important?

3. Chapter 15, page 181, beginning with "Al-Quds . . ." and ending with ". . . one of the mountains." Hayaat understands the importance of heritage. *Talkback*: Do you have any touchable or tangible objects that represent your own heritage? Show and explain its importance to the group.

4. Chapter 17, pages 220 to 223, beginning with "We're on our way . . ." and ending with ". . . looking at me." Hayaat recalls her friend's death and her own disfigurement. *Talkback*: What is your reaction to Hayaat's story?

5. Chapter 23, pages 306 and 307, beginning with "I am thirteen . . ." and ending with the chapter. Hayaat reflects on her experiences and who she is because of them. *Talkback*: Do you believe in Hayaat's resolve?

Interview writing series with author read aloud available
@ http://lrrpublic.cli.det.nsw.edu.au/lrrSecure/Sites/Web/view/learncast/resources/12247.htm

Discussion guide available @ http://www.panmacmillan.com.au/resources/RA-WhereTheStreetsHadAName.pdf

Author interviews available @

http://www.randaabdelfattah.com/interview-randa-abdelfattah.asp

http://electronicintifada.net/content/breaking-down-stereotypes-randa-abdel-fattah-interviewed/9912

http://justinelarbalestier.com/blog/2010/02/16/guest-post-randa-abdel-fattah-on-writing-identity/

http://www.youtube.com/watch?v=3b9sOON5N30&feature=related

Related Works

1. **Abdel-Fattah, Randa. *Ten Things I Hate about Me*.** New York: Scholastic Inc./Orchard Books, 2009. 304p. $16.99. ISBN-13: 978 0 545 05055 5. [fiction] JS, G. Jamie/Jamilah works to hide her Muslim identity, but discovers that she is a stronger and more likeable person if she is brave enough to be the girl she wants to be.

2. **Barakat, Ibtisam. *Tasting the Sky: A Palestinian Childhood*.** New York: Farrar, Straus and Giroux/Melamie Kroupa Books, 2007. 176p. $16.00. ISBN-13: 978 0 374 35733 7. [nonfiction] JS, CG. (*Genre Talks for Teens*, 2009, pages 283 to 285.) The main story extends from the first day of the Six Day War in 1967 to 1971 when the family finds a permanent home.

3. **Carmi, Daniella. *Samir and Yonatan*.** New York: Arthur A. Levine Books, 2000. 192p. $15.95. ISBN 0 439 13504 4. [fiction] MJ, CG. Samir, a Palestinian, and Yonatan, a Jew, supposedly

enemies can live in peace only in an imaginary world created by Yonatan.

4. **Marston, Elsa. *Santa Claus in Baghdad and Other Stories about Teens in the Arab World***. Bloomington, IN: Indiana University Press, 2008. 198p. $15.95. ISBN-13: 978 0 253 22004 2. [short stories] JS, CG. (*Value-Packed Booktalks*, 2011, pages 230 to 232.) Eight short stories express the universal coming of age choices and desires of Arab teens that live in societies with challenges different than our own.

5. **Zenatti, Valérie, and Adriana Hunter (trans.). *When I Was a Soldier: A Memoir***. New York: Bloomsbury Children's Books, 2005. 235p. $16.95. ISBN 1 58234 978 9. [nonfiction] JS, CG with high interest for girls. (*Booktalks and Beyond*, 2007, pages 241 to 244.) The author describes her compulsory military service in the Israeli army and the questions, pride, and maturity it brings to her.

ॐॐ

Amir (text) and Khalil (art). **Zahra's Paradise.**
New York: First Second, 2011. 255p. $19.99.
ISBN 978 1 59643 642 8. [graphic] S/A, CG

Themes/Topics: Bloggers, missing persons, protest, tyranny, Iran

Summary/Description

In June 2009, Tehran, Iran, a young man named Mehdi vanishes. His mother Zahra and his brother, the narrator and a blogger, search for him. Their journey exposes the greed, corruption, and cruelty of a regime which uses gang rape, beatings, torture, and secret executions clothed in religious righteousness to subdue protest. The volume has a glossary and an explanation of the significance of names. An extensive Afterword includes explanations of the following: the story's origin; Iran's 2009 presidential elections and the challenge, protest, and repression which followed; the phrase Allahu Akbar and its relationship to Arab Spring; Iranian execution by crane and a bar chart showing executions in several countries during 2010; the significance of Neda Agha Soltan's death; the conditions of "The Kahrizak Detention Center"; an In Memoriam section listing the thousands executed, shot during demonstrations or assassinated since the establishment of the Islamic Republic of Iran. Also listed are Web sites for additional information. The content could be considered controversial and requires a mature audience.

Values: The horrific journey emphasizes the need for truth and honesty in government.

Booktalk

Ask how many have heard of the major protest in Iran following the 2009 elections. Show pages 40 to 41. Many say that this protest planted the seeds of the Arab spring that toppled so many regimes in the Middle East. This is the story of one of the faces in this crowd. His brother and mother search for him. Do they find him? (*Wait for responses.*) Yes and no. Their journey shows the struggle for a peaceful life in an ancient world and the government lies, corruption, and brutality that make that life impossible. And in the middle of that struggle is a graveyard that offers a new beginning, *Zahra's Paradise*.

Book trailer available @ http://us.macmillan.com/zahrasparadise/
Amir

Read Aloud/Talkback

1. "Prologue," pages 7 to 14. The killing of the puppies is a symbol for the entire story. *Talkback*: What is the author communicating with this prologue?
2. "June 19, 2009," pages 53 to 55. Mehdi's brother reacts to the Supreme Leader's speech. *Talkback*: What does this section say about public performance and private action?
3. "June 22, 2009," pages 93 to 96. The brother and narrator remember Mehdi in his room. *Talkback*: What does Mehdi's room reveal about him?
4. "July 8, 2009," pages 215 to 222. Mehdi is buried. *Talkback*: What makes this conclusion significant?
5. "Epilogue," page 225. The brother leaves the country and the mother discovers her grandchild. *Talkback*: Is this a hopeful ending?

Chapters 1 and 2 available @ http://www.zahrasparadise.com/

Chapter 5 available @ http://www.jadaliyya.com/pages/
index/2679/zahras-paradise_part-two-

Discussion guide available @ http://media.us.macmillan.com/
discussionguides/9781596436428DG.pdf

Author interviews available @
http://www.youtube.com/watch?v=VaYBT7YCO70

http://www.huffingtonpost.com/2012/02/14/zahras-paradise-comic_n_1276511.html

http://www.jadaliyya.com/pages/index/2607/zahras-paradise_an-interview-with-amir-and-khalil

http://www.movements.org/blog/entry/interview-with-zahras-paradises-writer/

http://robot6.comicbookresources.com/2010/03/unbound-zahras-paradise-creator-speaks/

http://timeoutchicago.com/arts-culture/books/15215926/zahra%E2%80%99s-paradise-interview

http://www.egyptindependent.com/news/telling-tehrani-story

Related Works

1. **Gordon, Mathew S. *Islam*.** New York: The Rosen Publishing Group Inc., 2010. 112p. (Understanding Religions) $33.25. ISBN-13: 978 1 4358 5618 9. [nonfiction] JS, CG. Text and extensive pictures briefly explain the origins, conflicts, practices, and Western misunderstandings of Islam. The glossary explains unfamiliar terms. Web sites, Further Reading, and Bibliography provide additional sources.

2. **Lat. *Kampung Boy*.** New York: Roaring Brook Press/First Second, 2006. 142p. $16.95. ISBN 1 59643 121 0. [graphic] MJS, CG. (*Genre Talks for Teens*, 2009, pages 264 to 266.) Starting with his parents' marriage and ending with his journey to school, this first book in the *Kampung Boy* series outlines the life of a Muslim boy within a disappearing rural family life.

3. **Marston, Elsa. *Santa Claus in Baghdad and Other Stories about Teens in the Arab World*.** Bloomington, IN: Indiana University Press, 2008. 198p. $15.95. ISBN-13: 978 0 253 22004 2. [short stories] JS, CG. (*Value-Packed Booktalks*, 2011, pages 230 to 232.) Eight short stories express the personal crises of Arab teens who live in societies with challenges different than our own, but with universal coming-of-age choices and desires.

4. **Satrapi, Marjane. *Persepolis*.** New York: Random House/Pantheon, 2003. 153p. $11.95pa. ISBN 0 375 71457 X. [graphic memoir] JS/A, CG. The great-granddaughter of one of Iran's emperors, Satrapi recounts eight years of her life that witnesses the overthrow of the shah, the Islamic Revolution, and the war with Iraq.

5. **Siddiqui, Haroon. *Being Muslim*.** Toronto, ON: Anansi Press/Groundwood Books, 2006. 160p. (Groundwood Guide) $9.95pa. ISBN-13: 978 0 88899 786 9. [nonfiction] JS, CG. Siddiqui explains the politics affecting the faithful, the situation of European Muslims, Muslim beliefs, the role of women, the relationship between jihad

and terrorism, and the future of the movement. He includes source notes, a list of readings, and an index.

☙❧

Bruchac, Joseph (story), and Will Davis (illus.). Dawn Land.

New York: First Second, 2010. 313p. $19.99.
ISBN 978 1 59643 143 0. [graphic] JS, CG with high interest for boys.

Themes/Topics: Abenaki tribe, creation myth, family, good versus evil, prehistoric America

Summary/Description

Ancient giants kill the parents of Weasel Tale and Young Hunter. Weasel Tale hides and saves his baby cousin Young Hunter, but a giant infects Weasel Tale with evil from which he cannot fully recover. Eventually, he is banished from the community. At 17, Young Hunter is chosen to save the Salmon people from the ancient giants. He carries the long bow to the tribe and discovers that Weasel Tale finds tribes for the giants to destroy. With Young Hunter's support, Weasel Tale claims his humanity, turns on the giants, and dies. Young Hunter challenges the Salmon people to use the longbow, their new weapon, well.

Values: Young Hunter's journey demonstrates bravery, love, generosity, and justice.

Booktalk

It is 10,000 years ago. Young Hunter is chosen to save his people. Ancient giants and monsters ravage his land and murder his family. What do you think this hero looks like? (*Wait for responses.*) Young Hunter is small and weak, (*Show a picture.*) and he doesn't have a phone booth to change into a superhero. He wonders how he can save anyone. Why do you think he was chosen? (*Wait for responses.*) But he begins his journey of love and danger with a secret weapon that can destroy his own nation. As he travels, his body is beaten and battered, but his heart and head gradually grow stronger. Will they be strong enough to defeat the giants and monsters—to save the *Dawn Land*?

Book trailers available @

http://www.youtube.com/watch?v=URB6gMdzvdg&feature=related
http://www.youtube.com/watch?v=GgnAR-rwsj0&feature=relmfu

http://us.macmillan.com/dawnland/WillDavis

Read Aloud/Talkback

1. Part I, pages 36 to 38. This section tells the story of the stone people and the people of ash. *Talkback*: What is the lesson of the creation story?

2. Part II, page 114. Young Hunter is told to live in two worlds. *Talkback*: Does this advice apply to just Young Hunter and his culture?

3. Part III, pages 176 to 181. This is Weasel Tale's Story. *Talkback*: How does Weasel Tale's story speak of the struggle between good and evil?

4. Part III, page 191. The Buffalo Woman promises to support the hunter. *Talkback*: How does the Buffalo Woman's prayer speak to generosity and responsibility?

5. Part III, page 299. In the last frame, Young Hunter shows the Long Thrower and states its challenge. *Talkback*: How is Young Hunter's presentation of the Long Thrower universal?

Discussion guide available @ http://media.us.macmillan.com/ readersguides/9781596431430RG.pdf

Author interviews available @ http://www.teachingbooks.net/ tb.cgi?tid=26933

Related Works

1. **Bruchac, Joseph. *Dawn Land*.** Golden, CO: Fulcrum Publishing, 1993. 336p. $16.95 (audiobook: two cassettes). ISBN-13: 978 1 5591 149 2. [audio, myth] JS, CG with high interest for boys. Joseph Bruchac reads the story of *Dawn Land*.

2. **Bruchac, Joseph. *Wabi: A Hero's Tale*.** New York: Dial Books, 2006. 198p. $16.99. ISBN 0 8037 3098 5. [fiction] MJS, CG. (*Genre Talks for Teens*, 2009, pages 189 to 191.) Wabi tells his story, from hatching to the heroic human deeds that win his love.

3. **Lowenstein, Tom, and Piers Vitebsky. *Native American Myths and Beliefs*.** New York: Rosen Publishing, 2012. 144p. (World Mythologies) $39.95. ISBN 978 1 4488 5992 4. [nonfiction] JS, CG. This title within the six of the series addresses beliefs concerning the creation, maintenance, and legacy of Native American cultures. Pages 89 to 90 address some of the monsters, including a man-eating buffalo and the gift of the bow for defense against them. Illustrations, pictures, glossary, and suggestions for further reading and research as well as an index are included.

4. **Philip, Neil.** *In a Sacred Manner I Live: Native American Wisdom*. New York: Clarion Books, 1997. 93p. $20.00. ISBN 0 395 84981 0. [nonfiction] JS, CG. (*Booktalks and More*, 2003, pages 44 to 46.) This collection of poems, songs, and speeches from 1609 to 1995 reflects the respect for nature and language that allows Native Americans to live "in a sacred manner."

5. **Philip, Neil.** *The Great Mystery: Myths of Native America*. New York: Clarion Books, 2001. 145p. $25.00. ISBN 0 395 98405 X. [nonfiction] JS, CG with high interest for boys. (*Booktalks and More*, 2003, pages 103 to 105.) In the first chapter, "Trail of Beauty," Philip defines myth, explains its evolution, describes the purpose of related rituals, and identifies the common themes and motifs of Native American belief. Subsequent chapters focus on myths for each region of North America from the Southwest to the Arctic.

ↄ℔

Edwardson, Debby Dahl. My Name Is Not Easy.

Tarrytown, NY: Marshall Cavendish, 2011. 248p. $17.99.
ISBN 978 0 7614 5980 4. [fiction] JS, CG

Themes/Topics: Indians of North America, Alaska, 1959–1964,
interpersonal relations, Catholic schools,
boarding schools, grief

Summary/Description

Twelve-year-old Luke and his two brothers, Bunna and Isaac, are sent to a strict and often abusive Catholic boarding school whose staff views the students as must-be-converted heathens. Immediately, six-year-old Isaac is sent to foster care without the parents' knowledge of his location. Over the next four years, Luke overcomes rivalries and prejudices as he bonds with the other students, loses his brother Bunna in a plane crash, finds his own identity, and grows to appreciate the family structure and spiritual beliefs that supported him. Luke's story intertwines with those of his fellow students: Amiq, a daring Eskimo leader; Chickie, a blond outsider; and the observant, quiet, and studious Junior. Together, they forge change in the school and look forward to doing the same in the larger world.

Values: Luke learns that family and friends that become family are sources of spiritual and emotional strength.

Booktalk

Ask how many people ride a bus to school. (*Wait for a show of hands.*) Ask how many people have had a teacher mispronounce or forget their name. (*Wait for a show of hands and then ask how the person felt about that happening.*) Twelve-year-old Luke is Eskimo. He and his brothers live in the Arctic. They are about to take a plane, not a bus, to school. They might return home on breaks. No guarantee on how often. Luke knows that the teachers in this new school will not be able to pronounce his name. No white teacher has been able to pronounce it, yet. So he changes it to Luke. At home, each day he can leave the white world and find his tongue again. But at this new school, Father Mullen slaps down anyone who does not speak English—both the Eskimos and Indians who are at war with each other there. So Luke arrives at Sacred Heart School with a new name, a new language, and students and teachers who will gladly beat him just because he his Eskimo. His mother made him promise to care for his brothers, but he is having trouble surviving himself. He has much more to worry about than *My Name Is Not Easy*.

Author book trailer available @ http://www.youtube.com/ watch?v=CcsxHUgdymQ

Book trailer/booktalk available @ http://www.youtube.com/ watch?v=6KOoiKDzbDA

Read Aloud/Talkback

1. "My Name is Not Easy," pages 3 to 7, beginning with the chapter and ending with ". . . turns seven?" Luke introduces his family and reflects on his anxiety about Sacred Heart. *Talkback*: What is your impression about the family?

2. "Snowbird," pages 52 to 55, beginning with "The nuns are . . ." and ending with the chapter. Chickie reads Sister Kate's diary and reacts to Bunna's teasing. *Talkback*: What do these two incidents reveal about Chickie and the school?

3. "The Size of Things Back Home," pages 65 to 67, beginning with the chapter and ending with ". . . a little kid." Luke returns home after Isaac is taken. *Talkback*: How does this passage affect your feelings?

4. "The Meanest Heathens," pages 134 to 136, beginning with "And now Father . . ." and ending with the chapter. Father Mullen beats Sonny and Amiq. *Talkback*: How is this beating both horrible and ironic at this point in the novel?

5. "Epilogue—A New Gun," pages 242 to 243, beginning with "Isaac's right . . ." and ending with "Guess I am." Luke reflects on change. *Talkback*: What point or points does this passage make about Luke and his world?

Author read aloud available @

http://www.debbydahledwardson.com/my_name_is_not_ easy_107683.htm

Author interview available @ http://www.nationalbook.org/ nba2011_ypl_edwardson_interv.html#.UCUWg6GPVpA

Related Works

1. **Bruchac, Joseph.** *Jim Thorpe: Original All-American*. New York: Dial Books/Walden Media, 2006. 276p. ISBN 0 8037 3118 3. [biographical novel] JS, B. (*Value-Packed Booktalks*, 2011, pages 200 to 202.) After Jim Thorpe runs away from several Indian schools, his father sends him to the Carlisle Indian School in Pennsylvania where he begins his sports career.
2. **Carvell, Marlene.** *Sweetgrass Basket*. New York: Dutton Children's Books, 2005. 243p. $16.99. ISBN 0 525 47547 8. [novel, poetry] JS, G. (*Booktalks and Beyond*, 2007, pages 244 to 246.) Sent to the Carlisle Indian Industrial School in 1879 after their mother's death, two sisters encounter cruelty, prejudice, and ignorance.
3. **Edwardson, Debby Dahl.** *Blessing's Bead*. New York: Farrar, Straus and Giroux/Melanie Kroupa Books, 2009. 178p. $16.99. ISBN-13: 978 0 374 30805 6. [fiction] JS, CG with high interest for girls. (*Value-Packed Booktalks*, 2011, pages 236 to 239.) Blessing realizes the strength of family and culture through stories and symbols.
4. **Samantha Seiple.** *Ghosts in the Fog: The Untold Story of Alaska's WWII Invasion* [nonfiction] MJS, CG with high interest for boys. (Action/Adventure/Survival/War, pages 213 to 216.) Seiple relates the World War II Japanese invasion of Alaska, in which both the Japanese and the Americans discriminated against the Native American population.
5. **Sullivan, Paul.** *Maata's Journal*. New York: Atheneum Books for Young Readers, 2003. 240p. $16.95. ISBN 0 689 83463 2. [fiction] JS, G. Seventeen-year-old Maata, an Inuit, records her survival in an Arctic expedition from April to July of 1924 and the white man's focus on measuring nature rather than listening to it.

ය ౭

Flores-Galbis, Enrique. **90 Miles to Havana.**

New York: Roaring Brook Press, 2010. 292p. $17.99.
ISBN 978 1 59643 168 3. [fiction] MJ, CG with high interest for boys

Themes/Topics: Cuba, 1960s, family, coming of age,
revolution, bullies, immigrants

Summary/Description

Julian and his two older brothers leave Cuba through the Pedro Pan
program when Castro's revolution begins. Bullies run the overcrowded
American camp. The three are targets. Julian, with friends from Cuba,
sneaks out of the camp to work as a migrant laborer and meets Tomás
who lives on a boat. Julian's brothers protest the camp treatment and
are sent to a Denver orphanage. Julian and friends, encouraged by the
camp cook to work democratically, create a revolution. Julian learns that
he will also be transported out, but runs away to live with Tomás who
plans to bring his father and other refugees to the United States. Julian
helps him, and the two become heroes. Julian discovers that his mother
is now in Connecticut. He joins his mother and brothers, and they plan
to bring the father to the United States.

Values: Difficult times help Julian develop strength, self-
respect, and independence.

Booktalk

Julian's father is talented and wealthy. His mother indulges him. Their
faithful servant Bebo runs their home. Julian's two older brothers tease
him and sometimes put him down, but they also protect him. He has
a wonderful life in Cuba. Then comes Fidel Castro. What happens?
(*Wait for responses.*) Spies report to the government. Enforcement
squads roam the streets. The wealthy and talented line up to leave.
Julian's mother has a plan. Her sons will go to the United States where
camps with swimming pools and palm trees wait for them. The brothers will be safe and comfortable until the parents can join them. But
the truth is much different. Too many parents have the same plan. The
camps are crowded. The staff is small. Bullies run things. Julian's parents may never leave Cuba. Julian's brothers can't protect him. What
happens to Julian? (*Wait for responses.*) Julian needs a plan, and fast,

because dictators are just as powerful and dangerous *90 Miles* [from] *Havana.*

Alternative booktalk available @ http://www.youtube.com/watch?v=YpIUv3QaCPo&feature=related

Book trailers available @

http://www.youtube.com/watch?v=ozty5FRtpZs
http://www.youtube.com/watch?v=6JlkRj9-oMU
http://www.youtube.com/watch?v=BAQpVimVl9Y&feature=relmfu

Read Aloud/Talkback

1. "The Omelet," pages 21 to 23, beginning with "What is a *revolution*?" and ending with ". . . play somewhere else." Bebo uses the omelet to explain revolution. *Talkback*: How do you react to Bebo's explanation?

2. "Locked Up Tight," pages 38 to 40, beginning with "The next morning . . ." and ending with the chapter. Bebo tells Julian that he will be leaving and gives him advice. *Talkback*: What do you think of Bebo's advice?

3. "Dolores Democratic," pages 138 to 139, beginning with "Dolores leans in . . ." and ending with ". . . than my plan." Dolores encourages Julian to fight the democratic way. *Talkback*: Do you agree with Dolores? Why or why not?

4. "Heroes," pages 270 to 271, beginning with "It's late . . ." and ending with ". . . how things worked out." Armando plays a central role in their rescue. *Talkback*: Who is the hero?

5. "Connecti-Y-Cut," pages 276 to 292. Julian arrives at his new home and establishes himself. *Talkback*: How has Julian changed? How has his family changed?

Author read aloud available @ http://www.youtube.com/watch?v=mpcpJdmbtqQ&feature=related

Author presentation available @ http://www.youtube.com/watch?feature=endscreen&NR=1&v=yXh2vf1rw8w

Related Works

1. **Bruchac, Joseph.** *The Way*. Plain City, OH: Darby Creek Publishing, 2007. 164p. $16.95. ISBN-13: 978 1 58196 062 4. [fiction] MJS, CG with high interest for boys. (*Value-Packed Booktalks,*

2011, pages 213 to 215.) Cody LeBeau deals with bullying in his high school and becomes a hero when his uncle teaches him fitness through the Way.

2. **Calcines, Eduardo F. *Leaving Glorytown: One Boy's Struggle under Castro***. New York: Farrar, Straus and Giroux, 2009. 221p. $17.95. ISBN-13: 978 0 374 34394 1. [nonfiction] MJS, CG with high interest for boys (*Value-Packed Booktalks*, 2011, pages 216 to 218.) Calcines describes slow starvation, destruction of cultural and religious customs, nationalization of businesses, and violence visited on Cubans.

3. **Grant, Vicki. *Pigboy***. Victoria, BC: Orca Book Publishers, 2006. 101p. (Orca Currents) $8.95pa. ISBN-13: 978 1 55143 643 2. [fiction] MJ, CG with high interest for boys (*Genre Talks for Teens*, 2009, pages 103 to 105.) Bullied Dan Hogg joins his class for a field trip to a pig farm and becomes a hero.

4. **Lekuton, Joseph Lemasolai. *Facing the Lion: Growing up Maasai on the African Savanna***. Washington, DC: National Geographic, 2003. 123p. $15.95. ISBN 0 7922 5125 3. [nonfiction] MJS, CG with high interest for boys (*Booktalks and Beyond*, 2007, pages 234 to 236.) In Chapter 1, Lekuton relates a lion encounter that teaches him to confront other "lions" in his life.

5. **Osa, Nancy. *Cuba 15***. New York: Delacorte Press, 2033. 277p. $17.99. ISBN 0 385 90086 4. [fiction] JS, G. Fifteen-year-old Violet Paz learns her Cuban heritage when planning her ". . . quinceañero (KEEN-say-ahnYEH-ro) or quince . . ." a coming of age ceremony for womanhood.

Additional related works available @

http://www.schoollibraryjournal.com/slj/newslettersnewsletter
    bucketcurriculumconnections/888599–442/leaving_home_
    young_refugees_from.html.csp
http://www.cnbc.com/id/37062429/

ෆ෩

Goodman, Shawn. Something like Hope.
New York: Delacorte Press, 2011. 193p. $16.99.
ISBN 978 0 385 73939 9. [fiction] JS, CG with high interest for girls

Themes/Topics: Juvenile delinquents, juvenile detention homes, emotional problems, family problems, African Americans

Summary/Description

Violent and sullen, 17-year-old Shavonne closes herself off from love, kindness, and hope until she works with the sad and persistent psychologist, Mr. Delpopolo, who encourages her to open herself to positive emotions. He persuades her to control herself, not the system, and points out that every person is more than mistakes and poor decisions. He emphasizes that many of Shavonne's "mistakes" were the faults of adults who failed to support her. Reaching out to others, she receives support and respect. By the end of the story, she is leaving detention and reconnecting with the brother whom she thought she injured and lost.

Values: After experiencing only fear and anger, Shavonne opens herself to forgiveness and faith.

Booktalk

Seventeen-year-old Shavonne dreams about a secretarial job, a studio apartment with only one key, beautiful clothes, and a cat. Do these dreams seem unreachable or unusual? (*Wait for responses.*) Shavonne is dreaming this dream on a cold detention floor. She just busted her teacher's pretty face and has some bad bruises of her own. Her mother is a crack addict. Her baby went directly to foster care, and she doesn't know what happened to her brother. Where do you think she will spend her life? (*Wait for responses.*) But she meets a short, fat, kind of sad little man who has lost almost everything good in his life. He doesn't talk about his losses. He wants to hear about Shavonne's feelings and plans. And her questions are "Should I trust him? Should I trust *Something like Hope?*"

Book trailer available @ http://www.randomhouse.com/book/201951/something-like-hope-by-shawn-goodman

Read Aloud/Talkback

The selections include controversial language and situations.
1. Chapter 8, page 26, beginning with "I want to believe . . ." and ending with the chapter. Shavonne describes her warning, angry voices. *Talkback*: How would you label Shavonne's voices?
2. Chapter 9, pages 27 to 31. Cyrus Jacobs points out a pair of geese to a hostile audience. *Talkback*: Is Cyrus wasting his time? Why or why not?
3. Chapter 14, pages 47 to 50. Shavonne recalls losing her daughter. *Talkback*: What does this chapter tell you about Shavonne?

4. Chapter 19, pages 61 to 63. When asked to list what she feels guilt or shame about, Shavonne finds a connection with Mr. Delpopolo. *Talkback*: How is it possible that two such very different people have a connection?

5. Chapter 61, pages 181 to 182. Shavonne gives up her daughter. *Talkback*: Does Shavonne make the right decision?

Author interviews available @

http://cynthialeitichsmith.blogspot.com/2011/03/new-voice-shawn-goodman-on-something.html

http://dawnvandermeer.blogspot.com/2010/05/interview-author-shawn-goodman-2009.html

http://thebrownbookshelf.com/2012/01/26/a-conversation-with-shawn-goodman-author-of-something-like-hope/

http://author2author.blogspot.com/2011/01/fun-friday-interview-with-first-time-ya.html

Related Works

1. **Booth, Coe. *Kendra*.** New York: Scholastic Inc., 2008. 292p. $16.99. ISBN-13: 978 0 439 92536 5. [fiction] JS, G (*Value-Packed Booktalks*, 2011, pages 24 to 26.) Kendra fights for her mother's attention and becomes sexually active.

2. **Booth, Coe. *Tyrell*.** New York: Scholastic Inc./Push, 2006. 320p. $16.99. ISBN 0 439 83879 7. [fiction] JS, CG with high interest for boys. Fifteen-year-old Tyrell, who has grown up in the projects, unsuccessfully tries to hold his family and his love life together even though his father is in jail and his mother is self-centered and dysfunctional.

3. **Frost, Helen. *Keesha's House*.** New York: Farrar, Straus and Giroux/Frances Foster Books, 2003. 116p. $16.00. ISBN 0 374 34064 1. [poetry] JS, CG with high interest for girls (*Booktalks and Beyond*, 2009, pages 21 to 24.) Joe, accepted into this house when he was 12, offers refuge to troubled teens.

4. **Gantos, Jack. *Hole in My Life*.** New York: Farrar, Straus and Giroux, 2002. 200p. $16.00. ISBN 0 374 39988 3. [nonfiction] JS, CG with high interest for boys (*Teen Genre Connections*, 2005, pages 1 to 3.) Gantos admits his willingness to sell and deliver drugs, describes his subsequent incarceration, and explains his realization that his poor decisions could cancel any hope for a positive life.

5. **Nolan, Han. *Born Blue*.** New York: Harcourt Brace and Co., 2001. 177p. $17.00. ISBN 0 15 201916 2. [fiction] JS, G. (*Teen*

Genre Connections, 2005, pages 13 to 15.) Born to a heroin addict, Janie grows up in foster care and pursues a destructive life pattern, but decides to leave her baby with a stable family.

ʧʦ

Myers, Walter Dean. **Lockdown.**

New York: HarperCollins/Amistad, 2010. 247p. $16.99.
ISBN 978 0 06 121480 6. [fiction] JS, CG with high interest for boys

Themes/Topics: Juvenile delinquents, juvenile detention homes, conduct of life, friendship, self-perception, old age, African Americans

Summary/Description

Fourteen-year-old Maurice Anderson comes from a seriously dysfunctional inner-city family, and has served 22 months in Progress juvenile facility when he is offered a work release program in a nursing home. His work release and early release are jeopardized because he defends a younger inmate from the facility's bullies. A nursing home patient who tells him about surviving a Japanese occupation during World War II changes Maurice's fatalistic view about his situation and life. Maurice continues successfully to defend his friend, loses his early release, but crafts a life plan to keep himself out of trouble and send his little sister to college.

Values: Maurice learns the value of loyalty, integrity, and determination.

Booktalk

Reese will probably celebrate his 15th birthday in jail. He has spent 22 months in Progress juvenile facility and has a few to go, but this is his second arrest. The next step may be real jail. Mom is addicted. Dad is a drop-in who disowns him. His older brother works the streets, and now the Progress bullies are planning on jumping Reese's friend Toon. He doesn't think he can do much about any of it. What do you think his life chances are? (*Wait for responses.*) Then, he gets a break—work release in a nursing home. The patients don't have much of a future either. One patient, Mr. Hooft, tells him right out that he doesn't like African Americans or criminals, and he doesn't like Reese. Reese could make the man's life miserable, but Mr. Hooft has other things to say, too—about his war, fear, death, and survival. Mr. Hooft's life was filled with tough choices and some unhappy endings. But Reese starts to listen because Mr. Hooft survived the ultimate *Lockdown*.

Book trailers available @

http://www.youtube.com/watch?v=yzoKsHoZ6PI

http://www.youtube.com/watch?feature=endscreen&v=KhIWGPjp
Uxo&NR=1

Read Aloud/Talkback

1. Chapter 3, pages 20 to 21, beginning with "We were on . . ." and ending with ". . . world out." Maurice describes lockdown. *Talkback*: What does Maurice's view of lockdown say about his life?
2. Chapter 7, pages 56 to 62, beginning with "Hello, Pieter . . ." and ending with the chapter. Maurice meets Mr. Hooft. *Talkback*: What is your impression of Mr. Hooft?
3. Chapter 13, pages 90 to 97. In this chapter, Mr. Hooft tells about his boyhood experience during World War II. *Talkback*: How does Mr. Hooft's story affect you?
4. Chapter 20, pages 140 to 141, beginning with "James, you ever . . ." and ending with the chapter. Mr. Cintron uses the image of crabs in a basket to illustrate what will happen to Maurice. *Talkback*: Do you agree with Mr. Cintron?
5. Chapter 29, pages 207 to 209, beginning with "When I got to Mr. Hooft's room . . ." and ending with ". . . stories about you." Mr. Hooft and Maurice talk about made-up life. *Talkback*: Do you agree with Mr. Hooft's characterization of life?

Discussion guide available @ http://files.harpercollins.com/ PDF/ReadingGuides/0061214809.pdf

Author interviews available @

http://www.nationalbook.org/nba2010_ypl_deanmyers.html#
.T94dpxfY9kl

http://s3.amazonaws.com/wmnf/news_story_soundclips/3674/
walter_dean_myers_part_two.mp3

http://www.nationalbook.org/nba2010_ypl_deanmyers_interview
.html#.UCatVqGPVpA

http://ritahubbard.com/2010/black-history-month-walter-dean-
myers-in-the-house/

http://www.npr.org/player/v2/mediaPlayer.html?action=1&t=1&
islist=false&id=144944598&m=144949372

http://www.youtube.com/watch?v=9TLzoH1BnCA

Related Works

1. **Booth, Coe. *Tyrell***. New York: Scholastic Inc./Push, 2006. 320p. $16.99. ISBN 0 439 83879 7. [fiction] JS, CG with high interest for boys. Fifteen-year-old Tyrell, who has grown up in the projects, unsuccessfully tries to hold his family and love life together.

2. **Myers, Walter Dean. *Bad Boy: A Memoir***. New York: Harper Tempest, 2001. 206p. $6.95pa. ISBN 0 06 447288 4. [nonfiction] JS, CG with high interest for boys (*Teen Genre Connections*, 2005, pages 54 to 56.) In this autobiography, Myers tells about his family, education, passion for reading, dangerous choices, and social barriers.

3. **Myers, Walter Dean. *The Beast***. Scholastic Press, 2003. 176p. $16.95. ISBN 0 439 36841 3. [fiction] JS, CG. A senior at an exclusive prep school returns to his Harlem home and discovers that his girl-friend is a drug addict.

4. **Myers, Walter Dean. *Monster***. New York: HarperCollins Publishers, 1999. 281p. $15.95. ISBN 0 06 028077 8. [fiction] JS, CG with high interest for boys (*Booktalks and More*, 2003, pages 13 to 15.) The reader never knows if a young man accused of a crime is guilty or innocent.

5. **Sachar, Louis. *Small Steps***. New York: Delacorte Press, 2006. 257p. $16.95. ISBN 0 385 73314 3. [fiction] MJS, CG with high interest for boys (*Genre Talks for Teens*, 2009, pages 53 to 56.) Seventeen-year-old African American Theodore Johnson from *Holes* joins a ticket-scalping scheme, saves a singing star's life, becomes a hero, and considers how close he came to disaster.

Balance

de la Peña, Matt. **Mexican Whiteboy.**

New York: Delacorte Press, 2008. 248p. $8.99pa.
ISBN 978 0 440 23938 3. [fiction] S, CG with high interest for boys

Themes/Topics: Identity, self-acceptance, racially mixed people, baseball, fathers and sons, National City (California)

Summary/Description

When Danny's white mother moves in with a new white boyfriend, Danny heads to National City, California, for the summer to visit his father's Mexican family and reconnect with his father who left four years ago. In his private school, the high-achieving Danny is considered Mexican and ignored. Danny feels that his father left because Danny's whiteness embarrassed him. His confusion affects his pitching skill. In National City, he meets Uno whose father is black and whose mother is Mexican. Uno helps Danny get his life and his fastball under control. Danny's school success motivates Uno and others in the group to find direction in their lives. Some might consider the language and situations controversial.

Values: Danny realizes that his personal decisions can direct his life.

Booktalk

Danny is smart, a high achiever in an exclusive private high school, but he never talks to anyone there. Danny has a 95-mile-an-hour fastball, but can't control it. He watches his school's team on the sidelines. He just feels safer under the radar. Now, his white mother throws him a curve. She is moving in with her new white boyfriend. Danny and his sister can move with her, or they can visit their father's Mexican relatives in National City, California. Danny's sister chooses the boyfriend. Danny chooses National City even though he can't speak Spanish. Who makes the better choice? (*Wait for answers.*) In National City, Danny might have a chance to see and talk to someone—his father who left them four years ago. Danny is convinced that Dad left because of Danny's whiteness. But when he gets to National City, some half-black, half-Mexican kid wants to fight him, and a girl who can't speak English may want to date him. What kind of summer is it going to be for this *Mexican Whiteboy*? (*Wait for responses.*)

Book trailer available @ http://www.youtube.com/watch?v=uL2Gzjxr334

Read Aloud/Talkback

Some of these selections contain language that might be considered controversial.

1. "Home Run Derby: Uno's Time Has Come," Section 2, pages 8 to 10. Uno anticipates the home run derby. *Talkback*: What is your impression of the neighborhood?

2. "The Shot Heard Round the Cul-de-Sac," Section 7, pages 27 to 28. Danny comes to after the fight and writes to his father. *Talkback*: What does this section say about Danny?
3. "Mexican Whiteboy," Section 3, pages 88 to 91. Danny realizes his separation from the National City family. *Talkback*: Would Danny's life have been better in National City?
4. "Uno Gets Another Drunken Tongue-Lashing," Section 5, pages 146 to 147. Uno shows Danny the power of the train. *Talkback*: What does this passage tell you about Uno?
5. "A New Light on The Recycling Plant," pages 244 to 247. Danny and Uno watch the sunrise on the Recycling Plant. *Talkback*: Did you like this ending? Why or why not?

Discussion questions available @ http://www.randomhouse .com/catalog/teachers_guides/9780385733106.pdf

Author interviews available @

http://www.youtube.com/watch?v=tR8dhpQBCMc&feature=related
http://teens.denverlibrary.org/media/pena.html
http://www.kpbs.org/news/2010/apr/26/matt-de-la-penas-books-reach-young-readers/

Center for Fiction Presentations available @

http://www.youtube.com/watch?v=2WkDD_IPaEs&feature=related
http://www.youtube.com/watch?v=w_AgZ13Sj0Q&feature=relmfu
http://www.youtube.com/watch?v=r-4d8s-1yg0&feature=relmfu
http://www.youtube.com/watch?v=F-0X7lMd7JM&feature=relmfu

Related Works

1. **Alexie, Sherman, and Ellen Forney (illus.). *The Absolutely True Diary of a Part-Time Indian*.** New York: Little, Brown & Co., 2007. 228p. $16.99. ISBN-13: 978 0 316 01368 0. [fiction] JS, CG with high interest for boys (*Genre Talks for Teens*, pages 269 to 272.) Intellectually gifted but physically challenged Arnold Spirit (aka Junior) leaves the reservation school and attends Reardan, a more prosperous white school. Some language may be considered controversial.
2. **de la Peña, Matt. *Ball Don't Lie*.** New York: Delacorte Press, 2005. 280p. $16.95. ISBN 0 385 73232 5. [fiction] JS, CG with high interest for boys (*Booktalks and Beyond*, 2007, pages 68 to 70.) Seventeen-year-old Sticky, a white foster child with obsessive-compulsive behavior, focuses

his life in the Lincoln Rec where he is challenged, and eventually accepted by outstanding black street ball players.

3. **Myers, Walter Dean.** *Bad Boy: A Memoir*. New York: Harper-Tempest, 2001. 206p. $6.95pa. ISBN 0 06 447288 4. [nonfiction] JS, CG with high interest for boys (*Teen Genre Connections*, 2005, pages 54 to 56.) Myers tells about his passion for reading and writing, supportive adults, society's stereotypes, and his own poor choices.

4. **Soto, Gary.** *Buried Onion.* New York: Harcourt Brace, 1997. 149p. $17.00. ISBN 0 15 201333 4. [fiction] MJS, CG with high interest for boys (*Booktalks Plus*, 2001, pages 124 to 126.) Nineteen-year-old Eddie, challenged to avenge a friend's death, leaves the neighborhood.

5. **Woodson, Jacqueline.** *Miracle's Boys*. New York: G. P. Putnam's Sons, 2000. 131p. $15.99. ISBN 0 399 23113 7. [fiction] MJS, CG with high interest for boys (*Teen Genre Connections*, 2005, pages 28 to 30.) Three Puerto Rican brothers learn about each other and their guilt as they struggle to keep their household together after their mother's death.

✿✿

Molnar, Haya Leah. Under a Red Sky.

New York: Farrar, Straus and Giroux/Frances Foster Books, 2010. 302p. $17.99. ISBN 978 0 374 31840 6.

[biography] JS, CG with high interest for girls

Themes/Topics: Family, Romanian history, 1944–1989, communism

Summary/Description

In this memoir, Molnar's artistic Romanian family, who survived the World War II Holocaust, now suffers under the antireligious/anti-Semitic rule of Communist Romania. Molnar lives with her parents, grandparents, an aunt and uncle, and a housemaid. The family decides to teach Molnar about her Jewish identity. They want to prepare her for immigration to Israel, where they can work and practice their religion without discrimination. The hostile, red-tape-filled process, which highlights memories of World War II persecution and post-war labor camps becomes Molnar's journey of personal identity.

Values: Molnar's journey demonstrates the power of friendships, family, generosity, heritage, and religious belief.

Booktalk

Show a world map and point out Romania. Romanian Haya Leah Molnar is eight years old before she discovers that she is Jewish. Why? Because her grandparents, parents, and aunt and uncle lived through Hitler's Holocaust. (*Ask the group to share what they know about the Holocaust. Wait for responses.*) After World War II, they still suffer under anti-Semitic or anti-Jewish Communists. They have always thought that being labeled a Jew would hurt her. But now there is a reason for her to know—a new but ancient land called Israel, a promised land that celebrates the family's identity. (*Point out Israel on the map.*) In the Communist Romania of the 1950s, even asking to leave is dangerous for Jews. Because Haya's family is filled with eccentric, strong-minded artists, there is even more danger. Why do you think this would be true? (*Wait for possible responses.*) Will they be permitted to leave? Or once again, will prejudice trap the family, this time *Under a Red Sky*?

Book trailer available @ http://hayaleahmolnar.com/molnar-trailer.htm

Read Aloud/Talkback

1. "What Came First—Bucharest, Romania—November 1957," pages 3 to 4, beginning with "You were a lovely . . ." and ending with ". . . thing of all." Haya's grandfather gives advice. *Talkback*: Do you agree with the grandfather's advice?
2. "The Clock That Stopped," pages 65 to 68, beginning with "The most constant . . ." and ending with ". . . who wound it." Haya learns about Tata's World War II experiences. *Talkback*: How are the card and the clock central to Tata's wartime experiences?
3. On Earaches and Luck—December 1958," pages 101 to 103, beginning with "When I feel . . ." and ending with the chapter. Haya learns why she is lucky. *Talkback*: How does Haya's mother define luck?
4. "Tata Builds His Darkroom," pages 157 to 158, beginning with "I turn eight . . ." and ending with the chapter. Haya confronts her Jewish identity. *Talkback*: Why is this passage important to Haya's memoir?
5. "If All Jews Were Like You," pages 169 to 171, beginning with "What I learned . . ." and ending with the chapter. Haya's grandmother describes a Romanian slaughter that Nazi soldiers helped the family escape. *Talkback*: How did you react to the story?

Haya Leah Molnar explains her writing @

http://www.hayaleahmolnar.com/blog/

http://www.youtube.com/watch?v=alGyzBrg-ww&feature=relmfu

Author interview available @ http://www.blogtalkradio.com/
living-energy-works/2010/04/12/living-energy-interviews-haya-
leah-molnar-author-o

Related Works

1. **Baskin, Nora Raleigh.** *The Truth about My Bat Mitzvah*. New York: Simon & Schuster Books for Young Readers, 2008. 138p. $15.99. ISBN-13: 978 1 4169 3558 2. [fiction] MJS, G (*Value-Packed Booktalks*, 2011, pages 234 to 236.) After her grandmother wills her a gold Star of David, 12-year-old Caroline Weeks explores her Jewish heritage.

2. **Durbin, William.** *The Darkest Evening*. New York: Orchard Books, 2004. 240p. $15.95. ISBN 0 439 37307 7. [fiction] MJ, CG. An American family in the Depression relocates to Stalin's Russia and faces persecution and repression.

3. **Grimberg, Tina.** *Out of Line: Growing up Soviet*. Toronto, ON: Tundra Books, 2007. 128p. $22.95. ISBN-13: 978 0 88776 803 3. [nonfiction] JS, G. Tina Grimberg's memoir recalls personal relationships, the rules of a repressive government, and the Ukraine's complicated relationship with its Jewish community.

4. **Sís, Peter.** *The Wall: Growing up behind the Iron Curtain*. New York: Farrar, Straus and Giroux/Frances Foster Books, 2007. 56p. $18.00. ISBN-13: 978 0 374 34701 7. [graphic, nonfiction] MJS, CG (*Genre Talks for Teens*, 2009, pages 255 to 257.) In this illustrated memoir, Sís describes growing up in Soviet-controlled Czechoslovakia and the brief glimpses of Western culture that changed his thinking and life.

5. **Zenatti, Valérie, and Adriana Hunter (trans.).** *When I Was a Soldier: A Memoir*. New York: Bloomsbury Children's Books, 2005. 235p. $16.95. ISBN 1 58234 978 9. [nonfiction] JS, G (*Booktalks and Beyond*, 2007, pages 241 to 244.) At 18, according to Israeli law, Zenatti becomes a soldier and questions Israel's romantic self-characterizations.

ʕ˘ʔ˘ʔ

Lai, Thanhha. Inside Out & Back Again.

New York: HarperCollins Children's Books, 2011. 262p. $15.99.

ISBN 978 0 06 196278 3.

[novel in verse] MJS, CG with high interest for girls

Themes/Topics: Vietnamese Americans, emigration and immigration, Vietnam (1971–1980), Alabama, bullies, prejudice, choices, grief

Summary/Description

In a series of poems, 10-year-old Hà describes her family's adjustment to the United States in the pivotal year of 1975 when the family leaves Saigon. Their Alabama sponsor hires Hà's oldest brother as a mechanic. The family encounters both prejudice and support as they work hard and adjust to the new culture. By the end of the year, the mother gathers the family to declare their father, an officer in the Vietnamese army, dead. They look to the future in their new country. The author, Thanhha Lai, bases the story on her experiences.

Booktalk

Hà is 10 years old. It is 1975. Her father has been missing for nine years. They live in a war-torn Vietnam. As war comes closer to Saigon, they must leave the city they love. Where will they go? How will they go? They can go to France, Canada, or the United States. Which do you think the mother chooses? Why? (*Wait for responses.*) She sees the United States as a land of opportunity. And so the family crowds onto a boat. An American Navy ship rescues them. They are taken to Florida and wait for a sponsor. He finally comes, a man from Alabama who looks like an American cowboy. Hà's oldest brother will learn to be a mechanic and work for him. In Alabama, Hà enters a world of black and white. Where would Hà fit? (*Wait for responses.*) Hà creates a space for brown, her own space. She fights the bullies who try to take it from her, and accepts the not-so-perfect gifts from those who welcome her. Her family's journey is also her personal journey of strength and discovery, *Inside Out & Back Again*.

Book trailers available @

http://www.youtube.com/watch?v=ycdMqJ52ghY
http://www.youtube.com/watch?v=erjRxbX4CzM&feature=related

Read Aloud/Talkback

The entire book is appropriate for dramatic readings.
1. "Birthday," pages 26 to 29. The mother tells the family history. *Talkback*: What does this brief passage say about the family and their situation?

2. "Choice," pages 55 to 56. The family packs. *Talkback*: What possession would you take?
3. "A Kiss," pages 91 to 93. The U.S. Navy ship ensures their safety. *Talkback*: How would you answer Hà's question on page 93?
4. "Choose," pages 105 to 106. Mother decides on the United States. *Talkback*: Do you agree with the mother's choice?
5. "1976: Year of the Dragon." The family celebrates the New Year. *Talkback*: What are the strengths of this New Year ceremony?

Author read aloud available @ http://www.youtube.com/watch?
v=KEkjwu2WEIA&feature=related

**Brief author comments, two read alouds, and
pronunciation guide available @** http://www.teachingbooks
.net/tb.cgi?aid=15573

Discussion guide available @

http://files.harpercollins.com/HCChildrens/OMM/Media/
InsideOutandBack_DG_FINAL.pdf

Author interviews available @

http://www.schoollibraryjournal.com/slj/articles/interviews/
893040–338/the_inside_story_it_took.html.csp
http://www.nationalbook.org/nba2011_ypl_lai_interv.html
http://www.publishersweekly.com/pw/by-topic/authors/interviews/
article/47651-spring-2011-flying-starts-thanhha-lai.html

Related Works

1. **Burg, Anne E. *All the Broken Pieces*.** New York: Scholastic Press, 2009. 224p. $1699. ISBN-13: 978 0 545 08092 7. [novel in verse] MJS, CG. Adopted by a loving American couple, a young Vietnamese/American refugee copes with prejudice in the United States and the sorrow of leaving his mother and injured brother in Vietnam.
2. **Caputo, Philip. *10,000 Days of Thunder: A History of the Vietnam War*.** New York: Atheneum Books for Young Readers/A Byron Preiss Visual Publications Inc. Book, 2005. 128p. $22.95. ISBN-13: 978 0 689 86231 1. [nonfiction] JS, CG with high interest for boys. Philip Caputo explains the historical background, battles, context, politics, cultural influences, and cultural clashes of the Vietnam War.
3. **Schmidt, Gary D. *Trouble*.** New York: Clarion Books, 2008. 297p. $16.00. ISBN-13: 978 0 618 92766 1. [fiction] MJS, CG (*Genre Talks for Teens*, 2009, pages 292 to 295.) Fourteen-year-old Henry

Smith learns about the trials of the Cambodian refugee falsely accused of killing Henry's brother.

4. **Schmidt, Gary D. *The Wednesday Wars*.** New York: Clarion Books, 2007. 264p. $16.00. ISBN-13: 978 0 618 72483 3. [fiction] MJS, CG (*Genre Talks for Teens*, 2009, pages 56 to 59.) Holling Hoodhood, a seventh grader during the Vietnam War, discovers the meaning of faithfulness, true love, and open-mindedness.

5. **Shea, Pegi Deitz. *Tangled Threads: A Hmong Girl's Story*.** New York: Clarion Books, 2003. 236p. $15.00. ISBN 0 618 24748 3. [fiction] JS, G (*Teen Genre Connections*, 2005, pages 264 to 267.) Thirteen-year-old Mai Yang and her grandmother, forced to leave their Thailand refugee camp, face brutal soldiers and cultural misunderstandings.

෴

Meyerhoff, Jenny. Queen of Secrets.

New York: Farrar, Straus and Giroux, 2010. 230p. $16.99.

ISBN 978 0 374 32628 9. [fiction] JS, G

Themes/Topics: Identity, secrets, interpersonal relations, Jews, cousins, grandparents, orphans, conduct of life, high schools

Summary/Description

Fifteen-year-old Essie makes cheerleading and catches the eye of Austin King, the football team captain. Her estranged cousin Micah, the team kicker, threatens her "in-group" status because of his open devotion to Judaism. Essie hides her relationship to Micah from her new "friends," and the true relationship with Austin from her protective grandparents who raised her after her parents died. She plans an overnight with Austin after the Homecoming dance and faces the adult decision of whether or not to have sex. She refuses. Austin admits that he is also a virgin and tired of the peer pressure. But both Essie and Austin bow to pressure to toilet paper in Micah's house. The prank escalates. Essie apologizes to Micah's family for her part in the prank. Her aunt forgives her and apologizes for her bitterness over not being able to adopt Essie after her parents' deaths. All reconcile, but Essie has a more defined identity and real friends.

Values: Essie discovers the value of family, honesty, and her heritage.

Booktalk

Fifteen-year-old Essie just made cheerleading, and the captain of the football team notices her. What will that do for her social status? (*Wait for responses.*) All her new popularity could be wrecked by her cousin moving back to town. He insists on showing the world that he is a Jew. His parents, whom Essie can barely remember, are coming to the house. Her family talks about a religion and holidays she knows nothing about. What should she do? (*Wait for responses.*) Essie clams up. She can't tell her relatives where she is going or about the drinking, driving, or partying when she gets there. She can't let her new "friends" know that the guy wearing the "kippah" and praying during the games is her cousin. Her life is a train wreck waiting to happen, but lots of other people have secrets, too. And Essie may no longer be the *Queen of Secrets.*

Book trailer and alternative booktalk available @ http://www.teenreads.com/blog/2010/07/06/queen-of-secrets-book-trailer

Read aloud/Talkback

1. Chapter 10, pages 123 to 126, beginning with "That night we . . ." and ending with ". . . I ever would." Micah and Essie discuss identity. *Talkback*: What can Essie and Micah learn from each other?
2. Chapter 12, pages 140 to 143, beginning with "On Thursday . . ." and ending with ". . . find out?" Essie asks grandmother about religion in her life. *Talkback*: How are the family religious practices related to grief? Have you ever seen the same responses?
3. Chapter 13, pages 146 to 151, beginning with the chapter and ending with ". . . walked away." Sara challenges Essie and Micah about heritage and hazing. *Talkback*: Do you agree with Sara? What is the heritage of Essie's name?
4. Chapter 17, page 193, beginning with "Austin *did* . . ." and ending with the chapter. Essie rationalizes her inaction. *Talkback*: What is Essie risking in making her decision?
5. Chapter 19, pages 206 to 207, beginning with the chapter and ending with ". . . awesome night." Lara and Hayden show Essie that she isn't really part of the group. *Talkback*: What does Essie realize? Did the girls surprise you? Why or why not?

Author interviews available @
http://www.jennymeyerhoff.com/about.html

http://thebookscout.blogspot.com/2010/07/blog-tour-jenny-meyerhoff-queen-of.html

http://jewishbooks.blogspot.com/2010/06/queen-of-secrets-interview-with-jenny.html

http://laurenscrammedbookshelf.blogspot.com/2010/07/blog-tour-queen-of-secrets-by-jenny.html

http://www.readingrocks4me.com/2010/07/jenny-meyerhoff-joins-us-on-her-blog.html

http://www.bookingmama.net/2010/07/author-interview-jenny-meyerhoff.html

http://theirrepressiblewriter.com/2010/07/06/interview-jenny-meyerhoff-a-positive-journey/

Author guest blogs available @

http://cynthialeitichsmith.blogspot.com/2010/08/guest-post-jenny-meyerhoff-on-what-to.html

http://www.greenbeanteenqueen.com/2010/07/guest-post-jenny-meyerhoff.html

http://inbedwithbooks.blogspot.com/2010/07/jenny-meyerhoff-on-estrangement.html

Jenny Meyerhoff describes her writing process @
http://www.jennymeyerhoff.com/writers.html

Related Works

1. **Abdel-Fattah, Randa.** *Does My Head Look Big in This?* New York: Scholastic Inc./Orchard Books, 2007. 352p. $16.99. ISBN 13: 978 0 439 91947 0. [fiction] JS, G (*Genre Talks for Teens*, 2009, pages 259 to 262.) Eleventh grader, Amal Mohamed Nasrullah Abdel-Hakim, an Australian-Muslim-Palestinian, learns about herself and those around her when she decides to wear the hijab, the Muslim head scarf, full time.

2. **Abdel-Fattah, Randa.** *Ten Things I Hate about Me*. New York: Scholastic Inc./Orchard Books, 2009. 304p. $16.99. ISBN-13: 978 0 545 05055 5. [fiction] JS, G. Jamie/Jamilah works to hide her Muslim identity, but discovers that she is a stronger more likeable person if she is brave enough to be the girl she wants to be.

3. **Baskin, Nora Raleigh.** *The Truth about My Bat Mitzvah*. New York: Simon & Shuster Books for Young Readers, 2008. 138p. $15.99. ISBN 13: 978 1 4169 3558 2. [fiction] MJS, G (*Value-Packed Booktalks*, pages 234 to 236.) After her grandmother dies and leaves her a gold Star of David, 12-year-old Caroline Weeks explores her Jewish heritage.

4. **Singer, Marilyn (ed.).** *I Believe in Water: Twelve Brushes with Religion*. New York: HarperCollins, 2000. 280p. $24.89. ISBN 0 06 028398 X. [fiction] JS, CG. Twelve short stories examine how real life and spiritual beliefs can complement and collide.

5. **Yancy, Philip, and Tim Stafford (ed.).** *Student Bible: New International Version*. Grand Rapids, MI, 2001. 1440p. $32.99. ISBN 0 310 92784 6. In the book of Esther, pages 527 to 536, the minority girl whose beauty allowed her to become queen acts to save her people.

ርሃጊ

Oppel, Kenneth. Half Brother.
New York: Scholastic Press, 2010. 384p. $17.99.
ISBN 978 0 545 22925 8. [fiction] MJS with high interest for boys

Themes/Topics: Family relationships, interpersonal relations, animal experimentation, human behavior, animal behavior, human/animal relationships

Summary/Description

Thirteen-year-old Ben Tomlin's family moves and acquires a baby chimp when Ben's father, a behavioral scientist, decides to study a chimpanzee's ability to learn advanced language. The family treats the chimp, named Zan, as a family member. A staff of university students is hired to work with him. Ben becomes attached to Zan, but the experiment deteriorates. The father abandons the project, and the university sells Zan to another professor. The new owner secretly decides to sell Zan to an experimental lab. Ben, with the help of a university assistant who followed Zan to his new home, intervenes, and Zan eventually is sent to a sanctuary. Sorting out his feelings about Zan forces Ben to define his family relationships and friendships.

Values: Ben concludes that any successful relationship requires respect and responsibility.

Booktalk

Thirteen-year-old Ben is an only child. Mom and dad decide it's time for a brother. They move to accommodate the family's new addition. Ben has to leave his school and his friends. Complicated? How would you feel? (*Wait for responses.*) It gets worse. His new brother is a chimpanzee. It is hard enough to be the new kid in school without having a brother from the animal kingdom. Will the chimp make him a social chump? No way. Ben decides that in this eighth and ninth grade survival-of-the-fittest contest he is going to be on top—the dominant male. He is going to have popular friends and the prettiest girl. And where will he learn to do all this? Right at home from the new and amazing Zan, his better than human *Half Brother*.

Alternative booktalks available @

http://jamiethelibrarianreviews.wordpress.com/2011/10/25/half-brother-by-kenneth-oppel/

http://blog.scholastic.com/ink_splot_26/2010/10/half-brother.html

http://ec.libsyn.com/p/b/7/a/b7a63db2483a7a83/20110322_MCLHalfBrotherLC.mp3?d13a76d516d9dec20c3d276ce028e d5089ab1ce3dae902ea1d01cc833fd4cf584dc4&c_id=3136372

Book trailers available @

http://www.youtube.com/watch?v=eJhRA5jvbnc

http://www.youtube.com/watch?v=m6L-trj7MLI

Read Aloud/Talkback

1. Chapter 6, pages 72 to 74, beginning with "Windermere was a bit . . ." and ending with ". . . submitted to *him*." Ben attends Windermere for the first time. *Talkback*: What is your reaction to the school, Henry, and Ben?
2. Part Two, pages 81 to 82. In this introductory passage to Part Two, Ben assesses his strengths and weaknesses. *Talkback*: Do you agree with his assessment?
3. Chapter 10, pages 127 to 129, beginning with "Just then . . ." and ending with ". . . Zan's courage." Zan reacts to father's argument with Ben, and Ben reacts to the reaction. *Talkback*: What does this incident suggest about Zan, Ben, and his father?
4. Chapter 12, pages 157 to 158, beginning with "Before I went to bed . . ." and ending with ". . . was wrong." Ben reflects on the definitions of both human and person in relation to Zan. *Talkback*: Do you think the dictionary is wrong? Why might the definition be biased?
5. Chapter 26, pages 373 to 375, beginning with "A couple . . ." and ending with the novel. Ben dreams about Zan in his sanctuary. *Talkback*: What does this conclusion do for the novel?

Discussion guide and author interview available @

http://www.kennethoppel.ca/pages/novel%20studies/half_brother_discussion_guide.pdf

Author interviews available @

http://www.foodiebibliophile.com/2010/12/author-interview-kenneth-oppel.html

http://kennethoppel.blogspot.com/2010/12/half-brother-q-with-kenneth-oppel.html

Author article available @ http://www.huffingtonpost.com/kenneth-oppel/writing-half-brother-love_b_710856.html

Related Works

1. **Bruchac, Joseph. *Wabi: A Hero's Tale*.** New York: Dial Books, 2006. 198p. $16.99. ISBN 0 8037 3098 5. [fiction] MJS, CG (*Genre Talks for Teens*, 2009, pages 189 to 191.) Wabi tells the story of his life, from his hatching as an owl to his performing heroic human deeds that give him the love of a chief's headstrong daughter.

2. **Carey, Janet Lee. *The Beast of Noor*.** New York: Atheneum Books for Young Readers, 2009. 497p. $16.95. ISBN-13: 978 0 689 87644 8. [fiction] MJ, CG with high interest for boys. Fifteen-year-old Miles Ferrell and his 13-year-old sister Hanna discover their own magic and strengths in the human, animal, and supernatural worlds, as they struggle to destroy the Shriker, a huge and raging beast of the dark woods.

3. **Coville, Bruce (comp. and ed.). *Half-Human*.** New York: Scholastic Press, 2001. 224p. $15.95. ISBN 0 590 95944 1. [fiction] JS, CG (*Booktalks and More*, pages 101 to 103.) This collection of stories questions what makes a human being. "How to Make a Human," a poem by Lawrence Schimel appearing on pages 94 and 95, presents a negative view of man forgetful of his ties to nature.

4. **Napoli, Donna Jo. *Beast*.** New York: Atheneum Books for Young Readers, 2000. 260p. $17.00. ISBN 0 689 83589 2. [fiction] JS, CG (*Teen Genre Connections*, 2005, pages 171 to 173.) A Persian prince is turned into a lion for offending the gods and learns about suffering, love, and being truly human.

5. **Sonnenblick, Jordan. *Zen and the Art of Faking It*.** New York: Scholastic Press, 2007. 272p. $16.99. ISBN-13: 978 0 439 83707 1. [fiction] MJ, CG (*Value-Packed Booktalks*, 2011, pages 42 to 44.) Fourteen-year-old San Lee, a perpetual new student, poses as a Zen Buddhist to fit in and impress a girl in his social studies class, but his plan backfires.

ʕʗʔʗʔ

Selznick, Brian. Wonder Struck.

New York: Scholastic Press, 2011. 640p. $29.99.

ISBN 978 0 545 02789 2. [fiction] MJS, CG with high interest for boys

Themes/Topics: Deafness, families, museums, identity

Summary/Description

Two stories, one in text and one in illustrations, unfold and merge. The text story is set in Gunflint, Minnesota, 1977. After Ben Wilson's mother dies, he lives with his aunt and uncle, but finds evidence of the father he never knew. Trying to phone his father, Ben is struck by lightning and left totally deaf. He leaves the hospital where he is being treated and uses his mother's secret savings to seek his father in New York, but his money is stolen. He finds shelter in the museum which has a diorama depicting Gunflint Lake. An old woman visits it every day. Jamie, whose father works in the museum, shelters him in a storage room, and Ben finds clues about his parentage.

The illustrated story, set in Hoboken, New Jersey, 1927, involves a young deaf girl who runs away to New York to find her actress mother. The mother tries to send her home, but she escapes to the museum where she finds shelter with her older brother, an employee. With the brother's support, she attends a school for the deaf, marries, has a son, and makes dioramas for the museum. She is the old woman that Ben sees at the diorama. They unite. She tells him the story of his father, her son. Ben, Jamie, and Ben's grandmother, build new relationships.

Values: Ben learns the importance of both family and creativity.

Booktalk

Ask who in the group has read The Invention of Hugo Cabret. *Hold up the book.* If you have read the book, you know that author Brian Selznick blends words and pictures to tell his stories. In this book, he tells two stories, one with words and one with pictures. (*Turn the pages to show both words and pictures.*) The word story occurs in 1977. Ben's mother has died. He lives unhappily with his aunt, uncle, and cousin. He wants to find the father he never knew. In his search, he is struck by lightning. He wakes up deaf. He doesn't want to be in the hospital and he doesn't want to be with his aunt and uncle. So he takes the money his mother hid and goes to New York to find his father. What do you think are his chances? (*Wait for responses.*) The picture story occurs in 1927. In this story, an unhappy young deaf girl also runs away from home, but she seeks her actress mother. The mother wants to send her back to be hidden away. When can two such different but similar stories collide? (*Wait for responses.*) They can collide when both the boy and the girl are *Wonderstruck*.

Booktalk available @ http://www.gennasarnak.com/?p=3183

Booktalk through the stars available @ http://www.scholastic
.com/wonderstruck/stars.html

Book trailers available @

http://www.youtube.com/watch?v=9K2YaVxeTiM
http://www.youtube.com/watch?feature=endscreen&v=CEqTtrW
MicO&NR=1

Read Aloud/Talkback

1. Part 1, pages 16 to 18, beginning with the chapter and ending with "Ben silently agreed." The passage describes Ben's recurring wolf dream and his unhappy situation. *Talkback*: What forces push Ben?
2. Part 1, page 22, beginning with "We are all . . ." and ending with ". . . at the stars." Ben reflects on his mother's cryptic quotation. *Talkback*: What do you think the quotation means?
3. Part 1, pages 96 to 99, beginning with "Sitting on the edge . . ." and ending with ". . . Gunflint, Lake." Ben ponders the role of a curator as described in *Wonderstruck*. *Talkback*: According to this passage, are you a curator? Why are curators important?
4. Part 2, pages 440 to 441, beginning with "The next morning . . ." and ending with ". . . or your dad." Ben wishes for a neat and organized life. *Talkback*: What would be the advantage of life being organized according to the Dewey decimal system? What would be the disadvantages?
5. Part 3, pages 591 to 609, beginning with "Jamie looked from . . ." and ending with ". . . full of wonders." Ben realizes his bond with Jamie and Rose and the events that created it. *Talkback*: Is this trip manipulated by magic or common interests?

Read alouds, discussion guides, and interviews available @
http://www.teachingbooks.net/tb.cgi?tid=25731&a=1

Read aloud available @ http://minnesota.publicradio.org/www_
publicradio/tools/media_player/popup.php?name=minnesota/
news/features/2011/10/17/selznickreads_20111017_64

Discussion guides available @

http://www.wcmu.org/radio/childrens_bookshelf/cb_bookshelf_
questions_2012.html#wonderstruck

http://www.bookbrowse.com/reading_guides/detail/index.cfm/
book_number/2607/wonderstruck

http://www.scholastic.com/teachers/collection/vitural-field-trip-
teaching-resources#collection-block-try-these-wonderstruck-
classroom-activities

http://sweetonbooks.com/all-titles/699-wonderstruck.html

Brian Selznick booktalk and museum tour available @

http://www.scholastic.com/teachbrianselznick/assets/video.htm

Author interviews available @

http://www.youtube.com/watch?v=nXf9Cz8CF8k&feature=related

http://www.youtube.com/watch?v=OH5JR7XjnuM&feature=related

http://www.newsarama.com/comics/brian-selznick-1-wonderstruck-
111005.html

http://pajka.blogspot.com/2012/01/interview-with-wonderstruck-
author.html

http://blaine.org/sevenimpossiblethings/?p=2228

http://www.wonderstruckthebook.com/brian_interviews.htm

http://www.publishersweekly.com/pw/by-topic/authors/interviews/
article/48242-q—a-with-brian-selznick.html

http://minnesota.publicradio.org/display/web/2011/10/17/selznick-
wonderstruck/

Background essays available @ http://www.wonderstruck
thebook.com/essays.htm

Related Works

1. **Lawlor, Laurie. *Helen Keller: Rebellious Spirit***. New York: Holiday House, 2001. 168p. $22.95. ISBN 0 8234 1588 0. [nonfiction] MJS, CG with high interest for girls (*Teen Genre Connections*, 2005, pages 40 to 42.) Lawlor describes the Keller household, its post-Reconstruction Southern context, and the period's prejudice against "defectives."

2. **Muth, Joh. *Zen Shorts***. New York: Scholastic Press, 2005. 36p. $17.99. ISBN-13: 978 0 439 33911 7. [fiction, picture book] CMJS/A, CG. Three stories illustrate that consequences are unpredictable.

3. **Selznick, Brian.** *The Invention of Hugo Cabret*. New York: Scholastic Press, 2007. 544p. $22.99. ISBN-13: 978 0 439 81378 5. [fiction] M, CG (*Genre Talks for Teens*, 2009, pages 152 to 154.) Orphaned Hugo Cabret tries to repair his father's automaton, and with a new friend, resurrects the machine and the talents of a pioneer French movie maker thought to be dead.

4. **Tan, Shaun.** *The Arrival*. New York: Scholastic Inc./Arthur A. Levine Books, 2007. 128p. $19.99. ISBN-13: 978 0 439 89529 3. [wordless graphic] MJS, CG with high interest for boys. The story, told in pictures, communicates the joy of arrival to a new country and how that joy is passed to others.

5. **Tan, Shaun.** *Tales from Outer Suburbia*. New York: Scholastic Inc./Arthur A. Levine Books, 2009. 96p. $19.99. ISBN-13: 978 0 545 05587 1. [illustrated stories and poems] MJS/A, CG with high interest for boys (*Value-Packed Booktalks*, 2011, pages 174 to 176.) Fifteen off-the-wall tales explore the mystery and magic of cryptic advice, multiple cultures, creativity, nature, love, strangers, and just seeing and listening.

ↂↂ

Weitzman, David. Skywalkers: Mohawk Ironworkers Build the City.

New York: Roaring Brook Press, 2010. 124p. $19.99.
ISBN 978 1 59643 162 1. [nonfiction] MJ, CG with high interest for boys

Themes/Topics: Mohawk Nation, adaptation, tradition, 19th and 20th centuries, ironworkers, Canada, urban life, reservation life.

Summary/Description

The first two chapters briefly describe the Native American, most specifically Native American culture. The next four chapters explain how the Mohawks became involved in ironworking, which involved bridge building and eventually skyscrapers. The last chapter explains how their skills in building relate to their warrior traditions and their determination to adapt rather than to a natural desire to climb. The Author's Note characterizes the people. A Glossary explains terms. A list of sources and excerpt notes lead the reader to more sources. Black and white pictures depict their challenging work, and the index makes information readily accessible.

Values: The skywalkers value bravery, reliability, and cooperation.

Booktalk

How many of you are afraid of heights? (*Wait for responses.*) It is the second most common fear. The first is snakes. But the Native American Mohawk ironworkers seem to defy gravity and thrive. (*Show pictures from the book.*) They are a legend in our history. They built our bridges, our skyscrapers, and the modern age. They seem as fearless as they are strong, and yet many fall to their deaths every year. (*Show picture on page 88.*) What do you think makes them go up on those wires and beams every day? (*Wait for answers.*) That is what Mr. Weitzman wanted to know, too. And so he visited some of the biggest cities in the world and talked personally to the *Skywalkers.*

Alternative booktalk available @ http://chapterbooks.wordpress .com/2011/05/16/skywalkers-mohawk-ironworkers-build-the-city/

Read Aloud/Talkback

1. Chapter 2, pages 16 to 19, beginning with "The Mohawks found . . ." and ending with ". . . began to decline." The passage includes three primary source accounts which explore how the Mohawks deal with the world. *Talkback*: What does each primary source reveal about the Mohawks?
2. Chapter 4, "Time Seemed to Stop," pages 45 to 50. The bridge at Quebec collapses. *Talkback*: What about this disaster surprised you? Why?
3. Chapter 5, pages 56 to 57, beginning with the chapter and ending with ". . . at one time." Mohawks react to the Quebec disaster. *Talkback*: What does this passage reveal about the attitude of the ironworkers and the power of the women in their community?
4. Chapter 5, "Department of Immigration vs. Paul K. Diabo," pages 72 to 73. This passage describes why the Supreme Court gave the Mohawks the right to cross borders without restriction. *Talkback*: Do you agree with the court's decision? Explain your answer.
5. Chapter 7, "Breaking Away," pages 107 to 108. This section describes a young man leaving home to become an ironworker against his family's wishes. *Talkback*: What dynamics are operating in the scene? Does this scene need to apply just to ironworkers?

Related Works

1. **Alexie, Sherman (text), and Ellen Forney (illus.).** *The Absolutely True Diary of a Part-Time Indian*. New York: Little, Brown & Co., 2007. 228p. $16.99. ISBN-13: 978 0 316 01368 0. [fiction] JS, CG with high interest for boys (*Genre Talks for Teens*, 2009, pages 269 to 272.) Intellectually gifted but physically challenged Arnold Spirit leaves the reservation school to attend the more prosperous white school. His story shows a different side of modern Native American life.

2. **Bruchac, Joseph.** *Code Talker: A Novel about the Navajo Marines of World War Two*. New York: Dial Books, 2005. 231p. $16.99. ISBN 0 8037 2921 9. [fiction] MJS, CG with high interest for boys. This novel recounts the heroic lives of the Navajos in World War II.

3. **Bruchac, Joseph.** *Jim Thorpe: Original All-American*. New York: Dial Books/Walden Media, 2006. 276p. ISBN 0 8037 3118 3. [biographical novel] JS, B (*Value-Packed Booktalks*, 2011, pages 200 to 202.) In spite of prejudice, family dysfunction, cultural differences, and exploitation, Jim Thorpe becomes an Olympic champion and an American hero.

4. **Bruchac, Joseph.** *The Way*. Plain City, OH: Darby Creek Publishing, 2007. 164p. $16.95. ISBN-13: 978 1 58196 062 4. [fiction] MJS, CG with high interest for boys (*Value-Packed Booktalks*, 2011, pages 213 to 215.) Cody LeBeau moves from loser to hero when his Abenaki uncle arrives and teaches him to think like a winner.

5. **Edwardson, Debby Dahl.** *Blessing's Bead*. New York: Farrar, Straus and Giroux/Melanie Kroupa Books, 2009. 178p. $16.99. ISBN-13: 978 0 374 30805 6. [fiction] JS, CG with high interest for girls (*Value-Packed Booktalks*, 2011, pages 236 to 239.) In this story spanning from 1917 to 1989, an Iñupiaq family struggles to keep their traditions and beliefs as the world changes.

 CŞŞ

Yang, Gene Luen, and Thien Pham (art). Level Up.

New York: Roaring Brook Press/First Second, 2011. 160p. $19.99.
ISBN 978 1 59643 714 2. [graphic] JS, CG with high interest for boys

Themes/Topics: Family, fate, self-determination, video games, medicine

Summary/Description

Dennis's parents push him to high academic achievement, but Dennis's passion for video games eventually gets him dismissed from college. He recalls his father's ambitions for him and the grief he suffered after his father's death. A group of angels take over his life so that he can be successful in medical school, his destiny. Dennis becomes overwhelmed and determines that his father's ambitions for him came from his father's inability to live up to his own promises. Dennis drops out of medical school and returns to video games where he is successful but not fulfilled. He realizes that saving lives is more important than winning games, returns to school, reunites with a close friend, and finds his talent in the colonoscopy which requires video game dexterity.

Values: Dennis learns to balance his Asian values of hard work and self-discipline with his passion for video games.

Booktalk

Ask how many in the group play video games. How much time per day? What are their favorite games? How do the parents feel about the games and the time they put into them? Dennis loves video games, and he is the best. Mom and Dad want him to focus on medical school. But Dennis lives for the games, and so he flunks out of school. Then, Mom and Dad get some help. These little weird angels appear, an entire take-over-his-life crew. They hound Dennis to fulfill his destiny to be a doctor, even a gastroenterologist, the kind of doctor his father wants him to be. What would you choose? Dennis thinks he has two choices. The gaming gives him fun, but will it give him fulfillment? Medical school gives him fulfillment, but will it drive him crazy? Maybe there is a third choice, one with a challenge that is a *Level Up*.

Book trailer available @ http://us.macmillan.com/levelup/ GeneYang

Read Aloud/Talkback

1. "Level 1," pages 42 to 49, beginning with "Good morning Dennis." and ending with the last frame on page 49. The angels push Dennis to endure. *Talkback*: After reading these frames, whose side are you on?
2. "Level 1," page 55, beginning with "You know the best . . ." and ending with the last frame on the page. Dennis explains the draw of

video games. *Talkback*: How do you react to Dennis's reflection on video games?

3. "Level 2," pages 90 to 92, beginning with the first frame on page 90 and ending with the last frame on page 92. Dennis and his friend discuss destiny. *Talkback*: Do you agree with Dennis or his partner?

4. "Level 3," pages 121 to 130, beginning with the first frame on page 121 and ending with the first frame on page 130. Dennis realizes that the angels are his father's broken promises. *Talkback*: What does Dennis learn from the broken promises?

5. "Level 3," page 149, beginning with the second frame and ending with the last frame on the page. Dennis makes a distinction between the games and medicine. *Talkback*: How do you react to Dennis's conclusion?

Discussion guide available @ http://media.us.macmillan.com/discussionguides/9781596432352DG.pdf

Author interviews available @

http://www.publishersweekly.com/pw/by-topic/childrens/childrens-book-news/article/47726-gene-yang—s—level-up—videogames-angels-and-growing-up-asian-american.html

http://www.comicbookresources.com/?page=article&id=36651

http://www.8asians.com/2011/06/07/level-ups-gene-luen-yang-thien-pham-on-asian-parenting-video-games/

http://www.tor.com/blogs/2012/05/gene-luen-yang-on-chronicling-the-last-airbender-gangs-further-adventures

http://www.smcl.org/en/content/insider-series-interview-gene-luen-yang-part-1

http://www.smcl.org/en/content/insider-series-interview-gene-luen-yang-part-2

http://blog.schoollibraryjournal.com/goodcomicsforkids/2012/01/12/interview-gene-luen-yang-and-thien-pham/

http://hhhlteenreads.blogspot.com/2012/06/level-up-by-gene-luen-yang.html

Author interviews and read aloud available @

http://www.teachingbooks.net/tb.cgi?tid=23790&a=1

Related Works

1. **Na, An. *A Step from Heaven***. Asheville, NC: Front Street, 2001. 156p. $15.95. ISBN 1 886910 58 8. [fiction] JS, G (*Booktalks and More*, 2003, pages 33 to 35.) Young Ju, a Korean immigrant, relates her family's entry into life in the United States.

2. **Nam, Vickie (ed.).** *Yell-Oh Girls!* New York: HarperCollins/ Quill, 2001. 249p. $13.00pa. ISBN 0 06 095944 4. [nonfiction] JS, G (*Booktalks and More*, 2003, pages 262 to 264.) In essays and poetry, Asian American females express their joy, frustration, and determination in relation to their ancestry.

3. **Shea, Pegi Deitz.** *Tangled Threads: A Hmong Girl's Story.* New York: Clarion Books, 2003. 236p. $15.00. ISBN 0 618 24748 3. [fiction] JS, G (*Teen Genre Connections*, 2005, pages 264 to 267.) Thirteen-year-old Mai Yang tries to keep her balance between the Hmong culture of Thailand and the contrasting culture of the United States.

4. **Son, John.** *Finding My Hat.* New York: Scholastic Press/Orchard Books, 2003. 185p. (First Person fiction) $16.95. ISBN 0 439 43538 2. [fiction] MJS, CG with high interest for boys (*Booktalks and Beyond*, 2007, pages 254 to 257.) In a series of essays, Jin-Han tells about his integration into American life as a member of a Korean family.

5. **Yang, Gene Luen.** *American Born Chinese.* New York: Roaring Brook Press/First Second, 2006. 233p. $16.95. ISBN-13: 978 1 59643 152 2. [graphic] MJS, CG with high interest for boys (*Genre Talks for Teens*, 2009, pages 280 to 281.) Yang blends three stories to illustrate the difficulty in finding one's identity when caught between Asian and American cultures.

Index

About the Author

LUCY SCHALL is a retired high school and middle school English teacher, a book reviewer for VOYA, and the author of six other acclaimed booktalking guides, including *Value-Packed Booktalks* (Libraries Unlimited, 2011) and *Teen Genre Connections* (Libraries Unlimited, 2005), a selection for the VOYA Five Foot Bookshelf award. Ms. Schall holds a Bachelor of Arts with a major in English and a Master of Arts in Education from Allegheny College.

Made in the USA
Lexington, KY
21 October 2013